THE SELF ACROSS
PSYCHOLOGY

SELF-RECOGNITION,
SELF-AWARENESS,
AND THE SELF CONCEPT

ANNALS OF THE NEW YORK ACADEMY OF SCIENCES

Volume 818

THE SELF ACROSS PSYCHOLOGY

SELF-RECOGNITION, SELF-AWARENESS, AND THE SELF CONCEPT

Edited by Joan Gay Snodgrass and Robert L. Thompson

The New York Academy of Sciences
New York, New York
1997

Cover: *The illustration on the softcover edition of this book is Pablo Picasso's* Girl before a Mirror. *Boisgeloup, March 1932. 64 × 51¼" (162.3 × 130.2 cm). Oil on canvas. From the Museum of Modern Art, New York. Gift of Mrs. Simon Guggenheim. Photograph © 1997 The Museum of Modern Art.*

Library of Congress Cataloging-in-Publication Data

The self across psychology : self-recognition, self-awareness, and the
self concept / edited by Joan Gay Snodgrass and Robert L. Thompson.
    p. cm. — (Annals of the New York Academy of Sciences, ISSN
0077-8923 ; v. 818)
    Papers presented at a series of lectures of the Psychology Section
of the New York Academy of Sciences, 1994–96.
    ISBN 1-57331-034-4 (cloth : alk. paper). — ISBN 1-57331-035-2
(pbk. : alk. paper)
    1. Self.   2. Self-perception.   I. Snodgrass, Joan Gay.
II. Thompson, Robert L., 1926– .   III. New York Academy of
Sciences. Section of Psychology.   IV. Series.
BF697.S4215   1997
155.2—dc21   97-20571
                                                  CIP

&/PCP
Printed in the United States of America
ISBN 1-57331-034-4 (cloth)
ISBN 1-57331-035-2 (paper)
ISSN 0077-8923

ANNALS OF THE NEW YORK ACADEMY OF SCIENCES

Volume 818
June 18, 1997

THE SELF ACROSS PSYCHOLOGY:
SELF-RECOGNITION, SELF-AWARENESS, AND THE SELF CONCEPT[a]

Editors
JOAN GAY SNODGRASS AND ROBERT L. THOMPSON

CONTENTS

---

[a]This volume comprises papers presented at a series of lectures given during the 1994–96 meetings of the Psychology Section of the New York Academy of Sciences in New York, N.Y.

Preface

JOAN GAY SNODGRASS

Department of Psychology
New York University
New York, New York 10003

ROBERT L. THOMPSON

Department of Psychology
Hunter College and the Graduate Center of the
City University of New York
New York, New York 10021

This volume grew out of a two-year series of talks concerned with the topic of the Self given at meetings of the Psychology Section of the New York Academy of Sciences. The topic of the Self was selected as a focus of interest because it is sufficiently central to many areas of psychology and would thus serve those engaged in diverse fields of psychology and also illustrate how different areas of psychology vary in their approach to a single problem.

Because this volume surveys virtually every area of psychology, from comparative psychology to cognitive psychology to social and cultural psychology, the papers are not meant to represent the latest in highly technical experimental advances; rather, the articles serve as tutorials illustrating how a single topic can be addressed by a diverse range of methodologies. This is not to say that the papers avoid controversy or skirt difficult issues; indeed, particularly in Part II, which addresses the comparative animal studies, debate still rages over the meaning of the mirror-test of self-recognition in primates.

We are grateful to all of the contributors to this volume for their cooperation in submitting original and revised articles in good time. We are also grateful to Mr. Charles Weiner, who took photographs at all of the lectures.

Gay Snodgrass is Professor of Psychology at New York University and past Chair of the Psychology Section of the New York Academy of Sciences. She received her Ph.D. from the University of Pennsylvania in 1966 and has been at New York University ever since. Her research interests are in implicit and explicit memory, the role of imagery in memory, and the role of imagery as a causal component of memory deficits. She is the author of numerous articles and of two textbooks, The Numbers Game: Statistics in Psychology *and* Human Experimental Psychology.

Part I: The Self across Psychology

Introduction

JOAN GAY SNODGRASS

Department of Psychology
New York University
New York, New York 10003

This first part of this volume introduces the nature of the self and of self-knowledge and self-awareness. John Kihlstrom and Stanley Klein show how research from cognitive psychology can illuminate a difficult topic such as the self-concept. They propose four answers to the question of how the concept of the self is represented. The first derives from research in categorization, and proposes that the self is a fuzzy set of characteristics that may have a prototypical structure. The second is based upon the self as narrative (see Part IV), in which the stories about ourselves that we have constructed and recounted to others, based upon our autobiographical memories, represent the self. The third is based upon our images of ourselves (see the article by Ulrich Neisser) in which our notion of ourself interacts with the environment to produce our self-image. The fourth is based upon theories of semantic memory, in which the concept of the self is represented as a series of abstract propositions which can be accessed independently of the episodic knowledge upon which they are based.

In the second paper in the section, Ulrich Neisser also considers how the self-concept comes to be represented. He argues that the answers proposed by Kihlstrom and Klein enter into the development of the self-concept at various ages. The first and earliest of the representations of the self depend upon the self-image, which is developed by ecological perception (our view of our interaction with the environment as given in the optic array) and interpersonal perception (our view of our interaction with other people). In Neisser's view, the ecological self becomes defined through a series of interactions with the environment. These first interactions define the self as an active agent with a "body image" and a recognition of itself through agent–environment interactions. Later the self develops as it interacts with the most important of environmental influences—significant other people in the environment. Through this social interaction, the self defines itself as a social being, which influences, and is influenced by, others.

Neisser argues that these senses of self develop very early, and much earlier than another definition of self-awareness, recognition of the self in the mirror (see Part II). In his terms, ecological and interpersonal perception enable you to know what you are doing and where, but cannot represent

1

your beliefs about yourself. The self-concept consists of your beliefs about yourself, which may be best characterized by Kihlstrom and Klein's fourth way, and which in Neisser's system develops next. Finally, the self can also be represented as a narrative of episodic memory (the third way in Kihlstrom and Klein's system), which is a major focus of this volume (see Part IV).

John Kihlstrom is Professor in the Department of Psychology at Yale University and the University of California, Berkeley. He received his Ph.D. from the University of Pennsylvania, and previously held positions at Harvard, Wisconsin, and Arizona. His chief research interests are in cognition in a personal and social context, and he has special interests in unconscious mental processes, autobiographical memory, and the self. He is editor of Psychological Science, *the flagship journal of the American Psychological Society, and his many awards include the APA Distinguished Scientific Award for an early career contribution to psychology.*

Stan Klein is Associate Professor of Psychology at the University of California, Santa Barbara. Klein received his Ph.D. from Harvard University and has previously held jobs at Trinity University and the University of Illinois. His research interests are in social cognition with a particular focus on the mental representation of trait and behavioral knowledge about the self. A larger goal of this research is to examine the extent to which a common set of principles can explain the way in which knowledge of self and others is represented in the mind.

Self-Knowledge and Self-Awareness[a]

JOHN F. KIHLSTROM[b]

Department of Psychology
Yale University
New Haven, Connecticut 06520

STANLEY B. KLEIN

Department of Psychology
University of California, Santa Barbara
Santa Barbara, California 93106

T he self lies at the center of mental life. As William James (1890/1981, p. 221) noted in the *Principles of Psychology,*

> Every thought tends to be part of a personal consciousness. . . . It seems as if the elementary psychic fact were not *thought* or *this thought* or *that thought* but *my thought*, every thought being owned. . . . On these terms the personal self rather than the thought might be treated as the immediate datum in psychology. The universal conscious fact is not "feelings and thoughts exist" but *"I* think and *I* feel". . . .

In other words, conscious experience requires that a particular kind of connection be made between the mental representation of some current or past event, and a mental representation of the self as the agent or patient, stimulus or experiencer, of that event (Kihlstrom, 1995). It follows from this position that in order to understand the vicissitudes of consciousness, and of mental life in general, we must also understand how we represent ourselves in our own minds, how that mental representation or self gets linked up with mental representations of ongoing experience, how that link is preserved in memory, and how it is lost, broken, set aside, and restored.

The research program, described in this article (Kihlstrom & Cantor, 1984; Kihlstrom, *et al.*, 1988; Kihlstrom & Klein, 1994; Kihlstrom, Marchese & Klein, 1995; Klein & Loftus, 1993) begins with a simple question: What does the self look like? In answering this question, we assume that the self is one's mental representation of oneself—or, put another way, that the self represents our own knowledge of ourselves. Thus, the answer to the

[a]The point of view represented in this paper is based in part on research supported by Grant No. MH-35856 from the National Institute of Mental Health.

[b]Address for correspondence: Department of Psychology, Yale University, P.O. Box 208205, New Haven, Connecticut 06520-8205. Phone (203) 432-2596; fax (203) 432-7172; e-mail: Kihlstrm@Minerva.cis.Yale.edu

5

question of what the self looks like comes from the vast literature within cognitive psychology concerning the manner in which knowledge is represented in the mind.

THE SELF AS A CONCEPTUAL STRUCTURE

Within personality and social psychology, the self-concept is commonly taken as synonymous with self-esteem, but within the social-intelligence framework of personality (Cantor & Kihlstrom, 1987) the self-concept can be construed simply as one's concept of one's self, a concept no different, in principle, than one's concept of *bird* or *fish*. From this perspective, the analysis of the self-concept can be based on what cognitive psychology has to say about the structure of concepts in general (Smith & Medin, 1981).

From the time of Aristotle until only just recently, concepts were characterized as *proper sets*: summary descriptions of entire classes of objects in terms of defining features which were singly necessary and jointly sufficient to identify an object as an instance of a category. Thus, the category *birds* includes warm-blooded vertebrates with feathers and wings, while the category *fish* included cold-blooded vertebrates with scales and fins. But both philosophical considerations and the results of experiments in cognitive psychology have persuaded us not to think about concepts in terms of proper sets and defining features, but rather in terms of family resemblance, in which category members tend to share certain attributes, but there are no defining features as such. According to this view of categories as *fuzzy sets*, category instances are summarized in terms of a *category prototype* which possesses many, but not necessarily all, of the features which are characteristic of category membership.

In the late 1970s and early 1980s the idea that the self, too, was represented as a category prototype was popular, and some very interesting experiments were done based on the assumption (Rogers, 1981). But how does one talk about family resemblance, or abstract a prototype, when there is only one member of the category—oneself? The notion of self-as-prototype, taken literally, seems to imply that the self is not unitary or monolithic. We do not have just one self: rather, each of us must have several different selves, the characteristic features of which are represented in the self-as-prototype.

A dramatic example of this may be found in *The Three Faces of Eve*, a case of multiple personality disorder, played with Academy-Award-winning skill by Joanne Woodward in the 1957 film of the same title (cf. Thigpen & Cleckley, 1954). Two personalities, Eve White and Eve Black, were separated by an asymmetrical amnesia: Eve White knew nothing about Eve Black, but Eve Black knew all about Eve White. Testing with the semantic differential technique revealed that the two Eves had markedly different self-concepts. Eve White saw herself as bad, passive, and weak, while Eve Black saw herself as good, strong, and active (Osgood & Luria, 1954). During therapy a third personality, Jane, emerged, who seemed to blend the best qualities of the two Eves: she was strong and active, and recognized both her good and bad sides; in that sense, Jane might be construed as something like a self-prototype.

But one does not have to have a dissociative disorder to have a multiplicity of selves. Traditional personologists assume that behavior is broadly stable over time and consistent over space, and that this stability and consistency reflect traits which lie at the core of personality. Viewed cognitively, the self might be viewed as the mental representation of this core. But social psychologists have argued that behavior is extremely flexible, varying widely across time and place. If so, then the self-concept should represent this context-specific variability, so that each of us possesses a repertoire of context-specific self-concepts—a sense of what we are like in different classes of situations (Kihlstrom, Marchese & Klein, 1995). The self-as-prototype might be abstracted from these contextual selves. Thus, we might begin to think about a hierarchy of selves, with more or less context-specific selves at lower levels, and a very abstract prototypical self at the highest level.

This is all well and good, but maybe there is not a prototype after all. Another trend in cognitive psychology has been to abandon the notion entirely that concepts are summary descriptions of category members (Medin, 1989). Rather, according to the *exemplar view of categories*, concepts are only a collection of instances, related to each other by family resemblance perhaps, and with some instances being in some sense more typical than others, but lacking a unifying prototype at the highest level. Some very clever experiments have lent support to the exemplar view, but as yet it has not found its way into research on the self-concept. Nevertheless, the general idea of the exemplar-based self-concept is the same as that of the context-specific self, only lacking hierarchical organization or any summary prototype.

The three views of categorization presented so far—proper sets, fuzzy sets, and exemplars—all assume that the heart of categorization is the judgment of similarity. That is, instances are grouped together into categories because they are in some sense similar to each other. But similarity is not the only basis for categorization. It has been proposed that categorization is also based on one's theory of the domain in question, or, at least, that people's theories place constraints on the dimensions which enter into their similarity judgments (Medin, 1989). Application of this *theory-driven* view of categorization to the self was anticipated more than 20 years ago by Epstein (1973, p. 407), who argued that the self-concept is "a theory that the individual has unwittingly constructed about himself as an experiencing, functioning individual, and . . . part of a broader theory which he holds with respect to his entire range of significant experience."

Epstein's views have not been translated into programmatic experimental research on the self, but we can perhaps see examples of theory-based construals of the self in the variety of "recovery" movements in American society today (Kaminer, 1992). Whether we are healing our wounded inner child, freeing our inner hairy man, dealing with codependency issues, or coping with our status as an adult child of alcoholics or a survivor of child abuse, what links us to others, and literally constitutes our definition of ourselves, is not so much a set of attributes as a theory of how we got the way we are. And what makes us similar to other people of our kind is not so much that they resemble us but that they went through the same kind of formative process, and hold the same theory about *themselves* as we do of *ourselves*. Dysfunctional or not, it may well be that we all have theories—we might call them origin myths—about how we became what we are, and these theories are important parts of our self-concept. Such self-theories could give unity to our context-specific multiplicity of selves, explaining why we are one kind of person in one situation, and another kind of person in another (Kihlstrom *et al.*, 1995).

THE SELF AS A STORY

Something of the flavor of the self-as-theory is provided by a second form of mental representation, knowledge as stories. Recently, Schank and Abelson (1995, p. 80) have asserted that "from the point of view of the social functions of knowledge, what people know consists almost exclusively of stories and the cognitive machinery necessary to understand, remember, and tell them." As they expand on the idea (p. 1),

> (1) Virtually all human knowledge is based on stories constructed around past experiences; (2) New experiences are interpreted in terms of old stories; (3) The content of story memories depends on whether and how they are told to others, and these reconstituted memories form the basis of the individual's *remembered self*. Further, shared story memories within social groups define particular social selves, which may bolster or compete with individual remembered selves.

Schank and Abelson concede that knowledge also can be represented as facts, beliefs, lexical items like words and numbers, and rule systems (like grammar), but they also argue that, when properly analyzed, non-story items of knowledge actually turn out not to be knowledge (for example, they may constitute indexes used to organize and locate stories). Their important point is that from a functional standpoint, which considers how knowledge is used and communicated, knowledge tends to be represented as stories.

The idea of knowledge as stories, in turn, is congruent with Pennington and Hastie's story model (1993) of juror decision-making. According to Pennington and Hastie, jurors routinely organize the evidence presented to them into a story structure with initiating events, goals, actions, and consequences. According to Schank and Abelson (1995), each of us does the same sort of thing with the evidence of our own lives. From this point of view, the self consists of the stories we tell about ourselves—stories which relate how we got where we are, and why, and what we have done, and what happened next. We rehearse these stories to ourselves to remind ourselves of who we are; we tell them to other people to encourage them to form particular impressions of ourselves; and we change the stories as our self-understanding, or our strategic self-presentation, changes. When stories aren't told, they tend to be forgotten—a fact dramatically illustrated by Nelson's studies (1993) of the development of autobiographical memory in young children. Furthermore, when something new happens to us, the story we tell about it, to ourselves and to other people, reflects not only our understanding of the event, but our understanding of ourselves as participants in that event. Sometimes, stories are assimilated to our self-understanding; on other occasions, our self-understanding must accommodate itself to the new story. When this happens, the whole story of our life changes.

THE SELF AS AN IMAGE

Our discussion of the self as concept and as story illustrates a strategy that we have found particularly useful in our work: beginning with some fairly informal, folk-psychological notion of the self-concept, we see what happens when we apply our technical understanding of what that form of self-knowledge looks like. Much the same attitude (or, if you will, heuristic) can be applied to another piece of ordinary language: the self-image. Schilder (1938), p. 11) defined the self-image as "the picture of our own body which we form in our mind, that is to say, the way in which the body appears to ourselves." What follows from this?

First, there is the question whether, in talking about our mental images of ourselves, we should be talking about mental images *at all*. Beginning in the 1970s, a fairly intense debate raged about the way in which knowledge is stored in the mind. At this point, most cognitive psychologists are comfortable distinguishing between two forms of mental representation: meaning-based and perception-based (Anderson, 1983). Meaning-based representations store knowledge about the semantic relations among objects, features, and events, and take the form of propositions—primitive sentence-like units of meaning which omit concrete perceptual details. We will discuss these later. For now, we wish to focus on perception-based representations, which store knowledge about perceptual structure.

Perception-based representations are relatively unstudied in social cognition, but it is quite clear that we have them. For example, we have visual and auditory images of the faces and voices of people we know, which permit us to recognize these people as familiar. That we have perception-based representations of others makes it more likely that we have perception-based representations of *ourselves* as well. In fact, Head (1926) coined the term *body schema* to refer to our postural models of our own bodies—models which allow us to maintain stability and adjust to our environment, and which are distorted in the classical experiments on prism adaptation. The fact that we can adjust our movements when our vision is distorted, and that these adjustments persist when objective stimulus conditions change, indicates that we have internal representations of our bodies, and their parts, which are independent of sensory stimulation.

As with the self-concept, the self-image can be illustrated with clinical data. Acute schizophrenics often complain of distortions in their perception of their own bodies. In *autopagnosia*, a neurological syndrome associated with focal lesions in the left parietal lobe, the patient can name body parts touched by the examiner, but cannot localize body parts on demand. In *phantom limb pain*, amputees perceive their lost arms and legs as if they were still there. In *body dysmorphic disorder*, the patient complains of bodily defects where there really aren't any. In *eating disorders* such as anorexia and bulimia, the sufferer sees fat where the body is objectively normal, lean, or even gaunt.

But little of this clinical folklore has been studied experimentally. In the laboratory, studies of the self-image qua image are very rare. One exception is a fascinating study by Mita, Derner, and Knight (1977) on the mere exposure effect (Zajonc, 1968), in which subjects view a series of unfamiliar objects (for example, nonsense polygons or Turkish words), and later make preference ratings of these same objects and others which had not been previously presented. On average, old objects tend to be preferred to new ones, and the extent of preference is correlated with the number of prior exposures. In the experiment of Mita *et al.* (1977), subjects were presented with pairs of head-and-shoulder photographs of themselves and their friends, and asked which one they preferred. In each pair, one photo was the original, and the other was a left–right reversal. The result was that when viewing photos of their friends, subjects preferred the original view (that is, the view as seen through the lens of the camera), but when viewing photos of themselves, the same subjects preferred the left-right reversal (that is, the view as would be seem in a mirror). Thus, our preferences for pictures match the way we typically view ourselves and others. Mita took this as evidence for the mere exposure effect, which it is; but it is also evidence for a highly differentiated self-image which preserves information about both visual details and the spatial relations among them.

THE SELF AS ASSOCIATIVE NETWORK

For most of its history the study of memory has been the study of verbal learning. Accordingly, many psychologists have come to think of memory as a set of words (or phrases or sentences), each representing a concept, joined to each other by associative links representing the relations between them, the whole system forming an associative network of meaning-based knowledge (Anderson, 1983)—Schank and Abelson's (1995) theory of knowledge as stories is explicitly opposed to this conventional thinking. It is also commonplace to distinguish between two broad types of verbal knowledge stored in memory (Tulving, 1983). *Episodic* memory is autobiographical memory for a person's concrete behaviors and experiences: each episode is associated with a unique location in space and time. *Semantic* memory is abstract, generic, context-free knowledge about the world. Almost by definition, episodic memory is part of the self-concept, because episodic memory is about *the self*: it is the record of the individual person's past experiences, thoughts, and actions. But semantic memory can also be about the self, recording information about physical and psychological traits of the sort that might be associated with the self-concept.

Within the verbal-learning tradition, knowledge about other people has been studied extensively in a line of research known as *person memory* (Hastie, Ostrom, Ebbesen, Wyer, Hamilton, & Carlston, 1980). Several different models of person memory have been proposed (Kihlstrom & Hastie, 1993), and some of these have been appropriated for the study of memory for one's self (Kihlstrom & Klein, 1994; Klein & Loftus, 1993). The simplest person-memory model is an associative network with labeled links. Each person (or perhaps only his or her name) is represented as a single node in the network, and knowledge about that person is represented as fanning out from that central node. The person-nodes are also connected to each other, to represent relationships among them, but that is another matter. The point is that in this sort of model the various nodes are densely interconnected, so that each item of knowledge is associatively linked to a great number of other items. In theory, the interconnections among nodes form the basis for associative priming effects, in which the presentation of one item facilitates the processing of an associatively related one.

Of course, knowledge about a person can build up rather fast: consider how much we know about even our casual acquaintances. According to the spreading activation theory that underlies most associative network models of memory (Anderson, 1983), this creates a liability known as the *fan effect*: the more information you know about someone or something, the longer it takes to retrieve any particular item of information.

Is there any way around the fan effect in person memory? One possibility which has been suggested is that our knowledge about ourselves and others (especially those whom we know well) is organized in some way—perhaps according to its trait implications. There is some evidence that organization does abolish the fan effect (Smith, Adams & Schorr, 1978), but this evidence is rather controversial, and some have concluded that memory isn't really organized in this manner after all (Reder & Anderson, 1980). Nevertheless, the notion of a hierarchically organized memory structure is so sensible that many person-memory theorists, such as Hamilton and Ostrom, have adopted it anyway (see, for example, their contributions to Hastie *et al.*, 1980; see also Kihlstrom & Hastie, 1993).

How can we generalize from person memory to the structure of memory for the self? Actually, there are three possibilities here, distinguished particularly with respect to the relations between behavioral and trait information, or episodic and semantic knowledge. FIGURE 1A depicts the conventional wisdom: that memory for specific behavioral episodes is organized by their trait implications. In this model, nodes representing traits fan off the node representing the self, and nodes representing specific episodes which exemplify these traits fan off the trait-nodes. This *hierarchical* model implies that retrieval has to pass through traits to effect access to information about behaviors. Thus, traits will be activated in the course of gaining access to information about behaviors. FIGURE 1B depicts an alternative model, which holds that the self contains only episodic knowledge about experiences and behaviors, and that semantic knowledge about traits is known only indirectly, by inference. One such inferential process would involve sampling autobiographical memory, and integrating the trait implications of the memories so retrieved. In this *self-perception* model, retrieval must pass through behaviors in order to reach traits. Put another way, nodes representing behaviors will be activated in the course of recovering—to be precise, in the course of *constructing*—information about traits. FIGURE 1C depicts the original default model, in which episodic self-knowledge is encoded independently of semantic self-knowledge—or, put another way, in which knowledge of behaviors is represented separately from knowledge of traits.

An extensive series of studies by Klein and Loftus (1993) has produced a compelling comparative test of these models. These studies adapted for the study of the self the *priming* paradigm familiar in studies of language and memory, in which the presentation of one item facilitates the processing of another associatively related item. Subjects were presented with trait adjectives as probes, and performed one of three tasks. In the *define* task, they simply defined the word; in the *describe* task, they rated the degree to which the term described themselves; in the *recall* task they remembered an incident in which they displayed behavior relevant to the trait. For each probe, two of these tasks were performed in sequence—for example, *describe* might be followed by *recall*, or *define* by *recall*, or *recall* by *describe*. There were nine possible sequences, and the important datum was the subject's response latency when asked the second question of each pair.

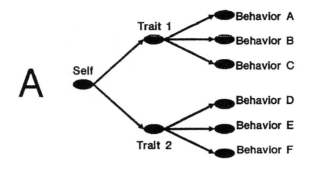

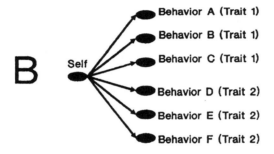

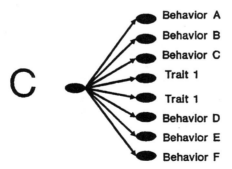

FIGURE 1. Three formats for representing episodic (behavioral) and semantic (trait) information about the self. **(A)** behaviors organized by traits; **(B)** traits inferred from behaviors, **(C)** behaviors and traits represented independently.

Because priming occurs as a function of overlap between the requirements of the initial task and the final task, systematic differences in response latencies will tell us whether activation passes through trait information on the way to behaviors, or vice versa, or by neither way. When the two processing tasks were identical, there was a substantial repetition priming effect of the first one on the second. But when Klein and Loftus (1993) examined the effect of *recall* on *describe*, they saw no evidence of semantic priming compared to the effects of the neutral *define* task. Nor was there semantic priming when they examined the effect of *describe* on *recall* (again, compared to the effects of the neutral *define* task). Contrary to the hierarchical model, the retrieval of autobiographical memory does not automatically invoke trait information. And contrary to the self-perception model, retrieval of trait information does not automatically invoke memory for behavioral episodes. Because self-description and autobiographical retrieval do not prime each other, Klein and Loftus concluded that items of episodic and semantic self-knowledge must be represented independently of each other.

This conclusion has received some additional support from an unusual source: Tulving's study of a neurological patient with an exceptionally dense amnesia (Tulving, 1993). The patient, known as K. C., was involved in a serious motorcycle accident at age 30. As a consequence, he suffered a dense anterograde amnesia affecting his memory for events which occurred since the time of the accident, but he also suffered a profound retrograde amnesia covering his entire personal history. To this day, K. C. remembers absolutely nothing of any of his experiences since birth. Interestingly, K. C. also underwent a marked change in personality. K. C.'s premorbid personality was quite extroverted, but his postmorbid personality was quite introverted. Tulving learned of the work of Klein and Loftus (1993) and wondered whether K.C. had any appreciation of his current personality.

With Klein's cooperation, Tulving (1993) assembled a list of personality trait adjectives and administered them to K. C. and his mother in a two-alternative forced-choice format. K. C. was asked to choose the adjective from each pair which better described himself as he is now. His mother was asked to complete the task twice, once for his premorbid personality, once for his postmorbid personality. K. C.'s choices were reliable, and agreed with his mother's judgments of his postmorbid personality, but disagreed with her judgments of his premorbid personality. This means that he has generic, semantic knowledge of what he is like *now* even though he cannot consciously recollect anything he has ever said or done. So he has acquired semantic knowledge of himself without retaining any episodic knowledge of the specific actions and experiences on which that self-knowledge is based.

More recently, Klein, Loftus, and Kihlstrom (1995) obtained similar findings from another patient, W. J., who, as a result of a severe head injury, suffered a temporary loss of her episodic memory. Both during her amnesia and following its remission, W. J. was asked to make trait judgments about herself. Because responses given when she could access episodic self-knowledge were reliable compared with responses given when she could not do so, Klein and his colleagues concluded that the loss of her trait-relevant behavioral memories did not greatly affect the availability of her trait self-knowledge.

These two cases of amnesia, taken together, offer strong support for the general proposition that knowledge of one's traits is represented and accessed independently from knowledge of one's behavior. Tulving (1993) interprets this outcome as support for his notion that episodic and semantic memory are represented in different memory systems of the brain. In the present context, it is also generally inconsistent with the self-perception theory of self-knowledge, and is consistent with the proposition that trait self-knowledge is encoded independently of behavioral self-knowledge.

WHAT DOES THE SELF LOOK LIKE?

To this question, cognitive psychology offers four answers:

1. *Viewed as a concept*, the self is a fuzzy set of context-specific selves, perhaps united by a prototypical self, or by an overarching theory of why we are one person in some situations, and another person in others.

2. *Viewed as a story*, the self is a narrative, or a set of narratives, which we have constructed, rehearsed to ourselves, and related to others, which answers Gaugin's three questions: Where do we come from? What are we? Where are we going? And perhaps a fourth: What does it all mean?

3. *Viewed as an image*, the self is a percept-based representation which stores knowledge about both spatial relationships and visual details about our faces, bodies and gestures.

4. *Viewed as an associative network*, the self is a bundle of propositions about our abstract traits, and our specific experiences, thoughts and actions, in which semantic self-knowledge is represented independently of episodic self-knowledge.

One feels a little like someone watching four blind people describe an elephant. But this is all right: why shouldn't self-knowledge be rich and multifaceted? In the end it's all neural connections anyway, but at the psychological level of analysis, which is where we as psychologists *should* be operating, there's no reason why we shouldn't consider different representational formats for different kinds of self-knowledge.

One thing is sure: the self, which plays such an important role in social interaction, is also a knowledge structure represented in the mind of the actor. Far from being a mystical entity, it appears that we can study and understand the self using the conceptual and methodological tools of modern cognitive psychology—bringing what we know about category structure, story understanding, image processing, and priming effects to bear on the self. And we can gather data for research on the self from a wide variety of sources: from conventional personality and social psychology, from conventional cognitive psychology, from cognitive neuropsychology, and from clinical psychology. So, both conceptually and empirically, the study of the self seems to serve a unifying function in psychology, bringing cognitive, social, personality, developmental, and clinical psychology together in common cause—just as William James thought it would.

ACKNOWLEDGEMENTS

We thank Robert Abelson, Mahzarin Banaji, Marilyn Dabady, David DiSteno, William Hirst, and Judith Loftus for their comments.

REFERENCES

ANDERSON, J. (1983). *The architecture of cognition*. Hillsdale, NJ: Erlbaum.

CANTOR, N. & KIHLSTROM, J. F. (1987). *Personality and social intelligence*. Hillsdale, NJ: Erlbaum.

EPSTEIN, S. (1973). The self-concept revisited: Or a theory of a theory. *American Psychologist, 28,* 404–416.

HASTIE, R., OSTROM, T. M., EBBESEN, E. B., WYER, R. S., HAMILTON, D. L. & CARLSTON, D. E. (EDS.). (1980). *Person memory: The cognitive basis of social perception*. Hillsdale, NJ: Erlbaum.

HEAD, H. (1926). *Aphasia and kindred disorders of speech*. Cambridge, MA: Cambridge University Press.

JAMES, W. (1981). *Principles of psychology*, (p. 221). Cambridge, MA: Harvard University Press. Original work published 1890.

KAMINER, W. (1992). *I'm dysfunctional, you're dysfunctional: The recovery movement and other self-help fashions*. Reading, MA: Addison-Wesley.

KIHLSTROM, J. F. (1995). Consciousness and me-ness. In J. Cohen & J. Schooler (Eds.), *Scientific approaches to the question of consciousness* (in press). Hillsdale, NJ: Erlbaum.

KIHLSTROM, J.F. & CANTOR, N. (1984). Mental representations of the self. In L. Berkowitz (Ed.), *Advances in experimental social psychology* (Vol. 17, pp. 1–47). New York: Academic Press.

KIHLSTROM, J. F., CANTOR, N., ALBRIGHT, J. S., CHEW, B. R., KLEIN, S. B. & NIEDENTHAL, P.M. (1988). Information processing and the study of the self. In L. Berkowitz (Ed.), *Advances in experimental social psychology* (Vol. 21, p. 145–177). San Diego, CA: Academic Press.

KIHLSTROM, J. F. & HASTIE, R. (1993). Mental representations of persons and personality. In R. Hogan, J.H. Johnson, & S. R. Briggs (Eds.), *Handbook of personality psychology*. Orlando, FL: Academic Press.

KIHLSTROM, J. F. & KLEIN, S. B. (1994). The self as a knowledge structure. In R. S. Wyer & T. K. Srull (Eds.), *Handbook of social cognition* (Vol. 1, pp. 154–208). Hillsdale, NJ: Erlbaum.

KIHLSTROM, J. F., MARCHESE, L. & KLEIN, S. B. (1995). Situating the self in interpersonal space. In D. Jopling & U. Neisser (Eds.), *The conceptual self in context.* Cambridge, UK: Cambridge University Press.

KLEIN, S. B. & LOFTUS, J. (1993). The mental representation of trait and autobiographical knowledge about the self. In R.S. Wyer & T.K. Srull (Eds.), *Advances in social cognition* (Vol. 5, pp. 1–49). Hillsdale, NJ: Erlbaum.

KLEIN, S. B., LOFTUS, J. & KIHLSTROM, J. F. (1995). Self-knowledge of an amnesic patient: Toward a neuropsychology of social cognition. *Journal of Experimental Psychology: General,* in press.

MEDIN, D. L. (1989). Concepts and conceptual structure. *American Psychologist, 44,* 1469–1481.

MITA, T. H., DERNER, M. & KNIGHT, J. (1977). Reversed facial images and the mere-exposure hypothesis. *Journal of Personality & Social Psychology, 35,* 597–601.

NELSON, K. (1993). The psychological and social origins of autobiographical memory. *Psychological Science, 4,* 7–14.

OSGOOD, C. E. & LURIA, Z. (1954). A blind analysis of a case of multiple personality using the semantic differential. *Journal of Abnormal Psychology, 49,* 579–591.

PENNINGTON, N. & HASTIE, R. (1993). The story model for juror decision making. In R. Hastie (Ed.), *Inside the juror: The psychology of juror decision making* (pp. 192–221). Hillsdale, NJ: Erlbaum.

REDER, L. M. & ANDERSON, J. R. (1980). A partial resolution of the paradox of interference: The role of integrating knowledge. *Cognitive Psychology, 12,* 447–472.

ROGERS, T. B. (1981). A model of the self as an aspect of human information processing. In N. Cantor & J. F. Kihlstrom (Eds.), *Personality, cognition, and social interaction* (pp. 193–214). Hillsdale, NJ: Erlbaum.

SCHANK, R. C. & ABELSON, R. P. (1995). Knowledge and memory: The real story. In R.S. Wyer (Ed.), *Advances in social cognition* (Vol. 8, pp.1–85). Hillsdale, NJ: Erlbaum.

SCHILDER, P. (1938). *Image and appearance of the human body.* London: Kegan Paul, Trench, and Tubner.

SMITH, E. E., ADAMS, N. & SCHORR, D. (1978). Fact retrieval and the paradox of interference. *Cognitive Psychology, 10,* 438–464.

SMITH, E. E. & MEDIN, D. L. (1981). *Categories and concepts.* Cambridge, MA: Harvard University Press.

THIGPEN, C. H. & CLECKLEY, H. (1954). A case of multiple personality. *Journal of Abnormal Psychology, 49,* 135–151.

TULVING, E. (1983). *Elements of episodic memory.* Oxford: Oxford University Press.

TULVING, E. (1993). Self-knowledge of an amnesic individual is represented abstractly. In T. K. Srull & R. S. Wyer (Eds.), *Advances in social cognition* (Vol. 5, pp.147–156). Hillsdale, NJ: Erlbaum.

ZAJONC, R.B. (1968). Attitudinal effects of mere exposure. *Journal of Personality & Social Psychology Monographs, 9* (2, Pt. 2), 1–27.

Ulric Neisser has recently returned to Cornell University (where he was Professor from 1967 to 1983) after thirteen years as Woodruff Professor of Psychology at Emory University in Atlanta. Widely regarded as one of the founders of cognitive psychology, Neisser is best known for his books Cognitive Psychology *(1967),* Cognition and Reality *(1976),* Memory Observed *(1982),* The School Achievement of Minority Children *(1986), and* The Perceived Self *(1993). He is a member of the National Academy of Sciences as well as a former Guggenheim and Sloan Fellow.*

The Roots of Self-Knowledge:
Perceiving Self, It, and Thou[a]

ULRIC NEISSER

Department of Psychology
Cornell University
Ithaca, New York 14853

If we are in search of the self, we can look either inward or outward. To look inward is to focus on private experience, on mental representations, on the self-concept. To look outward is to see the self as embedded in its environment, ecologically and socially situated in relation to other objects and persons.

These modes are not exclusive: people learn about themselves in both ways. Human beings have access to many forms of knowing about self and world—ecological perception, social perception, memory, verbal instruction, conception, reflection, introspective awareness. But philosophers concerned with the self have not treated all those forms with equal respect or given them equal time. From Descartes and Hume through James and Mead to modern cognitive science, theorists of the self have usually looked inward, trying to find the self inside the head. The results have been disturbing: the harder they look, the less self they find. Daniel Dennett (1991), one of the most articulate of the current crop of mentalists, puts it this way:

> Searching for the self can be somewhat like [this]. You enter the brain through the eye, march up the optic nerve, round and round in the cortex, looking behind every neuron, and then, before you know it, you emerge into daylight on the spike of a motor nerve impulse, scratching your head and wondering where the self is. (p. 355)

Dennett eventually concludes that the self simply does not exist; it is only a "narrative fiction." This outcome is hardly surprising: David Hume reached more or less the same position two hundred years ago on the basis of a similar argument. I think that such conclusions are inevitable as long as the search for the self is confined to the inside of the head. Fortunately, there is another place to look. Each of us is an active agent in a real environment, and we can directly see that this is the case. Thus we are–and know that we are–*ecological selves* (Neisser, 1988, 1991).

This approach—the definition of self in terms of one's real existence in

---

[a]An earlier version of this paper appeared in the Danish journal *Psyke & Logos* (1994, *15*, 392–407) under the title "Self-perception and self-knowledge."

the world—has its own philosophical roots. Merleau-Ponty and Heidigger come immediately to mind, and Martin Buber has made a particularly salient contribution. But I am not a philosopher, only a psychologist; my expertise is in the study of perception. My claim that the self can be directly perceived is based on an analysis of objectively existing information, and on experiments showing how that information is used. Such an analysis reveals two basic modes of self-perception, the *ecological* and the *interpersonal*. Available from earliest infancy, these modes are the foundation on which other forms of self-knowledge are built (Neisser, 1993).

Self-perception is such an unfamiliar concept that it is easily misunderstood. What I have in mind is nothing like self-evaluation or self-criticism; neither is it the kind of seeing that occurs when you look into a mirror. No mirror is necessary: we all perceive ourselves continuously and veridically without one. Although it has occasionally been suggested that self-awareness begins only with recognition of one's mirror image, I believe that this suggestion is deeply mistaken. Mirror recognition is a rather late step in development, one that depends on previously established forms of self-perception. To see why this is the case, we must first review some general principles of visual perception.

The ecological analysis of perception is based on the work of James J. Gibson, who was my friend and colleague at Cornell University for a number of years. It is radically different from the classical theories of vision. Gibson (1979) begins not with the image on the retina but with the *optic array*, the ocean of structured light in which all animals live and move. Except in pitch darkness, every point in the environment to which the eye of an animal might come is necessarily the center of a shell of optical structure: light reaches it from all directions. Because much of that light has been reflected from nearby surfaces, the structure of the array carries information about how those surfaces are arranged.

In the static case, the optic array can be defined as the infinite set of such points together with their shells of informative structure. But the static case is neither optimal nor typical: a great deal more information appears when the point of observation is allowed to move. Movement-produced changes in the array, collectively known as *optic flow*, uniquely specify both the layout of the environment and the perceiver's own path of motion. It is because we are mobile animals, not limited to static points of observation, that we can see the environment as it really is. In doing so, we also see our own path of motion. As Gibson put it: "Egoreception accompanies exteroception like the two sides of a coin. . . . One perceives the environment and coperceives oneself" (1979, p. 126).

There are several different kinds of optic flow. One type is produced by movements parallel to an extended surface, such as a nearby wall: every texture element in the corresponding sector of the array streams backward as the eye moves forward. Under natural conditions, this flow is completely reliable information for motion of the self. That is why it can so easily be used to produce illusions of self-motion, as in the so-called "moving room" experiments. If you stand on the (motionless) floor of David Lee's experimental room at the University of Edinburgh, you will sway in gentle synchrony with the walls as they move back and forth. With larger displacements of the walls you will have a compelling experience of self-motion although you are standing still, and may even have trouble keeping your balance (Lishman & Lee, 1973). The same thing happens in the familiar "railroad illusion," when a train on the next track begins to move.

Another important kind of motion-produced information is *occlusion* (J.J. Gibson, 1979). In a normally cluttered environment, an object that is fully visible from one point of observation may be shifted behind some other "occluding" object as the observer moves forward, eventually becoming invisible. These patterns of occlusion specify the relative positions of the objects involved: the one that becomes hidden is always farther away than the one that hides it. And even without actual occlusion, the changing visual directions of nearby stationary objects are enough to specify the perceiver's path of motion exactly (Cutting, Springer, Braren & Johnson, 1992).

A third form of optic flow, *looming* (Schiff, 1965), occurs when an object moves toward the observer. The sector of the array that corresponds to the approaching object gets larger and larger, until just before contact it fills the whole visual field. The rate of this magnification is especially informative; its inverse, which David Lee (1980) calls *tau*, specifies how soon the object will collide with the observer (that is, if there is no change in relative velocity). Thus the optic array can specify the perceiver's situation not only in the present but also as it will be in the immediate future (cf. Lee, 1993).

These forms of optic flow enable individuals to see their own situations in the real environment; that is, they specify the ecological self. What they specify is not always limited to the biological body: anything that moves along with you is likely to be accepted as part of your ecological self, especially if its motions are deliberately produced. Consider the case of clothing: it was *you* who just kicked the soccer ball, even though its only contact was with your shoe. This principle explains why the wearers of artificial limbs so naturally perceive them as parts of themselves. To the extent that the motions of a limb (or of anything else) are responsive to intentions and coordinated with shifts of viewpoint, it will be perceived as belonging to the ecological self. (It may nevertheless be considered alien to the *conceptual* self; as we shall see, that is a different matter.)

One surprising piece of evidence for this hypothesis comes from a form of childhood behavior that has been often described but even more often misunderstood. In a game-like situation, young children may cover their own eyes with their hands and say "You can't see me!" This behavior is often interpreted in terms of Piaget's concept of egocentricity: when a child can't see, it just assumes that you can't see either. The results of an experimental study by Flavell, Shipstead and Croft (1980) show, however, that this interpretation is wrong. When Flavell *et al.* asked their eyes-covered subjects "Can I see you?", most two- or three-year-old children did indeed answer "No." But the very same subjects answered "Yes" to many other questions about what the experimenter could see: "Can I see Snoopy [a nearby doll]?" Yes. "Can I see your leg?" Yes. "Your head?" Yes. "Can I see you?" No. These results suggest that "You can't see me" does not result from any childish egocentric misunderstanding; rather, it reflects the child's own conception of self. When my *eyes* are covered, you can't see *me*: what children call "me" is somewhere near what I have been calling the "point of observation."

Vision is not the only possible source of such information. Bats, unlike *Homo sapiens*, depend primarily on the acoustic array established by reflected sound. Despite this difference, bats' awareness of where they are—and of what is about to happen—seems to be at least as precise as our own. Echolocation (i.e., perception based on a reflected acoustic array) enables bats to pursue flying insects at high speed through a lacework of leafy branches, all in total darkness. It is sometimes suggested that the phenomenal world of an echolocating bat, based as it is on hearing rather than vision, must be very different from our own. That suggestion may be based on a mistaken premise. In J.J. Gibson's view (1979), perception does not depend on visual or auditory or any other kind of "sensations"—bits of modality-specific mental experience—but on *information*, which may well have the same structure in more than one stimulus array. Individuals perceive the real situation specified by that information, regardless of the input modality they happen to be using. If the life-world of bats differs widely from our own, it is not because they use hearing where we use vision; it is only because they fly among the trees while we walk on the ground.

Although this chapter focuses on vision, normal human perception of the ecological self is also supported by hearing and feeling and touch. This is true for everyone, but it is especially clear in the case of the blind. Given a reasonable amount of social support, many blind individuals manage fairly well without any vision at all. Among other things, they can make some use of information in the acoustic array. Using what is called "facial vision" (which is actually based on sound), a blind person can perceive some aspects of the near environment—a large object here, a wall over there. Nevertheless, the absence of vision is a serious handicap. Blind children are slow to explore their environments and slow to understand their immediate situations. They are also slow in using words like *I* and *you*, which depend on a clearly defined ecological self (Fraiberg, 1977; E.J. Gibson, 1978).

The ecological self is a perceiver, but it is also a doer—an active agent engaged with the surrounding world. As we act in and on the environment, we are aware of our actions and know them for our own. That is, we *perceive* them for our own, on the basis of what we see and hear and feel. I grasp a glass of water: the visual and auditory and tactile feedback thus produced coincides appropriately with the intention that drove the movement in the first place. That coincidence marks the movement as something I did myself; it also provides further information to guide my next movements as I bring the glass to my lips. Here, then, is another mode of self-perception. I know what I am *doing* as well as where I am *going*.

Perceptual awareness extends not only to actions in progress but to those we have not yet undertaken. J.J. Gibson (1979) coined a new technical term, "affordance," to describe this situation. Right now, for example, the floor of the office in which I sit affords walking, and its door affords passage. What this means is simply that I could walk across the room and go out the door (if I wanted to). Seeing a glass of water at hand I could drink from it, or for that matter throw it across the room. Affordances can often be directly perceived: I can *see* that the floor affords walking, the glass drinking. To be sure, I don't see everything. Every situation objectively offers infinitely many affordances for any given individual, of which only a few are perceived and even fewer realized in action.

It would be a fact that the glass affords throwing, even if throwing it had never occurred to me. By insisting on the objective existence of affordances, Gibson broke with a long-established tradition. Although phenomenologists have often noted that the world is perceived in terms of possible actions, they typically assign such possibilities to some nonphysical realm: to the "phenomenal field," for example, or the "behavioral world." As Gibson defined them, however, affordances are in the *real* world. They are perceived rather than invented. Indeed, they must be perceived if the individual is to survive.

To say that affordances are in the real world is not to say that they are properties of objects per se. They belong just as much to the individual. *I* can drink from the glass, but a paraplegic might not be able to do so; a small fish could swim in the glass, but I cannot. Just as interpersonal relations are essentially *between* one person and another—a topic to which we will turn shortly—so affordances are essentially *between* actors and environments. They are relations, not object properties.

Recent research has shown that such affordances are easily and accurately perceived. I see at a glance whether an object is within reach, whether a door is wide enough for me to walk through or a chair the right height to sit on. Ballplayers see how they must move to catch the ball, long jumpers adjust their strides to hit the take-off board. Another new concept must be introduced here: such perception is necessarily *body-scaled* (Warren & Whang, 1987). The distances that matter are not measured in centimeters or inches, but in relation to my own bodily dimensions and capabilities. Partly for this reason, the perception of affordances is subject to constant learning and recalibration. A floor that afforded only crawling to a baby at eleven months affords walking a few weeks later; a fence that afforded leaping when I was twenty-four affords only clambering when I am sixty-four. The body in "body-scaling" is that of the perceiver himself. To see an object as within reach is to see it as within *my* reach, given the length of *my* arm and the flexibility of *my* trunk. To see a flight of stairs as climbable is to see that *I* can climb it, given the length and strength of my own legs. This means that in perceiving affordances, we are again perceiving ourselves.

How is this possible? Our own bodies are rarely in the field of view: how do we manage to scale our perceptions to them so exactly? This problem has been only partly solved, but one important source of information has now been identified. It is *eye height*: the vertical distance from the ground to the eyes of the perceiver. Eye height is almost always fully specified in the field of view. To see that this is so, consider first the special case when you stand outdoors on a level plain. Your eye level is then marked by the visible horizon, so that, for example, any tree that happens to be bisected by the horizon is necessarily twice as tall as you are, regardless of its distance (Sedgwick, 1986). The same thing is possible indoors, or indeed almost anywhere. You can try it now: just look around. In whatever direction you may look, your level gaze will meet some object at some distance. You easily see where (that is, how high up) your gaze intercepts that object—so easily that there might as well be a white stripe painted around the whole field of view at eye level! People don't need mirrors to see how tall they are.

A slight digression is worth making here. The optic array does not specify eye height *absolutely*, but only in relation to visible objects. The same relationship can also be read the other way, to specify the sizes of objects in relation to the eye height of the observer (Wraga & Neisser, 1995). Some things are larger than you, others smaller. You have always seen the sizes of objects in this way, even when you yourself were much smaller than you are today. That is why the house you grew up in often seems so tiny when you return as an adult. The fireplace that once loomed so large is now of quite a conventional size, the endless hallway just a short corridor, the tree in which you climbed so high hardly more than a sapling. Nevertheless, there was and is no illusion. Your perception of object size was quite right on both occasions, scaled to the height of your gaze.

This example suggests that the principles of ecological perception apply as much to children as to adults. Indeed they do, and even to infants. Babies only three or four months old are aware of themselves as active agents in a real environment, just as we are ourselves. That fact has now been established by many elegant experiments. Nevertheless, it has not always been so obvious. Through most of psychology's history, from Locke to James to Freud to Piaget, the mental life of infants was regularly described as no better than a buzzing confusion. Where we (as adults) see real and persisting objects, babies were believed to see only blurs of visual sensation; where we experience ourselves as distinct individuals, they were thought to experience only "oneness" with their mothers. Realistic perception was described as a late intellectual achievement, based on the slow accumulation of memories and associations. These assumptions seemed reasonable enough—I once took them for granted myself—but they have all turned out to be wrong.

We now know that babies are sensitive to every major form of optic flow. Looming is a well-studied case in point: infants perceive an expanding optical display much as we do. What they see is a rapidly approaching object, so they flinch away from it (Ball & Tronick, 1971). Moreover, parallel optic flow specifies movement of the ecological self to children just as it does to adults. This is easily shown in the moving room, where a slight movement of the visible walls is enough to make a standing twelve-month-old fall down (Lee & Aronson, 1974). The seated posture of younger infants is equally affected (Bertenthal & Bai, 1989).

The case of occlusion is especially interesting, because it bears on what is often called "object permanence." When one object goes behind another, its surface disappears in a gradual and systematic way that J.J. Gibson called *texture-deletion-at-an-edge* (e.g., Gibson, Kaplan, Reynolds & Wheeler, 1969). As noted earlier, this specifies the relative positions of the two objects with respect to the self. The occluder (A) must be closer than the object being occluded (B). But Gibson also made another, more controversial claim: when all of B's texture has disappeared, the perceiver sees that B *has gone behind* A. At this point B is no longer visible, but its position in the environment is fully specified. Thus the fact that objects continue to exist after they go out of sight can be seen; it need not be inferred.

This claim was controversial for two reasons. First, it seems counterintuitive to claim that one can see the present locations of invisible objects. Second, Gibson's argument contradicted certain well-entrenched assumptions about object permanence. According to Piaget, our belief that things continue to exist after they go out of sight is just that—a belief, an intellectual achievement. Because young infants have not yet acquired this belief, objects that go out of sight no longer exist for them: out of sight is literally out of mind.

Recent experiments, testing for object permanence in new and ingenious ways, have supported Gibson's analysis rather than Piaget's. In these experiments, babies first see an object go behind a barrier. They are then shown a further event which would be impossible if the object were still there. For example, a wooden block may be placed behind a screen; the screen then folds down flat onto the table through the space where the block should be. Four-month-old infants exhibit great surprise on seeing such displays (Baillargeon, Spelke & Wasserman, 1985). Appropriate controls show that they are surprised for the same reason that we would be: what they have just seen is impossible. These and other studies demonstrate that babies have a realistic grasp of the environment. Their experience is no meaningless blur; on the contrary, they are ecologically located selves.

Infants also see what actions that environment *affords* them. The perception of affordances in infancy is especially interesting because babies' capacities for action are so different from our own and because they change so quickly with development. They reach for nearby objects, but only those that are within reach; they crawl onto surfaces that look capable of support, but not over the edges of cliffs. In short they are much like us where self-perception is concerned: aware of themselves, they also perceive the environment in terms of their own possibilities for action. Perception is not only the most dependable but also the earliest source of self-knowledge.

ᶎ𝄞

So far I have told only half the story. I have spoken of the self in the physical environment: of looking at *things*, and perceiving ourselves in terms of what those things afford. How about *people?* Human beings are social animals. In some societies, people spend their entire lives within earshot of one another. In all societies, the most meaningful occasions of life involve interaction with other persons. Those exchanges may be based on close physical contact, as when we embrace; on acoustical signals, as when we speak to one another; on visual information, as when we smile or exchange gestures; perhaps on other modalities too. Often, they involve several modalities at once.

Whatever their basis, these personal exchanges are what make life worth living. We would hardly be human without them. William James (1890) put it this way:

> No more fiendish punishment could be devised, were such a thing physically possible, than that one should be turned loose in society and remain absolutely unnoticed by all the members thereof. If no one turned round when we entered, answered when we spoke, or minded what we did, but if every person we met "cut us dead," and acted as if we were non-existing things, a kind of rage and impotent despair would ere long well up in us, from which the cruellest bodily tortures would be a relief; for these would make us feel that, however bad might be our plight, we had not sunk to such a depth as to be unworthy of attention at all (p. 293).

People do, usually, turn round when we enter and answer when we speak. We do the same for them. Mutuality of behavior is the rule, not only among humans but for many other species. Crickets call to crickets, frogs to frogs; dogs and apes and monkeys encounter each other in systematic, species-specific ways. Every such exchange brings something new into existence: namely, a series of reciprocated behaviors occurring at a particular time and place. Those social exchanges are *perceptible*. What is perceived is not merely the other's behavior, but its reciprocity with one's own. Both participants are engaged in a mutual enterprise, and they are aware of that mutuality.

Considered as a participant in a shared communicative activity, each member of the dyad is an *interpersonal self*. Where the ecological self is an active agent in the physical environment, the interpersonal self is an agent in an ongoing social exchange. That self, too, is perceived: we see ourselves as the target of the other person's attention, and as co-creator of the interaction itself. Though Gibson himself did not make this extension, his claim about ecological perception transposes easily to the social case. Egoreception accompanies alteroception like the other side of a coin; one perceives the other and coperceives oneself. This is true whether we are returning an embrace or just maintaining eye contact, improvising in a jazz group or just taking turns in a conversation.

Like its ecological counterpart, the interpersonal self is an active agent in a real environment. You are aware of your own interpersonal activity, and of what its result should be. You then perceive its actual result, the appropriate (or perhaps inappropriate) response of your partner. As in the nonsocial case, the fit between intentions and outcomes establishes a strong sense of agency, of personal effectiveness.

Human beings confirm one another's selfhood in so many ways that it is impossible to list them all. Almost every personal encounter is mutually regulated: X directs behavior toward Y, and Y to X, in a reciprocal pattern that both establish together and both perceive. This pattern exists objectively and observably: it requires no inferences. To be sure, some theorists have argued that these behaviors are the basis of what they call "nonverbal" or "spontaneous" communication (Buck, 1993). From this perspective, social behaviors are messages that carry information about the sender's motives and emotions to the receiver. This may indeed happen, but it is not what I have in mind here. Patterns of reciprocated behavior exist in their own right. A mutual embrace is a perceptible fact, whatever the true feelings of the embracing participants and whatever they may believe about each other. Interpersonal exchange is something that happens *between* people. To perceive such an exchange is to look not inside the other person but at the overt pattern of ongoing activity. The interpersonal self is not an inner state to be communicated nor a detector of such states in others: it is just a person aware of engaging in a social encounter.

Interpersonal perception, like ecological perception, begins very early in life. Even newborn babies are interested in human faces, and sometimes imitate their expressions (Meltzoff & Moore, 1989). By eight weeks or so babies have become exquisitely social, perhaps more than they ever will be again. They return their mother's embraces, listen to her voice, look at her face, maintain eye contact. Such infants are still a long way from speech, but when speech is addressed to them they may goo-goo cheerfully in return. These "protoconversations" (Bateson, 1975) between babies and mothers are by no means neutral in tone. They are often happy, punctuated with surges of joy that are systematically coordinated with the mother's own feelings. Such sustained and motivated behaviors testify to the innate human readiness for emotional relationships; they are clear cases of the interpersonal self in action.

A recent experiment by Lynne Murray and Colwyn Trevarthen (1985) illustrates the reciprocity of protoconversation especially well. The subjects of the experiment were Scottish mothers and their 6- to 8-week-old infants, interacting over closed-circuit television. Each partner saw a life-size full-face image of the other, and heard the other's voice as well. Under these conditions their exchanges were entirely natural: the babies smiled and goo-gooed at their mothers, who happily responded in kind. After a few minutes of this, real-time communication was interrupted. Instead the baby was shown a *videotape* of its mother, one which had been recorded during the successful interaction a few months earlier. The results were dramatic. The previously happy babies now became miserable: they looked away from the TV monitor, fidgeted, and generally seemed to wish that they were some-where else. This happened even though they were seeing the very same visual/auditory display that had given them so much pleasure before! Their un-happiness in the taped presentation suggests a hypothesis about what they had enjoyed so much before: it was, in part, their own ability to affect the exchange. Watching a videotape eliminates *agency*: taped mothers do not re-turn gestures or respond to vocalizations. Like the rest of us, 2-month-olds apparently know when they are—or are not—reciprocally engaged with an-other person.[b]

Encountering a person is very different from being engaged with the inanimate environment. Although both are occasions to perceive ourselves, they are quite different epistemologically. The information that specifies the ecological self is based on universal principles of optics. Those principles are the same for everyone: parallel optic flow means "I am moving" to any ani-mal with a developed visual system. Patterns of interpersonal action, in con-trast, are species-specific. Horses do not value eye contact as we do, and cats do not hold hands (or paws). The dominant male stare so important for pri-mates has no counterpart among spiders, probably not even among rabbits. These behavior patterns are consequences of natural selection (just as per-ceptual systems are), but they are different in different species. In every case, they are critical for the species' social life.

The emotional accompaniments of these two kinds of self-knowledge are different too. The ecological self is a fairly cool customer, competent rather than passionate. Navigating the world is occasionally exhilarating and some-times fear-provoking, but mostly it is just something we do. The environ-ment is always there for us, and we are always in touch with it. Encounters with persons, in contrast, are special. We do not entirely control them. They occur irregularly, in ways that depend on the presence and attitude of an es-

---

[b]Unfortunately, our own efforts to replicate the findings of Murray and Trevarthen (1985) have not been successful (Rochat, Neisser & Marian, in press).

sentially mysterious other. Only by the grace of that other can we reach the heights of joy that human contact may bring—or, for that matter, the corresponding depths of despair. This unpredictability must be especially poignant in the first year of life, before language, when the infant has no real grasp of other people's purposes and or the constraints on their actions. But it does not end with infancy: for most of us, interpersonal relations remain more than a little mysterious throughout life.

Although the notions of *encounter* and *between* may be unfamiliar to psychologists, they are well-known in the philosophy of dialogue. An especially powerful formulation is that of the Hasidic theologian Martin Buber, presented seventy years ago in his book *I and Thou* (Buber, 1923/1955). Buber distinguished two primary relations in human life, which he called *I-It* and *I-Thou*. The more familiar of these, *I-It*, is the relation between ourselves and some other person or object that we try to manipulate for purposes of our own. All of us relate to most of the world, most of the time, as *It*. Something very different happens on the rare occasions when we encounter another person directly, meeting them as a *Thou*. The relation *I-Thou* is one of immediate engagement, free of intellectual forethought or manipulation. It cannot be forced. The essential component of the encounter with *Thou* occurs *between* the participants; it is not to be found in either of them taken alone.

There is at least a superficial parallel between Buber's dichotomy and my distinction between ecological and interpersonal perception. The *I* of *I-It* is something like an ecological self, while the *I* of *I-Thou* is an acutely interpersonal one. To be sure, Buber's categories are much deeper than mine. His *It* includes not only the world of perceptible things but also that of ideas, analysis, and self-centered reflection. He notes that even our encounters with people are usually on the level of *I-It*; we tend to treat the other person as an object rather than as a *Thou*. On the other hand we can have an *I-Thou* encounter even with an inanimate object—a tree or a stone—if we approach it as a *Thou*. Buber believed that we also have such encounters with God; indeed, every *Thou* participates somehow in the divine.

Although I am not religious in Buber's sense, I also believe that interpersonal contact and social feeling have a special status in human life. Our immediate awareness of interpersonal engagement does not depend on anything else in experience: not on inference, not on reflection, not even on ecological perception. *Thou* cannot be reduced to a category of *It*. Even in early infancy—*especially* in early infancy—there is something unique about our relations with other people. The sense of mystery and unpredictability that characterizes genuine encounters with other persons begins in the first weeks of life. It may be some dim memory of that primary experience that allows us to resonate to Buber's categories—to feel, as he did, that there is something especially powerful about the encounter with *Thou*. After all, we can affirm the ecological self whenever we want to, just by looking around and moving about. The interpersonal self comes into being only by the grace and response of another human being.

Throughout this chapter, I have argued that people perceive their immediate ecological and social situations realistically and accurately. This claim may seem surprising. Nowadays the word *perception* is often used in a very different sense, to contrast as sharply as possible with *real*. When politicians believe that the public sees their behavior in an unfavorable light, for example, they do not necessarily change the behavior itself; instead they employ special consultants to change how it is perceived. In the same vein, advertisers spend large sums to ensure that products are favorably perceived even when they do not deserve to be. What's worse, many of those products themselves are specifically designed to mislead perceivers—to make us look younger than we really are, for example. Sometimes they are successful in doing so. We live in an age of deception, when almost nothing—at least nothing in public life—is what it seems. How then can I argue that perception and self-perception are veridical?

In fact, there are two fundamentally different forms of perception. One of these is the "direct" perception that guides and accompanies our immediate encounters with persons and things. Direct perception is dependable because it is based on invariant structures in the stimulus array. The other one—known in some terminologies as the "what" system—is chiefly responsible for recognition and interpretation. Primarily associative in function, it may indeed be subject to manipulation and deceit. These systems are very different—so different that they even depend on distinct neural circuitry in the brain (Ungerleider & Mishkin, 1982). More important here, however, is that they use different forms of information (Neisser, 1994).

As we have seen, direct perception depends on changes in the optic array that every real action must produce. Associative perception, in contrast, depends on relating what we see at this moment to concepts we already have—on recognizing, classifying, evaluating, thinking. That is why it can so easily be misled. What particular concept comes to mind on a given occasion depends on literally hundreds of variables, from cultural predispositions to personal past experiences to momentary moods. It is the ease with which such variables can be manipulated that can give "perception" a bad name.

This distinction is also important for knowledge of self. Ecological and interpersonal perception may enable you to know what you are doing and where, but there is much more to you than that. Much of what you believe about yourself is not and cannot have been directly perceived; instead it comprises your *self-concept* or *conceptual self* (Neisser, 1988). Loosely speaking, your self-concept consists of your beliefs about yourself—your appropriate roles, your personal attributes, your worth and value, and so forth. I believe, for example, that I am an American, a psychologist, a husband and father. But that's not all: I may also believe that I am handsome or ugly, stupid or smart, important or worthless; that I have a liver, a kindly disposition, an immortal soul. None of those beliefs is based on direct perception, and in principle they could all be mistaken. In actual fact, some of them may be mistaken indeed.

In addition to self-concepts there are also *self-narratives*, the stories we tell in order to extend the self into an otherwise vanished past (Neisser & Fivush, 1994). We are usually quite confident about those stories, but we do not always tell them in the same way and they may not always correspond to what actually happened. As a psychologist with a long interest in the study of memory, I can cite many examples of mistaken recall (cf. Neisser & Harsch, 1992). But that fallibility has not made the concept of narrative any less attractive to postmodern theoreticians; on the contrary, the narrative mode is currently very popular. Dennett's (1991) conclusion that the self is only a "narrative fiction" is a case in point. Given what has been said here about self-perception, that conclusion is surely wrong. Nevertheless we do *need* self-narratives, just as we need self-concepts; we would hardly be human without them.

At what age do we acquire self-concepts and self-narratives? The relevant learning begins quite early, but not so early as perception. I am inclined to place the beginnings of conceptual thought near the end of the first year of life. At that point, the ecological and interpersonal selves are already firmly in place. Conceptual thought would be impossible without the prior skills of perception: for one thing, children get most of their concepts from other people. This happens primarily on occasions of shared attention (Bruner, 1983; Tomasello & Farrar, 1986), when the child and its "tutor" are attending the same thing and both of them know it. Those occasions, which are critical for the acquisition of language as well as of concepts, depend for their very existence on the child's (and the tutor's) interpersonal perception.

How, then, does the *self*-concept originate? It probably begins in a subset of the occasions of shared attention just mentioned—namely, those in which the object of joint interest is the child herself (Tomasello, 1993). These are the occasions when a mother says "That's a good girl!" or "Did you do that?"—when she speaks *to* the child *about* the child. The result is that the child, like her mother, now takes herself as an object of thought. She begins to think of herself as having traits, attributes, worth and value. Not all the characteristics that will be important later attract her attention at first. It may be another year, for example, before she notices that her *facial appearance* matters to other people. Typically it is only then, when she is nearly two, that she begins to use her mirror image as information for her own appearance, and to display the behaviors that some theorists take as reflecting the beginnings of self-awareness (Gallup, 1970).

The self-narrative begins still later, sometime around the third year. It is then that children become interested in the past and the future, and begin to acquire the memory skills on which narrative depends. They start to tell their own stories, an activity that typically continues throughout life. Even as adults, every new experience has at least some potential for changing our self-narratives and our self-concepts. Certain kinds of encounters, like those with psychoanalysts and other therapists, may even be undertaken with that purpose explicitly in mind. I do not undervalue those efforts, nor do I dispute the importance of concept and narrative as sources of self-knowledge. But they are not the *first* such sources; that honor goes uncontestedly to ecological and interpersonal perception.

Even later, it is the perceived self to which all the more intellectual modes of knowing ultimately refer. Whose story does my self-narrative tell, if not that of the perceptible persisting self who is currently here, staring at his word-processor? What entity does my self-concept describe, if not that self-same individual? The perceived self is what those other selves are about, what they refer to, what they mean. Even when mystics deny that the things of this world have any importance, it is the ecological and interpersonal self that they must ultimately deny. What cannot be denied, I think, is that perception is first.

REFERENCES

BAILLARGEON, R., SPELKE, E. S. & WASSERMAN, S. (1985). Object permanence in five-month-old infants. *Cognition, 20,* 191–208.

BALL, W. A. & TRONICK, E. (1971). Infant responses to impending collision: Optical and real. *Science, 171,* 818–820.

BATESON, M. C. (1975). Mother-infant exchanges: The epigenesis of conversational interaction. In D. Aronson & R. W. Rieber (Eds.), Developmental psycholinguistics and communication disorders. *Annals of the New York Academy of Sciences, 263.*

BERTENTHAL, B. I. & BAI, D. L. (1989). Infants' sensitivity to optical flow for controlling posture. *Developmental Psychology, 25,* 936–945.

BRUNER, J. (1983). *Child's talk.* New York: Norton.

BUBER, M. (1955). *I and thou.* New York: Scribners. (First published in 1923.)

BUCK, R. (1993). Spontaneous communication and the foundation of the interpersonal self. In U. Neisser (Ed.), *The perceived self: Ecological and interpersonal sources of self-knowledge.* New York: Cambridge University Press.

CUTTING, J. E., SPRINGER, K., BRAREN, P. A. & JOHNSON, S. H. (1992). Wayfinding on foot from information in retinal, not optical, flow. *Journal of Experimental Psychology: General, 121,* 41–72.

DENNETT, D. C. (1991). *Consciousness explained.* Boston: Little, Brown.

FLAVELL, J. H., SHIPSTEAD, S. G. & CROFT, K. (1980). What young children think you see when their eyes are closed. *Cognition, 8,* 369–387.

FRAIBERG, S. (1977). *Insights from the blind: Comparative studies of blind and sighted infants.* New York: Basic Books.

GALLUP, G. (1970). Chimpanzees: Self-recognition. *Science, 167,* 86–87.

GIBSON, E. J. (1978). C'est moi: Review of Fraiberg's "Insights from the Blind." *Contemporary Psychology, 23,* 609–611.

GIBSON, J. J. (1979). *The ecological approach to visual perception.* Boston: Houghton Mifflin.

GIBSON, J. J., KAPLAN, G. A., REYNOLDS, H. N. & WHEELER, K. (1969). The change from visible to invisible: A study of optical transitions. *Perception and Psychophysics, 5,* 113–116.

JAMES, W. (1890). *Principles of psychology.* New York: Holt.

LEE, D. N. (1980). The optic flow field: the foundation of vision. *Philosophical transactions of the Royal Society of London, B 290,* 169–179.

LEE, D. N. (1993). Body-environment coupling. In U. Neisser (Ed.), *The perceived self: Ecological and interpersonal sources of self-knowledge.* New York: Cambridge University Press.

LEE, D. N. & ARONSON, E. (1974). Visual proprioceptive control of standing in human infants. *Perception and Psychophysics, 15,* 529–532.

LISHMAN, J. R. & LEE, D. N. (1973). The autonomy of visual kinaesthesis. *Perception, 2,* 287–294.

MELTZOFF, A. N. & MOORE, M. K. (1989). Imitation in newborn infants: Exploring the range of gestures imitated and the underlying mechanisms. *Developmental Psychology, 25,* 954–962.

MURRAY, L. & TREVARTHEN, C. (1985). Emotional regulation of interactions between two-month-olds and their mothers. In T. M. Field & N. A. Fox (Eds.), *Social perception in infants.* Norwood, NJ: Ablex.

NEISSER, U. (1988). Five kinds of self-knowledge. *Philosophical Psychology, 1,* 35–59.

NEISSER, U. (1991). Two perceptually given aspects of the self and their development. *Developmental Review, 11,* 197–209.

NEISSER, U. (Ed.). (1993). *The perceived self: Ecological and interpersonal sources of self-knowledge.* New York: Cambridge University Press.

NEISSER, U. (1994). Multiple systems: A new approach to cognitive theory. *European Journal of Cognitive Psychology, 6,* 225–241.

NEISSER, U. & FIVUSH, R. (Eds.) (1994). *The remembering self: Construction and accuracy in the self-narrative.* New York: Cambridge University Press.

NEISSER, U. & HARSCH, N. (1992). Phantom flashbulbs: False recollections of hearing the news about *Challenger.* In E. Winograd & U. Neisser (Eds.), *Affect and accuracy in recall: Studies of "flashbulb" memories.* New York: Cambridge University Press.

ROCHAT, P., NEISSER, U. & MARIAN, V. (in press). Are young infants sensitive to interpersonal contingency? *Infant Behavior and Development.*

SCHIFF, W. (1965). Perception of impending collision. *Psychological Monographs, 79,* No. 604.

SEDGWICK, H. A. (1986). Space perception. In K. Boff, L. Kaufman & J. Thomas (Eds.), *Handbook of perception and human performance.* New York: Wiley.

TOMASELLO, M. (1993). On the interpersonal origins of self-concept. In U. Neisser (Ed.), *The perceived self: Ecological and Interpersonal sources of self-knowledge.* New York: Cambridge University Press.

TOMASELLO, M. & FARRAR, J. (1986). Joint attention and early language. *Child Development, 57,* 1454–1463.

UNGERLEIDER, L. G. & MISHKIN, M. (1982). Two cortical visual systems. In D. J. Ingle, M. A. Goodale & R. J. W. Mansfield (Eds.), *Analysis of visual behavior.* Cambridge, MA: MIT Press.

WARREN, W. H. J. & WHANG, S. (1987). Visual guidance of walking through apertures: Body-scaled information for affordances. *Journal of Experimental Psychology: Human Perception and Performance, 13,* 371–383.

WRAGA, M. J. & NEISSER, U. (1995). *Effective eye height as a determinant of perceived size and distance: Four exploratory studies* (Report #32). Atlanta: Emory Cognition Project.

Robert L. Thompson is Professor Emeritus of Psychology at Hunter College and the Graduate School of the City University of New York. His research activity has ranged from neurobehavioral studies of basal ganglia function to analyses of avoidance behavior and learning in a variety of species. Over the last 20 years his work has centered on a behavioral approach to self-awareness and self-conception in monkeys and chimpanzees. He is a Fellow of the New York Academy of Sciences and a long time member of the Academy's Advisory Committee for the Psychology Section

Part II: Lessons from the Animal Laboratory

Introduction

ROBERT L. THOMPSON[a]

Department of Psychology
Hunter College and the
Graduate Center of the
City University of New York
New York, New York 10021

Robert Mitchell begins this section with a review of the essential procedural and interpretive aspects of the mark test (mirror-mediated mark-directed responding) as used with human and nonhuman primates to imply the presence or absence of self-recognition. He takes instances in which young children are described as attempting to touch a nonexistent mark on their own face after observing a mark on the face of another person as reasons to doubt the claim that passing the mark test invariably indicates self-recognition.

He next tells us that extant theoretical accounts of self-recognition reduce to two: *self-awareness theory*, which views self-recognition as a product of an already established self-awareness, and *kinesthetic–visual matching theory*, in which self-recognition arises from or with successful matching of visual inputs from one's bodily postures and movements. Both "theories" lead to a number of predictions of other classes of behavior: empathy, intentional deception, perspective-taking, pretending, and imitation among them.

Most importantly, Mitchell reviews some of the very extensive literature on behavioral abilities of autistic children to argue for support of the kinesthetic–visual matching view of self-recognition. His discussion leads to a focus on the production and discrimination of bodily/gestural imitative behavior in human and nonhuman animals. Because imitation also requires visual–kinesthetic matching, the demonstration of imitative behavior should be highly correlated with performance on the mark test. Because it is overt, imitative behavior is more objectively assessable than, say, intentionality, empathy, or perspective-taking. Although the data are few and the interpretations contentious, Mitchell tilts toward kinesthetic–visual matching as the better account of self-recognition.

Karyl Swartz begins with a review of the now standard account of the

[a]Address for correspondence: P.O. Box 393, Ridgefield, New Jersey 07657-0393.

events accompanying preparation for the mark test by introduction of a mirror into a naive chimpanzee's cage area. She is critical but accepting of the interpretation of a positive mark test as self-recognition, but she maintains that this need not imply self-awareness, a self-concept, or anything like a human understanding of the concept of self. She emphasizes species and individual differences in performance before mirrors and on the mark test, and makes the very important point that it may be inappropriate to continue to describe and define mirror self-recognition in other animal species based on chimpanzee behavior in front of a mirror. In this regard she discusses the often ambiguous or negative results of mark tests with gorillas and various species of macaque monkeys.

Swartz sees the way to a better comprehension of mirror self-recognition to be in comparative and developmental research focussing on analysis over time of the emergence of the animal's "understanding" of what it sees in a mirror and the accompanying cognitive capacities and mechanisms.

Gordon G. Gallup, Jr. is the author of the 1970 report that inspired if not initiated the ever-growing body of mirror (and video)-based empirical studies of self-recognition, self-awareness, and self-conception in animals and humans. Broadly, these topics lead to the questions of if and how we are to understand self-consciousness as an attribute of animal conduct, and broader still, how we are to understand the evolution of human consciousness. Gallup argued that mirror-mediated mark-directed responding indicated recognition of the reflection as one's own self, implying self-awareness and a self-concept. He argued too that mirror self-recognition was not a step toward self-conception but an elaboration of an already established self-concept. But the methodology of mirror self-recognition research and the inferences drawn from it have been criticized right from their beginning, and more so in recent years (see, for example, the two preceding discussions).

In this paper, Gallup acknowledges three major problem areas in dealing with the available data: the phyletic distribution of evidence for self-recognition, variance of the evidence within species, and the developmental characteristics of self-recognition. He further attempts to interpret these problems within an evolutionary account of "personal agency," drawing upon the "arboreal clambering hypothesis" of Povinelli and Cant (1995) and his own hypotheses concerning the relative social and reproductive advantages conferred by an evolving self-awareness. The whimsical title of Gallup's paper hints at the literal descent of self-awareness, coming down out of the trees and subsequently flourishing or diminishing through genetic drift.

Howard Rachlin's essay deals with describing and understanding human choices among opportunities for monetary payoffs in a social context having implications for altruistic or selfish outcomes. On this kind of understanding hangs the greater good of society. The principal experimental results are from a variant of the much-studied game of "prisoner's dilemma." Subjects either defect or cooperate. Procedures are described which enhance cooperation (a long-term mutually beneficial strategy when considered across the participants) rather than defection (a short-term beneficial strategy for the self).

In an uncommonly refreshing fashion the self is characterized in terms of interactions between behavior and the environment (i.e., short- and long-term probabilistically defined consequences). "Self" is an abstraction of one's present and past behavior, and the self-concept is taken as perception of those abstract relations. Rachlin is not concerned with how self is represented internally, but with how self-conception functions in the environment. One needs to consider oneself broadly over time rather than narrowly at this moment in time. What may be preferable now can be nonpreferable later (e.g., a drink now, a hangover later). To act in the interests of society or the community one must again consider one's actions over the long run. It is because there are inconsistencies between short- and long-term goals that there is a place for self-control and thus for a concept of self.

Rachlin's approach has its roots in radical behaviorism and the experimental analysis of self-control and commitment studied in the context of the operant behavior of laboratory animals (and human subjects) working under contingencies of choice (concurrent schedules of reinforcement).

Robert W. Mitchell is Associate Professor of Psychology at Eastern Kentucky University. He has studied social cognition in a variety of species, including humans, apes, monkeys, dolphins, and parrots, and has co-edited several volumes which compare human and nonhuman cognition: Deception: Perspectives on Human and Nonhuman Deceit *(1986),* Self-Awareness in Animals and Humans *(1994), and* Anthropomorphism, Anecdotes and Animals *(1997). Currently he is writing a book on the history of scientific attitudes toward anthropomorphism about animals, and researching children's understanding of pretense and false belief.*

A Comparison of the Self-Awareness and Kinesthetic–Visual Matching Theories of Self-Recognition: Autistic Children and Others

ROBERT W. MITCHELL

Department of Psychology
Eastern Kentucky University
Richmond, Kentucky 40475

THE PROBLEM

If a normal adult human being observes a novel mark on his or her face, he or she normally attempts to remove that mark. Unless the person is told of the mark by someone else, a mirror or a videotaped image of the person is usually required for the novel mark to be observed. When the person acts to remove the mark, one reasonably assumes that the image of his or her own body in the reflective or video medium has informed the person about the visual state of his or her own body. Such a person is said to recognize himself or herself, and exhibits the evidence for self-recognition by wiping the mark off his or her face.

This simple task of wiping a foreign mark off the face was used by Gallup (1970) and Amsterdam (1972) to support the idea that chimpanzees and young children self-recognize. Chimpanzees under anaesthesia were marked on one brow ridge and one ear (Gallup) and fully aware children were surreptitiously marked on the nose (Amsterdam); when later shown their image in a mirror, some of these organisms attempted to rid themselves of the mark by wiping it off after or while observing themselves in a mirror. This evidence is called "passing the mark test," and occurs in normal human children from about 12–22 months of age, with few successes prior to 15 months of age, and with 18 months as the average (Hart & Fegley, 1994; Lewis & Brooks-Gunn, 1978; Neuman & Hill, 1976).

The relationship between passing the mark test and self-recognition has often been assumed to be one of identity: if one has self-recognition, one passes the mark test; if one passes the mark test, one has self-recognition. Further tests with human children indicate, however, that this relationship is, surprisingly, somewhat ambiguous because some children also attempt to wipe a nonexistent mark off their nose after observing that another person has a mark on his or her nose. Seventeen of 59 children from ages 18–24 months of age touched their own unmarked nose after observing a mark on their mother's nose (Lewis & Brooks-Gunn, 1979, pp. 39, 57); and four of 48 children from ages 15–26 months of age touched their own unmarked nose after observing a mark on the nose of a same-age child on video (and only 11 of these 48 children touched their own marked nose after looking in the mirror) (Johnson, 1983, p. 217). Because young children may attempt to wipe a nonexistent mark off a particular location on their own face after observing that *another* person has a mark on his or her face in the same location, wiping a mark off one's face after observing oneself in a mirror need not indicate that one believes that the image in the mirror is an image of oneself (i.e., passing the mark test need not indicate self-recognition, Mitchell, 1993a). Otherwise, we would have to say that an attempt to wipe a mark off one's own nose after observing a mark on another's nose indicates that one believes that the image of the other's face is an image of oneself, in the same way that a mirror or videotaped image is.

Even though passing the mark test does not necessarily indicate self-recognition, passing the mark test remains the most commonly used indicator of self-recognition. Further tests with chimpanzees and children indicate that not all chimpanzees, and not all children, recognize themselves in mirrors (Lewis & Brooks-Gunn, 1979; Swartz & Evans, 1991). This fact raises complications for evaluating theories that predict that organisms that self-recognize have other psychological capacities, because typically the organisms tested for self-recognition are not the same as the organisms of the same species tested for these other psychological capacities.

THE THEORIES

Several theories have been elaborated to explain self-recognition and/or passing the mark test. I evaluate two theories here, in that other theories appear to be reducible to one of these two theories or make predictions that are contrary to evidence (see discussion in Mitchell, 1993b, pp. 368–371). The two theories discussed here are the self–awareness theory and the kinesthetic–visual matching theory.

The self-awareness theory of Gallup (1983, 1985; Gallup & Povinelli, 1993) assumes that passing the mark test is an indication of self-recognition, and that self-recognition is an indication that the organism can become the object of its own attention and is therefore self-aware. In this view, the organism's self-awareness is an explanation for its passing the mark test. But self-awareness is also viewed as an explanation for a variety of other psychological capacities, including theory of mind, intentional deception and concealment, reciprocal altruism, empathy, reconciliation, and pretending. These other psychological capacities are predicted by Gallup's theory because, in Gallup's view, organisms that are self-aware are aware of their own mental states, and model conspecifics' mental states on the basis of their own mental states.

The kinesthetic–visual matching theory, initially stated by Guillaume (1926/1971) and elaborated by Parker (1991) and Mitchell (1992, 1993a, 1993b), claims that passing the mark test is a result of kinesthetic–visual matching, that is, a capacity for matching between the kinesthetic, proprioceptive, and somasthetic sensations of one's own body's position and one's own bodily feeling, and visual images of one's own body and others' bodies. In this view, the organism's ability for kinesthetic–visual matching is an explanation for its passing the mark test.[1] Kinesthetic–visual matching would seem to provide capabilities for activities (in addition to bodily imitation and mirror-self-recognition) which require matching between the self and others, such as bodily pretense, recognition that one is being imitated, and planning, and seems a necessary ingredient for intentional (planned) deception, empathy, and perspective-taking (see Mitchell, 1993b; 1994; 1997). An organism with kinesthetic–visual matching can not only reproduce others' actions in pretense, but also presumably can translate from its own visual mental images of itself into action in planning, and from another's actions to its own similar actions to recognize that it is being imitated. An organism that pretends to be another may eventually gain some insight into the other's experience, and be able as a result to imagine the other's point of view and recognize that the other may experience some of the same feelings that the organism itself does. Such an organism may also be able to recognize how it appears to others (as suggested by Merleau-Ponty [1960/1982] and Wallon [1954/1984]), and therefore produce deceptive actions that are consistent with another's perspective. But there is no guarantee that an organism with kinesthetic–visual matching will necessarily take another's perspective, show empathy, or use its planning skills to intentionally deceive (Mitchell, 1993b).

Although both theories are clear about which psychological capacities are predicted from passing the mark test, and indeed predict that some of the same capacities are related to abilities necessary to pass the mark test (e.g., pretense, empathy, intentional deception), the theories differ in how they explain self-recognition (see extensive discussion in Mitchell, 1993a, 1993b). The self-awareness theory unfortunately does not specify how self-awareness leads to passing the mark test, in that the mental states an organism must be aware of to recognize itself in a mirror are never specified (see, for example, Gallup & Povinelli, 1993, in response to Mitchell, 1993a). The kinesthetic–visual matching theory, by contrast, specifies how an organism passes the mark test: the organism matches its kinesthetic sensations to its visual image in the mirror, and therefore predicts that, because these are the same, the mark on the nose of the image in the mirror indicates a mark on its own nose. Indeed, if the organism's recognition of the match between its own kinesthetic sensations and the visual image in the mirror is the mental state which the organism is aware of when it recognizes itself in the mirror, then the self-awareness theory of passing the mark test reduces to the kinesthetic–visual matching theory (Mitchell, 1993a).

Even if the self-awareness theory does not specify a means by which an organism passes the mark test, both it and the kinesthetic–visual matching theory specify psychological concomitants of passing the mark test.[2] Because evidence of intentional deception, pretense, theory of mind, and many other predicted psychological concomitants of self-recognition from nonhuman primates and normal human children has already been presented in relation to theories of self-recognition (Mitchell, 1993a, 1993b; Parker, 1991) and remains contentious (see Whiten & Byrne, 1988, and subsequent commentaries; Anderson, 1993; Gallup & Povinelli, 1993; Mitchell, 1993b; Premack, 1988), I instead focus my evaluation of the two theories on a little-discussed group: autistic children.

THE EVIDENCE FROM AUTISM

Autistic children present a good test case for the two theories because they frequently pass the mark test and have been tested on measures of imitation (of various forms), recognition of being imitated, pretense (bodily and other), intentional deception, empathy, theory of mind, planning, perspective-taking, and theory of mind. In addition, the evidence for self-recognition in autistic children is almost exclusively in the form of passing the mark test, rather than in the form of self-exploration, playing with their image, or verbal self-labeling observed in other children and animals (see Anderson, 1993; Gallup, 1970; Mitchell, 1993a, 1993b). The predictions from the two theories and evidence of the predicted psychological concomitants in autistic children are summarized globally in TABLE 1.

Note that TABLE 1 simply states whether autistic people typically show evidence of a psychological capacity, not whether they do so as frequently as or in the same way that normal children do. Autism is a highly variable syndrome. Some autistic people have written books and autobiographies, whereas others remain mute. Autistic children show profoundly disturbed social relationships, severely impaired communication skills, and ritualistic, obsessive, and stereotypic behavior (Spiker & Ricks, 1984), and often fail to generate, spontaneously, high frequencies of activities which they are nonetheless capable of performing. Consequently, they are often described as having "impaired" abilities compared to mental-age-matched children who are normal or have Down syndrome; but such impairment may have more to do with limited expression of present abilities. For example, although autistic children typically show little pretense about objects (Baron-Cohen, 1987), they understand pretense about objects (Jarrold, Smith, Boucher & Harris, 1994). To evaluate the two theories, what is important is

TABLE 1. Predictions from and Evidence for the Self-awareness and Kinesthetic–Visual Matching Theories, from Autistic Persons.

Psychological Abilities	Self-awareness Theory	Kinesthetic-visual Matching Theory	Autistic Children
Self-recognition	x	x	yes
Bodily/facial imitation		x	yes
Planning (deferred imitation)		x	yes
Pretend replication of another's acts		x	yes
Recognition that one is being imitated		x	yes
Perspective-taking	x	precursor	yes
Theory of mind	x	precursor	no
Intentional deception	x	precursor	no
Empathy	x	precursor	no

NOTE: "x" means that the theory predicts this psychological ability. "Precursor" means that kinesthetic–visual matching is viewed as a developmental precursor to the psychological ability, which depends upon other abilities for expression.

not whether autistic children produce the same frequency as normal children of actions indicating a particularly psychological ability (which they rarely do for *any* of the predicted psychological concomitants of self-recognition), but whether they *typically* produce some evidence of it. Also, given that most but not all autistic children pass the mark test (see below), the processes necessary to pass the mark test need not be found in all autistic children.

Unfortunately, as with most other organisms discussed in the literature, in most cases autistic children tested for self-recognition were not also tested for the proposed concomitants of self-recognition, so the relationship between self-recognition and the proposed concomitants is not directly tested. (However, this discrepancy is not the case for measures of self-recognition and imitation—see below.) In addition, because the ages at which autistic people evince self-recognition are highly variable, it is not always possible to show ontogenetic sequences of development. Thus, the evidence for the most part consists of whether or not autistic people in general are capable of the psychological concomitants predicted for self-recognition, rather than whether individual autistic people capable of the predicted concomitants are also capable of self-recognition (in the form of passing the mark test).

Self-Recognition

Four studies examined self-recognition in autistic children (Dawson & McKissick, 1984; Ferrari & Matthews, 1983; Neuman & Hill, 1976; Spiker

& Ricks, 1984). All children were participating in some program assisting autistic people; the seven autistic children in the Neuman and Hill study were being trained to imitate motor movements. Of the 89 autistic children in the four studies, 68.5% passed the mark test: 6 of 7 in front of a simultaneous videotape image of themselves, and 55 out of 82 in front of a mirror (see TABLE 2). (Note that 2 of the 11 children who passed the mark test in the Dawson and McKissick study also touched their nose in the control situation, that is, when in front of the mirror without a mark on their nose.)

Imitation, Planning, and Recognition of Another's Imitation of Self

Although autistic children are generally impaired in imitation of action (Smith & Bryson, 1994), the majority nevertheless still reproduce a variety of actions they observe (see TABLE 2). Most autistic children can imitate another person's (or a doll's) body movements, hand, or arm gestures (with or without objects), and nonsymbolic actions. About 33–40% of autistic children tested could perform unfamiliar actions and invisible facial gestures. Two autistic children, when trained to imitate bodily actions both with and without objects, generalized their abilities for imitation to actions (with and without objects) they had not been trained to perform (Metz, 1965). Most autistic children tested show deferred imitation (reproducing an action after it is no longer visible), which indicates that they develop plans for their own actions. Finally, relatively young autistic children (4 to 6 years of age) recognize when they are being imitated (as do normal children starting at 14 months of age [Meltzoff, 1990]) in that they gaze longer at an adult who imitates their actions on objects than they do at an adult who simply uses the same object as the child or an adult who acts with an object unrelated to the child (Tiegerman & Primavera, 1984).

Pretense

Autistic children can pretend that they themselves or a doll are doing something they have seen another doll do: when shown a doll performing actions, 4 or 5 of 10 autistic children made another doll reproduce those actions, and 7 or 8 of 10 imitated the action of the doll (Riguet, Taylor, Benaroya, & Klein, 1981), thus indicating that autistic children can translate from the visual image of another body to either their own or another's body. When actions with imaginary objects were modeled for them, in one study only 2 of 8 autistic children showed imitation of the pretend use of an imaginary object (Hammes & Langdell, 1981), but in another study in which 24 autistic children's responses were pooled, 38% of responses were pantomimic (as if actually holding an object), 54% of responses used a body part to

TABLE 2. Number of Autistic Children Exhibiting, and Tested on, Various Forms of Kinesthetic–Visual Matching

	No. Showing	No. Tested	Age Range Year–Month	Reference
Passing the mark test	6	7	5-6 to 11-5	Neuman & Hill, 1976
	11	15	4-1 to 6-8	Dawson & McKissick, 1984
	8	15	3-6 to 10-5	Ferrari & Matthews, 1983
	36	52	3-7 to 12-8	Spiker & Ricks, 1984
Spontaneous imitation	22	48	3-7 to 12-8	Spiker & Ricks, 1984
Imitation of	10	10	5-9 to 10-6	Jones & Prior, 1985
bodily/hand/arm	5	12	4-9 to 12-0	Curcio, 1978
gestures	9	9	3-6 to 6-11	DeMyer, et al., 1972
	24	24	5-10 to 15-7	Curcio & Piserchia, 1978
Imitation of action with	8	8	ave.:9-10	Hammens & Langdell, 1981
object	9	9	3-6 to 6-11	DeMyer et al., 1972
Imitation of unfamiliar	3	12	4-9 to 12-0	Curcio, 1978
actions	8	15	4-1 to 6-8	Dawson & McKissick, 1984
Generalized imitation of actions	2	2	7-0	Metz, 1965
Imitation of invisible	5	12	4-9 to 12-0	Curcio, 1978
facial gestures	4	15	4-1 to 6-8	Dawson & McKissick, 1984
Deferred imitation	7	8	ave.:9-10	Hammes & Langdell, 1981
Imitation of doll's actions	7	8	ave.:9-10	Hammes & Langdell, 1981
	7-8	10	6-9 to 12-9	Riguet et al., 1981
Causes doll to imitate observed acts	4-5	10	6-9 to 12-9	Riguet et al., 1981
Imitation of pretend use	2	8	ave.:9-10	Hammes & Langdell, 1981
of imaginary object	22-24	24	5-10 to 15-7	Curcio & Piserchia, 1978
Recognition of another's imitation of one's own actions	5	5	4-0 to 6-0	Tiegerman & Primavera, 1984

NOTE: In the Jones and Prior study, apparently all autistic people showed some imitation of hand/arm gestures and dynamic movements; although they showed less imitation than chronological and mental age controls, autistic children on average showed 15.5(s = 3.17) gestural imitations out of 20 gestures, and 8.6 (s = 2.53) dynamic movement imitations out of 12 dynamic movements. Thus, apparently *some* autistic children achieved maximum imitation scores, and most achieved greater than 50% correct. In the DeMyer *et al.* study, schizophrenic children were included in the presentation of results. Average scores on easy, mid-range, and difficult bodily imitation tasks for nine autistic and three schizophrenic children were 59, 30 and 13%; average scores on easy, mid-range, and difficult imitations of actions with objects ("motor object imitations") were 84, 48 and 34%. It is assumed that all autistic children were at least able to perform some bodily and motor object imitations.

represent the object (e.g., used a finger to represent a knife) and otherwise pretended to perform the action, and only 8% of responses were not pretense (Curcio & Piserchia, 1978). Pantomime is typical of normal 3-year-old children, occurring well over a year after they recognize themselves in mirrors.

Self- Recognition and Imitation

There is evidence of a relationship between imitative abilities and self-recognition. All seven autistic children in the Neuman and Hill (1976) study were being trained in imitating motor actions, and six of these passed the mark test. More significantly, of the 22 children in the Spiker and Ricks (1984, p. 218) study who showed spontaneous imitation in their classrooms, 16 passed the mark test; and of eight autistic children in the Dawson and McKissick (1984) study who showed Piagetian stages 5 or 6 on gestural imitation, seven passed the mark test. This last study indicates that autistic children who imitate facial and/or unfamiliar gestures are more likely to pass the mark test than not. Overall, 23 of 30 autistic children who showed some imitative ability pass the mark test ($\chi^2(1, N = 30) = 7.5$ [corrected for continuity], $p<.05$). (Note that failure to spontaneously imitate in the classroom, or to produce Piagetian stage 5 or 6 imitations, does not indicate an inability to imitate in these ways.[3])

Perspective-Taking and Theory of Mind

Autistic children do well on visual perspective-taking tasks (moving an object to show another person various requested facets of it), as well as on some cognitive perspective-taking tasks (telling about what another feels or perceives) (Hobson, 1984; Reed & Peterson, 1990; Reed, 1994). However, autistic children have difficulty understanding others' intentions and thoughts, usually taken as evidence of theory of mind (Baron-Cohen, 1991; Reed & Peterson, 1990; Reed, 1994). For example, when autistic children, children with Down syndrome and normal children were asked to arrange a series of four cartoon panels into a logical sequence, autistic children did worse than did Down syndrome and normal children when the panels depicted a sequence that required the attribution of mental states such as intentionality or surprise, but were either better than or equivalent to the other children when the panels depicted a mechanical or behavioral sequence (Baron-Cohen, Leslie & Frith, 1986). In addition, when confronted with a situation in which they had, or another person could be expected to have, a false belief, such as finding out that a box that appeared to contain candy actually contained a toothbrush, autistic children accurately stated their own prior belief that the box contained candy, but persisted in believing that another would think the box contained a toothbrush (Leslie & Thaiss, 1992; Naito, Komatsu & Fuke, 1994). (After age 4, normal children understand that they and others can have false beliefs.) Most profoundly, autistic children appear to lack the mechanism envisioned in the self-awareness theory as necessary for all the predicted behaviors: they typically do not extrapolate from their own experience to that of another (Baron-Cohen, Tager-Flusberg & Cohen, 1993; Frith, 1989; Harris, 1989).

Intentional Deception

As might be expected from their inability to extrapolate from their own experience, autistic children almost always fail to deceive intentionally. In the typical test of intentional deception, a child is told that a competitor wants a piece of chocolate which is in one of two boxes; the child can see which box contains the chocolate, but the competitor cannot. If the child points to the box containing the chocolate, the competitor will take it away; if the child points to the box which does not contain the chocolate, the child can have the chocolate. Of 11 autistic children examined, only one deceived by pointing in all 20 trials; by contrast, seven pointed to the box containing the chocolate (i.e., failed to deceive) in all 20 trials, one deceived only 8 times (spread throughout the 20 trials), and two deceived 3 times or less, and these only during the first 4 trials (Russell, Mauthner, Sharpe & Tidswell, 1991). Comparable evidence is found when autistic children must deceive verbally (Baron-Cohen, 1992; Sodian & Frith, 1992).

Empathy

Although high-functioning autistic children develop empathic understanding of others (but less than do normal children; see Yirmiya, Sigman, Kasari & Mundy, 1992), the "most general description of social impairment in autism is a lack of empathy. Autistic people are noted for their indifference to other people's distress, their inability to offer comfort" (Frith, 1989, p. 154). Indeed, autism is a "disorder of empathy," resulting not from any inability of autistic children to feel their own emotions, but instead from a difficulty in understanding that others have inner worlds (Gillberg, 1992).

Summary

Overall, the evidence from autistic children supports the kinesthetic–visual matching theory, and does not support the self-awareness theory. Some of the evidence from autistic children suggests that perhaps only an ability to imitate gestures is necessary for self-recognition (rather than an ability to imitate unfamiliar actions and invisible facial gestures) but, because of the variability in findings from autistic children, more evidence is needed.

KINESTHETIC–VISUAL MATCHING ABILITIES IN OTHER HUMANS AND ANIMALS

Given the success of the kinesthetic–visual matching theory, I wish to re-examine the evidence of kinesthetic–visual matching for normal human children and nonhuman species. Several organisms exhibit imitative behavior suggestive of kinesthetic–visual matching, comparable to what Galef (1988, p. 23) calls "imitation of motor patterns." Although I do not think that all such suggestions of imitation are strong evidence of kinesthetic–visual matching, it is important to evaluate these suggestions as potential evidence against the kinesthetic–visual matching theory. As will be observed, the evidence of kinesthetic–visual matching is most firm for humans and great apes, particularly chimpanzees and orangutans, and least adequate for rats.

Humans

Normal human children show evidence of kinesthetic–visual matching in imitation, pretense, planning (deferred imitation), and recognition of being imitated by 14 months of age (see Hart & Fegley, 1994; Meltzoff, 1990, 1993; Mitchell, 1993a, 1993b, 1994) and self-recognition usually begins at 15 months (Lewis & Brooks-Gunn, 1979). Indeed, passing the mark test is correlated with children's imitations of gestures, in that the latter begins to develop elaborately just prior to passing the mark test (Hart & Fegley, 1994). Retarded children also pass the mark test (Hill & Tomlin, 1981; Loveland, 1987), and can learn to imitate bodily and facial gestures (Baer, Peterson & Sherman, 1971).

Humans show a great ability to form a match between their kinesthetic (proprioceptive) feelings and dislocated visual images of their own body, as when they wear prisms which distort the visual field (Harris, 1965; also, see intriguing discussion of the development of the match between kinesthesis and vision in Wallon, 1954/1984). Once they see their arm dislocated through a prism, for example, people actually experience their kinesthetic stimulation in a new location (where they *see* their arm); that is, they maintain the match between kinesthesis and vision even when they know that the match is nonsensical. When subjects looking through a prism continuously observe their displaced hand pointing toward various locations over several trials (such that the hand becomes adapted to the deviation) and are then tested on their other (nonadapted) hand, they tend not to make an error (which, if made, would be indicative of transfer of adaptation) with the non-adapted hand. However, when subjects are only allowed to observe their completed point over several trials (called terminal exposure), they tend to transfer the error to the nonadapted hand (Kornheiser, 1976, p. 793). The explanation for these differences has to do with which sensory modality subjects take as veridical: if the visual modality is taken as veridical (as it would be in the continuous observation task, as vision is the most salient perception), subjects map their kinesthetic sensations to the visual (and therefore do not transfer to the other hand); however, if the kinesthetic modality is taken as veridical (as it would be in the terminal exposure task, as kinesthesis is the only perception the subject experiences for most of the task), subjects map the visual sensations to the felt kinesthetic sensations (and therefore transfer to the other nonadapted hand: kinesthetic perceptions are apparently not as easily separable into parts as visual perceptions are). Surprisingly, and by contrast to other children and adults, autistic children in the continuous observation task appear to extend the translocation of kinesthetic feelings of the arm they did not view to that arm when perceived through the prism: they make errors with the nonadapted hand, and thereby show transfer, when they have continuously observed their other hand point to a location over several trials (Masterton & Biederman, 1983). This unique transfer indicates that autistic children accept kinesthetic perceptions as more veridical than visual perceptions. (Cross cultural studies of persons for whom nonvisual perceptions are taken as most veridical might provide an interesting comparison to autistic children—see Howes [1991].)

Kinesthetic–visual matching appears to be localized in the parietal area of the left hemisphere of the brain. Adult humans with parts of their parietal region destroyed show a form of ideomotor apraxia in which they are incapable of imitating gestures; the parietal area is presumed to contain "visuokinesthetic motor engrams, where motor acts may be programmed" (Heilman, Rothi & Valenstein, 1982, p.342). When people with ideomotor apraxia and left brain damage were asked to imitate meaningless gestures of a hand toward a face on themselves or on a mannikin, they generally failed on both tasks, indicating a generic incapacity to imitate bodily gestures (Goldenberg, 1995).

Great Apes

The only species of great apes that have been evaluated extensively for imitation based on kinesthetic–visual matching are chimpanzees and orangutans. The orangutan Chantek was taught to imitate the sounds, effects, and motor patterns of his caregivers upon their gesturally signed request to DO-THE-SAME-THING, and was able to imitate a variety of actions (many nonvisible), including patting the top of his head, touching his tongue with his finger, blinking his eye, and jumping (Miles, Mitchell & Harper, 1996). In some of these imitations, Chantek produced the bodily or facial movement via a different means because he was unable to perform the activity: in imitating blinking his eye, he pushed his eyelid down with his finger (apparently not having voluntary control over his eyelids), and in imitating jumping he lifted his feet off the ground while holding himself up with his hands (apparently not being able to jump). Chantek produced his first imitation of a sign at 15 months, and first recognized himself in a mirror at 25 months (Miles, 1994). Chantek continued to show spontaneous evidence of kinesthetic–visual matching near the end of his third year: he produced some gestural signs without having these gestures molded (shaped) by his caregivers at 35 months, and touched his own nose while looking at a picture of a gorilla touching its nose at 40 months (Miles *et al.*, 1996). Other orangutans, rehabilitants being returned to the wild in Borneo, imitated a variety of activities, some of which indicate kinesthetic–visual matching: brushing teeth, applying insect repellent on head and appendages, and holding a burning stick to a cigarette held with lips (Russon & Galdikas, 1993). Although neither of these studies proves that orangutans can imitate novel acts in that the acts the animals used may, in other contexts, have been familiar to them, the generalizability of the imitative ability to novel actions seems a reasonable expectation (see discussion by Russon & Galdikas, 1993; Miles *et al.*, 1996). Many early observational and experimental studies of chimpanzees (discussed in Custance, Whiten & Bard, 1995; Mitchell, 1994; Whiten & Ham, 1992) indicate that chimpanzees could model a human's behavior rather specifically, and more recent experiments indicate that chimpanzees produce arbitrary (and nonvisible) actions based on kinesthetic–visual matching, including closing eyes, protruding lips, touching the nose, puffing out cheeks, and touching an ear (Custance *et al.*, 1995). Although gorillas apparently can imitate novel bodily, facial and manual actions on the first trial and after a delay (Chevalier-Skolnikoff, 1977, p. 169), only one specific action is described: touching the ear (p. 179), and this by a gorilla who also recognizes herself in a mirror (Patterson & Cohn, 1994). Similarly, one bonobo has shown behavioral evidence of spontaneous imitation of another's gestures and actions (Savage-Rumbaugh, 1984).

Macaques

Three observations of imitation suggesting kinesthetic–visual matching are found for macaques, two of which are *Macaca mulatta*. One instance is based upon animals producing a strange behavior like that of another animal: when a rhesus macaque with a distinctive tic of touching its forehead with its hand was placed among 32 other laboratory rhesus monkeys, within 3 months another monkey was making similar movements, and within 1.5

years three additional monkeys were also making the same movements (Rivers, Bartecku, Brown & Ettlinger, 1983, p. 8). Another instance shows a concurrent matching by one rhesus of another: one free-ranging female rhesus monkey holding half of a coconut shell followed behind a mother carrying her own infant; the following female held the coconut shell in the same position the mother held her infant, and when the mother moved the infant and held it in a different way, the female moved her coconut shell to conform to the position of the infant on the mother (Breuggeman, 1973, p. 196). Finally, the last suggests delayed imitation by an unidentified species of macaque: one juvenile monkey which, after watching another sub-adult monkey look up and down a road, place its hand over its eyes and then "jauntily amble . . . in a curious three-legged stride down the road," moved to where the sub-adult had been, covered its eyes and followed the sub-adult with the same "odd gait" (Burton, 1992, p. 39). Only one study has attempted to test a macaque for imitation: the long-tailed macaque Rodrique was conditioned to scratch *when* a human model scratched, but failed to learn to scratch *where* the model scratched (Mitchell & Anderson, 1993). However, the three observations of spontaneous imitation are suggestive, and indicate that imitation may be present in some macaques, though it is rare. Perhaps only a very few macaques show a limited ability for kinesthetic–visual matching, or perhaps the few instances mentioned are happenstance.

Bottlenosed Dolphins

Bottlenosed dolphins (*Tursiops aduncus*) in captivity were observed to imitate a variety of different postures and behaviors of seals and humans (Tayler & Saayman, 1973) in a manner suggestive of kinesthetic–visual matching. Imitated by the dolphins were the sleeping, grooming, and swimming patterns of a cape fur seal, and the actions of humans cleaning the windows of the dolphins' tank (including putting the flipper against the window frame while cleaning the window with an object, much as human divers put their hand against it while cleaning). These actions are extremely atypical for a dolphin, which is in part why their imitativeness was so salient, and clearly suggest kinesthetic–visual matching. Bottlenosed dolphins (*Tursiops truncatus*) also show observational learning, including repetition of inconsequential actions of a demonstrator (Adler & Adler, 1978), but kinesthetic–visual matching need not be implicated.

Parrots and Budgerigars

Perhaps the most surprising claim of imitation based on kinesthetic–visual matching comes from an African grey parrot named Okíchoro

(Moore, 1992). The parrot when alone showed behaviors similar to those of his caregiver, and said a verbal label associated with the behaviors. These verbal "labels" were used only with particular movement patterns (p. 253). Kinesthetic–visual matching is implicated for some behaviors: waving wings or foot when saying "Ciao," moving its foot up (like the model holding up food) when saying "Peanut," opening its beak when saying "Look at my tongue," shaking its head left and right when saying "Shake," and moving its head up and down when saying "Nod." Not all of these movement–sound combinations need to have derived from kinesthetic–visual matching. For example, the action of moving a foot up when saying "Peanut" may have derived from the parrot's own activity of grabbing a peanut when offered, and simply saying "Look at my tongue" may, with some of the parrot's vocal variations, have produced an open mouth. In addition, the movement of foot and wings while saying "Ciao" may have derived from the parrot's own movements as well. When I worked with the parrot Alex studied by Pepperberg, one common reaction of Alex to someone's leaving (and to many stressful events) was to lift up his foot or wave his wings; Okíchoro may have produced a similar response upon another's leave-taking, and associated "Ciao" with that event. Unfortunately, no reliability measures are presented. Given the difficulty in providing reliable discriminations between avian behaviors using the same appendage (Galef, Manzig & Field, 1986, pp. 194–195), reliability would surely help in ascertaining that the "Ciao" waving and "Peanut" foot-lifting, or "Shake" head shakes and "Nod" head nods, were indeed different behaviors. With all of these problems, the evidence that African grey parrots can imitate human actions based on kinesthetic–visual matching is not convincing. However, the evidence *is* suggestive, and deserves experimental replication. Other research (Galef *et al.*, 1986) evaluating whether budgerigars could imitate the same motor patterns as budgerigar "demonstrators" found only a limited replication of two motor patterns, which disappeared after the second trial. Whether budgerigars can learn to produce numerous imitations on demand (or with a vocal cue) is unknown.

Rats

Kinesthetic–visual matching is implicated by researchers studying rats' imitations. Observer rats watched demonstrator rats push a joystick consistently in a given direction to receive a food reward, and then were allowed in the observer's area with the joystick in the same or a perpendicular location. The observer rats significantly more than chance pushed the joystick in the same direction as had the demonstrator rat. The researchers suggest that "observer rats tend to push the joystick in the same direction relative to their own bodies as did their demonstrator" (Heyes, Dawson & Nokes,

1992, p. 236) even "when the joystick moves through a plane perpendicular to that in which it was moved by the demonstrators" (p. 238). The idea that rats push in a direction relative to their own body, after having visually observed the demonstrator, suggests kinesthetic–visual matching. However, rats are very good at spatial knowledge (Olton, 1978), and could instead have learned to "push the joystick *that way* in relation to the mesh or background closest to the joystick" (Mitchell, 1995a). Thus, the rats most likely never learned to match their body kinesthetically to the visual image of the other; rather, they integrated the spatial positions of the joystick and background, an interpretation more in keeping with what we know about rat cognition.

KINESTHETIC–VISUAL MATCHING AND SELF-RECOGNITION AGAIN

From these data, it appears that rats do not show evidence of kinesthetic–visual matching, that some great apes do, that some dolphins (*Tursiops aduncus*) probably do, that some parrots might, and that very few if any macaques do. As support for the kinesthetic–visual matching theory, the data can be examined in two ways. First, by seeing if any members of these species show both bodily/gestural imitation and passing the mark test; and second, by looking at which species show some evidence of both bodily/gestural imitation and passing the mark test.

Bodily/Gestural Imitation and Passing the Mark test in Individuals

There is now clear evidence of a connection between having gestural imitation abilities and passing the mark test in human children (Hart & Fegley, 1994) and, as discussed above, in autistic children (see also Mitchell, 1993a). In addition, several chimpanzees, an orangutan, a bonobo, and a gorilla tested for both bodily/gestural imitation and mirror-self-recognition provide evidence for both capacities (Custance & Bard, 1994; Hyatt & Hopkins, 1994; Miles, 1994; Patterson & Cohn, 1994).

Bodily/Gestural Imitation and Passing the Mark test in Species

If one ignores the organisms showing evidence of both bodily/gestural imitation and passing the mark test, which species have members who show evidence of one or the other? Human children, including normal, retarded, and autistic ones, show bodily/gestural imitation, and some evince self-recognition (see, for example, Boysen, Bryan & Shreyer, 1994; Gallup,

1987; Lethmate & Dücker, 1973; Miles, 1994; Suarez & Gallup, 1981, Swartz & Evans, 1991). Gorillas largely fail the mark test (although see Swartz & Evans, 1994) and bonobos engage in self-directed behaviors indicative of self-recognition (Hyatt & Hopkins, 1994; Walraven, Elsacker & Verheyen, 1995), but neither have been tested for bodily/gestural imitation. Macaques largely fail to show any indication of bodily/gestural imitation, and largely fail the mark test (Gallup, 1987). Although a few macaques have apparently had limited success in passing the mark test (Boccia, 1994, Howell, Kinsey & Novak, 1994; Thompson & Boatright-Horowitz, 1994), these animals merely touch the mark (in one case, only the vicinity of the mark), and contact is fleeting. Indian Ocean bottlenosed dolphins (*Tursiops aduncus*) exhibit bodily imitation, but have not been tested for self-recognition; and Atlantic Ocean bottlenosed dolphins (*Tursiops truncatus*) have not been tested for bodily imitation, but appear to pass one form of the mark test (Marten & Psarakos, 1994, 1995). The evidence here, however, is somewhat contaminated by use of a tactile dye, which provides the dolphins with an additional perceptual modality by which to recognize their own image (see Mitchell, 1995b). Whether or not parrots show bodily imitation is unclear, and although parrots appear to understand some properties of mirrors (Pepperberg, Garcia, Jackson & Marconi, 1995), they have yet to be tested for self-recognition. Finally, rats fail to show bodily/gestural imita-

TABLE 3. Evidence of Bodily/Gestural Imitation and Passing the Mark Test in at Least Some Human Children and at Least Some Members of Other Species

Organisms	Bodily/Gestural Imitation	Pass Mark Test
Normal 15-month-old children	√	√
Autistic children	√	√
Mentally retarded children	√	√
Chimpanzees	√	√
Gorillas	√	√
Orangutans	√	√
Bonobos	√	?
Indian Ocean bottlenosed dolphins	√	?
Atlantic Ocean bottlenosed dolphins	?	√
Macaques	~	~
African Grey parrots	~	?
Budgerigars	~	?
Rats	—	?

NOTE: "√" indicates the presence of the activity in some organisms of this type or species; "—" means that the best evidence does not support the presence of the activity in any species members; "?" means that organisms of this species have yet to be tested for the presence of the activity; "~" means that organisms of this species fail to show extensive behavioral evidence for the presence of the activity.

tion, but have never been tested on self-recognition (although one expects they would fail).

CONCLUSION

All in all, predictions from the kinesthetic–visual matching theory are in line with current evidence (TABLE 3). Bodily/gestural imitation and self-recognition (in the form of passing the mark test) appear to derive from kinesthetic–visual matching; passing the mark test does not appear to result from self-awareness, unless it is an awareness of the match between one's kinesthetic experiences and the visual image of oneself in the mirror. Autistic children, as a test case, support the kinesthetic–visual matching theory, and disprove the self-awareness theory. Even though more exacting evidence is desirable for firm support, the kinesthetic–visual matching theory is at present our best bet for understanding why organisms pass the mark test.

REFERENCES

ADLER, H. E. & ADLER, L. L. (1978). What can dolphins (*Tursiops truncatus*) learn by observation? *Cetology, 30*, 1–10.

AMSTERDAM, B. (1972). Mirror self-image reactions before age two. *Developmental Psychobiology, 5*, 297–305.

ANDERSON, J. R. (1993). To see ourselves as others see us: A response to Mitchell. *New Ideas in Psychology, 11*, 339–346.

ANISFELD, M. (1991). Neonatal imitation. *Developmental Review, 11*, 60–97.

BAER, D. M., PETERSON, R. F., & SHERMAN, J. A. (1971). The development of imitation by reinforcing behavioral similarity to a model. In A. Bandura (Ed.), *Psychological modeling: Conflicting theories* (pp. 128–150). Chicago: Aldine/Atherton.

BARON-COHEN, S. (1987). Autism and symbolic play. *British Journal of Developmental Psychology, 5*, 139–148.

BARON-COHEN, S. (1991). Do people with autism understand what causes emotion? *Child Development, 62*, 385–395.

BARON-COHEN, S. (1992). Out of sight or out of mind? Another look at deception in autism. *Journal of Child Psychology and Psychiatry, 33*, 1141–1155.

BARON-COHEN, S., LESLIE, A. M. & FRITH, U. (1986). Mechanical, behavioural and intentional understanding of picture stories in autistic children. *British Journal of Developmental Psychology, 4*, 113–125.

BARON-COHEN, S., TAGER-FLUSBERG, H. & COHEN, D. J. (1993). *Understanding other minds: Perspectives from autism.* Oxford: Oxford University Press.

BARTSCH, K. & WELLMAN, H.M. (1995). *Children talk about the mind.* Oxford: Oxford University Press.

BOCCIA, M.L. (1994). Mirror behavior in macaques. In S. T. Parker, R. W. Mitchell, & M. L. Boccia (Eds.), *Self-awareness in animals and humans* (pp. 350–360). New York: Cambridge University Press.

BOYSEN, S. T., BRYAN, K. M. & SHREYER, T. A. (1994). Shadows and Mirrors: Alternative avenues to the development of self-recognition in chimpanzees. In S.T. Parker, R.

W. Mitchell, & M. L. Boccia (Eds.), *Self-awareness in animals and humans* (pp. 227–240). New York: Cambridge University Press.

BREUGGEMAN, J. A. (1973). Parental care in a group of free-ranging rhesus monkeys. *Folia Primatologica, 20,* 178–210.

BURTON, F.D. (1992). The social group as information unit: Cognitive behaviour, cultural processes. In F. D. Burton (Ed.), *Social processes and mental abilities in non-human primates* (pp. 31–60). Lewiston: The Edwin Mellen Press.

CHEVALIER-SKOLNIKOFF, S. (1977). A Piagetian model for describing and comparing socialization in monkey, ape, and human infants. In S. Chevalier-Skolnikoff & F. E. Poirier (Eds.), *Primate biosocial development: Biological, social, and ecological determinants* (pp. 159–187). New York: Garland.

CURCIO, F. (1978). Sensorimotor functioning and communication in mute autistic children. *Journal of Autism and Childhood Schizophrenia, 8,* 281–292.

CURCIO, F. & PISERCHIA, E. A. (1978). Pantomimic representation in psychotic children. *Journal of Autism and Childhood Schizophrenia, 8,* 181–189.

CUSTANCE, D & BARD, K. A. (1994). The comparative and developmental study of self-recognition and imitation: The importance of social factors. In S. T. Parker, R. W. Mitchell & M. L. Boccia (Eds.), *Self-awareness in animals and humans* (pp. 207–226). New York: Cambridge University Press.

CUSTANCE, D.M., WHITEN, A. & BARD, K. A. (1995). Can young chimpanzees (*Pan troglodytes*) imitate arbitrary actions? Hayes & Hayes (1952) revisited. *Behaviour, 132,* 837–859.

DAWSON, G. & MCKISSICK, F. C. (1984). Self-recognition in autistic children. *Journal of Autism and Developmental Disorders, 14,* 383–394.

DEMYER, M. K., ALPERN, G. D., BARTON, S., DEMYER, W E., CHURCHILL, D. W., HINGTGEN, J. N., BRYSON, C. Q., PONTIUS, W. & KIMBERLIN, C. (1972). Imitation in autistic, early schizophrenic, and non-psychotic subnormal children. *Journal of Autism and Childhood Schizophrenia, 2,* 264–287.

FERRARI, M & MATTHEWS, W. S. (1983). Self-recognition deficits in autism: Syndrome-specific or general developmental delay? *Journal of Autism and Developmental Disorders, 13,* 317–324.

FRITH, U. (1989). *Autism: Explaining the enigma.* Oxford: Basil Blackwell.

GALEF, B.G. (1988). Imitation in animals: History, definition, and interpretation of data from the psychological laboratory. In T. A. Zentall & B. G. Galef (Eds.), *Social learning in animals* (pp. 3–28). Hillsdale, NJ: Lawrence Erlbaum.

GALEF, B. G., JR., MANZIG, L. A. & FIELD, R. M. (1986). Imitation learning in budgerigars: Dawson and Foss (1965) revisited. *Behavioural Processes, 13,* 191–202.

GALLUP, G. G., JR. (1983). Toward a comparative psychology of mind. In R. L. Mellgren (Ed.), *Animal cognition and behavior* (pp. 473–510). Amsterdam: North-Holland Publ.

GALLUP, G. G., JR. (1985). Do minds exist in species other than our own? *Neurosciences and Biobehavioral Review, 9,* 631–641.

GALLUP, G. G., JR. (1987). Self-awareness, In G. Mitchell & J. Erwin (Eds.), *Comparative primate biology, Vol. 2, Part B: Behavior, cognition, and motivation* (pp. 3–16). New York: Liss.

GALLUP, G. G., JR. & POVINELLI, D. J. (1993). Mirror, mirror on the wall, which is the most heuristic theory of them all? A response to Mitchell. *New Ideas in Psychology, 11,* 327–335.

GILLBERG, C. L. (1992). Autism and autism-like conditions: Subclasses among disorders of empathy. *Journal of Child Psychology and Psychiatry, 33,* 813–842.

GOLDENBERG, G. (1995). Imitating gestures and manipulating a mannikin—The representation of the human body in ideomotor apraxia. *Neuropsychologia, 33,* 63–72.

GUILLAUME, P. (1926/1971). *Imitation in children*, 2nd ed. Chicago: University of Chicago Press.

HAMMES, J. G. W. & LANGDELL, T. (1981). Precursors of symbol formation and childhood autism. *Journal of Autism and Developmental Disorders, 11*, 331–346.

HANNA, E. & MELTZOFF, A. N. (1993). Peer imitation by toddlers in laboratory, home, and day-care contexts: Implications for social learning and memory. *Developmental Psychology, 29*, 701–710.

HARRIS, C. S. (1965). Perceptual adaptation to inverted, reversed, and displaced vision. *Psychological Review, 72*, 419–444.

HARRIS, P. (1989). *Children and emotion: The development of psychological understanding.* Oxford: Basil Blackwell.

HART, D. & FEGLEY, S. (1994). Social imitation and the emergence of a mental model of self. In S. T. Parker, R. W. Mitchell, & M. L. Boccia (Eds.), *Self-awareness in animals and humans* (pp. 149–165). New York: Cambridge University Press.

HEILMAN, K. M., ROTHI, L. J. & VALENSTEIN, E. (1982). Two forms of ideomotor apraxia. *Neurology, 32*, 342–346.

HEYES, C. M., DAWSON, G. R. & NOKES, T. (1992). Imitation in rats: Initial responding and transfer evidence. *Quarterly Journal of Experimental Psychology, 45B*, 229–240.

HILL, S. D. & TOMLIN, C. (1981). Self-recognition in retarded children. *Child Development, 52*, 145–150.

HOBSON, R. P. (1984). Early childhood autism and the question of egocentrism. *Journal of Autism and Developmental Disorders, 14*, 85–104.

HOBSON, R. P. (1991). Against the theory of "Theory of Mind." *British Journal of Developmental Psychology, 9*, 33–51.

HOWELL, M., KINSEY, J. & NOVAK, M. A. (1994). Mark-directed behavior in a rhesus monkey after controlled, reinforced exposure to mirrors. *American Journal of Primatology, 13*, 216.

HOWES, D., Ed. (1991). *The varieties of sensory experience: A sourcebook in the anthropology of the senses.* Toronto, Canada: University of Toronto Press.

HYATT, C. W. & HOPKINS, W. D. (1994). Self-awareness in bonobos and chimpanzees: A comparative perspective. In S. T. Parker, R. W. Mitchell & M. L. Boccia (Eds.), *Self-awareness in animals and humans* (pp. 248–253). New York: Cambridge University Press.

JARROLD, C., SMITH, P., BOUCHER, J. & HARRIS, P. (1994). Comprehension of pretense in children with autism. *Journal of Autism and Developmental Disorders, 24*, 433–455.

JOHNSON, D. B. (1983). Self-recognition in infants. *Infant Behavior and Development, 6*, 211–222.

JONES, S. S. (1996). Imitation or exploration? Young infants' matching of adults' oral gestures. *Child Development, 67*, 1952–1969.

JONES, V. & PRIOR, M. (1985). Motor imitation abilities and neurological signs in autistic children. *Journal of Autism and Developmental Disorders, 15*, 37–46.

KORNHEISER, A. S. (1976). Adaptation for laterally displaced vision: A review. *Psychological Bulletin, 83*, 783–816.

LESLIE, A. M. & THAISS, L. (1992). Domain specificity in conceptual development: Neuropsychological evidence from autism. *Cognition, 43*, 225–251.

LETHMATE, J. & DÜCKER, G. (1973). Untersuchungen zum Selbsterkennen im Spiegel bei Orangutans und einigen anderen Affenarten. *Zeitschrift für Tierpsychologie, 33*, 248–269.

LEWIS, M. & BROOKS-GUNN, J. (1979). *Social cognition and the acquisition of self.* New York: Plenum Press.

LOVELAND, K. A. (1986). Discovering the affordances of a reflecting surface. *Developmental Review, 6,* 1–24.

LOVELAND, K. A. (1987). Behavior of young children with Down syndrome before the mirror: Finding things reflected. *Child Development, 58,* 928–936.

MARTEN, K. & PSARAKOS, S. (1994). Evidence of self-awareness in the bottlenose dolphin (*Tursiops truncatus*). In S. T. Parker, R. W. Mitchell & M. L. Boccia (Eds.), *Self-awareness in animals and humans* (pp. 361–379). New York: Cambridge University Press.

MARTEN, K. & PSARAKOS, S. (1995). Using self-view television to distinguish between self-examination and social behavior in the bottlenose dolphin (*Tursiops truncatus*). *Consciousness and Cognition, 4,* 205–224.

MASUR, E. F. (1993). Transitions in representational ability: Infants' verbal, vocal, and action imitation during the second year. *Merrill-Palmer Quarterly, 39,* 437–456.

MASTERTON, B. A. & BIEDERMAN, G. B. (1983). Proprioceptive versus visual control in autistic children. *Journal of Autism and Developmental Disorders, 13,* 141–152.

MELTZOFF, A. N. (1990). Foundations for developing a concept of self: The role of imitation in relating self to other and the value of social mirroring, social modeling, and self practice in infancy. In D. Cicchetti & M. Beeghly (Eds.), *The self in transition: Infancy to childhood* (pp. 139–164). Chicago: University of Chicago Press.

MELTZOFF, A. N. (1993). Molyneux's babies: Cross-modal perception, imitation and the mind of the preverbal infant. In N. Eilan, R. McCarthy & B. Brewer (Eds.), *Spatial representation* (pp. 219–235). Oxford, UK: Blackwell.

MELTZOFF, A. N. & MOORE, M. K. (1977). Imitation of facial and manual gestures by human neonates. *Science, 198,* 75–78.

MERLEAU-PONTY, M. (1960/1982). The child's relations with others. In J. M. Edie (Ed.), *The primacy of perception* (pp. 96–155). Illinois: Northwestern University Press.

METZ, J. R. (1965). Conditioning generalized imitation in autistic children. *Journal of Experimental Child Psychology, 2,* 389–399.

MILES, H. L. (1994). ME CHANTEK: The development of self-awareness in a signing orangutan. In S. T. Parker, R. W. Mitchell & M. L. Boccia (Eds.), *Self-awareness in animals and humans* (pp. 254–272). New York: Cambridge University Press.

MILES, H. L., MITCHELL, R. W. & HARPER, S. E. (1996). Simon says: The development of imitation in an enculturated orangutan. In A. E. Russon, K. A. Bard & S. T. Parker (Eds.), *Reaching into thought.* Cambridge: Cambridge University Press.

MITCHELL R. W. (1992). Developing concepts in infancy: Animals, self-perception, and two theories of mirror-self-recognition. *Psychological Inquiry, 3,* 127–130.

MITCHELL, R. W. (1993a). Mental models of mirror-self-recognition: Two theories. *New Ideas in Psychology, 11,* 295–325.

MITCHELL, R. W. (1993b). Recognizing one's self in a mirror? A reply to Gallup and Povinelli, de Lannoy, Anderson, and Byrne. *New Ideas in Psychology, 11,* 351–377.

MITCHELL, R. W. (1994). The evolution of primate cognition: Simulation, self-knowledge, and knowledge of other minds. In D. Quiatt & J. Itani (Eds.), *Hominid culture in primate perspective* (pp. 177–232). Boulder: University Press of Colorado.

MITCHELL, R. W. (1995a). *Bodily imitation, kinesthetic-visual matching, and animals.* Invited presentation for symposium on *Social learning and tradition in animals,* 67th Annual Meeting of the Midwestern Psychological Association, Chicago, IL.

MITCHELL, R. W. (1995b). Evidence of dolphin self-recognition and the difficulties of interpretation. *Consciousness and Cognition, 4,* 229–234.

MITCHELL, R. W. (1996). Anthropomorphism and anecdotes: A guide for the perplexed.

In R. W. Mitchell, N.S. Thompson & H. L. Miles (Eds.), *Anthropomorphism, anecdotes, and animals*. Albany: SUNY Press.

MITCHELL, R. W. (1997). Kinesthetic-visual matching and the self-concept as explanations of mirror-self-recognition. *Journal for the Theory of Social Behavior, 27,* 101–123.

MITCHELL, R. W. & ANDERSON, J.R. (1993). Discrimination learning of scratching, but failure to obtain imitation and self-recognition in a long-tailed macaque. *Primates, 34,* 301–309.

MOORE, B. R. (1992). Avian movement imitation and a new form of mimicry: Tracing the evolution of a complex form of learning. *Behaviour, 122,* 231–263.

NAITO, M., KOMATSU, S. & FUKE, T. (1994). Normal and autistic children's understanding of their own and others' false belief: A study from Japan. *British Journal of Developmental Psychology, 12,* 403–416.

NEUMAN, C. J. & HILL, S. D. (1978). Self-recognition and stimulus preference in autistic children. *Developmental Psychobiology, 11,* 571–578.

NISBETT, R. E. & WILSON, T. D. (1977). Telling more than we can know: Verbal reports on mental processes. *Psychological Review, 84,* 231–259.

OLTON, D. S. (1978). Characteristics of spatial memory. In S. H. Hulse, H. Fowler & W. K. Honig (Eds.), *Cognitive processes in animal behavior* (pp. 341–373). Hillsdale, NJ: Lawrence Erlbaum.

PARKER, S. T. (1991). A developmental approach to the origins of self-recognition in great apes. *Human Evolution, 6,* 435–449.

PARKER, S. T., MITCHELL, R. W. & BOCCIA, M. L., Eds. (1994). *Self-awareness in animals and humans*. New York: Cambridge University Press.

PATTERSON, F. G. P. & COHN, R. H. (1994). Self-recognition and self-awareness in lowland gorillas. In S. T. Parker, R. W. Mitchell & M. L. Boccia (Eds.), *Self-awareness in animals and humans* (pp. 273–290). New York: Cambridge University Press.

PEPPERBERG, I. M., GARCIA, S. E., JACKSON, E. C. & MARCONI, S. (1995). Mirror use by African Grey Parrots. *Journal of Comparative Psychology, 109,* 182–195.

POVINELLI, D. J. (1995). The unduplicated self. In P. Rochat (Ed.), *The self in early infancy* (pp. 161–192). Amsterdam: North Holland-Elsevier.

PREMACK, D. (1988a). "Does the chimpanzee have a theory of mind?" revisited. In R. Byrne & A. Whiten (Eds.), *Machiavellian intelligence* (pp. 160–179). New York: Oxford University Press.

PRIEL, B. & DESCHONEN, S. (1986). Self-recognition: A study of a population without mirrors. *Journal of Experimental Child Psychology, 41,* 237–250.

REED, T. (1994). Performance of autistic and control subjects on three cognitive perspective-taking tasks. *Journal of Autism and Developmental Disorders, 24,* 53–66.

REED, T. & PETERSON, C. (1990). A comparative study of autistic subjects' performance at two levels of visual and cognitive perspective taking. *Journal of Autism and Developmental Disorders, 20,* 555–567.

RIGUET, C. D., TAYLOR, N. D., BENAROYA, D. & KLEIN, L. S. (1981). Symbolic play in autistic, Down's, and normal children of equivalent mental age. *Journal of Autism and Developmental Disorders, 11,* 439–448.

RIVERS, A., BARTECKU, U., BROWN, J. V. & ETTLINGER, G. (1983). An unexpected "epidemic" of a rare stereotypy: Unidentified stress or imitation? *Laboratory Primate Newsletter, 22,* 5–7.

RUSSELL, J., MAUTHNER, N., SHARPE, S. & TIDSWELL, T. (1991). The "windows task" as a measure of strategic deception in preschoolers and autistic subjects. *British Journal of Developmental Psychology, 9,* 331–349.

RUSSON, A. E. & GALDIKAS, B. (1993). Imitation in free-ranging rehabilitant orangutans. *Journal of Comparative Psychology, 107,* 147–160.

SAVAGE-RUMBAUGH, E. S. (1984). *Pan paniscus* and *Pan troglodytes:* Contrasts in preverbal communicative competence. In R. L. Sussman (Ed.), *The pygmy chimpanzee: Evolutionary biology and behavior* (pp. 395–413). New York: Plenum Press.

SMITH, I. M. & BRYSON, S. E. (1994). Imitation and action in autism: A critical review. *Psychological Bulletin, 116,* 259–273.

SODIAN, B. & FRITH, U. (1992). Deception and sabotage in autistic, retarded and normal children. *Journal of Child Psychology and Psychiatry, 33,* 591–605.

SPIKER, D. & RICKS, M. (1984). Visual self-recognition in autistic children: Developmental relationships. *Child Development, 55,* 214–225.

SUAREZ, S. D. & GALLUP, G. G., JR. (1981). Self-recognition in chimpanzees and orangutans, but not gorillas. *Journal of Human Evolution, 10,* 175–188.

SWARTZ, K. B. & EVANS, S. (1991). Not all chimpanzees (*Pan troglodytes*) show self-recognition. *Primates, 32,* 483–496.

SWARTZ, K. B. & EVANS, S. (1994). Social and cognitive factors in chimpanzee and gorilla mirror behavior and self-recognition. In S. T. Parker, R. W. Mitchell & M. L. Boccia (Eds.), *Self-awareness in animals and humans* (pp. 189–207). New York: Cambridge University Press.

TAYLER, C. K. & SAAYMAN, G. S. (1973). Imitative behaviour by Indian Ocean bottlenose dolphins (*Tursiops aduncus*) in captivity. *Behaviour, 44,* 286–298.

THOMPSON, R. L. & BOATRIGHT-HOROWITZ, S. L. (1994). The question of mirror-mediated self-recognition in apes and monkeys: Some new results and reservations. In S. T. Parker, R. W. Mitchell & M. L. Boccia (Eds.), *Self-awareness in animals and humans* (pp. 330–349). New York: Cambridge University Press.

TIEGERMAN, E. & PRIMAVERA, L. H. (1984). Imitating the autistic child: Facilitating communicative gaze behavior. *Journal of Autism and Developmental Disorders, 14,* 27–38.

UŽGIRIS, I. Č. (1973). Patterns of vocal and gestural imitation in infants. In L. J. Stone, H. T. Smith & L. B. Murphy (Eds.), *The competent infant: Research and commentary* (pp. 599–604). New York: Basic Books.

WALLON, H. (1954/1984). Kinesthesia and the visual body image in the child. In G. Voyat (Ed.), *The world of Henri Wallon,* (pp. 115–131). New York: Jason Aronson.

WALRAVEN, V., ELSACKER, L. VAN, & VERHEYEN, R. (1995). Reactions of a group of pygmy chimpanzees (*Pan paniscus*) to their mirror-images: Evidence of self-recognition. *Primates, 36,* 145–150.

WHITEN, A. & BYRNE, R. W. (1988). Tactical deception in primates. *Behavioral and Brain Sciences, 11,* 233–244.

WHITEN, A. & HAM, R. (1992). On the nature and evolution of imitation in the animal kingdom: Reappraisal of a century of research. *Advances in the Study of Behavior, 21,* 239–283.

WITTGENSTEIN, L. (1953). *Philosophical investigations.* New York: The Macmillan Co.

YIRMIYA, N., SIGMAN, M. D., KASARI, C. & MUNDY, P. (1992). Empathy and cognition in high-functioning children with autism. *Child Development, 63,* 150–160.

ENDNOTES

1. Several significant errors of fact are presented in Povinelli's (1995, p. 178) discussion of Mitchell's (1993a) ideas about explanations of self-recognition.

(*1*) Contrary to Povinelli (1995, p. 178), kinesthetic–visual matching is not "present at birth," as noted in Mitchell (1993a; 1993b). In a recent review of neonatal imitation studies, Anisfeld (1991) argues that the only consistent evidence for neonatal imitation of others is for tongue protrusion, and that there are at least three hypotheses other than matching between kinesthetic and visual modalities which can more convincingly account for imitation of tongue protrusion. More recently, Jones (1996) has shown that tongue protrusion is an exploratory response to any object moving toward an infant's face, which indicates that no "imitations" or "matching" of any kind is present. Although Meltzoff (1993) argues that a very limited ability for kinesthetic–visual matching is present in neonatal imitation of tongue protrusion (nothing like that required by Mitchell [1993a] for passing the mark test), he also claims (in the articles cited by Povinelli, 1995) that such neonatal imitation of tongue protrusion is based on representational abilities exactly like those which Povinelli (1995, p. 163) claims occur only in children at 18–24 months of age. Thus, evidence of "imitation" in neonates, if assumed to be evidence of kinesthetic–visual matching, is also evidence of the representational abilities which Povinelli's model predicts will occur much later.

(2) One sort of "elaborated" kinesthetic–visual matching ability Mitchell (1993a, p. 303) suggests for his model is when "organisms can imitate in relation to their own body apparently innumerable visually unfamiliar acts of another, using visually unknown parts of their own body." Contrary to Povinelli's claim, this form of imitation (comparable to Piagetian stages 5–6 imitation—see Parker, 1991) is not, as Povinelli (1995, p. 178) states, "quite elaborated by 9–14 months," but rather shows up in some children only beginning at 14 months, and is shown by most children at 17–18 months (Hanna & Meltzoff, 1993; Hart & Fegley, 1994, Masur, 1993; Užgiris, 1973, pp. 600–601). Passing the mark test starts at 15–18 months and, as Povinelli argues, most children pass the mark test by 18–24 months.

(3) Contrary to Povinelli (1995, p.178), Mitchell (1993a) does not assume that understanding of mirrors is necessary for passing the mark test (see 1993a, pp. 300, 302–303). Indeed, Povinelli (with Gallup) previously expressed surprise at Mitchell's (1993a) statement that understanding mirrors may not be necessary for passing the mark test:

> Mitchell [1993a] asserts that as far as humans are concerned, "experience with mirrors is not necessary to pass the mark test" (p. 302). Putting aside the fact that a literal interpretation of this statement would imply that humans somehow have innate knowledge of the properties of mirrors, the study he cites (Priel & de Schonen, 1986) in support of this position is less than convincing. Although Priel & de Schonen (1986) discarded some children based on reports from mothers about the presence of things in the home that might have provided them with access to their reflections (e.g., toys, tin cans, bottles), their study provides no assurance that the children in the rural sample did not have experience with their reflections in automobile hubcaps, chrome bumpers, and rearview mirrors, as well as reflections emanating from a variety of other objects outside the house. (Gallup & Povinelli, 1993, p. 328).

In Povinelli (1995), however, the study by Priel and de Schonen is depicted as quite convincing evidence that infants can recognize themselves in mirrors even when they have never previously experienced mirrors.

(4) Mitchell's (1993a, pp. 298–299) model, like Povinelli's, also assumes that "the kinds of sensitivity to contingency that are necessary for self-recognition are in place long before 18–24 months" (Povinelli, 1995, p.178), so there is not a "direct contrast" here between the models. Indeed, not one of the differences claimed by Povinelli between his model and Mitchell's model is accurate.

2. Note particularly that attribution of mental states to another does not indicate that

this attribution is based on extrapolation of one's own mental states to another (see, for example, Bartsch & Wellman, 1995, pp. 181–185). Problems with the idea that self-recognizing organisms model others' mental states based on their own mental states are discussed in Mitchell (1993a, 1993b). Problems with the idea that understanding other minds depends on reflective extrapolation from one's own experience are discussed in Wittgenstein (1958), Hobson (1991), and Mitchell (1996). The idea that we experience many of our own mental processes is itself contrary to evidence (Nisbett & Wilson, 1977).

3. The skeptical reader will, of course, wonder about the self-recognition skills of the children who did not show spontaneous imitation in the classroom or Piagetian stages 5 or 6 on gestural imitation. Of the 26 subjects in the Spiker and Ricks (1984) study who failed to show spontaneous imitation in the classroom, 18 passed the mark test; and of the 7 subjects in the Dawson and McKissick (1984) study who showed Piagetian stages 2 or 3 (none showed stage 4), 4 passed the mark test. Overall, 22 out of 33 children who showed limited or no imitative ability passed the mark text ($\chi^2(1, N = 33) = 3.67$, ns), suggesting that there is no relationship between imitation and passing the mark test: children who show little or no imitation are as likely to pass the mark test as not. However, children's failure to show imitation in these studies is problematic as evidence against an ability for kinesthetic-visual matching: in the Spiker and Ricks study, a child may fail to "spontaneously imitate" in the classroom but still be capable of imitation; and in the Dawson and McKissick study, a child may be unwilling to imitate an unfamiliar experimenter's gestures, though she or he can imitate actions. Thus, it is unclear whether autistic children who failed to show these activities in the above studies are incapable of performing them. Given autistic children's overall low level of imitative response in the midst of a clear ability to imitate (Smith & Bryson, 1994), children should be tested repeatedly on imitation tasks under a variety of situations before it is concluded that they are unable to imitate at advanced levels.

Karyl B. Swartz is currently Associate Professor of Psychology at Lehman College and the Graduate School of the City University of New York, and director of the Laboratory for Comparative Cognition at Lehman College. She serves on the editorial board of The Journal of Comparative Psychology. *Her research interests focus on comparative cognition in primates. She has published articles on attachment in nonhuman primates, perception and cognition in human infants and children, cognitive factors underlying social perception in infant macaques, and learning and memory in adult macaques, and has written many critical discussions of mirror self-recognition in great apes.*

What Is Mirror Self-Recognition in Nonhuman Primates, and What Is It Not?

KARYL B. SWARTZ

Department of Psychology
Lehman College of the
City University of New York
Bronx, New York 10468

Since Gallup first described it in 1970, the phenomenon of mirror self-recognition in nonhuman primates has been a provocative, and at times, seemingly intractable phenomenon. Theoretical interpretations provide thoughtful but different perspectives on the issue (see, for example, Gallup, 1977, 1982; Mitchell, 1993). Even empirical investigations of the phenomenon have provided controversy (Swartz & Evans, 1991, 1997). Investigators have attempted to determine which species demonstrate the phenomenon and which do not (see Anderson, 1984; Parker, Mitchell, & Boccia, 1994), and have attempted to explain unexpected failures to find it in species for whom it was considered robust (Swartz & Evans, 1991, 1994, 1997). In the present paper, an overview of the phenomenon will be presented, species and individual differences will be discussed, and some measurement issues will be presented. Although suggestions for interpretation of the phenomenon will be proposed, the reader will determine his or her own interpretation.

The phenomenon itself consists of two behavioral patterns, described well by Gallup (1970): behavior during mirror exposure and behavior during the mark test (described below). Gallup reported that during the initial exposure to the mirror, chimpanzees exhibited social behaviors directed toward the mirror image. These social behaviors suggested that the animals perceived the mirror image to be an unfamiliar conspecific. Following several hours of exposure to the mirror, the social behaviors waned and behaviors that Gallup called "self-directed" appeared. These self-directed behaviors involved exploration of previously unseen parts of the body, using the mirror for visual inspection and to guide the hands for manual exploration. Examples of self-directed behaviors were grooming the eyes, blowing bubbles with the mouth while watching the mirror image, and making faces. More recently, investigators have discussed a third class of behavior, termed contingent behavior, to describe gross motor movements made in front of the mirror while watching the mirror image (Lin, Bard & Anderson, 1992; Povinelli, Rulf, Landau & Bierschwale, 1993). Some of these behaviors were included in Gallup's self-directed category. Contingent behaviors may occur in conjunction with self-directed behaviors, and may provide additional information to the animal regarding the nature or source of the mirror image. Gallup (1970) interpreted the presence of self-directed behaviors as evidence that the chimpanzees recognized themselves in the mirror.

In order to support the somewhat subjective interpretation of mirror behavior, Gallup (1970) devised a more objective measure of mirror self-recognition, termed the "mark test." He anesthetized the chimpanzees and placed a red mark on an eyebrow and the opposite ear, locations that could only be seen with the use of the mirror. Following recovery from the anesthesia and a non-mirror control period, the animals were presented with the mirror. All subjects made multiple mark touches in the presence of the mirror, compared to only one mark touch by one animal during the control period. Gallup (1970) interpreted this finding to support his initial suggestion that the chimpanzees recognized themselves in the mirror.

Gallup's interpretation of the phenomenon went beyond the animal's knowledge of the mirror image. He suggested that mirror self-recognition implied the presence of a self-concept. According to Gallup (1975) mirror self-recognition can be shown only by organisms who have a sense of identity and who therefore recognize the identity of the mirror image. He further expanded the theoretical interpretation (Gallup, 1982). Passing the mark test indicated self-recognition, which, he claimed was an index of self awareness. He suggested that consciousness is bidirectional, that is, that it translates into awareness and self-awareness. These capacities, Gallup (1982) suggested, provide the demonstration of mind in nonhuman animals. Mind was defined as "the ability to monitor your own mental states" (Gallup, 1982, p. 242). This ability to be privy to one's own state of mind suggested to Gallup that such organisms should be able to attribute similar states of mind to other organisms. This suggestion, related to Premack and Woodruff's (1978) discussion of theory of mind, has been tested empirically by Povinelli, Nelson, and Boysen (1990), with equivocal results (see Heyes, 1993; Swartz, in preparation). Although they showed that chimpanzees could discriminate between two people who had different knowledge states, they were unable to demonstrate the basis for the performance. Further, closer analyses of the data suggest that the animals were not performing the task consistently above chance (Swartz, in preparation).

The question here is whether such a rich interpretation of the chimpanzee's self-knowledge (mark test performance) is necessary to understand how an individual chimpanzee comes to comprehend the nature of the mirror image. Other interpretations are possible (see Mitchell, 1993). The present chapter is an attempt to support the case that this behavior can legitimately be called self-recognition, but that it does not imply self-concept or a psychological experience identical to that which humans experience when they talk about self. To make this case, the phenomenon will be discussed in more detail.

What do we know specifically about the phenomenon itself? First, there are species differences in the demonstration of mirror self-recognition. The most puzzling case is that of the gorilla who does not readily provide evidence for mirror self-recognition, either with behavior during mirror exposure or passing the mark test (Ledbetter & Basen, 1982; Suarez & Gallup, 1981). Only one gorilla has unequivocally demonstrated self-recognition, with some evidence from others that gorillas are capable of mirror self-recognition (Parker, 1994; Patterson & Cohn, 1994; Swartz & Evans, 1994). The question about the gorilla, which opens questions about mirror self-recognition, is why it is so difficult to obtain mirror self-recognition in a great ape species with a social structure that would seem to support such a capacity and with cognitive capacities very similar to that of the chimpanzee (Rumbaugh & Rice, 1962). As Swartz & Evans (1994) suggest, the answer may be related to the testing situation and to the individual gorilla's history. It may also be based on the historical precedent of defining this phenomenon on the basis of chimpanzee behavior. The subtlety of the gorilla's behavior may have masked mirror behaviors because investigators have been looking for chimpanzee-like behaviors in front of the mirror. A more careful analysis of the gorilla's behavior may lead to different conclusions than previously drawn.

Other than the great apes (primarily common chimpanzees and orangutans), nonhuman primates have not demonstrated unequivocal evidence of mirror self-recognition (Anderson, 1984; Gallup, 1991). The genus receiving most attention has been macaque monkeys (*Macaca*). Gallup (1970) provided ten macaque monkeys with mirror exposure but none of the monkeys showed self-directed behavior or passed the mark test. More recently, four macaque monkeys who were given extensive experience and/or remediation with mirrors showed brief or equivocal mark touches (Boccia, 1994; Howell, Kinsey, & Novak, 1994; Itakura, 1987; Thompson & Boatright-Horowitz, 1994). Despite the report of mark-directed behavior in these macaque monkeys, there are significant differences between the topography of the macaques' mark touches and those of chimpanzees. In one case, only one brief mark touch occurred immediately after inspection of the mirror image, and it did not appear that the mirror was used to direct the behavior to the mark (Thompson & Boatright-Horowitz, 1994). Despite reporting that one monkey made mark-directed responses in the presence of the mirror, Itakura (1987) found this result insufficient to support the conclusion that monkeys use the mirror to guide their responses to their own body. In another instance, although one mark touch appeared to be guided by the mirror, three mark-directed touches were equivocal and could have been incidental to self-aggression (Howell et al., 1994). In contrast, the topography of mark-directed behavior by chimpanzees involves using the mirror to direct the hand to the mark. In some cases, touching the mark is followed by looking at or sniffing the fingers that contacted the mark, a behavior that is of great significance to Gallup (1975) who suggested that the inspection of the hand that touched the mark would make sense only if the animal perceived that the mark was on its own body. At present, it is not clear under what circumstances macaque monkeys show mirror self-recognition, if at all.

In addition to observed species differences, there are also individual differences in the demonstration of mirror self-recognition. Swartz & Evans (1991) failed to replicate Gallup's (1970) findings with chimpanzees. In contrast to the implication that this phenomenon is a robust phenomenon in chimpanzees, we failed to find evidence of mirror self-recognition in several chimpanzees provided with mirror exposure. Further, we had difficulty getting this study published (see Swartz & Evans, 1997). At the time that we submitted our manuscript in 1987, only 14 chimpanzees had been reported to demonstrate mirror self-recognition with the mark test (four in Gallup, 1970; two in Hill, Bundy, Gallup & McClure, 1970; three in Gallup, McClure, Hill & Bundy, 1971; three in Suarez & Gallup, 1981; two in Lethmate & Ducker, 1973), yet our failure to replicate the phenomenon was taken to imply more about our study than about the phenomenon. Further, the existing data for orangutans also showed some failures to find mirror self-recognition. In 1987, there were two reports with orangutan subjects, one that reported positive mark tests with two orangutans (Lethmate and Ducker, 1973), and one that obtained self-directed behavior and a successful mark test with only one of two orangutans (Suarez and Gallup, 1981). The finding of individual differences in chimpanzees has been replicated (Povinelli et al., 1993) but Gallup (1994) still reports the orangutan data as a strong demonstration of the phenomenon, failing to note that one of four did not demonstrate the phenomenon.

Species differences and individual differences have not yet been adequately characterized or explained. Further investigation of a wide range of individuals reared and tested in various contexts will provide a richer understanding of the phenomenon. The situation, of course, is bidirectional. The study of species and individual differences will help define the phenomenon and allow the development of new theoretical treatments of this phenomenon. Conversely, theoretical treatments of the phenomenon must take into account the obtained species and individual differences across nonhuman primate groups. The extreme position taken by Gallup (e.g., 1982, 1994) does not seem warranted at this point. To suggest that mirror self-recognition implies the presence of a self-concept or identity, which leads to self-awareness and mind, suggests that only some chimpanzees, some orangutans, and some gorillas under some circumstances have self-concepts, self-awareness, and mind.

Mirror self-recognition does not imply self-concept, nor is it appropriate to treat it theoretically in the comparative domain as we treat self-recognition, self-concept, sense of self in humans. However, the phenomenon can legitimately be termed self-recognition in that it implies something about the animal's understanding of itself in its environment, and it is a phenomenon worthy of investigation. What evidence supports the interpretation that the presence of self-directed behavior can be legitimately termed self-recognition? First, the behavior is directed back to the self, *using the mirror as a guide*. Second, the demonstration of self-directed behavior requires some experience with the mirror image. Although not yet determined, the nature of this experience, including the time course and the unfolding of specific behavioral patterns, is of great importance. Third, the demonstration of spontaneous self-directed behaviors in great apes but not other animals is an important finding.

The behavior seen in many chimpanzees, orangutans, and some gorillas provisionally can be labeled self-recognition. What is meant by that term? Minimally, that the animal differentiates itself from other environmental objects. There must be cognitive capacities that underlie this phenomenon, and by addressing those, we will come to a better understanding of the phenomenon and how to characterize it. Some of this work is ongoing (see chapters in Parker *et al.*, 1994 and in this volume). Most important is what is *not* meant here, and that is an interpretation of mirror self-recognition that involves human levels or types of self-awareness, self-concept, and mind.

Can it be concluded that nonhuman primates show self-recognition? The contention in this chapter is *yes*, with certain qualifications. Some individuals of some species spontaneously use a mirror to address their own bodies. Rather than responding directly to the mirror image, they use the mirror image to inspect or to guide behavior back to the body. The simplest explanation of this behavior is that these organisms can use the mirror as a tool for autogrooming or related behaviors (see Thompson & Boatright-Horowitz, 1994, for a discussion of the mirror as a tool).

A more enriched interpretation is that the organism understands the nature of the mirror image, that is, understands that the mirror image is a reflection of its own body. To call this self-recognition does not necessarily imply the presence of a self-concept, self-awareness, or mind, nor does it imply that nonhuman primates who show mirror self-recognition have self conceptions similar or identical to those demonstrated by humans who show mirror self-recognition.

Explanations based on identity or self-concept are inadequate. Rather, the cognitive capacities involved in being able to understand the nature of the mirror image must be defined.

It is important to spend time and effort on determining, across species and across development, how mirror self-recognition arises. The time course and form of specific behaviors that fall into the gross categories of social behaviors, contingent behaviors, and self-directed behaviors must be documented. By documenting the development of mirror self-recognition as it appears in individual organisms, we can determine how the nonhuman primate discovers the attributes of the mirror and develops an understanding of the nature of the mirror image. In so doing, we can then address some unanswered questions about the phenomenon, such as the meaning of inconsistencies between self-directed behaviors during mirror exposure and passing the mark test. An important step in that direction will be the establishment of rigorous and agreed-upon criteria for mirror self-recognition that take into account species differences (see Gallup, 1994; Swartz & Evans, 1994).

REFERENCES

ANDERSON, J. R. (1984). Monkeys with mirrors: Some questions for primate psychology. *International Journal of Primatology, 5,* 81–98.

BOCCIA, M. (1994). Mirror behavior in macaques. In S. T. Parker, R. W. Mitchell & M. L. Boccia (Eds.), *Self-awareness in animals and humans: Developmental perspectives* (pp. 350–360). New York: Cambridge University Press.

GALLUP, G. G., JR. (1970). Chimpanzees: Self-recognition. *Science, 167,* 86–87.

GALLUP, G. G., JR. (1975). Towards an operational definition of self-awareness. In R. H. Tuttle (Ed.), *Socioecology and psychology of primates* (pp. 309–342). The Hague, the Netherlands: Mouton.

GALLUP, G. G., JR. (1977). Self-recognition in primates: A comparative approach to the bidirectional properties of consciousness. *American Psychologist, 32,* 329–338.

GALLUP, G. G., JR. (1982). Self-awareness and the emergence of mind in primates. *American Journal of Primatology, 2,* 237–248.

GALLUP, G. G., JR. (1991). Toward a comparative psychology of self-awareness: Species limitations and cognitive consequences. In G. R. Goethals & J. Strauss (Eds.), *The self: An interdisciplinary approach* (pp. 121–135). New York: Springer-Verlag.

GALLUP, G. G., JR. (1994). Self-recognition: Research strategies and experimental design. In S. T. Parker, R. W. Mitchell & M. L. Boccia (Eds.), *Self-awareness in animals and humans: Developmental perspectives* (pp. 35–50). New York: Cambridge University Press.

GALLUP, G. G., JR., MCCLURE, M. K., HILL, S. D. & BUNDY, R. A. (1971). Capacity for self-recognition in differentially reared chimpanzees. *The Psychological Record, 21,* 69–74.

HEYES, C. M. (1993). Anecdotes, training, trapping and triangulating: Do animals attribute mental states? *Animal Behaviour, 46,* 177–188.

HILL, S. D., BUNDY, R. A., GALLUP, G. G., JR. & MCCLURE, M.K. (1970). Responsiveness of young nursery reared chimpanzees to mirrors. *Proceedings of the Louisiana Academy of Sciences, 33,* 77–82.

HOWELL, M., KINSEY, J. & NOVAK, M. (1994). *Mark-directed behavior in a rhesus monkey after controlled, reinforced exposure to mirrors.* Paper presented at annual meeting of the American Society of Primatologists, Seattle, WA, July, 1994.

ITAKURA, S. (1987). Use of a mirror to direct their responses in Japanese monkeys (*Macaca fuscata fuscata*). *Primates, 28,* 343–352.

LEDBETTER, D. H. & BASEN, J. A. (1982). Failure to demonstrate self-recognition in gorillas. *American Journal of Primatology, 2,* 307–310.

LETHMATE, J & DÜCKER, G. (1973). Untersuchungen zum Selbsterkennen im Spiegel bei Orang- utans und einigen anderen Affenarten. *Z. Tierpsychol., 33,* 248–269.

LIN, A. C., BARD, K. A. & ANDERSON, J. R. (1992). Development of self-recognition in chimpanzees (*Pan troglodytes*). *Journal of Comparative Psychology, 106,* 120–127.

MITCHELL, R. W. (1993). Mental models of mirror self- recognition: Two theories. *New Ideas in Psychology, 11,* 295–325.

PARKER, S. T. (1994). Incipient mirror self-recognition in zoo gorillas and chimpanzees. In S. T. Parker, R. W. Mitchell & M. L. Boccia (Eds.), *Self-awareness in animals and humans: Developmental perspectives* (pp. 301–307). New York: Cambridge University Press.

PARKER, S. T., MITCHELL, R. W. & BOCCIA, M. (Eds.) (1994). *Self-awareness in animals and human: Developmental perspectives.* New York: Cambridge University Press.

PATTERSON, F. G. & COHN, R. H. (1994). Self-recognition and self-awareness in lowland gorillas. In S. T. Parker, R. W. Mitchell & M. L. Boccia (Eds.), *Self-awareness in animals and humans: Developmental perspectives* (pp. 273–290). New York: Cambridge University Press.

POVINELLI, D. J., NELSON, K. E. & BOYSEN, S. T. (1990). Inferences about guessing and knowing by chimpanzees (*Pan troglodytes*). *Journal of Comparative Psychology, 104,* 203–210.

POVINELLI, D. J., RULF, A. B., LANDAU, K. & BIERSCHWALE, D. (1993). Self-recognition in chimpanzees (*Pan troglodytes*): Distribution, ontogeny, and patterns of emergence. *Journal of Comparative Psychology, 107,* 347–372.

PREMACK, D. & WOODRUFF, G. (1978). Does the chimpanzee have a theory of mind? *Behavioral and Brain Sciences, 4,* 515–526.

RUMBAUGH, D. M. & RICE, C. P. (1962). Learning set formation in young great apes. *Journal of Comparative and Physiological Psychology, 55,* 866–868.

SUAREZ, S. D. & GALLUP, G. G., JR. (1981). Self-recognition in chimpanzees and orangutans, but not gorillas. *Journal of Human Evolution, 10,* 175–188.

SWARTZ, K. B. (In preparation). Theory of mind in nonhuman primates: What is the evidence?

SWARTZ, K. B. & EVANS, S. (1991). Not all chimpanzees (*Pan troglodytes*) show self-recognition. *Primates, 32,* 583–496.

SWARTZ, K. B. & EVANS, S. (1994). Social and cognitive factors in chimpanzee and gorilla mirror behavior and self-recognition. In S. T. Parker, R. W. Mitchell & M. L. Boccia (Eds.), *Self-awareness in animals and humans: Developmental perspectives* (pp. 189–206). New York: Cambridge University Press.

SWARTZ, K. B. & EVANS, S. (1997). Anthropomorphism, anecdotes, and mirrors. In R. W. Mitchell, H. L. Miles & N. Thompson (Eds.), *Anthropomorphism, anecdotes, and animals* (pp. 296–306). Albany, NY: SUNY Press.

THOMPSON, R. L. & BOATRIGHT-HOROWITZ, S. L. (1994). The question of mirror-mediated self-recognition in apes and monkeys: Some new results and reservations. In S. T. Parker, R. W. Mitchell & M. L. Boccia (Eds.), *Self-awareness in animals and humans: Developmental perspectives* (pp. 330–349). New York: Cambridge University Press.

Gordon G. Gallup, Jr., is a Professor of Psychology at the State University of New York at Albany, and a former editor of the Journal of Comparative Psychology. *In addition to his work on primate cognition, his research interests are quite diverse (e.g., predator-prey relations, animal models of psychopathology, reproductive strategies). Much of his current work focuses on human behavior from an evolutionary perspective.*

On the Rise and Fall of Self-Conception in Primates

GORDON G. GALLUP, JR.[a]

Department of Psychology
State University of New York at Albany
Albany, New York 12222

INTRODUCTION

Since the original report of self-recognition in chimpanzees almost three decades ago (Gallup, 1970), numerous studies of mirror self-recognition have been conducted on humans, nonhuman primates, and other animals (for some reviews of different aspects of this literature see Anderson, 1986, 1994; Gallup, 1991; Povinelli, 1987). This research has revealed three curious aspects of what is now known about the distribution, pattern, and emergence of self-recognition. One concerns the highly restricted phyletic distribution of this capacity, the second involves the presence of considerable within-species variation in the expression of this capacity, and the third relates to the ontogeny or life-span developmental characteristics of self-recognition. The purpose of this paper is to briefly review and attempt to integrate all three of these features of self-recognition in the context of an ingenious recent attempt by Povinelli and Cant (1995) to trace the evolution of self-conception from what may appear to be some very unlikely origins.

PHYLOGENY OF SELF-RECOGNITION

Despite a recent attempt to discredit self-recognition research (Heyes, 1994) as a result of what amounts to a desperate and unsuccessful effort to salvage radical behaviorism as a failed paradigm (see Gallup, Povinelli, Suarez, Anderson, Lethmate & Menzel, 1995), there is a substantial and convincing body of evidence that chimpanzees, orangutans, and humans are capable of correctly deciphering mirrored information about themselves. Most other species seem incapable of realizing that they are the source of what they see when they confront themselves in mirrors and persist in responding to the image as if it represented another member of the same species (see Anderson, 1994). In contrast to chimpanzees, which often begin to show signs of self-recognition within an hour to several days of mirror

[a]Address for correspondence: Department of Psychology, S.U.N.Y. at Albany, Albany, New York 12222; phone (518) 442-4852.

exposure (Povinelli *et al.*, 1993), rhesus macaques with years of continuous exposure to themselves in mirrors continue to react to the reflection as if confronted by another monkey (Gallup & Suarez, 1991).

INDIVIDUAL DIFFERENCES IN SELF-RECOGNITION

Among species that can recognize themselves in mirrors there are rather substantial individual differences in the presence or absence of this capacity. Not all chimpanzees (or even all humans) are capable of correctly deciphering mirrored information about themselves. Across different studies of chimpanzees, the proportion of subjects showing evidence of self-recognition ranges from 100 percent (Gallup, 1970) to less than one of ten (Swartz & Evans, 1991). It is difficult, however, to compare these studies because they are typically based on small samples that differ in terms of important methodological details, and critical information about the past rearing history of the subjects is often inadequate or unavailable (see Gallup, 1994 for a further discussion of these problems). The most comprehensive study of self-recognition in chimpanzees was recently published by Povinelli and his associates and involved data obtained from more than 100 captive chimpanzees (Povinelli, Rulf, Landau & Bierschwale, 1993). Collapsing across age, approximately 50 percent of the chimpanzees in this sample exhibited compelling signs of self-recognition.

The situation is much less clear for orangutans because far fewer studies have been conducted and sample sizes have typically been even smaller than in those that have employed chimpanzees. But on the basis of the available evidence it appears that most of the orangutans that have been tested do show self-recognition (Lethmate & Dücker, 1973; Miles, 1994; Shillito, Shumaker & Gallup, unpublished data; Suarez & Gallup, 1981).

Unlike orangutans and chimpanzees, most gorillas fail tests of mirror self-recognition (Ledbetter & Basen, 1982; Lethmate & Dücker, 1973; Shillito, Shumaker & Gallup, unpublished data; Suarez & Gallup, 1981). However, there are several reports of individual exceptions to this pattern of results. Patterson (1984) claims that the hand-reared female gorilla named Koko can recognize herself in a mirror, and Swartz and Evans (1994) report some preliminary data that they interpret as being suggestive of self-recognition in another captive gorilla named King. Other claims concerning self-recognition in gorillas (e.g., Law & Lock, 1994; Parker, 1994) are difficult to evaluate because the evidence is not based on rigorous procedures (see Gallup, 1994).

Even among humans the capacity for self-recognition is not a universal trait. There are instances of individuals who are mentally retarded, as well as those with other mental and emotional disturbances who fail tests of self-recognition and persist in responding to themselves in mirrors as though they were seeing other people (for a review see Gallup, 1979). Among chimpanzees and humans there are also notable individual differences in self-recognition as a function of age (see following section). Thus the picture that has begun to emerge is one in which most humans, many orangutans, about half of the chimpanzees, and maybe a few isolated gorillas exhibit evidence of self-recognition. To date no one has reported compelling evidence of self-recognition in any other species (primate or otherwise).

ONTOGENY OF SELF-RECOGNITION

There is a striking difference in emphasis between the human and the nonhuman primate literature on self-recognition. Most of the published studies on humans focus on the ontogeny of self-recognition or the question of when, in the course of psychological development, this capacity first emerges. In contrast, the animal literature has focused almost entirely on the issue of phylogeny or the question of which species can or cannot recognize themselves in mirrors.

Although the methods that have been used to assess self-recognition in human infants are not as rigorous as those that have been developed for use on animals (see Gallup, 1994 for a critique of the methodology used in these areas), there is a high degree of correspondence across different studies of human children in showing the emergence of mirror self-recognition between the ages of 18 to 24 months (for a review see Anderson, 1984). At the other end of the life-span developmental spectrum in humans, there are data that show the ability to correctly decipher mirrored information about the self can be lost as a result of progressive age-related dementia. For example, Biringer and Anderson (1992) report that among patients with Alzheimer's disease the transition from stage 5 to 6 on the Global Deterioration Scale is associated with the loss of mirror self-recognition, and that the ability of such patients to recognize themselves under conditions of a noncontingent video image is lost at even earlier stages of dementia.

THE RISE OF SELF-CONCEPTION:
THE CLAMBERING HYPOTHESIS

Povinelli and Cant (1995) have theorized that the orangutan may be the closest approximation to the now extinct common ancestor to humans and great apes. They contend that an examination of the unique features of orangutan ecology contains a clue as to what prompted the evolution of self-conception. Unlike other great apes, orangutans characteristically spend much if not most of their time in the trees. Whereas many primates live in the arboreal world, great apes are unlikely inhabitants because of their size.

As they move about the forest canopy orangutans are in constant danger of falling owing to the deformation of that habitat because of their large body mass, which in the case of some male orangutans can approach 80 kg or more. Not only does their body mass increase the fragility of the substrate in the canopy, but it exacerbates the consequences of falling by increasing the likelihood of sustaining serious injury as a result.

To put the unique situation that the orangutan confronts in perspective, Povinelli and Cant present a detailed comparative analysis of the locomotor patterns employed by several arboreal primate species. Whereas most primates employ a set of relatively fixed, stereotyped patterns of locomotion that can be combined in various ways to deal with the specific demands imposed at different junctures in the canopy, the orangutan represents a dramatic exception. Orangutans employ a methodical, carefully executed series of nonstereotyped, highly flexible responses for moving through the trees called clambering, in which they carefully test and evaluate various features (such as limbs and vines) of the canopy in terms of whether they will provide adequate support. Povinelli and Cant reason that this kind of strategy requires an "on-line," continuous monitoring of various options that necessitates a sense of personal agency (i.e., the realization that you can exercise some control over various outcomes) and that this is what led to the emergence of self-conception.

SELF-CONCEPTION AND MENTAL STATE ATTRIBUTION: THE REPRODUCTIVE HYPOTHESIS

I have argued on several occasions that self-awareness may have evolved because it conferred a reproductive advantage (Gallup, 1982, 1985). According to my model, human evolution came to increasingly emphasize a unique combination of strategies for purposes of securing scarce resources. Whereas some species have evolved to emphasize competition as the principle means of adaptation, others (e.g., the social insects) have followed a trajectory which placed a premium on cooperation. Human evolution came to favor a unique combination of both of these strategies. Although they might appear to be strange bedfellows, the marriage of cooperation and competition is what favored the development and elaboration of self-conception. Organisms that were aware of being aware and could represent limited aspects of their own mental and emotional worlds found themselves in the unique position of being able to generate introspective/inferential models of the experience and mental states of others. The advantages that would accrue from a strategy such as this have been nicely set forth by Humphrey (1976) and the evidence for a relationship between self-conception and mental state attribution has been recently reviewed by Povinelli (1993).

Aside from the arboreal clambering hypothesis, Povinelli and Cant

(1995) claim that no one has "produced a compelling, testable proposition concerning the evolutionary emergence of self-conception" (p. 394). However, an account based on reproductive competition does have a number of testable, and therefore potentially falsifiable, implications. First, if the use of introspectively based social strategies confers a reproductive advantage, then one would expect individual differences in self-conception (e.g., presence or absence of self-recognition) to correlate with corresponding differences in the production of descendants. For example, it would be a relatively simple matter to measure differential reproduction among humans and chimpanzees as a function of whether they recognize themselves in mirrors.

Another obvious prediction that would follow from this model is that if this capacity evolved to enable individuals to take into account the experiences, desires, beliefs, and intentions of others as a means of both facilitating cooperation and competition among each other for access to reproductive opportunities, then the development of self-conception within an individual ought to precede or at least coincide with the onset of puberty. Most humans show a highly precocial onset of self-awareness. However, there is growing evidence that once the process of self-conception begins in humans at about 18 to 24 months of age with the emergence of self-recognition, other more complex processes underlying self-awareness follow. These include extension, elaboration, and fine-tuning of a variety of increasingly complex cognitive strategies based on more subtle and sophisticated instances of mental state attribution. These complex strategies may ultimately serve to prepare the individual for life in a complex interpersonal milieu which involves competing and cooperating among one another over issues of politics, mating, and economics—the outcome of which can have profound reproductive consequences.

Although the developmental sequence is different for chimpanzees, it is nevertheless consistent with the model. Whereas until recently the development of self-recognition in chimpanzees was largely ignored and unknown, the comprehensive life-span developmental study by Povinelli *et al.* (1993) of captive chimpanzees show that self-conception emerges at or about the onset of puberty. Descriptions of chimpanzee reproductive tactics under natural and semi-natural conditions reveal the apparent use of a variety of introspectively derived strategies for maximizing individual access to resources and mating opportunities (e.g., de Waal, 1982).

Finally another testable implication of the reproductive model concerns the failure to find self-recognition in gorillas. Since humans and great apes appear to share a now-extinct ancestor in common, it is reasonable to suppose that the protohominid precursor of the human–great ape clade was self-aware (Gallup, 1991; Povinelli & Cant, 1995). If this is true, then it would follow that at some point during their evolutionary history, gorillas, like chimpanzees, orangutans, and humans, were self-aware; but somewhere along the line they lost the capacity. The alternative account of the data showing self-recognition to chimpanzees, orangutans, and humans, but not gorillas, would be to suppose that rather than being a shared trait derived from a common ancestor, self-conception evolved independently on three separate occasions. Although a possibility, this is a far less plausible and parsimonious account of the species differences among members of the human–great ape clade.

The next question is that if gorillas evolved from a self-aware ancestor, why did they lose the capacity for self-conception? Biologically speaking, I suspect that self-awareness is an organizationally and energetically expensive trait in the sense that it requires a considerable commitment of complicated neurological material (frontal cortex) that functions at a considerable metabolic cost. If these commitments and costs are not outweighed by corresponding reproductive benefits, then it would not take long for random mutations (genetic drift) to lead to the disappearance of the trait. Povinelli (1994) has theorized that the ancestral trait for self-conception still exists in gorillas and, as is true for the female gorilla Koko, early environmental enrichment and stimulation may provide a means of recapturing that trait. But even if that is the case, it still leaves unanswered the question of why gorillas lost the capacity in the first place? One possibility that would be consistent with my model is that gorilla social organization and socioecology has changed in such a way that there is no longer a reproductive advantage to being self-aware and as a consequence the trait has been lost (again through genetic drift). Thus my model would predict that the key to understanding the distribution of the trait among great apes, which have descended from the trees, can be found in terms of a comparative analysis of the natural history of their respective social dynamics and social organization. Reproductive strategies among gorillas are very different from those that typify chimpanzees. Accounts of gorillas living under natural conditions (e.g., Schaller, 1964) reveal that gorilla social structure involves the development of male-dominated harems, and there appears to be little or no direct competition among gorillas for resources or the opportunity to copulate. Nor does copulation itself seem to be driven by powerful proximate motivational mechanisms among gorillas.

The gorilla anomaly represents a clear and pivotal difference between the account of self-conception offered by Povinelli and Cant (1995) and my own. The clambering hypothesis provides a detailed and elegant set of reasons for the emergence of self-conception, but it is relatively silent about the underlying reasons for the contemporary distribution of this ability both between and within species of great apes and humans (see p. 416). Alternatively, if self-awareness among terrestrial apes served as the foundation for the emergence of a cognitive ensemble that conveys a set of strategic social/reproductive advantages, then once the trait appeared it could only be maintained to the extent that the considerable organizational and energetic costs of self-conception were outweighed by corresponding advantages.

THE RISE AND FALL OF SELF-CONCEPTION:
COMING DOWN OUT OF THE TREES

If Povinelli and Cant (1995) are right about the emergence of a sense of personal agency (as one of the primary ingredients to self-conception) as a means of dealing with life in an arboreal habitat on the part of a creature that is in constant danger of falling because of its substantial body mass and the effect this has in terms of rendering branches and other means of support fragile, then it would follow that while life in the arboreal mode may have been what prompted self-conception, in order for the capacity to flourish in a cognitive sense it would require coming down out of the trees.

For an orangutan life in the trees is predicated on maintaining a state of more or less never-ending vigilance concerning habitat deformation. Orangutans have to remain "on-line" in the sense of continually testing and evaluating the adequacy of support provided by the substrate as they move through the trees. Unlike an orangutan, I can walk from my office to the library and think about all sorts of things along the way (e.g., about the organization of a lecture I will be giving that afternoon, about a promotion and tenure case I have been asked to review by another university, about what I need to get at the grocery store on my way home, etc.). In other words, I can use the time spent traversing the distance between my office and the library engaged in a variety of other parallel but more or less independent mental operations. The analogue to what the orangutan confronts would be a situation in which you had to carefully concentrate, monitor, and tentatively test in a continuous fashion every step you took to get from one place to another. As a result you would never have the time to think about yourself in relation to other objects and/or events. Thus, to my mind one of the most intriguing, but unacknowledged implications of the analysis offered by Povinelli and Cant (1995) is that the capacity for self-conception ought to either flower or flounder once you come down out of the trees. Once removed from its point of origin or genesis in the arboreal world (as in the case of re-terrestrialization), the trait either must come to serve some derived function or it is in danger of being lost through genetic drift.

Although orangutans remain largely arboreal, the other descendants of this now extinct orangutan-like ancestor have all ventured down out of the trees. Humans, chimpanzees, and gorillas have, to varying degrees, abandoned life in the arboreal world. Humans are the furthest removed in the sense that they are the only primates that do not even return to the trees to sleep at night. During the day, gorillas are largely confined to the terrestrial mode. Although they too spend most of their time on the ground, chimpanzees still occasionally venture back into the trees to forage for certain kinds of food.

In the case of humans, self-conception has flourished in the terrestrial mode. Humans have obviously followed an interpersonal and social psychological trajectory that has placed a premium on self-conception and mental-state attribution as a means of competing with one another for scarce resources. When it came to the elaboration of this trait, humans became the source of their own intelligence. As noted previously, however, the trait appears to have been lost by gorillas. Chimpanzees may not be far behind. In chimpanzees the trait appears to be in the process of being lost. Both the distribution and ontogeny of self-recognition are precisely what one would expect for a trait that is undergoing disintegration and/or disorganization through genetic drift. Recall that only about 50% of chimpanzees exhibit self-recognition, and that the emergence of this ability in chimpanzee development is considerably retarded/delayed relative to humans (Povinelli *et al.*, 1993). Whereas humans begin to show signs of self-recognition at about 18 to 24 months of age, chimpanzees show self-recognition at a much later point in life and there is also much more variability among chimpanzees in the age of onset. Povinelli *et al.* (1993) have shown that a few chimpanzees may show signs of self-recognition as early as 3.5 years of age, but many do not begin to recognize themselves in mirrors until early adolescence (7–8 years of age). Moreover, unlike humans, the proportion of chimpanzees passing tests of self-recognition rises during adolescence and then drops precipitously during adulthood. Thus a significant number of chimpanzees fail to show evidence of mirror self-recognition [although not nearly as large a proportion as Swartz and Evans (1991) suggest], and among those that do come to recognize themselves in mirrors the onset is developmentally delayed relative to humans and its loss in later life is greatly accelerated. An obvious implication of this account of the evolution of self-conception and mental-state attribution is that we may be witnessing a relatively pure case of "use it or lose it."

Povinelli and Cant (1995) contend that because orangutans continue to live under conditions that place a premium on self-conception, one would expect orangutans to more closely resemble humans in terms of the distribution and development of self-recognition. Unfortunately, there are so few studies of self-recognition in orangutans that it is not possible to reach any firm conclusions about population or distribution parameters. But as my extension of their analysis would suggest, free-ranging orangutans, unlike humans, should have little time to elaborate and extend their capacity for self-conception to other cognitive domains (e.g., mental-state attribution) because of the need to maintain a continuous, on-line focus on body weight–induced habitat fragility and deformation. Thus a novel and potentially testable prediction derived from my extension of the clambering hypothesis would be that captive orangutans, now unencumbered by the demands of being in imminent danger of falling from the forest canopy, are in a position (at least in principle) to excel relative to their feral counterparts on a variety of cognitive tasks related to self-conception and mental-state attribution.

Contrary to what many people have been led to believe, the orangutan may be closer to being our intellectual equal than the chimpanzee. Although orangutans have not been the subject of much research on cognitive processes, there is an unsubstantiated but widely circulated anecdotal story among people who have worked with all three species of great apes, and this anecdote captures the essence of the differences that are implicated by the present analysis. According to the story, if a captive gorilla is given a screwdriver, the gorilla will ignore it. If a chimpanzee is given a screwdriver, the chimpanzee will play with it. But if an orangutan is given a screwdriver, the orangutan will proceed later that night to use it to dismantle its cage.

REFERENCES

ANDERSON, J. R. (1984). The development of self-recognition: A review. *Developmental Psychobiology, 17:* 35–49.

ANDERSON, J. R. (1994). The monkey in the mirror: A strange conspecific. In *Self-awareness in animals and humans.* S. Parker, R. Mitchell & M. Boccia (Eds.), (pp. 315–329). New York: Cambridge University Press.

BIRINGER, F. & ANDERSON, J. R. (1992). Self-recognition in Alzheimer's disease: A mirror and video study. *Journal of Gerontology, 47,* 385–388.

DE WAAL, F. (1982). *Chimpanzee politics.* New York: Harper and Row.

GALLUP, G. G., JR. (1979). Self-recognition in chimpanzees and man: A developmental and comparative perspective. In *Genesis of behavior, Vol. 2: The child and its family.* M. Lewis & L. Rosenblum, (Eds.) (p. 107–126). New York: Plenum.

GALLUP, G. G., JR. (1982). Self-awareness and the emergence of mind in primates. *American Journal of Primatology, 2,* 237–248.

GALLUP, G. G., JR. (1985). Do minds exist in species other than our own? *Neuroscience Biobehavioral Reviews, 9,* 631–641.

GALLUP, G. G., JR. (1991). Toward a comparative psychology of self-awareness: Species limitations and cognitive consequences. *In The self: An interdisciplinary approach.* G. R. Goethals & J. Strauss (Eds.), (pp. 121–135). New York: Springer-Verlag.

GALLUP, G. G., JR. (1994). Self-recognition: Research strategies and experimental design. *In. Self-awareness in animals and humans.* S. Parker, R. Mitchell & M. Boccia (Eds.) (pp. 35–50). New York: Cambridge University Press.

GALLUP, G. G., JR. POVINELLI, D. J., SUAREZ, S. D., ANDERSON, J. R., LETHMATE, J. & MENZEL, E. W., JR. (1995). Further reflections of self-recognition in primates. *Animal Behaviour, 50,* 1525–1532.

GALLUP, G. G., JR. & SUAREZ, S. D. (1991). Social responding to mirrors in rhesus monkeys (*Macaca mulatta*): Effects of temporary mirror removal. *Journal of Comparative Psychology, 105,* 376–379.

HEYES, C. M. (1994). Reflections on self-recognition in primates. *Animal Behaviour, 47,* 909–919.

HUMPHREY, N. (1976). The social function of intellect. *In. Growing points in ethology.* P. P. G. Bateson & R. A. Hinde (Eds.) New York: Cambridge University Press.

LAW, L. E. & LOCK, A. J. (1994). Do gorillas recognize themselves on television? *In Self-awareness in animals and humans.* S. Parker, R. Mitchell & M. Boccia, (Eds.) (pp. 308–312). New York: Cambridge University Press.

LEDBETTER, D. H. & BASEN, J. A. (1982). Failure to demonstrate self-recognition in gorillas. *American Journal of Primatology, 2,* 307–310.

LETHMATE, J. & DÜCKER, G. (1973). Untersuchungen am sebsterkennen im spiegel bei orangutans einigen anderen affenarten. *Zeitschrift für Tierpsychologie, 33:* 248–269.

MILES, H. L. W. (1994). ME CHANTEK: The development of self-awareness in a singing orangutan. In, *Self-awareness in animals and humans.* S. Parker, R. Mitchell & M. Boccia, (Eds.), (pp. 254–272). New York: Cambridge University Press.

PARKER, S. T. (1994). Incipient mirror self-recognition in zoo gorillas and chimpanzees. In, *Self-awareness in animals and humans.* S. Parker, R. Mitchell & M. Boccia, (Eds.), (pp. 301–307). New York: Cambridge University Press.

POVINELLI, D. J. (1987). Monkeys, apes, mirrors, and minds: The evolution of self-awareness in primates. *Journal of Human Evolution, 2,* 493–507.

POVINELLI, D. J. (1993). Reconstructing the evolution of mind. *American Psychologist, 48,* 493–509.

POVINELLI, D. J. (1994). How to create self-recognizing gorillas (but don't try it on macaques). *In, Self-awareness in animals and humans.* S. Parker, R. Mitchell & M. Boccia, (Eds.), (pp. 291–300). New York: Cambridge University Press.

POVINELLI, D. J. & CANT, J. G. H. (1995). Arboreal clambering and the evolution of self-conception. *Quarterly Review of Biology, 70,* 393–421.

POVINELLI, D. J. RULF, A. B., LANDAU, K. R. & BIERSCHWALE, D. T. (1993). Self-recognition in chimpanzees (*Pan troglodytes*): Distribution, ontogeny, and patterns of emergence. *Journal of Comparative Psychology, 107:* 347–372.

SCHALLER, G. B. (1964). The Year of the Gorilla. University of Chicago Press.

SUAREZ, S. D. & GALLUP, G. G., JR. (1981). Self-recognition in chimpanzees and orangutans, but not gorillas. *Journal of Human Evolution 10:* 175–188.

SWARTZ, K. B. & EVANS, S. (1994). Social and cognitive factors in chimpanzees and gorilla mirror behavior and self-recognition. In *Self-awareness in humans and animals.* S. Parker, R. Mitchell & M. Boccia, (Eds.), (pp. 189–206). New York: Cambridge University Press.

*Howard Rachlin, a New York City (Bronx) native, received a
bachelor's degree in mechanical engineering from Cooper Union in
1957, an M.A. in psychology from the New School of Social Research
in 1962, and a Ph.D. from Harvard University in 1965. After
teaching at Harvard for three years, he came to the State University
of New York at Stony Brook, where he is now Professor of Psychology.
He has published many articles and books reporting research in
behavioral economics, animal and human choice, gambling and self-
control. His most recent book,* Behavior and Mind, *is published by
Oxford University Press. He is currently working on a book
provisionally titled* Principles of Self-Control and Altruism.

Self and Self-Control

HOWARD RACHLIN

Department of Psychology
State University of New York at Stony Brook
Stony Brook, New York 11794

In this article the self is construed as a functional interaction between behavior and environment. The relation between behavior and the reflection (or feedback) of that behavior by the environment has been called "reafferent stimulation." Perhaps the most primitive form of reafferent stimulation is reflection in an ordinary mirror. We move and our reflection moves correspondingly. It was thought, for a while, that the ability of certain organisms to spontaneously recognize themselves in a mirror's reflection would be a good test of their ability to conceive of themselves. (Only humans and certain species of monkeys seem able to do it.) But a self must be something more than simple reflection of movements in an ordinary mirror. To function in the development of a self, feedback must not only reflect behavior, it must reflect behavior in a meaningful way, positively or negatively. Reinforcement is just another name for positive reafferent stimulation; the value of the feedback is higher than the value of the behavior itself (the bread is worth more to you than what you pay for it). Punishment is just another name for negative reafferent stimulation; the value of the feedback is lower than the value of the behavior itself.

All objects in the environment, including other organisms, other people, may serve as functional (positively or negatively valued) mirrors of our behavior. We step on the tines of the rake and the handle comes back and hits us on the head—a distorted reflection of our own behavior; we say, "Good morning," and our environment (in the form of a person we meet on the street) reflects back, "Good morning." More significantly, we have too much to drink at a party and our spouse provides immediate feedback—reflecting our unpleasant behavior in unpleasant words (to be backed up later by the unpleasant sensations of a hangover). It is as if the world were a funhouse with distorting mirrors moving this way and that, and our conception of ourselves depended on steering our way through William James's "booming buzzing confusion" reflected back upon us. From the present viewpoint, then, our selves are nothing but abstractions (reflected by the environment) of our own present and past behavior; our self-concepts are perceptions of those abstract reflections.

This view of the self is a drastic departure from tradition (at least since St. Augustine). Traditionally, self-perception was conceived as a wholly internal process; better self-understanding was supposed to come through better introspection. From the present viewpoint, however, the hermit who retires from the world in order to understand himself better is actually abandoning the set of mirrors—human society—from which he could best gain self-understanding. When we focus on inner dialogue, on inner pictures, we necessarily ignore our closest friends, our most intimate relations, the ones who see us and interact with us every day—mirrors where our selves are precisely and truly reflected.

The present article's viewpoint, although it departs from tradition, does not differ very much from that of most of the participants in this symposium. The difference between the present view and that of the other participants lies, largely, in where we go from here. We agree that self-reflection gives rise to a person's self-concept. But others are mostly concerned with how the self-concept is internally represented while I am mostly concerned with how the self-concept functions in the environment, that is, with self control.[1]

SELF-CONTROL AS A FUNCTIONAL ABSTRACTION OF ENVIRONMENTAL FEEDBACK

The reafferent stimulation provided by our environments reflects both our immediate behavior and our behavior in the long run. Such stimulation, like a symphony or an opera, or a novel, can be perceived on many levels. You might listen to a symphony for an individual melody or read a novel for an exciting turn of plot. On a wider level, you might listen for the structure of a movement or read for the plot of a chapter. On a still wider level, you might listen for the structure of the symphony itself or read for the structure of the novel itself—or, going still further, for the place of this piece in the work of the composer or author and the work of the composer or author in the history of symphonies or novels. Similarly, you might perceive yourself reflected narrowly in the emotions of an evening or widely in the pattern of stimulation extending over a day, a month, a year, a lifetime, or beyond a lifetime.

Biological evolution has arranged matters so that for most species, most of the time, and for humans, some of the time, behavior adaptive for the moment is also adaptive beyond the moment. The squirrel saves nuts not because its self-concept extends beyond the autumn and into the winter but rather because it wakes up one morning and suddenly finds burying nuts to be valuable in itself. The temporal breadth of an animal's interest can, most of the time, remain narrow while Mother Nature takes care of the long view. A squirrel does not have and does not need a broad concept of self.

In human life, however, a conflict frequently arises between the long and short runs. An alcoholic may strongly prefer activity X (say, having a scotch) to activity Y (having a soft drink) but also prefer pattern A (strict sobriety) to pattern B (alcoholism). The preferred long-term pattern (strict sobriety) is inconsistent with the preferred short-term act (having a scotch). It is only when such inconsistencies arise that conformity to the preferred long-term pattern is labeled "self-control." If such inconsistencies rarely or never arose (as in the life of the squirrel) there would be no need for self-control, hence no need for a concept of self extending beyond the moment.

DEGREES OF SELF-CONCEPT

It would be more correct to say that our human concept of self (deriving from the necessity for self-control in our environment) may be narrower or wider and that the squirrel actually has a concept of self, a narrow one, sufficient to its needs. Even a hungry rat rewarded for pressing a lever by a food is to an extent controlling itself. The pattern of pressing the lever and eating takes longer (necessarily) than the act of pressing the lever alone. Pressing the lever, considered alone, is "dispreferred" to just sniffing in the corner of the cage; hence pressing the lever for food to be delivered within a fraction of a second is an instance of self-control and an instance of self-conception (albeit, a narrow one) by the rat. Correspondingly, even a slug has a concept of self—on a microscopic level.

At the other extreme the examples cited above of pattern A (strict sobriety) and pattern B (alcoholism) may both be narrow relative to still more valuable and wider patterns (social drinking, presumably). The alcoholic's difficulty lies in the fact that drinking a single glass of scotch may be part of a pattern of drunkenness or a pattern of social drinking. Until it unfolds, the alcoholic himself cannot be sure (even though he has resolved to become a social drinker) that the new pattern will emerge. He may therefore be safest by being a teetotaler, which is *always* (moment-to-moment) inconsistent with drunkenness. Social drinking requires (by supposition) a more complex concept of the self in time than does strict sobriety and is thus more difficult to achieve.

This is not to say that a person's concept of self is equally wide in all areas. You could, over the same period of time, be an alcoholic, a non-smoker, and (in a third area) a moderate gambler, taking risks some times, avoiding them at others. Our concepts of our selves are multidimensional but their essence is always behavioral patterning—behavior over time. Behavioral patterning in the context of local "temptations" (local preferences inconsistent with the pattern) is not just a reflection or a sign of self-control. It *is* self-control. A person cannot be a drunkard inside his body and a teetotaler outside, nor the reverse. People *are* (abstractly and in the long run) what they *do*. (The qualifier, "in the long run" distinguishes between the alcoholic and the social drinker who are both at the moment having a scotch.)

It is sometimes supposed that in a perfect world there would be no conflict between immediate desires and long-term values. The image of a natural human being living a natural life has behind it, I believe, this sort of framework—a place where our immediate desires are in harmony with our long-term best interests. But, as Plato pointed out (*Philebos*, 21c), life in such a world would be the life of a slug. In such a world we would have no need for a wide concept of self and we would therefore not have one. A person's concept of self is not a mental appendix or mental decoration but a necessity, a functional aspect of human life. Willpower—the ability to behave right now in conformance with a valuable long-term pattern of behavior—to turn down the scotch despite its immediate value, to choose sobriety over drunkenness, arises not from any introspection on our part, not from *insight* but rather from what might better be called *outsight*, from our ability to abstract, from the booming buzzing confusion of the environment, reflections of our own behavior over long stretches of time.

SELF-CONTROL AND SOCIAL CONTROL

It is customary to distinguish between self-interested behavior, consistent with the goals of an individual, and altruistic behavior, consistent with the goals of someone else. Where these interests are in harmony (as in normal economic interchange), apparent altruism is normally explained in terms of self-interest. It is not considered altruistic to pay the grocer if he gives you something you want in return. But behavior where nothing is apparently received in return (such as volunteering at a hospital, donating to charity, rushing into a burning building to save a child) is considered altruistic because there is presumably no personal benefit, no benefit to the *self*, but only social benefit involved. The personal satisfaction that we may derive from such acts is considered to be dependent not on fundamental self-interest but on socially imposed conscience (or super-ego), or an innate altruistic motive built into us and, by its very nature, distinct from our selfish motives.

This conception of altruism as opposed to self-interest presumes that the unit of self-interest is in the first place our own individual bodies. But just as the temporal extent of the relation between behavior and reinforcement may vary from one situation to the next, so may the spatial (or the social) extent. And because this variation clearly jumps back and forth across genetic lines it seems unlikely that genetic correspondences *directly* determine degree of altruism. (However they may do so indirectly through their action on functional aspects of the environment.)

Part of the goal of this article is to show how apparently altruistic behavior actually serves a crucial function for *individuals*. In pursuit of this goal, however, it is necessary to empirically demonstrate the relation between the breadth of the concept of self and temporal patterning. I hope the reader will bear with a few descriptions of experiments. First, I present an informal demonstration that the functional self may extend beyond the limits of a person's skin. We asked 100 Stony Brook undergraduates to answer one of four questions below (25 subjects answered each question):

1. Which would you choose? (circle A or B)
   A: $100 for yourself
   B: $300 shared among yourself and the 5 people (friends and family) who you feel closest to ($50 to each).

2. Which would you choose? (circle A or B)
   A. $100 for yourself
   B. $300 shared among yourself and 5 randomly selected students in this class ($50 to each).

3. Which would you choose? (circle A or B)
   A. $100 for yourself
   B. $300 shared among yourself and 5 randomly selected members of the Stony Brook community ($50 to each).

4. Which would you choose? (circle A or B)
   A. $100 for yourself
   B. $300 shared among yourself and 5 people randomly selected from across the United States ($50 to each).

The results were what you would expect. Question 1 was answered "un-selfishly" (B circled) by 20 of 25 subjects, while all of the other questions were answered "selfishly" (A circled) by at least 23 of 25 subjects.

It seems that people's concepts of their selves *may* include other people with whom they function together. Of course there is much more genetic overlap among families (Question 1) than classmates or schoolmates (Question 2 or 3) or fellow citizens (Question 4), but the same results ("un-selfish" responses) apply when Question 1 is rephrased to exclude blood relatives and only include the subject's spouse and closest friends. The clearest connection here is a functional one. Imagine that the subject is a member of a basketball team needing equipment. Obviously $300 would buy more equipment than $100. The functional unit in this case is the team, not the individual. The same applies to families and close friends. Although individuals are units of *choice*, groups of individuals may be units of reinforcement or punishment. Coaches of teams are always trying to get individual players to play as a unit—to make choices as individuals for the benefit of the group.

Perhaps the clearest case of apparent opposition between individual and group interest is the much-studied game known as the "prisoner's dilemma." The second experiment I would like to describe involved pairs of subjects (this time, female undergraduates at the University of Rhode Island) playing this game one-on-one. The subjects faced each other across a table and each was given a stack of ordinary playing cards. The game was simple. Each subject chose a card and placed it face down on the table; then, at the experimenter's signal, they simultaneously turned the cards over. Only the color of the cards (red or black) was meaningful. If both subjects played a red card, each was given 3 poker chips (later convertible to cash) by the experimenter. If both played a black card, each was given 2 poker chips. However, if one subject played red while the other played black, the one who played red was given only 1 chip while the one who played black was given 4 chips. A continuously visible chart (Fig. 1a) illustrated these contingencies. Then the game was played over and over again, 60 times. (The subjects were not told exactly how many games would be played.) In the language of the mathematicians, economists, and psychologists who study prisoner's dilemma games, playing red is called "cooperating" and playing black is called "defecting." In what sense are these terms appropriate and why is the game called a dilemma? Imagine that a subject consulted a lawyer to advise her how to play. The lawyer might well reason as follows. "Your opponent can only cooperate or defect. Let us first suppose that she cooperates. If you cooperate too you will get 3 chips, but if you defect you will get 4 chips. Therefore if your opponent cooperates you should defect. Now let us suppose your opponent defects. If you cooperate you will get 1 point while if you defect you will get 2 points. Therefore if your opponent defects you should defect too. In either case, whether your opponent cooperates or defects, you should defect. Thus, logic says that you should always "defect." If this subject followed her lawyer's advice and if the other subject also hired a lawyer and got the same advice, both subjects would always defect (and get 2 chips each on each trial). The dilemma arises when we realize that if both

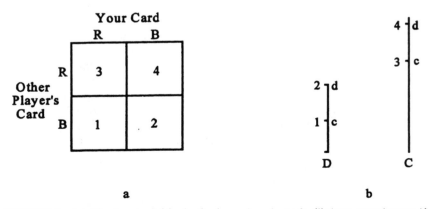

FIGURE 1. (*a*) Chart reviewed by both players in prisoner's dilemma experiment; (*b*) How other player's choice (D or C) affects a player's alternatives (d or c).

subjects had ignored their lawyers' advice and cooperated on each trial they would have gotten 3 chips instead of 2 chips per trial.

Before going further into the details of the experiment let me ask you to imagine that you are playing this game. Consider two kinds of opponent who might be playing against you. First, imagine your opponent's choices are preprogrammed. Your opponent plays in a machine-like way and is completely insensitive to whether you cooperate or defect. In playing against such an opponent your lawyer's advice would be good advice. You should always defect. FIGURE 1b shows your options (differently from FIGURE 1a) on two scales of value. The two vertical lines (labeled D and C) represent your opponent's choice. The two points on each line labeled d and c represent your choices. As you can see, regardless of your opponent's choice (D or C) you would get one more chip by defecting (d) than by cooperating (c). When there is nothing you can do to influence your opponent's choice, you should follow your lawyer's advice (i.e., follow logic) and always defect.

But let us now suppose that you *can* influence your opponent's choice. Your opponent might be employing a strategy aptly named "tit-for-tat." Tit-for-tat applies only over a series of repeated games; it consists of cooperating in the first game and thereafter simply mimicking in this game whatever the other player played in the game before. An opponent who plays tit-for-tat is thus a sort of mirror that reflects your behavior back to you, with a delay of one game. FIGURE 1b makes it clear that under such circumstances you would have two conflicting motives. First, you would want to get your opponent to cooperate. That is, you would want to be on the right-hand line, choosing between 3 and 4 chips rather than on the left-hand line, choosing between 1 and 2 chips. Second, you would prefer to defect yourself and gain one more chip (2 versus 1 or 4 versus 3).

In theory, the first motive (to get your opponent to cooperate) should dominate the second (to defect yourself). Going from D to C (from the left to the right line of FIGURE 1b) you gain an average of 2 chips (jumping from an average of 1.5 chips to an average of 3.5 chips) while going from c to d, you gain only 1 chip (1 to 2 or 3 to 4). If your opponent were in fact playing tit-for-tat, and you knew it, there would be only one way to get her to cooperate on the next trial—cooperating yourself on this trial. By cooperating you sacrifice 1 chip now (on this trial) for 2 chips later (on the next trial).

From the point of view of the group (of two players) mutual cooperation is the best solution to the prisoner's dilemma. Two cooperating players together would earn 6 chips per trial (3 each), which is the highest of all possible combinations in FIGURE 1. If one player cooperates and one defects they earn 5 chips together (4 plus 1); if both players defect they earn 4 chips together (2 each). In the Rhode Island experiment (Silverstein, Cross & Rachlin, unpublished) in a preliminary procedure, some subjects played against the experimenter, who played tit-for-tat. Slowly but surely these subjects learned to consistently cooperate. We have found, in general, that if one player persistently and doggedly plays tit-for-tat it is rare that the other player will not come around to consistent cooperation.

However, when neither player consistently plays tit-for-tat, as in the Rhode Island experiment when subjects played each other, the eventual result was mutual defection, the worst result from the point of view of the group (i.e., the pair of subjects)—the worst result, but nevertheless quite understandable. First, if your opponent is not already playing tit-for-tat you have to ask yourself, what is the probability that your cooperating on *this* trial will actually cause your opponent to cooperate on the *next* trial. By cooperating you are essentially gambling—you are making a small sacrifice on this trial on the chance of a larger gain on the next. If your opponent is a stranger having no common interest with you, the chance may well not be worth taking. Second, in real life as opposed to the laboratory, prisoner's-dilemma type games may not be rapidly repeated. You might not be willing to sacrifice a small gain this time for the possibility (not even the certainty) of a larger gain next week or next year.

Failures to cooperate are thus common in real-life prisoner's dilemmas. A form of prisoner's dilemma occurs in real life among larger groups of people. In a notorious case, New Bedford fishermen each profited maximally by buying and sending out as many boats as possible but ultimately when all the fishermen began to do this, the common resource (the available fish) became depleted and the group suffered as a whole (the industry was devastated). The fishermen did have a common interest (in restraining their fishing), but that interest was not clear to them (the few surviving fishermen still deny it). It is thus of crucial social importance (and a goal of my research) to understand how social situations may be manipulated to cause people to (*a*) perceive a common interest with others and (*b*) to trust others to cooperate.[2]

Success or failure to sacrifice individual to group interest in the prisoner's dilemma game (a version of the conflict inherent in all social activities) corresponds to success or failure to sacrifice momentary small gain for eventual long-term gain (i.e., to self-control).[3] In other words, cooperation on the social level corresponds to self-control on the individual level. In our prisoner's dilemma experiment, Silverstein, Cross and I found that the same procedural variation that had (in previous experiments) engendered better self-control and less risk-avoidance also engendered more social cooperation. This variation consisted of grouping sequences of repeated games in temporal patterns (subjects making 3 or 4 choices rapidly, followed by a wait) rather than spacing games equally.[4]

ALTRUISM RECONSIDERED

Why should such patterning (or grouping) increase social cooperation? In terms of this article and the questions asked in this volume, why should temporal patterning of choices (a seemingly irrelevant process) expand the boundaries of a person's self-concept? To see how this might work, imagine a single individual at successive moments in time, ranging from past to future, as if they were different individuals. Clearly, these conceptual individuals (Person, P, at $t_{-n} \ldots, t_{-3}, t_{-2}, t_{-1}, t_0, t_1, t_2, t_3 \ldots t_n$) have a common interest; they all inhabit the same skin. Good habits benefit P over a sum of times (that is what we mean by good habits) even though they may impose a sacrifice at t (now). Bad habits do the reverse. Individual development consists of a better and better perception of what might be called mutual self-interest (the interest of P at *all* times) while retaining an interest (nowadays considered "healthy") in our immediate self (the interest of P at t_0). As George Ainslie has pointed out, these narrow versus long-term interests must often face the same (prisoner's) dilemma as the individual does versus society (Ainslie, 1992). Consider P at t_0 (now) and P at t_1 (tomorrow morning, say). To see the analogy with FIGURE 1, let us suppose P is an alcoholic and arbitrarily assign points to events in his life as follows:

Drinking while not having a hangover	10 points
Not drinking while not having a hangover	0 points
Drinking while having a hangover	−10 points
Not drinking while having a hangover	−20 points

Hangover or no hangover, the alcoholic is clearly better off drinking than not drinking (letting "hangover" stand for all of the many deleterious effects of drinking). If he has no hangover, he can enjoy himself, put some pleasure in his life (going from 0 to 10 points). If he has a hangover he can ameliorate its pain (by going from −20 to −10 points). In either case he will be better off *now* if he drinks *now*.

But his body is playing tit-for-tat with him. If he drinks now he will have a hangover tomorrow. Thus if he keeps drinking he will be in a continuous hangover state and collect −10 points every day while if he never drinks he will collect 0 points every day (and, in the real world, be fit to pursue other pleasures). Just as the primary object of the prisoner's-dilemma player (of FIGURE 1) should have been to get her opponent to cooperate, the primary object of the alcoholic should be to avoid hangovers. But, as we said, the alcoholic's body is essentially playing tit-for-tat with him. If he chooses to defect (to have a drink now), his choices tomorrow will be just as if a prisoner's-dilemma opponent had defected in return. If he chooses to cooperate (remain sober), his choices tomorrow will be just as if an opponent had cooperated in return.

When we take these sorts of self-control situations into the laboratory, we find that the same patterning procedures (grouping trials together) that engender cooperation in the social prisoner's dilemma task also engender cooperation in the individual game.[5] People with extremely narrow self-conceptions would frequently make choices consistent with the interests of their narrow selves and in conflict with their wider selves. They would be generally impulsive rather than self-controlled. All of us are successfully tempted, at times, by narrow interests; now, at the present moment (at t_0), we fail to cooperate with our past and future selves (t_{-n} to t_n). Just as the Stony Brook students who answered the questionnaire could not conceive of common interests with other Stony Brook students so people with narrow self-concepts (all of us, at times) do not perceive the common interests of our present selves with our selves of last year and next year.

As the previous section's analysis shows, the rewards of *social* cooperation are both delayed and probabilistic. Where rewards to an *individual* are delayed or probabilistic, patterning of trials serves to forcibly broaden self-perception. A person forced to make four decisions at a time (without feedback) cannot make one decision at a time. A drinker or dieter who must decide in advance on a month-long pattern of drinking or eating is by definition better able to control himself than one who decides anew about each drink or each meal. That person is effectively making a group decision (P from t_{-n} to t_n) rather than an individual decision (P at t_0). Similarly, the person who develops good social habits benefits from those habits.

On an individual level, persons who commit themselves to a sanitarium (where eating or drinking will be rigidly controlled) are attempting to break a pattern of repeated defection in their normal environment by choosing in advance a weekly or monthly (self-cooperative) pattern. They expect that once they have begun to cooperate they will keep cooperating outside of the institution. On a social level, such commitment processes are not generally available. It is not possible, for instance, to move to an authoritarian society (like Singapore) where social cooperation is rigidly enforced, and then back to a permissive society (like ours).[6] The best alternative of course would be to consistently cooperate within the permissive society. As I have argued above, this alternative is not just best for society, but also best for the individual for purely selfish reasons—*provided* we perceive our selfish selves broadly rather than narrowly in time.

Among cognitive-decision theorists it is thought to be a puzzle why people habitually leave tips at restaurants (say on a highway) where they will never eat again. Leaving a tip at a restaurant where you know you will never eat again is clearly irrational when doing so is considered as an individual, isolated act. In fact, leaving a tip at a restaurant where you *do* intend to eat again is irrational from the point of view of your self considered wholly at the present moment; you benefit now; it is only that *other* guy, the one who will inhabit your body at a later time, who may suffer. The recent book and movie *Clockers* vividly illustrate the devastating effects of an environment where short-term social interactions dominate long-term ones. There, powerful short-term rewards (drugs, money, daily survival) overwhelm vague and abstract long-term rewards (health, family, friends). Consequently, everyone's self-concept is narrow in time, controlled by the clock rather than by the calendar.

Leaving tips in general is a pattern that (usually) serves us well in our society, a pattern in aid of individual self-control. It may seem as though there is no connection between the benefit our tip confers on the next person who wanders into the restaurant where we will never return and the benefit conferred on us by the previous person's tip. But there *is* a connection—in the pattern we maintain in our behavior. It would be bad for us *personally, selfishly,* if we decided individually each time we went into a restaurant whether or not we should leave a tip. Decisions on a case-by-case basis are exactly the sort of (pseudo-rational) behavior (the lawyer's prisoner's dilemma advice) that would get us defecting all of the time. It is not possible to tease apart the individual and social benefits of such acts. Most altruistic acts are, like tipping, personally profitable a lot of the time. Giving to charity is often observed and frequently rewarded by society. But the relation between generosity and its rewards is vague and indistinct. Generosity for most of us (like sobriety for the alcoholic) is not profitable and would not be chosen considering only its case-by-case (its narrow) reinforcement. Consequently the way for most of us to profit from generosity (and the way for an alcoholic to profit from sobriety) is to pattern our behavior abstractly—to choose to be a generous (or a sober) person. It is in aid of making such choices that narrative—biographical and autobiographical—derives its function. Others in this volume have discussed the *mechanism* by which a personal narrative may gain control of a person's behavior. Here we are concerned with the *function*, the purpose of that mechanism in human life. Saying, "I am a generous [or sober] person provides a discriminative stimulus that functions to group generous (or sober) behavior into positively (if vaguely and indistinctly) reinforced patterns—to classify behavior into acts consistent versus inconsistent with one's self—acts reinforced in the long run and as a group versus acts not so reinforced.

But in order to pattern our behavior in this way (and reap the rewards for so doing) we must forego making decisions on a case-by-case basis. Once we abandon case-by-case decisions, there will come times in choosing between selfishness and generosity when we will be generous even when generosity is explicitly unreinforced or even punished. In other words, we will behave altruistically. But such altruism is not only compatible with a wider selfishness, it is a *necessary* component of a wider selfishness.

In an environment (like at least some of ours) where tit-for-tat behavior (do unto others as they do unto you) is more or less the norm, altruism is clearly selfish. Those of us who live in such environments can come to perceive the social good as our good in the same way as we can come to perceive our long-range good as our immediate good—by developing good habits. But good habits require a certain kind of faith in the future. If you were born yesterday and were going to die tomorrow (a case approached by some of the characters in *Clockers*) there would be no advantage in behaving well—such behavior would have no function. But our larger society demands a wider sense of self. The mother who without thinking twice runs into the burning building to save someone else's child is behaving altruistically, but she is also behaving selfishly. *By* her behavior she has teased out of her booming, buzzing environment an abstract reflection of herself.

REFERENCES

AINSLIE, G. (1992). *Picoeconomics: The strategic interaction of successive motivational states within the person.* New York: Cambridge University Press.

KUDADJIE-GYAMFI, E. & H. RACHLIN. (1996). Temporal patterning in choice among delayed outcomes. *Organizational Behavior and Human Decision Process, 65,* 61–67.

RACHLIN, H. (1995a). Self control: Beyond commitment. *Behavioral and Brain Sciences, 18,* 109–159.

RACHLIN, H. (1995b). The value of temporal patterns in behavior. *Current Directions in Psychological Science, 4,* 188–191.

RACHLIN, H., A. W. LOGUE, J. GIBBON & M. FRANKEL. (1986). Cognition and behavior in studies of choice. *Psychological Review, 93,* 33–45.

SILVERSTEIN, A., D. V. CROSS & H. RACHLIN. Prior experience and patterning in a prisoner's dilemma game. Unpublished manuscript.

ENDNOTES

1. This is not to say that pleasure-seeking and pain-avoidance are the only motives that count in the formation of a self-concept or that a desire for self-knowledge is not a fundamental component of human nature. On the contrary, desire for self-knowledge is a far more important determinant of a person's self-concept than is the desire to seek pleasure or avoid pain. However, the present article takes a wholly pragmatic view of truth. From the present viewpoint, if a given belief does not function to make our lives better, either we do not truly believe it or it is not true—it may be belief but it is not knowledge. Self-knowledge that does not help us to live better lives is thus not really knowledge.

2. The classic prisoner's dilemma is pertinent here. In the classic (hypothetical) situation two prisoners would (supposedly) each get a moderately high sentence if they both confessed (defected), turned each other in, and plea-bargained; they each would get a moderately low sentence if both held out (cooperated with each other) and refused to testify against each other; however, if one confessed (defected) while the other held out (cooperated), the defector would go free and the cooperator would get a severe sentence. Interestingly, defecting from the small group (consisting of the two prisoners) is the same as cooperating with the prosecutors and (presumably) society as a whole. The case is not unusual. Small groups (families, for instance) often have interests in conflict with society as a whole—a young person might act selfishly with respect to his or her family, but be doing exactly what a larger society desires. This corresponds, in the personal sphere, with apparently impulsive actions (taking a drink, taking a day off) inconsistent with larger patterns (strict sobriety, success at a job), but consistent with still-larger ones (social drinking, living a balanced life). Such ambiguities are what make self-control so difficult (Rachlin, 1995a).

3. It may seem as though there are two factors causing failure of social cooperation—*delay* to the next encounter, and *probability* that others will respond to your cooperation by cooperating themselves. But many researchers, including myself, have argued that *risk avoidance* (overreacting to less-than-unit probabilities) and *impulsiveness* (overreacting to

greater-than-zero delays) are fundamentally the same motive (Rachlin, Logue, Gibbon & Frankel, 1986).

4. When playing each other half of the pairs of subjects made one choice (to cooperate or defect) at a time. After each choice the other player's choice was revealed and each was given a number of chips as shown by Figure 1a. The other half of the pairs of subjects made 4 choices at a time (played 4 games at a time) without seeing the other subject's choice and without being paid their chips. Then each of the 4 choices was revealed successively and subjects were paid. Then the next set of 4 choices was made by both subjects. The subjects who played 4 games at a time cooperated significantly more than those who played one game at a time (Rachlin, 1995b).

5. We use points convertible to money rather than actual drinks and hangovers. A subject's choice to cooperate or defect influences *all* alternatives on subsequent trials. (Cooperation gains less now, but makes all alternatives better in the future; defection gains more now, but makes all alternatives worse in the future.) (Kudadjie-Gyamfi & Rachlin, 1996.)

6. It is far from clear, moreover, that such shuttling would work. The stimuli of the Singapore environment may well gain control of social cooperation while those of the United States continue to signal rewards for defection.

Part III: Development of the Self Concept

Introduction

JOAN GAY SNODGRASS

Department of Psychology
New York University
New York, New York 10003

In this section, we explore the development of the self-concept from infancy to adolescence. In her paper, Katherine Nelson adopts a somewhat different definition of the self concept. In contrast to earlier accounts, which argue that the foundations of the self concept develop very early, Nelson argues that an objective sense of self as an enduring object in space and time requires both a concept of others as similar and different from the self and a construction of the self that has a past and future.

Nelson considers how the autobiographical self comes to be developed and concludes that this development occurs much later than does self-recognition, as measured by the mirror recognition test, occurring as it does in the middle of the preschool years. She argues that a neccessary ingredient in the human concept of the self is an autobiographical self, which projects the representation of the self forward and backward in time. On the basis of research on the development of episodic memory in childhood, Nelson concludes that this autobiographical self is established through conversational narratives between the child and others, and self-narratives which the child has with him or herself. She relates this view to data on acquisition of language and the child's theory of mind.

In the next paper, Michael Lewis considers another milestone in the development of the self—the emergence of the self-conscious emotions of shame, pride, guilt, and embarrassment. He finds that these self-conscious emotions emerge only after children have passed the "mirror-test" of self-recognition. In his earlier work, Lewis pioneered the application of the mirror-test to children, and found that children "passed" this test somewhere between 2½ to 3 years. Lewis argues that the elicitation of these self-conscious emotions requires a sense of self.

Lewis points out that study of these emotions has only just begun. One of the problems with studying the self-conscious emotions is that they differ from the earlier developing emotions of joy, anger, fear and disgust, which have characteristic facial and behavioral patterns and can be elicited fairly consistently by standard stimuli. In contrast, the self-conscious emotions are much less well differentiated in terms of both facial and behavioral patterns and their eliciting stimuli. Lewis considers some ways of characterizing these emotions in a model of the self-conscious emotions as a way of establishing the enterprise.

*Katherine Nelson is Distinguished Professor of Psychology at the
Graduate Center of the City University of New York. She was
previously Professor and Program Head of the Developmental
Psychology program at CUNY, and was Associate Professor at Yale
University from 1975 to 1978. She was editor of the journal*
Cognitive Development *from 1991 to 1995, and has written or
edited a total of eight books and monographs, including* Language in
Cognition Development: The Emergence of the Mediated Mind
(1996) and Narratives from the Crib *(1989). Her research interests
are early language development, particularly lexical development;
concept development; and development of memory and social
cognition.*

Finding One's Self in Time

KATHERINE NELSON

Developmental Psychology Program
City University of New York Graduate Center
33 West 42nd Street
New York, New York 10036

As the contributions to this volume indicate, there is a great deal of current interest and research on the topic of self-knowledge and the development of self-knowledge in all branches of psychology. Students of infant development have in recent years emphasized that self-awareness begins early and self-recognition, as evaluated by the mirror test, for example, is only one rather late manifestation of such awareness (e.g., Butterworth, 1990). At the same time, I and others have argued that the mirror test itself, indicating self-recognition at about 18 to 21 months, is but an early manifestation of self in relation to the world and as distinct from other people, the development of which continues for many years into adulthood (Nelson, 1993; Tessler & Nelson, 1994). We have emphasized the different aspects of consciousness of self that is realized in terms of the projection of self in time—forward, backward, and ongoing. It is this historical self, or autobiographical self, that is constitutive of a represented self that endures over a life span.

This perspective emerges from the studies of young children's memory for past events and their construction of events, narratives, stories, scripts, and imagined futures. Research on children's event knowledge, episodic memory, narrative language, and autobiographical memory all suggest a relation between self-representation and the temporal dimension. But the historical perspective is also based on the study of specific linguistic representations of and on the self, and of and by others. Recent research on these topics has focused on a developmental period in early childhood that is, furthermore, dramatic in its phase shifts in many domains of personal knowledge (Nelson, 1996).

The general claim is this: a sense of self as an enduring object in space and time begins in infancy but takes on an objective character—a representation of a self-concept—only when the child constructs others as both like and different from the self, and at the same time constructs a self that has both a past and a future. These two constructions, it is claimed, are integrally related and emerge together from the experience of exchanging accounts of understandings of the world with other people, a process that begins only in the middle of the preschool years as the child gains competence with language in extended discourse genres. This thesis is explicated here through a summary review of evidence from memory, from language uses, from narrative, and from the child's theory of mind.

MEMORY OF SELF

Memory in the early years of life has become a topic of intense interest in the past decade or so, for both pragmatic and theoretical reasons. In contrast to our understanding 20 years ago, we now know that infants remember action-object contingencies over many weeks, and that toddlers remember specific event sequences over several months (Bauer, Hertsgaard & Dow, 1994; Rovee-Collier, 1995; Sheffield & Hudson, 1994). As soon as children can talk in short sentences they can tell about memories for specific people, locations, and activities in their lives (DeLoache, 1986; Nelson, 1989a; Nelson & Ross, 1980). By three years of age they are able to engage in talk with parents and others about experienced events from the past, and contribute organized information about such events to the collaborative construction of a narrative (Fivush, 1993).

Is this evidence of episodic memory not also evidence of a self-concept, as Howe and Courage (1993) claimed? Howe and Courage based their claim on the assertion that autobiographical memory (and the resultant offset of infantile amnesia) begins at age two years. However, as I have argued elsewhere (Tessler & Nelson, 1994), their interpretation of the evidence is flawed: they have conflated autobiographical memory with a more general type of episodic memory, for which there is ample evidence in children of two years. Evidence for autobiographical memory—a continuous self-history—is generally found no earlier than 3½ years and for many people is not present until six or even eight years.

Consider in this regard the claim by Tulving (1983; see also Fraser, 1987) that humans are the only creatures that can revisit the past in their own lives and reexperience prior events in the same way. What can this claim mean? Do we ever actually experience the same events in the same way? Or do we reconstruct the past from bits and pieces set into a schema, as Bartlett (1932) claimed? Can infants do this reconstructing or reexperiencing as well as adults? These questions, and the question of why adults cannot remember anything from their first years of life, are those that are addressed in the contemporary literature on memory in early childhood. Tulving stated the claim as a general proposition about episodic memory, but it is more appropriately restricted to a subclass of memories that are significant for the self, whatever they may be.

What the literature on childhood memory reveals is that parents often engage their children in talk about the past and the future as early as the third year of life, and that both the amount and type of talk about remembered events contributes to the children's further development of memories (Fivush & Hamond, 1990). In particular, mothers who engage children in constructing elaborated narratives about the past encourage the development of enduring memories of experienced events (Fivush, 1993). The conclusion from these studies is that children learn to remember about their own past lives through talking with others, and that it is this practice that initiates the individual's autobiographical memory, the memory that emerges from infantile amnesia to become memory of an earlier self lasting into adult life.

The further implication is that it is memory of one's own past life that provides a self-history and thus a concept of a self that exists not only in the present but in a past and on into a future, and one with a *there* and *then* existence as well as a *here* and *now*. This self is recognized as both the same and yet as different from the ongoing experiencing self; it is a self that was once a baby and that will become an adult. A nonhistorical self is only an experiencing self, a self with a repertoire of knowledge about being in the world, a repertoire based on prior experience that guides action in the present; but not a self with a specific past and a specific imagined future. It is the self with a specific past that is endowed with the unique capacity to reexperience the past, unlike that of other creatures who can *use* past experience but not reexperience it.

LANGUAGE OF THE SELF

Beginning in the second year of life children acquire lexical terms that refer to themselves and to others. Most children have little difficulty distinguishing *I* and *you* although some normally developing children do temporarily confuse the two. Many children go through a stage of referring to the self by name, or using *me* rather than *I* in the subject position of their sentences. These uses and confusions have sometimes been overinterpreted because they have not been viewed within an understanding of language development that recognizes distinctions between forms and functions.

Gerhardt (1989), Budwig (1985), and I (Nelson, 1989b) have each discussed these uses from the perspective that the child is making functional distinctions among forms that are different from those made in the adult language. In particular, Budwig claims on the basis of her analysis of six children's early self-reference, that the child's name and *my* are used in utterances where control or volition are expressed, whereas *I* is used to mark deviations from the prototypical agentive perspective.

In contrast, Gerhardt (1989) analyzed one child's (Emily's) two-year-old distinction between the use of *Emmy/my* (these two were alternative forms in similar frames) and *I* as a functional distinction between the self as an experiencer in someone else's frame ("Emmy contexts," a very usual experiential position for a young child) in contrast to the active agent *I*. In an extension of this analysis, I found that the use of *Emmy/my* declined over two months following her second birthday, and that it was accompanied by an upswing in the use of *we* as contrasted to *I* in the subject position reporting on experience, both past and anticipated (Nelson, 1989b). Thus the emerging distinction mirrored the adult language more closely, but it substituted a different contrast—the singular *I* versus the group *we*.

A point to be noted is that, in contrast to the conclusion that is often drawn from the use of personal references in the early years, neither of these reported contrasts reflects a subjective/objective self distinction. There is no evidence that the use of the child's name for self-reference in any way indicates that the child views or represents himself or herself from an objective distance or as an object among other person-objects. Rather, the evidence indicates that these are all ways of referencing the *experiencing* self, sometimes as an experiencer in other people's activities, and sometimes as an active agent in an event.

A particularly interesting finding from the analysis of Emily's pre-sleep monologues at two to three years (Nelson, 1989b) was the coincidental acquisition of temporal language, including tense forms for the past in contrast to the ongoing present, at the same time that Emily was accommodating her self-reference to the adult language forms. This transition to the use of past tense and contrasting present progressive for ongoing events took place over a brief period between 23 and 25 months. Prior to this time Emily had used inconsistent past verb forms in contexts where she was talking about the "not now" but did not use them consistently, nor did she use the regular past *-ed* form. By 24 months contrasts of tense and the use of temporal adverbial expressions such as *now* were common in her narratives about her experience, as in the following excerpt from 23 months:

> when my slep
> and and Mormor came
> then Mommy coming
> then get up
> time to go home
> time to go home
> drink p-water [Perrier]
> yesterday did that

As this extract indicates, Emily had started to use forms such as *yesterday* to mark temporal distance, but the semantics of the terms was not yet sorted out (the quoted narrative was actually based on an episode from the same day). As the tense forms became regularized and established, these adverbial expressions fell into disuse. We (Levy & Nelson, 1994) have speculated that as she became sensitive to the temporal contrasts specified by tense she became uncertain about the denotation of the adverbial expressions. The latter began to appear again in her narratives at a later point in the third year, with greater semantic precision evident. This process follows a sequence of meaning acquisition in which "use without meaning" is a beginning acquisition strategy for words without obvious concrete reference.

The narrative quoted here enables us to see two aspects of time that relate to the self: locating the self in a temporal space that is distinct from ongoing experience; and within that space locating the sequence of actions in relation to one another. Both of these may be specified in terms of tense uses; the latter also often relies on sequencers such as *before, after, then, when* and so on. Sequencers are used in a variety of contexts indicating how things happen in general (scripts), what may happen in the future, what is happening in the present, pretending what is happening, and projecting a fictional story line, as well as what has happened in the past. The sequential aspect of organized memory is thus related to all forms of conceptualizing events, and not only to one's own remembered past. Yet it is critical to that construction. When the sequence of "what happened" cannot be kept straight, one cannot "relive the experience" in the way that it happened. By three years most children are capable of reporting a series of actions in order, and use common sequencing terms such as *and, so,* and *then* to indicate the order. They use the same sequencing devices to order specific episodes from their past experience as for their accounts of familiar routine scripts (French & Nelson, 1985; Nelson, 1986).

There is a more advanced form of temporal sequencing in which the order of events themselves is maintained, that is, where a person may be able to report that event A happened before event B and after event C. For example, an adult may be able to say that he or she took a vacation in France after moving to a new city but before taking one's present job. Of course adults have many cues for these events, as Barsalou (1988) and Conway (1993) have documented. Among other supports, adults use epoch markers such as "my first marriage" or "my college years" to organize their memories. School and job progressions are particularly useful as a sort of metaphorical measuring rod along which episodes from one's life may be located. Young children do not have the advantage of this kind of support—they have neither experienced epochs, nor do they have multiple experiential grade-marked contexts to use as indicies. For these reasons, even the memories that are retained from the preschool years, which may be well-ordered in themselves, may also be confused so that the order among them is difficult to untangle. Adults often report that they do not know how old they were when they experienced remembered events from early life unless they have salient markers such as moves to different homes to keep the record straight. These problems, however, do not identify a failing of the preschoolers' memory but a lack of an external or dual mode of representing large-scale temporal sequences.

THE NARRATIVE SELF

Thus far I have attempted to bolster the claim that children learn to remember their lives, and thus themselves, and that they acquire the language that enables them to enter into talk about these lives with other people, as well as to organize their own memories for recalling at a later time. What has come to be viewed as especially important in this overall process is the making of narratives about one's experiences. Thus the process is seen as one of constructing a "life story" composed of individual memorable event stories involving events that somehow have significance to one's understanding of self over the course of developmental time. Of course, what is of significance to a 3-year-old may not be to the 30-year-old, yet often the 3-year-old's memories are retained as "the beginning" of the "real" story of one's life.

The important idea here is that to become a part of the life story each episode must somehow be formulated as part of an ongoing overarching narrative. The narrative takes on significance in terms of life goals, achievements, failures, joys, and tragedies. Within it are contained representative or idiosyncratic episodes that in themselves are mini-narratives about what happened at one time in the past.

The narrative form is characterized by a goal orientation and by a sequence of events that are in general causally ordered toward an outcome with an evaluative component. The evaluation tags the episode as happy, sad, embarrassing, frustrating, exciting, and so on. An experience without an evaluative component does not become a part of the life story.

The question has arisen as to whether narrative is itself a natural form of human cognition, whether in fact it organizes memory to begin with (e.g., Bruner, 1986). My view is that narrative is primarily a linguistic product, one that is culturally formulated in different ways, and one that children learn through experience with stories, tales, memory talk and other discourse in the narrative genre (Nelson, 1996). Indeed, there is now a good deal of evidence that the children of parents who engage in narrative-type talk about ongoing as well as past experiences remember more of the experiences and remember it in a more organized form than children whose parents use more paradigmatic formulas in talk about ongoing or past experience (Fivush, 1993; Tessler & Nelson, 1994).

Of critical importance to the process of beginning and continuing the life story are two questions: (1) Whose story is it? and (2) What role do others play in providing the evaluative component that makes it one's own? Let me address the first question at once because it is of longstanding concern among students of early memory.

The skeptical view is that many if not most early memories have been implanted through family talk, photographs, videos, films, and so on. (Why this seems more plausible than a child's actual memory is unclear; what theoretical assumptions does this skeptical attitude rest on?) The claim that memory talk is learned and is therefore the basis for the foundation of auto-biographical memory implies just such a vulnerability to this sort of "implantation" as well as to subtle and not-so-subtle forms of suggestibility (Ceci & Bruck, 1993). But as Hudson (1990) proposed, the discourse-based claim is that children learn not *what* to remember but *how* to remember. Children bring to the memory-sharing experience their own memories, however fragmented these may be. Often the sharing with another appears to be of two separate experiences, although they were experienced in the same place together simultaneously. The child appears simply to have had a different experience from that of the adult (hardly a startling suggestion). Thus, coordinating the fragments of an episodic memory with the verbal hints from another who shared the experience may be quite difficult for a young child. But to the extent that the child can organize his or her own memory fragments around the scaffolding offered by the adult, the process is best seen as one of reorganization rather than of imposition or even of re-composition.

Nonetheless, both recomposition and original composition (or imposition) do take place sometimes (Leichtman & Ceci, 1995). A famous example of composition through social construction was reported by Jean Piaget who "remembered" for many years that as a young child he had been the target of an attempted kidnapping while in the care of a nursemaid who valiantly fought off the attacker when they were out for a walk. As an adult he learned that this episode had been a figment of his nurse's imagination, made up and told to his parents for reasons of advancing her regard in their eyes, and thus it became part of the family lore and a part of Piaget's "own" remembered childhood. Only as an adult did Piaget learn that the incident had never happened.

In a similar vein, Miller *et al.* (Miller, Fung, Hoogstra, Mintz & Potts, 1990) have spoken of the appropriation of others' stories by young children, an example being of a child telling as his own an episode of falling off a stool, heard from his mother as an account of her childhood experience. In other cases, preschool children have been observed to repeat the stories told by their playmates as though they happened to themselves. In some cases these appropriated recounts may be told with full knowledge that they are borrowed. However, in other cases, it is likely that they are absorbed into the child's own representational system as experiences undifferentiated from his own, representing "source errors" in Johnson's and Hirst's (1993) terms.

I have speculated that these source errors are particularly likely during the time (usually around 2½ to four years) when the child is becoming able to use language as an independent source of the representation of knowledge, in this case knowledge about an experienced event, albeit experienced by someone else. At the outset, the linguistically formulated account may enter into the child's memory before linguistic and action-based representations have been differentiated in the cognitive system. Such an undifferentiated cognitive system may also account for the greater tendency of young children to be susceptible to suggested fictions, which during this vulnerable period cannot be easily separated from what was actually experienced. Obviously, given this account of the status of the young child's representational system, the status of a self-concept must be very fragile, subject to invasion by others' experiences. But note that this "invasion" becomes feasible only when language can be used as a representation of experience "handed on" from person to person, a possibility that emerges only in the middle to late preschool years.

These speculations bear also on the second question, raised earlier: Who can provide the evaluative component of the narrative? The answer is crucial to the emerging self-concept. Of course from very early on—certainly from the toddler years—the child is building up a sense of others' valuations of his or her behaviors. But the verbal attribution by another, particularly by an adult, of one's emotional states, moral actions, or social appraisals in the context of the telling of or commenting on a narrativized episode is common among young children and may have a special impact on the child's self-concept and emerging representation of what kind of enduring self that is. Fivush (1993), for example, has provided evidence that in general boys and girls receive quite different commentaries on their behaviors and attitudes, and the likelihood is that such attributions have long-term effects once the child's life story has begun to be constructed.

A SELF AMONG OTHERS

Consider the possibility that talk with others about the self in past events and ongoing present experiences makes manifest different experiential perspectives and thus puts a new light on self, including the realization that what was "me" (pre-enlightenment) is no longer "me" and cannot be reconstituted in the present. An essential aspect of this enlightenment must be that others are different from the self in an important new way: they are not just different actors in an experienced event but are themselves *different experiencers.* Just such a realization is the topic of what has come to be called the study of the child's *theory of mind.* This should properly be described as the child's theory of other people's minds or experiential perspectives, although some theories of the theory of mind claim that the child does not have an understanding of his or her own mind until he or she has an understanding of others' minds. Let us attempt to untangle the complex issues involved by considering what is at stake in theory of mind studies.

The simplest way of explaining what is involved is to describe one of the prototypical tasks used to evaluate a child's status with respect to understanding the concept of mind, namely the "representational change" or Smarties" task. ("Smarties" are a kind of candy, similar to American M&Ms, in a distinctive tubular package well-known to European and Canadian children.) The preschool child is shown a Smarties box and asked to say what he or she thinks is inside. After he or she answers "Smarties," the experimenter opens the box and shows the child that there are really pencils inside. Two test questions follow. The child is asked what he or she thought was inside before the box was opened. Three-year-olds typically reply that they thought there were pencils, while 4-year-olds typically reply correctly that they thought there was candy. Then the child is asked what another child will think is inside before he or she opens the box. Again the younger child typically says he or she will think there are pencils while the older child typically says the child who has not seen the box opened will think there is candy inside. In each case the older child is credited with having a theory of mind, that is, an understanding that others have knowledge or belief states that may differ from one's own and from what is really the case; whereas the younger child does not have this understanding. The attribution of a false belief to others or *to oneself at a prior time* is considered to be diagnostic of a reasonably mature theory of mind or understanding of mental states as distinct from states in the real world.

What is incorporated in the theory of mind achieved by the 4-year-old, and how does that achievement come about? One facet of this level of knowledge about other minds is clearly the realization that others may be different from oneself with respect to their states of knowledge and by virtue of this fact are conceptually differentiated from oneself, not only in terms of their possibly different perspective on an ongoing scene but in what they know or think about a commonly shared situation. This understanding, and the related understanding that one's self was in a different knowledge state at a prior time, rests on taking time into account in one's representations of events, and of people's experience and understanding of events. Temporal perspective is critical because of the relation of sources of belief—one's own and other's—at different points in time, a point exemplified in the case of the Smarties task, for example, before and after looking at the box's contents. It is just this temporal perspective that underlies the objectivity of the self-perspective, as outlined previously. But where does this objectivity come from?

My claim is that the simplest source of knowledge of self and other as objects that differ over time and in relation to each other—the source that takes the least complex representational reasoning—is the talk of other people about their own beliefs about commonly shared events, whether past or present. It is worth noting that to the extent that the child has constructed a concept of permanent objects, the attainment of a belief in changeable objects such as is required to take changing mental states into account, must violate this more basic concept. Take the example described earlier of the mother who tells her child about having fallen from a stool when she was a little girl. The report of Miller, Fung, Hoogstra, Mintz & Potts (1990) of this instance indicated that the child repeated the story as one that happened to himself, thus having appropriated it to his own experience. This is a seemingly odd bit of behavior that suggests a severely undifferentiated self-other condition. But perhaps this is not rampant self-other confusion but reflection of a point along the path toward a differentiation of the represented self and other. The represented self, as distinguished from the experiential self, must be distinguished as well from other represented selves in stories about past, present, or future realities and fiction.

Briefly then, to tell another person a story about oneself is to represent oneself in an objective, differentiated framework. Similarly, to hear a story from someone else and to maintain it as a story about that person is to represent that person in an objective, differentiated sense. To tell or hear a story about both self and other where each is represented as an objective differentiated agent acting independently, each with different goals, knowledge, and beliefs, is a critical step toward the representation of self and other that goes beyond the recognition of different perspectives on the same shared ongoing experience.

That the temporal perspective is an essential part of this development can be seen in the representational change (theory of mind) situation. If the child has only an experiencing self among other persons in the ongoing scene (whether an "I" or a "me"—an agent or a patient), the role of prior experience in one's representational system is quite different from that of an objective, ongoing self that is continuous over time. In the earlier experiencing self, previous episodes are represented, as we know, but they bear on the present only with respect to what they contribute to present knowledge states. Specific past knowledge states or the knowledge states of others are of no interest to the present where action and interaction are located. If a parent, for example, relates a belief at odds with the child's, that belief can be questioned and adjudicated in the present. An account of a prior experience, even if it reports on something the child did not know at the time, may be of interest from the perspective of a narrative, but not from the perspective of knowledge, one's own or other's. It is only when the past becomes connected with the present through the continuation of the self that prior knowledge states "count." And it is through the talk of others about one's self at different times and in different places, with different people, that continuity with the present is first securely attained.

SELF AS A CATEGORY OF KNOWLEDGE

The discussion throughout this paper rests on the general theoretical claim that the child's initial mental model is constructed in terms of event representations that guide action in the present and anticipate the immediate future (Nelson, 1986). This theory also claims that categorical or paradigmatic knowledge may be derived from event knowledge by abstracting from general event representations, or "slot-filler categories," of items that recur in the component slots of familiar events (Lucariello, Kyratzis & Nelson, 1992). As an example, there is evidence from Emily's crib monologues that she constructed a "slot-filler category" of breakfast foods, revealed in the talk between Emily and her father about the foods that she would eat for breakfast on the following day (Nelson, 1996).

Similarly, there is evidence that emerges late in her third year that Emily has begun to construct a self-concept that reflects some of her experiences at home and at her preschool with other children. It is important to the general theoretical proposal here that in both of these cases the categorical knowledge is derived from *talk* about the *events*—both the talk and the event are critical. What is said (by parents, teachers, or peers) articulates the parts of the event and evaluates its components. In the case of self-knowledge, the evaluation is particularly significant, as it may become part of one's own self-concept and it may mark an episode as important in one's self-history.

Consider the following excerpt of Emily's father's bedtime talk when the child was almost two years old:

> What, why are you crying Emily? Cause you're a big girl now, why are you crying? . . . Does Carl [friend] cry when he goes to sleep? . . . Not very much. No . . . cause Carl's a big boy, and you're a big girl . . . and big boys and girls don't cry. Stephen [baby brother] cries when he goes to sleep because he's a little baby, but Emily and Carl . . . Carl's a big boy and Emily's a big girl! They don't cry. . . . You're such a good girl. . . .

In this excerpt Father conveys in specific terms *rules* and *definitions* (big girls and boys don't cry), *labels* distinguishing between self and others (big girls, babies), and *evaluative terms* for self (good girl). These are all potential input to Emily's self-category. But Emily was left with the problem of resolving the conflict between the *evaluative label* "big girl," the evaluative *label* "good girl," the behavioral *rule* "don't cry" and her own actual behavior, crying (a characteristic of her experiential self). In a pre-sleep monologue after her father left the room this conflict was specifically addressed as Emily repeated her father's rule about who cries (babies) and who doesn't (big kids). Then she stated:

> I big kid but I, I, I, I, I, . . . Ahhh ah ahhh kid . . . I big kid but I do cry [very very soft].

Thus she apparently recognized the conflict, although she did not resolve it.

When Emily was 2½ years old, crying reemerged as an issue that distinguished Emily from her friend, after they started nursery school:

> See Charlotte, . . . her mommy and dad, Charlotte's mom and dad all leave, and she's going too, then she'll cry and call for [teacher] so ?? her daddy or mommy will . . . stay the whole time . . . but my mommy and daddy don't. They just tell me what's happening and then go right to work. Cause I don't cause I don't cause I don't cry.

Now Emily's represented self conforms to the parental belief system as well as to her own experiential self. The conflict is resolved.

A further example of emerging self-concept as differentiated from others comes from when Emily was almost 3 years old:

> Anyway so then I, then they decided to do with me when I'm cranky because they don't like me to crank. They don't like Em. They don't like me's.

Here Emily applies to herself the evaluative term "cranky" and seems to conclude that "they" don't like her. She may be uncertain as to whether this is only when she's cranky or as a general case. Although the fragment provides little context, it suggests that a new level of reflection on an objective self differentiated from, but very much in relation to, others is emerging from the experiential self. These brief examples from one child's crib monologues are provocative but cry out for further exploration of the relation between the experiential self, the evaluations by others formulated through talk about self and other, and the construction of a category of self-knowledge in childhood.

CONCLUSIONS

The general proposal put forward here can be summarized as follows: knowledge of self as separate from others begins in infancy in self-other interactions. It is confirmed during the second and third years in ways revealed in self-recognition mirror tests and in linguistic self-reference, which include the use of both the agentive "I" and the patient "me." These achievements confirm an *experiential self* as an actor independent of other actors in events. The objective *represented self* is an achievement of the later preschool years, constructed collaboratively with others in conjunction with developments in personal memory and in understanding differentiated mental states (theory of mind). The critical constructions involve an understanding of self and other as continuous but changeable over time, differentiated from one another not only in ongoing present experiences but in present and past mental states, which may have implications for the present. Once the continuous self is established, a future self may be imagined; thus talk about tomorrow may begin to have a new significance for anticipating events, and a grown-up self may even be contemplated. These later developments have yet to be explored within this framework.

REFERENCES

BARSALOU, L. W. (1988). The content and organization of autobiographical memories. In U. Neisser & E. A. Winograd (Eds.), *Remembering reconsidered: Ecological and traditional approaches to the study of memory* (pp. 193–243). New York: Cambridge University Press.

BARTLETT, F. C. (1932). *Remembering: A study in experimental and social psychology.* Cambridge: Cambridge University Press.

BAUER, P. J., HERTSGAARD, L. A. & DOWN, G. A. (1994). After 8 months have passed: Long-term recall of events by 1- to 2-year old children. *Memory, 2,* 353–382.

BRUNER, J. S. (1986). *Actual minds, possible worlds.* Cambridge, MA: Harvard University Press.

BUDWIG, N. (1985). I, me, my and "name": Children's early systematizations of forms, meanings and functions in talk about the self. *Papers and Reports on Child Language Development, 24.*

BUTTERWORTH, G. (1990). Self-perception in infancy. In D. Cicchetti & M. Beeghly (Eds.), *The self in transition* (pp. 99–119. Chicago: University of Chicago Press.

CECI, S. J. & BRUCK, M. (1993). Suggestability of the child witness: A historical review and synthesis. *Psychological Bulletin, 113,* 403–409.

CONWAY, M. A. & RUBIN, D. C. (1993). The structure of autobiographical memory. In A. F. Collins, S. E. Gathercole, M. A. Conway, & P. E. Morris (Eds.) *Theories of memory* (pp. 103–139). Hillsdale, NJ: Erlbaum.

DELOACHE, J. S. (1986). Memory in very young children: Exploitation of cues to the location of a hidden object. *Cognitive Development, 1,* 123–137.

FIVUSH, R. (1993). Emotional content of parent-child conversations about the past. In C. A. Nelson (Ed.), *Memory and affect in development* (Vol. 26, pp. 39–77). Hillsdale, NJ: Erlbaum.

FIVUSH, R. & HAMOND, N. R. (1990). Autobiographical memory across the preschool years: Toward reconceptualizing childhood amnesia. In R. Fivush & J. A. Hudson (Eds.), *Knowing and remembering in young children* (pp. 223–248). New York: Cambridge University Press.

FIVUSH, R. & HUDSON, J. A. (1990). *Knowing and remembering in young children.* New York: Cambridge University Press.

FRASER, J. T. (1987). *Time the familiar stranger.* Amherst: University of Massachusetts Press.

FRENCH, L. A. & NELSON, K. (1985) *Young children's understanding of relational terms: Some ifs, ors and buts.* New York: Springer-Verlag.

GERHARDT, J. (1989). Monologue as a speech genre. In K. Nelson (Ed.), *Narratives from the crib* (pp. 171–230). Cambridge, MA: Harvard University Press.

HOWE, M. L. & COURAGE, M. L. (1993). On resolving the enigma of infantile amnesia. *Psychological Bulletin, 113,* 305–326.

HUDSON, J. A. (1990). The emergence of autobiographic memory in mother-child conversation. In R. Fivush & J. A. Hudson (Eds.) *Knowing and remembering in young children* (pp. 166–196). New York: Cambridge University Press.

JOHNSON, M. K. & HIRST, W. (1993). Mem: Memory subsystems as processes. In A. F. Collins, S. E. Gathercole, M. A. Conway, & P. E. Morris (Eds.), *Theories of memory* (pp. 103–139). Hillsdale, NJ: Erlbaum.

LEICHTMAN, M. D. & CECI, S. J. (1995). The effects of stereotypes and suggestions on preschoolers' reports. *Developmental Psychology, 31,* 568–578.

LEVY, E. & NELSON, K. (1994). Words in discourse: A dialectical approach to the acquisition of meaning and use. *Journal of Child Language, 21,* 367–390.

LUCARIELLO, J., KYRATZIS, A., & NELSON, K. (1992). Taxonomic knowledge: What kind and when. *Child Development, 63,* 978–998.

MILLER, P. J., FUNG, H., HOOGSTRA, L., MINTZ, J., & POTTS, R. (1990). Narrative practices and the social construction of self in childhood. *American Ethnologist, 17,* 292–311.

NELSON, K. (1989a). Monologue as representation of real-life experience. In K. Nelson (Ed.) *Narratives from the crib* (pp. 27–32). Cambridge, MA: Harvard University Press.

NELSON, K. (1989b). Monologue as the linguistic construction of self in time. In Nelson, K. (Ed.), *Narratives from the crib* (pp. 284–308). Cambridge, MA: Harvard University Press.

NELSON, K. (1993). Developing self-knowledge from autobiographical memory. In T. K. Srull & R. Wyer (Eds.), *The mental representation of trait and autobiographical knowledge about the self* (vol. 5, pp. 111–120). Hillsdale, NJ: Erlbaum.

NELSON, K. (1996). *Language in cognitive development: The emergence of the mediated mind.* New York: Cambridge University Press.

NELSON, K. & ROSS, G. (1980). The generalities and specifics of long term memory in infants and young children. In M. Perlmutter (Ed.), *Children's memory: New directions for child development* (vol. 10, pp. 87–101). San Francisco: Jossey-Bass.

ROVEE-COLLIER, C. (1995). Time windows in cognitive development. *Developmental Psychology, 31,* 147–169.

SHEFFIELD, E. G. & HUDSON, J. A. (1994). Reactivation of Toddlers' Event Memory. *Memory, 2,* 447–466.

TESSLER, M. & NELSON, K. (1994). Making memories: The influence of joint encoding on later recall. *Consciousness and Cognition, 3,* 307–326.

TULVING, E. (1983). *Elements of episodic memory.* New York: Oxford University Press.

Michael Lewis is University Distinguished Professor of Pediatrics and Psychiatry, and Director of the Institute for the Study of Child Development at the Robert Wood Johnson Medical School—University of Medicine and Dentistry of New Jersey. Professor Lewis is a Fellow of the New York Academy of Sciences, the American Psychological Association, the American Association for the Advancement of Science, and the Japan Society for the Promotion of Science. Michael Lewis has been one of the leaders in the study of child development, particularly in emotional development, and is the author of Children's Emotions and Moods; Shame, The Exposed Self; *and* Altering Fate: Why the Past Does Not Predict the Future.

The Self in Self-Conscious Emotions

MICHAEL LEWIS

*Institute for the Study of Child Development
Robert Wood Johnson Medical School of the
University of Medicine and Dentistry of New Jersey
New Brunswick, New Jersey 08903*

Although emotional development has recently begun to receive attention, there is a paucity of work on models of development. I have presented a model of emotional development elsewhere (Lewis, 1992b; Lewis, 1993; Lewis, Stanger, Sullivan & Weiss, 1989) so that I shall here present only the outlines of the theory, saving most of my discussion for the topic of the role of the self in self-conscious emotions. The first half of this paper deals with the model, the second with the role of self in self-conscious emotions.

THE EARLY EMOTIONS

In the model presented in FIGURE 1, I mean to indicate that many of the adult emotions such as pride, embarrassment, shame, and humiliation—those having to do with what Darwin called self-conscious—emerge in the human child by the time he or she is 3 years of age. As Darwin (1872) said, "the nature of the mental states of shyness, shame, and modesty have as their emotional element self-attention. It is not the simple act of reflecting on our own appearance, but the thinking what others think of us, which excites a blush" (p. 325). Such mental acts, reflecting on our own appearance and thinking about others thinking about us, require sophisticated cognitive abilities, abilities which are likely to emerge around the second and third year of life. Again quoting Darwin, "I have received authentic accounts of two little girls blushing at the ages of between 2 and 3 years. . . . It appears that the mental powers of infants are not as yet sufficiently developed to allow of their blushing" (p. 310). In other words, the mental powers or acts necessary for these emotions as exemplified by blushing are emerging in the child by 3 years of age. Such views argue for a developmental approach to the study of emotions in general and self-conscious emotions in particular.

In treating any model of emotional development we need be concerned with the appropriate markers for the emotions we wish to observe. Are we making reference solely to emotional expressions or are we talking about emotional states or experiences? Given the content of our inquiry—namely, the study of the emergence of emotions in the first three years of life—we

119

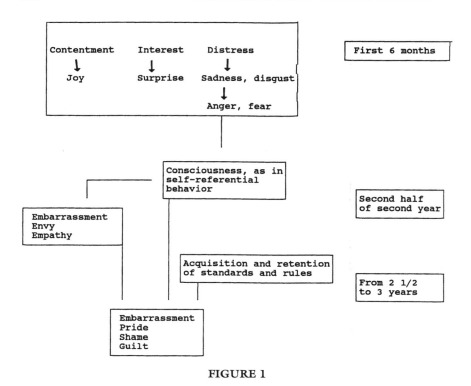

FIGURE 1

are presented with a difficulty. The ability to do more than observe the emitted behaviors of the child is all that is possible. In order to get emotional experiences, we need language in the form of "I am sad" or "I am ashamed." Because the language of the child is quite limited during this period, the study of emotional experience is difficult. Likewise, the study of emotional states is difficult to undertake because internal states remain a hypothetical construct not yet demonstrated. There has been little success in finding a unique configuration of neurophysiological events which mark unique emotions in adults, let alone children and infants.

What we are left observing is emotional expression and behavior. However, all does not appear lost, especially if we observe emotional behavior in context. This allows us, at least from the perspective of the adult meaning system, to assume that the child's expression reflects something more than a surface manifestation of the emotion (Lewis & Michalson, 1983). Observation of fear over the approach of a stranger or joy when a mother appears allows us to accept that an internal state of fear or joy exists. With these limitations in mind, the following discussion and mapping of emotional development can proceed.

Following Bridges (1932), we assume that at birth the child shows a bipolar emotional life. On one hand, there is general distress, marked by crying and irritability. On the other hand, there is pleasure marked by satiation, attention, and responsivity to the environment. Attention to the environment and interest in it appears from the beginning of life and we can place interest either in the positive pole or, if we choose, we can separate it, thus suggesting a tripartite division with pleasure at one end, distress at the other, and interest as a separate dimension.

By 3 months, joy emerges. Infants start to smile and appear to show excitement/happiness when confronted with familiar events, such as faces of people they know or even unfamiliar faces (Lewis, 1969). Also by 3 months, sadness emerges, especially around the withdrawal of positive stimulus events. Three-month-old children show sadness when mothers stop interacting with them (Tronick, Als, Adamson, Wise & Brazelton, 1978). Disgust also appears in its primitive form, a spitting out and getting rid of unpleasant tasting objects placed in the mouth. Thus, by 3 months, infants are already showing interest, joy, sadness, and disgust, and exhibiting these expressions in appropriate contexts.

Anger has been reported to emerge between 4 and 6 months (Stenberg, Campos & Emde, 1983). Anger is manifest when children are frustrated, in particular when their hands and arms are pinned down and they are prevented from moving. Lewis, Alessandri, and Sullivan (1990), however, have shown anger in 2-month-old infants when a learned instrumental act was blocked. Anger is a particularly interesting emotion since, from Darwin on, it has been associated with unique cognitive capacity. Anger is thought to be both a facial and motor/body response designed to overcome an obstacle. Notice that in this definition of anger, the organism has to have some knowledge in regard to the instrumental activity toward a goal. For anger to be said to be adaptive it has to be a response that attempts to overcome a barrier blocking a goal. In some sense then, means–ends knowledge has to be available and the demonstration of anger at this early point in life reflects the child's early knowledge acquisition relative to this ability (Lewis, 1990).

Fearfulness seems to emerge still later. Again, fearfulness reflects further cognitive development. Schaffer (1974) has shown that in order for children to show fearfulness they have to be capable of comparing the event that causes them fearfulness with some other event, either internal or external. Thus, for example, in fear of strangers the infant has to compare the face of the stranger to that of its internal representation of memory of faces. Fear occurs when the face is found to be discrepant or unfamiliar relative to all other faces that the child remembers. Children's ability to show fearfulness, therefore, does not seem to emerge until this comparison ability emerges. Around 7 to 8 months, children begin to show this behavior, although it has been reported by some to occur even earlier, especially in children who seem to be precocious.

Surprise also appears in the first 6 months of life. Children show surprise when there are violations of expected events; for example, when infants see a midget (a small adult) walking toward them, they are reported to show interest and surprise rather than fear or joy (Brooks & Lewis, 1976). Surprise can be seen when there is violation of expectancy or as a response to discovery as in an "aha" experience. Lewis, Sullivan, and Michalson (1984) showed that when children were taught an instrumental arm-pulling response, they showed surprise at the point when they discovered that the arm-pull could turn on a slide. Surprise can reflect both a violation as well as a confirmation of expectancy. In the first 8 or 9 months of life, children's emotional behavior reflects the emergence of the six early emotions, called by some primary emotions or basic emotions (Izard, 1978; Tomkins, 1962, for example). There is no question that cognitive processes play an important role in the emergence of these early emotions even though these processes are limited.

THE EMERGENCE OF OBJECTIVE SELF-AWARENESS

FIGURE 1 indicates that new cognitive capacities emerge and are utilized somewhere in the second half of the second year of life, in particular, the emergence of objective self-awareness (Lewis & Brooks-Gunn, 1979). The topic of self-awareness requires that we pay attention to what we might mean by the term, "objective self-awareness," and how it differs from other types of self-awareness. Human beings are complex, multilevel, self-regulating organisms capable of perceiving, emoting, thinking, remembering, and learning. We possess elaborate feedback loops that do not require our objective self-awareness in order to operate. For example, we regulate our bodily functions as well as our cognitive ones without focusing on the fact that we are doing so (indeed, most of the time we are unaware of this aspect of our being). All living creatures have similar processes. However, at some point ontogenetically, human beings gain a new capacity: awareness of their own operations. The capacity for objective self-awareness allows humans to process information and to decide on the best action (whether it be motor behavior, thought, or emotion). The objective self can reflect on and reject any solution generated by the subjective process. It allows us to stand back from our own processing and thereby increases the possibility of generating new solutions.

Although human adults have this capacity for objective self-awareness, or reflection, most of the time, for most of our organizing and regulating functions, we do not avail ourselves of this capacity. Moreover, there are times when its use can actually lead to difficulty. For example, when we try to listen to what we are saying while we are talking, we block our ability to continue to talk.

Attempts to delineate different features of the self are not new. Freud's contributions, especially his conception of the unconscious mind, extended and broadened our idea of self, enabling us to understand diverse behaviors as a product of the self's action. He forced us to recognize that the self acts, plans, knows, and believes without apparent awareness. There are, of course, problems with the psychoanalytic notion of an unconscious. The tripartite division of the self into id, ego, and superego, each with a life of its own, competing and warring, is both appealing and puzzling. Such a division requires that these features of the self stand as separate entities with separate goals and desires, and also necessitates some overall and overriding mechanism by which they are controlled. Freud assigned the ego the task of organization; and he gave the ego both a conscious function, that of monitoring the world in which we live, and an unconscious function, namely controlling and organizing libidinal impulses (Freud, 1959).

Lewis and Michalson's (1983) discussion of the distinction between emotional experiences and emotional states is helpful in framing the problems of a complex self. Emotional states operate at the level of subjective self-awareness. These states have goals; they learn and profit from experience; they control functions and react to events, including people. The processes are unknown to us, but they require learning and can be made to change. The experience of our states is the equivalent of objective self-awareness. The distinction between states and experiences or between subjective versus objective self-awareness can be explored at a biological level. Recently, certain states (rather than experiences) have been tied to the stimulation of different locations in the brain.

Karl Pribram describes a patient in whom the medial part of the temporal lobe, including the amygdala, had been removed bilaterally.

Because of the removal of this area, humans and animals are known to gain large amounts of weight, sometimes as much as 100 pounds. He asked the patient how it felt to be so hungry, and [to] one patient who had gained more than 100 pounds in the several years since surgery, he spoke at lunchtime and asked her "[Was she] hungry?" She answered, "No." Would she like a piece of rare, juicy steak?" "No." "Would she like a piece of chocolate candy?" She answered, "um-hum," but when no candy was offered she did not pursue the matter. A few minutes later when the examination was completed, the doors to the common room were opened, and she saw the other patients already seated at a long table eating lunch. She rushed to the table, pushed the others aside, and began to stuff food into her mouth with both hands. She was immediately recalled to the examining room, and questions about food were repeated. The same negative answers were obtained again, even after they were pointedly contrasted with her recent behavior at the table. Somehow the lesion had impaired the patient's feelings of hunger and satiety, and this impairment was accompanied by excessive eating! (Pribram, 1984, p. 25).

Here we can see a distinction between the patient's objective self experiences and her behavior and state of hunger.

More recent work by LeDoux (1989) also points to specific brain regions as responsible for what I have called specific emotional states (mediated by subjective self-awareness) and also emotional experiences (mediated by objective self-awareness). Working with rats, LeDoux and his colleagues found that even after the removal of the auditory cortex, the animals were still able to learn an association between an auditory signal and shock. After just a few trials, the rats showed a negative emotional response to the sound. Removal of the visual cortex followed by a visual sign and shock also resulted in learning. These findings indicate that fear conditioning—the production of a fear state—is mediated by subcortical, probably thalamic–amygdala sensory pathways. Similar findings have been reported in humans and point to different brain areas for experiences and states. Weiskrantz (1986), among others, has reported on a phenomena called "blindsight." Patients who lack a visual cortex, at least in one hemisphere, are asked if they can see an object placed in their blind spot. All such patients report that they cannot. When, however, they are asked to reach for an object they cannot see, they show that they have the ability to reach, at least some of the time, for the object. These findings suggest that separate brain regions are responsible for the production and maintenance of emotional states and the experiences of these states. LeDoux believes that emotional states and experiences may be mediated by separate but interacting areas of the brain. "The computation of stimulus significance takes place prior to and independent of conscious awareness . . . the amygdala may be a focal structure in the affective network. . . . Emotional experiences, it is proposed, result when stimulus representations affect representations, and self representations coincide in working memory" (LeDoux, 1989, p. 265).

Such a view of modularity, supported by different brain regions, provides evidence for different types of awareness. Duval and Wicklund (1972) use the term *objective self-awareness* to mean the organism's act of turning attention toward the self, to what the self knows, to what plans or desires the organism has, and they use the term *subjective self-awareness* to mean processes and systems that know about the world but to which we do not or cannot pay attention.

From an epistemological point of view, we have knowledge of many things, but it is our human capacity to have knowledge of knowledge that constitutes a unique mode of consciousness—from an ontogenetic and a phylogenetic sense, the highest mode. Given these definitions of objective and subjective self-awareness, we are confronted with the following question: Is all information that is subjectively known capable of being objectively known? From an epistemological point of view, the general issue of knowledge takes a similar turn. Benjamin Lewis pointed this out to me. For example, when I say "I know X," is it the case that I know that I know X? Is it the case that when I know X, I *must* know that I know X? Or is it the case that when I know X, I *can* know that I know X? If it is the case that when I know X, I *can* know that I know X, when is it the case that I *do* know that I know X? These kinds of epistemological questions require different ways of knowing. Such questions are difficult to answer, and we do not have enough information to answer them satisfactorily. On the one hand, it seems that there are many bodily functions of which there may be subjective awareness which we cannot make objective. Certain biochemical functions that take place in our body and which alter states, moods, and the like may not ever be objectively known. Having said that, however, this conclusion may need to be modified, given the research in behavioral medicine. If we could be taught or could train ourselves to focus on certain sensations and processes, there might be no limit to our ability to convey them from subjective to objective awareness. The same applies to the self-system that has knowledge and therefore can function in the world, but also has the capacity to reflect upon itself. The uniqueness of shame (and hubris, guilt, and pride) is its relationship to a self that can reflect on itself.

For the last 20 years, my colleagues and I have been studying the problem of self-development and emotional life (Lewis & Brooks-Gunn, 1979; Lewis & Michalson, 1983). Our interest in empirically exploring the origins of self started with our interest in self-recognition. Given that infants and very young children do not have the capacity for language, it is very difficult to study the acquisition of these concepts of the self that I have been discussing. While it is true that we can observe mother–child interaction, or children's interactions with objects, our observations, while informative, do not give us a clear idea of the developmental sequence. Accordingly, we decided to look at children's behavior in the presence of reflective surfaces. It seemed to me that if children could be shown to recognize themselves in a mirror without any prompting, then it might be said that they were able to view themselves, to refer to themselves; and we saw this self-referential behavior as the best possible marker of objective self-awareness. We undertook a large number of studies starting more than two decades ago. Our results indicate that objective self-awareness as defined by self-referential behavior, does not emerge until the second half of the second year of life.

In our procedures, we watched children's responses to mirrors, as well as their responses to television images and still photographs. Our method involved placing some dye on the child's nose without its awareness, and then observing its behavior in front of a mirror and classifying it as self-directed or mirror-directed. Many animals react to their mirror images as though the images were other animals. For example, chickens eat more in the presence of other chickens and also when in the presence of a mirror image of themselves than they do when alone (Tolman, 1965). Furthermore, animals behave as though the mirror images are not only social objects but animals like themselves. For example, fish, birds, and monkeys will display aggression to their mirror image just as they do to others like them. Some species, specifically primates, respond as though the images were unfamiliar, rather than familiar, members of their species. Self-directed behavior in the mirror indicates that the organism recognizes that the image in the mirror belongs to the self in another space. Thus, when the dye is applied to the animal's nose, we can observe whether the animal uses the mirror to touch its own nose. This is called self-recognition or self-directed behavior.

Using the same technique as Gordon Gallup (1977), we found that infants from 15 to 24 months of age touched their bodies or faces when placed in front of a mirror after their faces were marked, with more infants touching their faces following the marking process than before (Lewis & Brooks-Gunn, 1979). Their reaction is similar to chimpanzees' use of the mirror to visually locate and touch marked parts of their bodies. Infants begin to imitate their marked image by making faces, sticking out their tongues, or watching themselves disappear and reappear at the side of the mirror around 15 to 18 months of age. These behaviors seem to indicate a growing awareness of the properties of reflections. At the same time they begin to imitate, children also start to touch the mark on the face. The results from several of our studies were surprisingly consistent: mark-directed behavior was never exhibited in infants younger than 15 months. Between 18 and 24 months, a dramatic increase occurred, with approximately 75% of the 18-month-olds and all of the 24-month-olds exhibiting mark recognition.

We also studied visual self-recognition using pictures of the self. Studies of pictorial recognition almost always concentrated on the face because even adults have considerable difficulty in recognizing body parts other than their face. The ability of preverbal children to recognize their faces in pictures is best inferred by comparing their responses to pictures of themselves to their responses to pictures of others. The "others" that are used for comparison purposes should be as similar to the subjects as possible, to guard against differential responding based on aspects other than self-perception. Infants respond quite differently to adults than to children, for example, and therefore may differentiate between themselves and adults on the basis of age features, not features specific to themselves.

Zazzo (1948) showed his son pictures of himself throughout the first years of life to see when he would recognize them. Zazzo reported such recognition around 3 years of age. Using a bit more sophisticated procedure, we presented 9- to 24-month-old infants with slides of themselves, same-sex peers, and opposite-sex peers. The pictures we used showed only the face and shoulder area. Children responded differentially to pictures of themselves and other babies; they smiled more to their own pictures by 2 years. Early pictorial self–other differentiation may require perceptual–cognitive support structures other than feature recognition. Some of the infants differentiated between pictures of themselves and pictures of infants of the opposite sex, but not between pictures of themselves and pictures of infants of the same sex. Pictorial self–other differentiation in the first year of life seems to be dependent on perceptual structures, such as age and gender. In the middle of the second year of life, children seem to be capable of recognizing their own pictures on the basis of feature differences alone.

Children's verbal responses were studied by asking infants to point out and label their own picture in a set that included their own and others' pictures (Lewis & Brooks-Gunn, 1979). As many language researchers have found, comprehension preceded verbal production. Almost all infants could point to their own picture, as opposed to another's picture, by 18 months of age. Most infants did not label their own pictures until 21 to 24 months of age, although a few exceptions labeled as early as 15 months. Personal pronouns, although appearing at the end of the second year, were not used by a majority of the children until 30 to 36 months of age, a finding also reported by Gessell (1928). Personal-pronoun usage is an interesting milestone, not only in the acquisition of subjective self-knowledge but also in terms of a linguistic representation of self. Although children are referred to by others as "you," "he," or "she," and never as "I" or "me," and although they hear others refer to themselves as "I," but not as "you," "he," or "she," most do not refer to themselves as "you," or to others as "I." Interestingly, autistic children and blind children have been observed using personal pronouns incorrectly, "I" for others and "you" for self (Fraiberg & Adelson, 1976).

Examination of the use of personal pronouns seems to indicate that the first-person pronoun, "I," appears around 20 to 24 months of age, and second- and third-person pronouns, "you," "he," and "she," appear about two months later. When asked questions like "Where is my hair?," "Where is your hair?," and "Where is her hair?," toddlers responded to the "your" question earlier than to the "my" question, even though in spontaneous conversations they used "I" correctly earlier than they used "you." It seems that toddlers focus on the consistencies in speech, using "I" and "you" appropriately, rather than just imitating others' speech. Additionally, when the self is being referred to ("I" when the child is speaking, "you" when the adult is speaking), the personal-pronoun usage is more likely to be correct and to occur earlier than when another is being referred to ("you" when the child is speaking, "I" when the adult is speaking).

We studied children's self-recognition responses in movies and videotapes (Lewis & Brooks-Gunn, 1979). In Zazzo's study of his own son, home movies as well as pictures were shown to the child. He was found to recognize himself in these home movies in his third year of life. Today, videotapes have replaced home movies as the preferred medium for studying self-recognition and moving representations. In one of our videotape studies, infants between 9 and 24 months were seated in front of a television screen and saw, among other tapes, a videotape of themselves in the same setting made a week earlier or a videotape of a same-sex, same-aged infant in the same setting. In another videotape, the same procedure was utilized, with one interesting addition: an unfamiliar person silently approaches either the self or the other infant from behind, with the approach being visible on the television screen although, of course, the person was not actually present. Infants were more likely to pay attention to and turn toward the stranger when they saw the videotape of the other than the tape of themselves, while they were more likely to make sounds in response to and to imitate play with the tape of themselves than with that of the other. Differential responses to the tape of themselves and those of others occurred at around 15 to 18 months of age and reflect objective self-awareness. These studies suggest an ontogenetic sequence of self-recognition, which we use as an index of the acquisition of self-referential behavior, or objective self-awareness.

THE EMERGENCE OF LATER EMOTIONS

As FIGURE 1 shows, the rise of objective self-awareness leads to a new class of emotions. These have been called *self-conscious emotions* and include embarrassment, empathy, and envy. Although little work has been done in the development of these emotions, several studies exist that support the emergence of embarrassment at this point in time. Lewis *et al.* (1989) have shown that the emergence of embarrassment takes place only after self-recognition, the marker of consciousness, occurs. In a study of children 9–24 months of age, we have been able to demonstrate that embarrassment is related to the emergence of self-recognition. Empathy, too, emerges in relation to self-recognition and not before (Bischoff-Köhler, 1991). The emergence of these self-conscious emotions is related uniquely to the cognitive milestone of consciousness or mental acts (Lewis, 1992a). FIGURE 1 also shows a second cognitive milestone that occurs sometime between 2 to 3 years of age. This ability is characterized by the child's capacity to evaluate its behavior against a standard. This new capacity of evaluation gives rise to a second set of emotions called *self-conscious evaluative* emotions. It is these self-conscious emotions that I shall focus on for the remainder of this article.

In summary, the model I have proposed suggests that by 3 years of age the emotional life of the child has become highly differentiated. From the original tripartite set of emotions, we find that the child, within three years, comes to possess an elaborate and complex emotional system. While the emotional life of the 3-year-old will continue to be elaborated and will expand, the basic structures necessary for this expansion have already been formed. New experiences, additional meaning, and more elaborate cognitive capacities will all serve to enhance and elaborate the child's emotional life.

THE SELF-CONSCIOUS EMOTIONS

Having suggested a model for the emergence of emotional life in the first three to four years of life, I now focus on those emotions that emerge late and that require certain cognitive abilities for their elicitation. While the emotions that appear early—such as joy, sadness, fear, and anger—have received considerable attention, this set of later-appearing emotions that I will discuss has received relatively little attention. There are likely to be many reasons for this; one reason is that these self-conscious emotions cannot be described solely by examining a particular set of facial movements, necessitating the observation of bodily action as well as facial cues.

A second reason for the neglect of study of these later emotions is the realization that there are no clear specific elicitors of these particular emotions. Thus, while happiness can be elicited by seeing a significant other, and fear can be elicited by the approach of a stranger, there are a few specific situations that will elicit shame, pride, guilt, or embarrassment. These self-conscious emotions are likely to require classes of events that only can be identified by the individuals themselves. Consider pride. What conditions are necessary to elicit pride? Pride requires a large number of factors, all having to do with cognitions related to the self. Pride requires that one make a comparison or evaluate one's behavior *vis-à-vis* some standard, rule, or goal. Pride occurs when one evaluates one's behavior against a standard and finds that one has succeeded, and when one concludes that he or she is the cause of the success. For example, it is unlikely that a person will feel proud of winning the lottery. One might feel happy, but not proud, since for a person to feel proud he or she needs to feel responsible for the success and winning the lottery involves luck, not ability. Thus, the feeling experienced is less likely to be pride. The same can be said for shame or guilt which occurs when such an evaluation leads to the conclusion that one has failed and is the cause of the failure.

The elicitation of self-conscious emotions involves elaborate cognitive processes that have, at their heart, the mental "act" of self. While some theories, such as psychoanalysis (see Freud, 1936 and Erickson, 1950), have argued for some universal elicitors of shame, such as failure at toilet training or exposure of the backside, the idea of an automatic non-cognitive elicitor of these emotions does not make much sense. Cognitive processes must be the elicitors of these complex emotions (Lewis, 1992a). It is the way we think or what we think about that becomes the elicitor of pride, shame, guilt, or embarrassment. There may be a one-to-one correspondence between thinking certain thoughts and the occurrence of a particular emotion; however, in the case of this class of emotions, the elicitor is a cognitive event. This does not mean that the earlier emotions, those called primary or basic, are elicited by non-cognitive events. Cognitive factors may play a role in the elicitation of any emotion; however, the nature of cognitive events are much less articulated and differentiated in the earlier ones (Plutchik, 1980).

Recently, there has been an attempt to clarify those specific aspects of self that are involved in self-conscious emotions, in particular, the self-conscious *evaluative* emotions (Lewis, 1992b). Self-conscious evaluative emotions first involve a set of standards, rules, or goals (SRGs). These SRGs are inventions of the culture which are transmitted to the child and involve the child's learning of and willingness to consider these SRGs as their own. This process of incorporating the SRGs has been discussed recently by Stipek, Recchia, and McClintic (1992). What is apparent from the work of Stipek *et al.* is that the process of incorporation starts quite early in life. Standards, rules, and goals imply self-evaluation, for it would make little sense if we had SRGs but no evaluation of our action *vis-à-vis* them.

Having self-evaluative capacity allows for two distinct outcomes; we can evaluate our behavior and hold ourselves responsible for the action which is being evaluated, or we can hold ourselves not responsible. In the attribution literature, this distinction has been called either an internal or an external attribution (Weiner, 1986). If we conclude that we are not responsible, then evaluation of our behavior ceases. However, if we evaluate ourselves as responsible, then we can evaluate our behavior as successful or unsuccessful *vis-à-vis* the SRGs. The determination of success and failure resides within the individual on the basis of the nature of the standard that is set. For example, if I believe that only receiving an A in an exam constitutes success, then my receiving a B grade represents a failure for me. On the other hand, a B grade may be considered a success by another. Still another cognition related to the self has to do with the evaluation of one's self in terms of specific or global attributions. *Global self-attributions* refer to the whole self, while *specific self-attributions* refer to specific features or actions of the self (see Dweck & Leggett, 1988; Weiner, 1986). In every one of these processes, a concept of objective self-awareness needs to be considered.

The need for cognitive elicitors having to do with the self was known to Darwin (1872/1965). Darwin saw these latter emotions as involving the self, although he was not able to distinguish among the various types (see also Tomkins, 1963 and Izard, 1977 for similar problems). His observation in regards to blushing indicates his concern with two issues; the issue of appearance and the issue of consciousness. He repeatedly makes the point that these emotions depend on sensitivity to the opinion of others whether good or bad. Thus, the distinction between emotions that require opinion or thought of others versus emotions that do not suggest that two different kinds of cognitive processes are involved.

Trying to distinguish among the different types of self-conscious emotions (e.g., embarrassment, shyness, shame, and guilt) is difficult. As Darwin's analysis makes clear, all of these emotions are likely to produce blushing, and so blushing will do little good in distinguishing among them.

FIGURE 2 presents the structural model from which we define various self-conscious emotions. The three factors, A, B, and C, represent cognitive processes that serve as stimuli for these emotions.

Standards, Rules, and Goals

The first feature of the model has to do with the SRGs that govern our behavior. All of us have beliefs about what is acceptable for others and for ourselves in regard to standards having to do with action, thought, and feeling. This set of beliefs, or SRGs, constitutes the information one acquires through acculturation. SRGs differ across different societies, across groups within societies, across different time epochs, and between individuals of different ages. The standards of our culture are varied and complex, yet each of us knows at least some of them. Moreover, each of us has his or her own unique set. To become a member of any group requires that we learn them. I can think of no group that does not have SRGs, and, if violated, does not impose negative sanctions on the violator. These SRGs are acquired through

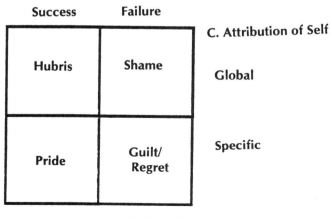

A. Standards and Rules

B. Evaluation

	Success	Failure	
	Hubris	Shame	**C. Attribution of Self** Global
	Pride	Guilt/Regret	Specific

FIGURE 2

a variety of processes. They are always associated with human behavior, including thinking, action, and feeling. They are prescribed by the culture, including the culture at large, as well as by the influences of specific groups, such as clan, peers, and family.

It is safe to claim that, by the age of 1 year, children are beginning to learn the appropriate action patterns reflecting the SRGs of the culture. By the second year of life, children show some understanding about appropriate and inappropriate behavior (Heckhausen, 1984; Kagan, 1981; Stipek *et al.*, 1992). The acquisition of these SRGs continues across the life span; however, some emerge early.

Evaluation

The evaluation of one's actions, thoughts, and feelings in terms of SRGs is the second cognitive evaluative process that serves as a stimulus for self-conscious evaluative emotions. Two major aspects of this process are considered; the first has to do with the internal and external aspects of evaluation. First, for the model to work in describing the process of eliciting emotions, internal evaluation, as opposed to either no evaluation or external evaluation, is necessary. Individuals differ in their characteristic evaluative response. Moreover, situations differ in the likelihood that they will cause a particular evaluative response. The second consideration has to do with how individuals make a determination about success or failure in regard to any specific standard.

Internal versus External Blame

Within the field of attributional studies, the problem of internal versus external attribution has received a good deal of attention (Weiner, 1986). People violate standards, rules, and goals, but often do not attribute the failure to themselves. They may explain their failure in terms of chance or through the actions of others (Seligman, 1975; Seligman *et al.*, 1984). Internal and external evaluations are both situationally determined and a function of individual characteristics. There are people who are likely to blame themselves no matter what happens. Dweck and Leggett (1988), in studying causes of success and failure within academic fields, found many children who blame their success or failure on external forces, although there are as many who are likely to evaluate success and failure in terms of their own actions. Interestingly, strong sex differences emerge. In academic achievement, boys are more apt to hold themselves responsible for their success and others for their failure, whereas girls are apt to thank others for their success and blame themselves for their failure.

Success or Failure

Another feature of the self-evaluation process has to do with the "socialization" of what constitutes success or failure. When people have assumed responsibility (internal evaluation), exactly how they come to evaluate their actions, thoughts, and feelings as success or failure is not well understood. This aspect of self-evaluation is particularly important because the same standards can result in radically different feelings, depending upon whether we attribute to ourselves success or failure.

Many factors are involved in producing inaccurate or unique evaluations of success or failure. These include early failures in the self-system leading to narcissistic disorders (see Morrison, 1989), harsh socialization experiences, and high levels of reward for success or punishment for failure (see Lewis, 1992b). The evaluation of one's behavior in terms of success and failure is a very important aspect of the organization of plans and the determination of new goals and new plans.

Attribution About Self

Another attribution in regard to the self has to do with "global" or "specific" self-attribution. The terms *global* and *specific* are used to specify the tendency of individuals to make global as opposed to specific evaluations about the self (Beck, 1967, 1979; Seligman, 1975). *Global* refers to an individual's propensity to focus on the total self. Thus, for any particular behavior violation, some individuals, some of the time, are likely to focus on the totality of the self; and they use such self-evaluative phrases as, "Because I did this, I am bad [or good]." Janoff-Bulman's (1979) distinction between characterological and behavioral self-blame is particularly relevant here.

In global attributions, the focus is upon the self. The self becomes embroiled in the self. The focus is not upon the individual's behavior, but upon the total self. There is little wonder that in using such global attribution one can think of nothing else, and one becomes confused and speechless (H. B. Lewis, 1971). We turn to focus upon ourselves, not upon our action. Because of this, we are unable to act and are driven from the field of action into hiding or disappearing.

Specific, in contrast, refers to the individual's propensity to focus on specific actions of the self. It is not the total self that has done something wrong or good, it is specific *behaviors* that are judged. At times like these, individuals will use such evaluative phrases as, "What I did was wrong, I mustn't do it again." Notice that, for such occurrences, the individual's focus is not on the totality of the self but on the specific behavior of the self in a specific situation.

Global versus specific focus of the self may be a personality style. Global attributions for negative events are generally uncorrelated with global attributions for positive events (Peterson *et al.*, 1982). It is only when positive or negative events are taken into account that relatively stable and consistent attributional patterns are observed. There are some individuals who are likely to be stable in their global and specific evaluations. Under most conditions of success or failure, these subjects are likely to maintain a global or specific posture in regard to self-attribution. In the attribution literature, such dispositional factors have important consequences upon a variety of fixed "personality patterns." So, for example, depressed individuals are likely to make stable, global attributions, whereas non-depressed individuals are less likely to be stable in their global attribution (Beck, 1979).

In addition to the dispositional factors relating to specific or global attributions, there are likely to be situational constraints as well. Some have called these prototypic situations. That is, although there are dispositional factors, not all people all the time are involved in either global or specific attributions. Unfortunately, these situational factors have not been well studied. It seems reasonable that there should be certain classes of situation more likely than others to elicit a particular focus. Exactly what these classes of stimuli are remains unknown (see Lewis, 1992b).

Given these three sets of activities—establishing one's SRGs, the evaluation of success or failure of one's action in regard to these, and the attribution of the self—it is now possible to see how these factors combine to produce the self-conscious evaluative emotions. It is important to point out that this model is symmetrical relative to positive and negative self-conscious emotions. Because of this, it focuses not only upon shame and guilt, but upon the other side of the axis, hubris and pride. It is the cognitive-evaluative process of the organism itself that elicits these states. The immediate elicitors of these self-conscious emotions are cognitive in nature.

The model distinguishes among four emotional states. Shame results from failure and global evaluation of the self. Guilt results from failure and specific evaluation of the self's action. A parallel exists as a consequence of success. When success is evaluated and the person makes a global attribution, hubris (pridefulness) is the resulting emotion; while if the person makes a specific attribution, pride is the resulting emotion. So, for example, if I say to success, "I am a great person," we would call this hubris, while if to the same success I say "I was able to see how I could do it to get it right," we would call this pride.

Shame

Shame is the product of a complex set of cognitive activities: the evaluation of an individual's actions as failure in regard to their SRGs and their global evaluation of the self. The phenomenological experience of the person having shame is that of a wish to hide, disappear, or die (H.B. Lewis, 1971; Lewis, 1992b). It is a highly negative and painful state which also results in the disruption of ongoing behavior, confusion in thought, and an inability to speak. The physical action accompanying shame is a shrinking of the body as though to disappear from the eye of the self or the other. Because of the intensity of this emotional state, the global attack on the self system, all that individuals can do when presented with such a state is to attempt to rid themselves of it. However, since it is a global attack on the self, people have great difficulty in dissipating this emotion. Shame is not produced by any specific situation, but rather by the individual's interpretation of the event. Even more important, shame is not related necessarily to the event's being public or private. While many hold that shame is a public failure, this need not be so. Failure, attributed to the whole self, can be either public or private. Shame may be public, but it is as likely to be private. Each of us can think of private events when we say to ourselves "I'm ashamed for having done that." Shame can occur around moral action as well. Thus, when a person violates some moral SRG, he or she is ashamed.

There are specific actions individuals employ when shamed that "undo" the shame state (see Lewis, 1992a). There are many ways of getting rid of shame, some of which we use every day. Denial is one example that is used in many ways. For example, once shame has occurred we can stop focusing on it. A colleague has a paper rejected from a journal and puts it into a drawer never to be seen again. She is using a lack-of-focus procedure in order to forget and, therefore, deny the shame. This act of denial through forgetting is an important way of separating the self from the feeling. Denial also can be used to prevent shame from occurring in the first place. One can deny that he or she violated the standard or that he or she even *had* a standard.

Laughter is another mechanism by which acknowledged shame can be reduced or eliminated. First, laughing at one's self serves to distance one's self from the emotional experience. Because laughter is such a powerful stimulus it allows us to focus on another emotion and thereby allows us to "defocus" the shame. Second, laughter, especially laughter around one's transgression as it occurs in a social context, provides the opportunity for the person to join others in viewing the self. In this way, the self metaphorically moves from the site of the shame to the site of observing the shame with the other. Consider the example of a person who slips on her own scarf. Others around her laugh at her clumsy behavior. This laughter serves to humiliate the woman and she immediately feels shame; however, by laughing at herself, she joins the others; now, rather than being the object of others' laughter, she becomes, with the others, one who laughs at the misfortune of another. It is as if the self moves from the position of being shamed, of having others' eyes on one, to a position where one is with the others, the observing eyes. Such a movement allows for the identification with the observer rather than with the observed, and has a very similar mechanism to that which Freud reported as identification with the aggressor. By laughing, the person identifies with the observer rather than with the observed; with those laughing at the one shamed, not the one shamed.

A third feature of laughter is its social significance. Experiencing someone's shame is itself shameful. The observers, seeing the person trip and seeing her shame, are in turn shamed. There is a contagious effect, such that the woman who tripped, shamed over having tripped, causes those watching to become shamed for her. This spiral of shame can be broken through the laughter of the one initially shamed. It is as if the woman says to the observers, "See, I'm not shamed; there's no reason for you to be shamed by my shame." In other words, laughter, as employed here, is used to break the spiral of the observer and the observed shame exchange (Chapman, 1976).

Confession, like laughter and forgetting, is an attempt to deal with shame once it is acknowledged. In confession, we go to others and tell about an event that has shamed us. This public acknowledgment of the transgression and the shame that accompanies it appears to be a successful way of dealing with shame. Certainly the use of confession by certain religions is an indication of its success in dealing with shame. In a sense, confession is like laughter. The degree to which people confess their transgressions to others is the degree to which they join in with the others in observing themselves. This allows the self to move from the self; that is, from the source of the shame to the other. This, in turn, allows the self as the "confessee" to look upon the self as the object rather than the subject.

Guilt

The emotional state of guilt or regret is produced when individuals evaluate their behavior as failure, but focus on the specific features of the self or on the self's action that led to the failure. Unlike shame, where the focus is on the global self, here the individual focuses on the self's actions and behaviors that are likely to repair the failure. From a phenomenological point of view, individuals are pained by their failure, but this pained feeling is directed to the cause of the failure or the object of harm. Because the cognitive attributional process focuses on the action of the self rather than on the totality of self, the feeling that is produced—guilt—is not as intensely negative as shame and does not lead to confusion and to the loss of action. In fact, the emotion of guilt always has associated with it a corrective action, which the individual can do but does not necessarily do, to repair the damage of failure. Rectification of the failure and preventing it from occurring again are the two possible corrective paths. Whereas in shame we see the body hunched over itself in an attempt to hide and disappear, in guilt we see individuals moving in spaces as if trying to repair their action (see Barrett & Zahn-Waxler, 1987). The postural differences that accompany guilt and shame are marked and are helpful both in distinguishing these emotions and in measuring individual differences.

Because in guilt the focus is on the specific, individuals are capable of ridding themselves of this emotional state through action. The corrective action can be directed toward the self as well as toward the other; thus, unlike shame, which is a melding of the self as subject and object, in guilt the self is differentiated from the object (Tangney, 1995).

Hubris

Hubris is defined as exaggerated pride or self-confidence, often resulting in retribution. It is an example of pridefulness, something dislikeable and to be avoided. Hubris is a consequence of an evaluation according to success at one's standards, rules, and goals where the focus is on the global self. In this emotion, the individual focuses on the total self as successful. It is associated with such descriptions as "puffed up." In extreme cases, it is associated with grandiosity or with narcissism (Morrison, 1989). In fact, the word *hubristic* signifies insolence or contemptuousness. Because of the global nature of this emotion, it is likely to be transient, and in order to be able to maintain this state the individual must either alter standards or re-evaluate what constitutes success. Unlike shame, it is highly positive and emotionally rewarding; that is, the person feels good about him- or herself. Hubris is, however, an emotion difficult to sustain since there is no specific action that precipitates the feeling. Because such feelings are addictive, persons prone to hubris derive little satisfaction from the emotion. Consequently, they seek out and invent situations likely to repeat this emotional state. This can be done either by altering one's SRGs or by re-evaluating what constitutes success of one's actions, thoughts, or feelings.

Pride

The emotion labeled pride is the consequence of a successful evaluation of a specific action. The phenomenological experience is "joy over an action, thought, or feeling well done." Here, again, the focus of pleasure is specific and related to a particular behavior. In pride, the self and object are separated, as in guilt. Unlike shame and hubris, where subject and object are fused, pride focuses the organism on its action. The organism is engrossed in the specific action that gives it pride. Some investigators have likened this state to achievement motivation (Heckhausen, 1984; Stipek *et al.*, 1992 for example). Its association with achievement motivation seems particularly apt. Because this positive state is associated with a particular action, individuals have available to themselves the means by which they can reproduce the state. Notice that, unlike hubris, pride's specific focus allows for action. Because of the general use of the term "pride" to refer to hubris, efficacy, and satisfaction, the study of pride as hubris has received relatively little attention. Dweck and Leggett (1988) similarly have approached this problem through the use of individuals' implicit theories about the self which are cognitive attributions that serve as the stimuli for the elicitation of the self-conscious emotion of mastery.

Embarrassment

For some, embarrassment is closely linked to shame (Izard, 1979; Tomkins, 1963). The most notable difference between embarrassment and shame is the intensity level. While shame appears to be an intense and disruptive emotion, embarrassment is clearly less intense and does not involve the disruption of thought and language that shame does. Secondly, in terms of body posture, people who are embarrassed do not assume the posture of one wishing to hide, disappear, or die. In fact, their bodies reflect an ambivalent approach and avoidance posture. Repeated looking and then looking away accompanied by smiling behavior seems to index embarrassment (see Edelman, 1987; Geppert, 1986; Lewis, Stanger, & Sullivan, 1989). Rarely in a shame situation do we see gaze aversion accompanied by smiling behavior. Thus, from a behavioral point of view, these two emotions appear to be different.

Phenomenologically, embarrassment is less differentiated from shame than from guilt. People often report that embarrassment is "a less intense experience of shame." Similar situations that invoke shame are found to invoke embarrassment, although, as we have mentioned, its intensity, duration, and disruptive quality are not the same. It is important to differentiate two types of embarrassed behavior since this may help us distinguish embarrassment from shame; these are called (1) embarrassment as self-consciousness and (2) embarrassment as mild shame (Lewis, 1995).

Embarrassment as Self-Consciousness

In certain situations of exposure, people become embarrassed. This is not related to negative evaluation, as is shame. Perhaps the best example is seen in response to being complimented. One phenomenological experience of those who appear before audiences is that of embarrassment caused by the positive comments of the introduction (see Buss, 1980; Lewis et al., 1989). Consider the moment when the person is introduced; the person introducing the subject extols his or her virtues. Surprisingly, praise, rather than displeasure or negative evaluation, elicits embarrassment!

Another example of this type of embarrassment can be seen in our reactions to public display. When people observe someone looking at them, they are apt to become self-conscious, look away, and touch or adjust their bodies. When the observed person is a woman, she will often adjust or touch her hair; men are less likely to touch their hair, but may adjust their clothes or change their body posture. In few cases do the observed people look sad. If anything, they appear pleased by the attention. This combination, gaze turned away briefly, no frown, and nervous touching, looks like this first type of embarrassment.

A third example of embarrassment as exposure can be seen in this experiment. When I wish to demonstrate that embarrassment can be elicited just by exposure, I announce I am going to randomly point to a student. I repeatedly mention that my pointing is random and that it does not reflect a judgment about the person. I close my eyes and point. My pointing invariably elicits embarrassment in the student pointed to. In each of these examples there is no negative evaluation of the self in regard to SRGs. In these situations, it is difficult to imagine embarrassment as a less intense form of shame. Since praise cannot readily lead to an evaluation of failure, it is likely that embarrassment due to compliments, to being looked at, or to being pointed to, has more to do with the exposure of the self than with evaluation. Situations other than praise come to mind, but in most cases a negative evaluation can be inferred, although it may not be the case. Take, for example, walking into a room before the speaker has started to talk. It is possible to arrive on time only to find people already seated. When walking into the room, eyes turn toward you, and you may experience embarrassment. One could say that there is a negative self-evaluation, "I should have been earlier; I should not have made noise [I did not make noise]." I believe, however, that the experience of embarrassment in this case may not be elicited by negative self-evaluation, but simply by public exposure.

Embarrassment as Mild Shame

The second class of embarrassment, which we call embarrassment as less intense shame, seems to me to be related to a negative self-evaluation. The difference in intensity is likely due to the nature of the failed SRG. Some standards are more or less associated with the core of self; for me, failure at driving a car is less important than is failure at helping a student. Failures associated with less important and central SRGs result in embarrassment rather than shame. If this analysis is correct, then it is possible that each of the four self-conscious emotions has a less intense form.

It may well be that embarrassment may not be the same as shame. From a phenomenological stance they appear very different. On the other hand, there is the possibility that embarrassment and shame, in fact, are related and that they only vary in intensity. It is safe to say that, as a working definition, there appears to be at least two different types of embarrassment.

SUMMARY

The study of self-conscious emotions has only recently begun. The model outlined here offers an opportunity to consider and to define carefully some of the self-conscious emotions. Unless we develop a more accurate taxonomy, we will be unable to proceed in our study of these emotions. Given the renewed interest in emotional life, it is now appropriate to consider these more complex emotions rather than the more "primary" or "basic" ones. Moreover, as others have pointed out, these self-conscious emotions are intimately connected with other emotions, such as anger and sadness (see for example, H.B. Lewis, 1971; Lewis, 1992b; Morrison, 1989). Finally, given the place of self-evaluation in adult life, it seems clear that the self-conscious evaluative emotions are likely to stand in the center of our emotional life (Dweck & Leggett, 1988; Heckhausen, 1984).

REFERENCES

BARRETT, K. C. & ZAHN-WAXLER, C. (1987). Do toddlers express guilt? Poster presented at the meetings of the Society for Research in Child Development (April).

BECK, A. T. (1967). *Depression: Clinical, experimental, and theoretical aspects.* New York: Harper & Row.

BECK, A. T. (1979). *Cognitive therapy and emotional disorders.* New York: Times Mirror.

BISCHOF-KÖHLER, D. (1991). The development of empathy in infants. In M.E. Lamb & H. Keller (Eds.), *Infant development: Perspectives from German speaking countries* (pp. 245–273). Hillsdale: Lawrence Erlbaum Associates.

BRIDGES, K. M. B. (1932). Emotional development in early infancy. *Child Development, 3,* 324–334.

BROOKS, J. & LEWIS, M. (1976). Infants' responses to strangers: Midget, adult and child. *Child Development, 47,* 323–332.

BUSS, A. (1980). *Self-consciousness and social anxiety.* San Francisco, CA: W.H. Freeman.

CHAPMAN, D. J. (ED.) (1976). *Humor and laughter: Theory, research, and applications.* London: Wiley.

DARWIN, C. (1872/1965). *The expression of the emotions in man and animals.* Chicago: University of Chicago Press.

DUVAL, S. & WICKLUND, R. A. (1972). *A theory of objective self-awareness.* New York: Academic Press.

DWECK, C. S. & LEGGETT, E. L. (1988). A social-cognitive approach to motivation and personality. *Psychological Review, 95,* 256–273.

EDELMAN, R. J. (1987). *The psychology of embarrassment.* Chichester, England: Wiley.

ERICKSON, E. H. (1950). *Childhood and society.* New York: Norton.

FRAIBERG, S. & ADELSON, E. (1976). Self-representation in young blind children. In Z.

Jastrzembska (Ed.), *The effects of blindness and other impairments on early development* (pp. 48–96). New York: American Foundation for the Blind.

FREUD, S. (1936). *The problem of anxiety*. New York: Norton.

FREUD, S. (1959). The ego and the id. In J. Strachey (Ed. and Trans.), *The complete psychological works of Sigmund Freud* (Vol. 19, pp. 241–258). London: Hogarth Press. (Original work published in 1925.)

GALLUP, G. G., JR. (1977). Self-recognition in primates: A comparative approach to the bidirectional properties of consciousness. *American Psychologist, 32,* 329–338.

GEPPERT, U. (1986). *A coding system for analyzing behavioral expressions of self-evaluative emotions* (Technical Manual.) Munich: Max-Planck Institute for Psychological Research.

GESSELL, A. (1928). *Infancy and human growth*. New York: Macmillan.

HECKHAUSEN, H. (1984). Emergent achievement behavior: Some early developments. In J. Nicholls (Eds.), *The development of achievement motivation* (pp. 1–32). Greenwich, CT: JAI Press.

IZARD, C. E. (1977). *Human emotions*. New York: Plenum Press.

IZARD, C. E. (1978). Emotions and emotion-cognition relationships. In M. Lewis & L. A. Rosenblum (Eds.), *The development of affect* (pp. 389–413). New York: Plenum.

IZARD, C. E. (1979). *The Maximally Discriminative Facial Movement Coding System (MAX)*. Newark, DE: Instructional Resources Center, University of Delaware.

JANOFF-BULMAN, R. (1979). Characterological versus behavioral self-blame: Inquiries into depression and rape. *Journal of Personality and Social Psychology, 37,* 1798–1809.

KAGAN, J. (1981). *The second year*. Cambridge: Harvard University Press.

LEDOUX, J. (1989). Cognitive and emotional interactions in the brain. *Cognition and Emotion, 3,* 265–289.

LEWIS, H. B. (1971). *Shame and guilt in neurosis*. New York: International Universities Press.

LEWIS, M. (1969). Infants' responses to facial stimuli during the first year of life. *Developmental Psychology, 1,* 75–86.

LEWIS, M. (1990). The development of intentionality and the role of consciousness. *Psychological Inquiry, 1*(3), 231–248.

LEWIS, M. (1992a). The self in self-conscious emotions. A commentary in Stipek, D. J., Recchia, S. & McClintic, S. Self-evaluation in young children. *Monographs of the Society for Research in Child Development, 57,* (1, Serial No.226).

LEWIS, M. (1992b). *Shame, The Exposed Self*. New York: The Free Press.

LEWIS, M. (1993). The emergence of human emotions. In M. Lewis & J. Haviland (Eds.), *Handbook of emotions* (pp. 563–573). New York: Guilford Press.

LEWIS, M. (1995). Embarrassment, the emotion of self exposure. In J. P. Tangney & K. W. Fischer (Eds.), *Self-conscious emotions: The psychology of shame, guilt, embarrassment, and pride* (pp. 198–218). New York: Guilford Press.

LEWIS, M., ALESSANDRI, S. & SULLIVAN, M. W. (1990). Violation of expectancy, loss of control, and anger in young infants. *Developmental Psychology, 26*(5), 745–751.

LEWIS, M. & BROOKS-GUNN, J. (1979). *Social cognition and the acquisition of self*. New York: Plenum.

LEWIS, M. & MICHALSON, L. (1983). *Children's emotions and moods: Developmental theory and measurement*. New York: Plenum.

LEWIS, M., STANGER, C. & SULLIVAN, M. W. (1989). Deception in 3-year-olds. *Developmental Psychology, 25,* 439–443.

LEWIS, M., SULLIVAN, M. W. & MICHALSON, L. (1984). The cognitive-emotional fugue. In C. E. Izard, J. Kagan, & R. Zajonc (Eds.), *Emotion, cognition, and behavior* (pp. 264–288). New York: Cambridge University Press.

LEWIS, M., SULLIVAN, M. W., STANGER, C. & WEISS, M. (1989). Self-development and self-conscious emotions. *Child Development, 60,* 146–156.

MORRISON, A. P. (1989). *Shame: The underside of Narcissism.* Hillsdale, NJ: Analytic Press.

PETERSON, C., SEMMEL, A., VONBAEYER, C., ABRAMSON, L. Y., METALSKY, G. I. & SELIGMAN, M. E. P. (1982). The attribution style questionnaire. *Cognitive Therapy and Research, 6,* 287–300.

PLUTCHIK, R. (1980). A general psychoevolutionary theory of emotion. In R. Plutchik & H. Kellerman (Eds.), *Emotion: Theory, research, and experience* (Vol. 1, pp. 3–33). New York: Academic Press.

PRIBRAM, K. H. (1984). Emotion: A neurobehavioral analysis. In K. R. Scherer & P. Ekman (Eds.), *Approaches to emotion* (pp. 13–38). Hillsdale, NJ: Erlbaum.

SCHAFFER, H. R. (1974). Cognitive components of the infant's response to strangeness. In M. Lewis & L. A. Rosenblum (Eds.), *The origins of fear* (pp. 11–24). New York: Wiley.

SELIGMAN, M. E. P. (1975). *Helplessness: On depression, development, and death.* San Francisco: Freeman.

SELIGMAN, M. E. P., PETERSON, C., KRASLOW, N., TANENBAUM, R., ALLOY, L. & ABRAMSON, L. (1984). Attributional style and depressible symptoms among children. *Journal of Abnormal Psychology, 39,* 235–238.

STENBERG, C. R., CAMPOS, J. J. & EMDE, R. N. (1983). The facial expression of anger in seven-month-old infants. *Child Development, 54,* 178–184.

STIPEK, D. J., RECCHIA, S. & MCCLINTIC, S. (1992). Self-evaluation in young children. *Monographs of the Society for Research in Child Development, 57,* (1, Serial No. 226).

TANGNEY, J. P. (1995). Shame-proneness, guilt-proneness, and interpersonal processes. In J. P. Tangney & K. W. Fischer (Eds.), *Self-conscious emotions: Shame, guilt and pride* (pp. 114–139). New York: Guilford Press.

Part IV: Telling About the Self: Narrative Approaches

Introduction

JOAN GAY SNODGRASS

Department of Psychology
New York University
New York, New York 10003

The two papers in this section—"A Narrative Model of Self Construction" by Jerome Bruner and "The Social Construction of the Remembered Self: Family Recounting" by William Hirst—have in common the assumption that narrative is an important, even necessary construction for developing the self-concept.

In his paper, Jerome Bruner first reviews a set of cues or indicators of selfhood, and then shows that these are constituents of well-formed narrative. He argues that the narratives that people construct of their life are also based upon the popular narratives of a culture's fiction in a celebration of the dictum, life imitates art. One way of imagining how people construct a story of their life is to posit an implicit life story in the memory which is used to construct whatever stories are necessary at the time, for example, to account for why I became a psychologist. Yet Bruner doubts that such a stored implicit life story exists, and argues instead that narratives are constucted "on-line" through meta-memorial processes. In that sense, then, he suggests that there are a multiplicity of selves which can be constructed whose narratives will differ depending upon the purpose at hand.

William Hirst and his colleagues consider a larger unit for developing and supporting the self concept—that of the family. Hirst *et al.* have taken on the difficult and time-consuming task of studying the role of individual family members in recounting their shared experiences. They show that family member often adopt different roles in recounting a shared past, and that these roles have a decisive influence over whose version of events is adopted by the family. Thus if a family member consistently adopts the role of Narrator, this member's memory of the shared event dominates.

In a subsequent set of studies, using unrelated groups, Hirst and his colleagues show that these group interactions actually affect subsequent memory. Thus, group discussion of a target event (a narrative passage) produced additional memories recounted by individuals in a later recall task. Taken together, these studies show that social interaction can affect how we remember an event in our lives, and thus can affect how we form our narrative of the autobiographical self.

Jerome Bruner is Research Professor of Psychology and Senior Research Fellow in Law at New York University and has served as co-director in the Center for Cognitive Studies at Harvard. He has played a major role in shaping the development of cognitive psychology and is the author of numerous books, including the autobiographical In Search of Mind, *and the 1956 classic with Jacqueline Goodnow and George Austin,* A Study of Thinking. *He is presently engaged in the study of narrative thought and the structure of narrative genres. He is past President of the American Psychological Association and the Society for the Psychological Study of Social Issues, and is the recipient of the APA's Distinguished Scientific Award among many others.*

A Narrative Model of Self-Construction

JEROME BRUNER

Department of Psychology
New York University
New York, New York 10003

I

The notion of "Self" is an oddball one for philosophers and psychologists alike. For though it seems phenomenologically familiar, it is a familiarity that evaporates when we examine it closely. Does my Self include my kin, my car, my alma mater? Does it include my pleasure in participating in this New York Academy of Sciences' symposium? Nor does this indefinability of the limits of Self get less troubling simply by granting that the self is only an idiosyncratic record of what got built into each person as a result of his or her varied experiences—a function of so-called individual differences. If that were all there were to it, then different selves would be so radically different from each other that the "other minds" problem would become virtually intractable. So, even granting that selves are in some respects constructed, how can we go about trying to understand what it is that, on the one hand, makes selves sufficiently alike to make them intersubjectively communicable, yet sufficiently unique to be distinctively individual.

With respect to the first of these, intersubjective communicability, self-construction seems often to be in some degree a byproduct of other-oriented activities, like finding where you belong in the social order, or justifying to others your intentions, or rationalizing your disappointments. So to know about Self, your own or somebody else's, you surely have to know about a lot more than just your own inner feelings, or those of somebody else. Self is, as it were, not only inside you, but "in the world," in some sort of real world. In this sense, it is both private and public.

But the sheer *existence* of a self-concept must surely depend upon some phylogenetic readaptation that makes it possible for Self to develop in the course of ontogenesis. For humans seem to be uniquely able to distinguish "Self" from "world" in the extended way that they do. Do all organisms have selves? Do newborn infants, severe autists, or the severely brain impaired?[a] What is it that develops?

---

[a] For a fuller discussion of the interplay of cultural and biological factors in the phylogenesis and ontogenesis of Self construction, see Bruner (1995) and Bruner and Kalmar (in press); also see Campbell (1994).

There seems now to be an emerging consensus on these topics. I think most would agree that the Self is indeed constructed through interaction with the world rather than being just there immutably, that it is a product of transaction and discourse (E. M. Bruner, 1986; Goodwin & Duranti, 1992; Markus & Kitayama, 1991; Ochs, 1988; Shore, 1996). Most would also agree that its construction would not occur without there being something special in the human genome. To the philosopher's favorite question, "How do I recognize that I am the 'same' self as the one that went to bed the night before, or that went to the analyst the year before?" We typically invoke both genomic and experiential factors—that our self system is intrinsic and self-maintaining, but that we elaborate it and reconstruct it with a view to maintaining and stabilizing our relationship to the world, particularly the social world. So robust is Self that fugue states and split personalities make news.

Yet, despite all this, the self, although seemingly continuous, strikes one as curiously unstable when considered over extended lengths of time. Autobiographies, for example, are typically marked by accounts of turning points featuring presumably profound changes in selfhood: "After that, I was a different person." As many as a third of self-referent sentences in the corpus of spontaneous autobiographies with which I have worked contain markers of doubt and uncertainty about identity—expressions containing subjunctives, models of uncertainty, outright Hamlet-like questions, and so on. So it may well be that the more temporally extended self poses problems for the maintenance of self-continuity.

Some writers even go so far as to say that the cohesion of the self over long periods poses a special problem under conditions of rapid cultural change (Lifton, 1993). Selves have, of course, always been taken to be representative of their times, as many students of autobiography have insisted (Misch, 1950). But it may well be that there is a limit to how much world change any given Self can absorb without undergoing a pathological crisis. If this is so, then it is altogether appropriate that the New York Academy of Sciences should now be devoting a series of lectures, collected in this volume, to the topic of Self. The series itself is probably a sign that the culture's very view of Self is undergoing a revolution, presumably in response to our rapidly changing world. It is altogether proper, then, that we explore this matter as seriously as we can.

II

Scientists, quite naturally, want to demystify Self. For demystification is our job. But the challenge is to demystify it without obscuring its complexities—particularly its seemingly unmanageable mix of the public and the private. For no doubt Self is an odd mix of the "outer" and the "inner." Our outer knowledge of Self comes principally from statements that other people make—whether in interviews, in replies to questionnaires, in autobiographies, and even by their so-called "self-revealing" acts in response, say, to praise or blame. Our knowledge of other selves must surely be based to some degree on our self-knowledge, because in making inferences about or in "perceiving" other selves we doubtless rely on our inner knowledge of our own Selves. But conversely, as many have remarked, we also model our conceptions of our own selves on what we observe in others. This poses a puzzling transactional problem with which we shall be much concerned in what follows.

Yet another problem. Even though we would all agree that Self grows out of our encounters with events and circumstances of the worlds in which we live, we also know that those events and circumstances do not, as it were, come ready-made. They are themselves constructed, products of self-generated meaning-making. The events of a life cannot be taken as its givens; they are themselves fashioned to fit our growing conceptions of our Selves, even filtered at the entry port by our perception of the world (Bruner, 1992; Neisser, 1988; Niedenthal & Kitayama, 1994). So the experienced world may produce Self, but Self also produces the experienced world. And part of that world is the Other, to whom we offer the justifications, excuses, and reasons that are so crucial to self-formation. So even the interpersonal setting of our self-accounting makes a difference.

The culture, moreover, prescribes its own genres for self-construction, ways in which we may legitimately conceive ourselves and others. When the Japanese describe themselves, they tend to emphasize their affiliations; we Americans emphasize our individuality (Markus & Kitayama, 1991). These cultural genres even implicate the ways in which we may deviate from them—the rebel, dreamer, seducer. A perceptive poet I once interviewed began his autobiographical story by telling me that the attending obstetrician at his birth slapped him on his back to get him breathing—and broke two of his ribs, unaware that he was suffering prenatal osteoporosis. "It's the story of my life," he went on, "people breaking my bones to do me good, which is how it is when you're a homosexual." The genre of the suffering victim of society served him well, right back to the moment of his birth!

Yet, there is a sense in which these cultural genres of selfhood also provide an external source of continuity to our conceptions of Self. For they give cultural continuity and stability to our place or position in the cultural world. My attention was drawn to this stabilizing feature of self-telling in Philippe Lejeune's searching discussion of what he calls the "autobiographical pact," a canonical notion of how to *tell* the story of yourself, which, of course, is also a prescription for how to construct one's own self (Lejeune, 1989). Here is his version of the pact: "DEFINITION: Retrospective prose narrative written by a real person concerning his [sic] own existence, where the focus is his individual life, in particular the story of his personality" (p. 4). This almost sounds like the "felicity conditions" on an acceptable self-telling speech act, or more simply, it is a canonical version of how to think about Self in our kind of culture. In another sense, it is a description of the "self-currency" that we bring to the open market of discourse in order to trade some version of our self for the distinctions that the culture has to offer, to use the terms of Pierre Bourdieu (1984). On his view, we offer our conventionalized resources of selfhood to trade on "symbolic markets" in exchange for symbolic "distinctions." Such trading leads to the formation of what Bourdieu calls our "habitus," a kind of commodity—i.e., I am not only *me*, but a professor, a speaker at the New York Academy of Sciences, etc.

This preliminary excursion into selfhood leads to some interesting tentative conjectures, if not to conclusions. The first is that self may not be as "private" or as ineffable as is sometimes supposed. For whatever else it may be, Self seems also to be a cultural product—even a product of the discourse in which we engage (Ochs & Schieffelin, 1983). It seems to serve as much a *cultural* as an *individual* function, particularly in regulating interpersonal transactions (even institutionalized ones, as in the law, where such concepts as "responsibility" further standardize our sense of selfhood, as when minors and felons are denied civil selfhood, and as when minors and felons are denied civil selfhood in the legal sense). Self, moreover, seems not just to develop in reaction to a given "real" world-out-there, but rather, to our *making* of events in conformity with the culture's semiotic codes and genres. Yet, for all that, the self thus constructed has great stability (Savage-Rumbaugh *et al.*, 1993; Tomasello, 1992).

One expression of that stability is that we cannot resist perceiving ourselves as selves, or perceiving others in that way. These selves seem irresistibly to be operating under their own direction, and even exceptions to this rule presuppose it—as when we see somebody or ourselves as "duped" or "coerced" (Astington, 1994). Our very view of the social world is built around this fundamental notion of selves interacting with each other. We seem to be organized in such a way as to "see" signs of that self-direction everywhere in our own acts and in the acts of others. What are these signs or cues of selfhood that we find so compelling, and how do they combine to give us such a unique view of ourselves and our conspecifics (Humphrey, 1983, 1986; Ricoeur, 1992)? They must indeed be ubiquitous and redundant to trip off our perceptions so easily and reliably. So, what makes us think we are in the presence of selfhood?[b] I want to turn to this question now, to the cues that we ordinarily take as indicative of selfhood.

[b]I do not mean to take a stance on the "reality" of the Self by posing these questions; such ontological issues need not concern us now. In certain ways, the questions posed are akin to Turing's test of how you can tell whether it is a human operator or a computer that you are interacting with.

III

For reasons that I will make clearer presently, let me propose the following list of cues or indicators of selfhood.

i. *Agency* indicators seem to refer to acts of free choice, to voluntary actions, and to initiatives freely undertaken in pursuit of a goal. They are legion, ranging from signs of mere hesitation to expressions of intentions. They take the form of language, as in models of obligation; we judge the vicarious trial and error (VTE) of the rat as agentive; and we regard approach–approach conflict in humans in a similar way. Indeed, agency indicators are so familiar and so varied that they scarcely need to be summarized here. Obviously, signs of impeded agency are seen as fitting the same category.

ii. *Commitment* indicators are about an agent's adherence to an intended or actual line of action, an adherence that transcends momentariness and impulsiveness. Commitment indicators tell about steadfastness, delay of gratification, sacrifice, or of flightiness and inconstancy.

iii. *Resource* indicators speak to the powers, privileges, and goods that an agent seems willing to bring or actually brings to bear on his commitments. They include not only such "external" resources as power, social legitimacy, and sources of information, but "inner" ones as well, like patience, perspective, forgiveness, persuasiveness and the like.

iv. *Social reference* indicators tell where and to whom an agent looks in legitimizing or evaluating goals, commitments, and resource allocation. They may reference "real" groups like one's classmates, or cognitively constructed reference groups like "people who care about law and order" (Merton, 1968).

v. *Evaluation* indicators provide signs of how we or others value the prospects, outcomes, or progress of intended, actual, or completed lines of endeavor. They may be specific (as with signs of being satisfied or dissatisfied with a particular act) or highly general (as with a sense that some large enterprise as a whole is satisfactory or not). These indicators tell about *situated* affect as it relates to the conduct of life in the small or large.

vi. *Qualia* indicators are signs of the "feel" of a life—mood, pace, zest, weariness, or whatever. They are signs of the subjectivity of selfhood. "Observed" in another they range from posture and pace to highly stylized verbal expressions, intentional or otherwise. Observed in ourselves, they are indicators of mood, fatigue, general activation. When they are relatively unsituated with respect to external events, they are notoriously subject to context effects.

vii. *Reflexive* indicators speak to the more metacognitive side of Self, to the reflective activity invested in self-examination, self-construction, and self-evaluation. We say of another that they are thoughtful or mindful (Langer, 1989), or that they live well-inspected lives, or that they seem shallow. In experiencing our own self, we distinguish between giving matters at hand "very close consideration" in contrast to "shooting from the hip."

viii. *Coherence* indicators refer to the apparent integrity of one's acts, commitments, resource investments, self-evaluations, etc. We say of somebody else that he or she seems "all of a piece" or of our own Self that some particular line of endeavor is "very much a part of me." These indicators are taken to reveal the internal structure of a larger self-concept and are presumed to indicate how the particulars of various endeavors cohere in a "life as a whole."

ix. *Positional* indicators are presumed to reveal how an individual locates himself or herself in time, space, or the social order—where one stands in the "real" world. Most usually, positional indicators become salient when we sense a discrepancy between our own sense of position and some publicly prescribed one—as when we act out of role, or somebody is seen as "uppity."

IV

This seemingly motley lot of self-indicators surely suggests a deeper system that operates when we process cues about selfhood. Such a system can, I think, be characterized more abstractly, in more general, even more functional terms. Let me propose some of the characteristics of such a general system better to elucidate how it generates such a profusion of self indicators as I have just listed.

1. *Innate modifiability.* It seems to be the case that the experience of Self, one's own or another's, is an "output" from some sort of preadapted processing system. This system initially accepts as input only a highly constrained set of indicators, as seen in infancy, or even in higher primates. It includes such sensory triggers as eyes (Eibl-Eibesfeld, 1975), voice qualities (Fernald, 1989, 1991), and various forms of movement (Johannson, 1973). These early inputs can be conceived as initial "tokens" of what will later grow into more inclusive category types whose limits, although initially highly constrained, grow larger through some form of learning or linguistic reconstruction. The early set of indicators grow eventually into something like our self-indicator list. The range and variety of viable tokens that fit particular indicator types come under the control of cultural equivalency rules once language is learned. Looked at functionally, such a self-system seems to fulfill two functions: a species maintenance function and an individual function. To these we turn next.

2. *Enhancement of species mutuality.* Such a self-system as we are considering has as one of its major functions maintaining the viability of a species that adapts culturally to its world. For speciation, wherever it is found, is based upon mutuality and enhanced intraspecific communication (Mayr, 1982). In the human species, with its cultural adaptation, this function is served by mutual self-systems governed by the rule that "other humans are

like us in being selves," that other minds operate as ours do, that we can share attention with others, and that as the system grows, we share common beliefs, expectations, and other intentional states. At a more evolved level, the mark of such viable cultural "speciation" seems to require not only mutuality, but also the establishment of a shared conception of legitimacy: what particular beliefs may be expected of others and what they may expect of us, what endeavors can be legitimately pursued, how values should be applied, etc. Legitimacy, under the circumstances, even enters into our way of conceiving our own and others' selfhood: it creates a cultural community where there can even be "forbidden thoughts."

3. *Individuation of self.* In human–cultural adaptation, self-individuation is a complement of cultural speciation: we are individual selves in a community of selves. Individuation has two sides, one epistemic and the other deontic. The epistemic is what we each know and believe individually: our own background knowledge and beliefs. The deontic is what we value, expect, care about, fear, love, etc. The epistemic side has to do with understanding the present, predicting the future, and interpreting the past. We expect ourselves and others, as Selves, to be individuated in both the epistemic and deontic senses. Knowing one's own self is to be consistent in a manner to minimize the helter-skelter of immediacy and impulsiveness of response. Being a good judge of your fellows reduces the surprise stemming from the acts of others. The deontics of individuation—what one values and expects as legitimate—is a poorly understood topic. Efforts to understand what others value and believe to be legitimate have often generated such overly intellectualized doctrines as Rational Choice Theory, Utilitarianism, theories of reinforcement, and the rest. Epistemic and deontic individuation (as experienced in oneself or in others) is (quite anomalously) often ritualized or institutionalized in customs and exemplary myths. Individuation is even preserved in a culture's social system, as in constitutional rights to privacy and in such doctrines as contracts and property rights.

Our list of self-indicators is a catalogue of the classes of major cues signalling the presence of enculturated and individuated selfhood. *Agency* indicators are doubtless the most primitive. Even invertebrates can discriminate between their shaking a twig themselves and the twig's shaking them (von Holst, 1973; see especially Chapter 3, "The reafference principle," written in collaboration with Horst Mittelstaedt). Indeed, such "primitive" agency may constitute what Neisser refers to as the "sensory self" (Neisser, 1988). The other indicators become differentiated as aspects of what Neisser calls the Conceptual Self.

V

Interestingly enough, the catalogue of self-indicators mentioned earlier comprises what is generally taken to be in their ensemble the "constituents" of well-formed narrative. They comprise, to borrow the terminology of the great narratologist, Vladimir Propp (1968), the "functions" of a narrative. Not that a well-formed story needs all of them, as Propp has noted. For they are often redundant, and it is in the nature of story that it makes possible reasonable inferences about missing constituents. *Beowulf*, for example, has little to say about the experiential qualia induced by the mayhem it portrays. Nor do Aesop's fables say much about the social positioning of its protagonists. Fictional narratives, indeed, can be made notoriously more "realistic" by leaving some self-indicators unspecified and subject to the imagination of the reader.

Recall that a narrative as classically defined by Burke (1945) for fiction, by Hayden White (1981) for history, and by Ricoeur (1984) in general, represents the interaction of the following constituents:

An *Actor* with some degrees of freedom;
An *Act* upon which he has embarked, with
A *Goal* to whose attainment he is committed;
Resources to be deployed in the above, in
A *Setting* affecting all the above, with
A presupposition of *Legitimacy,*
Whose violation has placed things in *Jeopardy.*

Could it be, then, that what we recognize as Self (in ourselves or in others) is what is convertible into some version of a narrative? Any account that lacks indicators of agentivity, or indicia of commitment, or information about resource deployment, or any indication of social referencing or evaluation, or is without qualia, or any signs of coherence or metacognitive reflexiveness, or finally, any indication of the social positioning of protagonists—such accounts are judged to be not only without a "story," but as with "no one there." In brief, such accounts are both without Selves and without narrative.

One might even speculate that the specialized genres of selfhood to which reference was made earlier represent ways of highlighting different sets of self-indicators. Emphasis on *agency* signals an adventurous self; a focus on *commitment* signals a dedicated self; specialization on *resources* signals either a profligate or a miserly self; too much *social referencing* bespeaks the in-grouper and/or the snob; preoccupation with *qualia* is the self-contained aesthete. Indeed, what some literary theorists (Spengemann, 1980) like to call the "original autobiography," St. Augustine's *Confessions,* is famous for balancing all our self-indicators.

What can we say regarding the modifiability of the self-indicators mentioned earlier? What accounts for the protean shapes that our conception of Self takes— the *extended* Self of William James's famous chapter (1890), or Kenneth Gergen's "saturated self" (1991), or Ciarán Benson's "absorbed self" (1993)? How does self get extended, saturated, absorbed, or whatever?

I want to begin our consideration with an autobiographical fragment borrowed from a recent article of my own. I described myself in childhood as something of a "water rat," for at about age eleven or twelve I began "hanging out" with a few friends at a certain small-boat dock in my home town. We all learned to perform chores for one Frank Henning who, by some unspoken contract, let us in return keep a clumsy old dory there. We spent a lot of time on the water. The "sea-going self" that began forming then continues even today. It includes such resources as being able not only to tie a few basic nautical knots, but also being able to do so in the dark, upside down, and quite automatically. In the course of things I also became a better-than-average celestial navigator, a skill now made obsolete by satellite navigation. Both my automatized knot-tying and my equally automatized skill with a sextant also contribute to my sea-going self. I am, for reasons that totally elude me, very proud of these skills. But that self is not just subjectively in memory. I pay rather stiff annual dues faithfully and dutifully each year to two rather self-congratulatory cruising clubs to which I was solemnly elected on my "sailing record." I attend the meetings of neither: their doings embarrass me a bit. Why don't I resign? Well, I'm not sure.

How did I (my Self) get from the "there" of Frank Henning's dock to the "here" of my present, rather embarrassed sea-going self? There are some odd archaisms that I have to account for in the passage. What am I to make, for example, about the ironic satisfaction that I get from being a celestial navigator in an age of satellites? Is the irony essential to maintaining continuity? I even know how to caulk a wooden boat in an age when boats are mostly built of fiberglass and other synthetics. Why does that give me ironic satisfaction? It is surely not that I like antiques, or even antique skills. Indeed, I even have a great fondness for e-mail, for postmodern novelists, for good rap—all of which seem to be at odds with my pride in anachronistic and useless skills. How do I get these all together? Or do these things all live in separate compartments, separate Selves?

How many selves are there, anyway? In an almost forgotten volume, Sigmund Freud once proposed that a person could be conceived as a "cast of characters," as in a novel or play. He then proposed that what a playwright or novelist does is to decompose himself into a constituent cast of characters, and then construct a story that somehow brings them all together (Freud, 1956). I think Freud's account probably comes closer to what we do in constructing our Selves (or the Selves of others) than to what a novelist or playwright does. Be that as it may, I think his account provides a suggestive model. And it may also tell us something about the difficulties people encounter in constructing a "long-term" self, a matter mentioned earlier.

For the only way I seem to be able to manage the fusion of the "Self" of that twelve-year-old at Frank Henning's dock and the "me" who is writing this paper is by telling a story. And the moment I start doing so, I become easy prey to the library of such stories that my culture has on offer. I can tell the story in the genre of "the adult (reluctantly) setting aside the playthings of youth." Or I can use the "conversion–displacement" model of the dynamic psychologist, with my present self being a disguised version of me at age twelve. Indeed, an afternoon in the literary stacks of a university library could easily provide me with quite a stock of other story models that might serve. Some of them would be "righter" than others, in the sense of fitting better, or sounding more "authentic." But none of them would be "true" in any procedurally manageable sense of that word—no more so than any narrative can be true or false.

VII

So let us look a bit more closely into the nature and structure of narrative. Vladimir Propp (1968) argues (as already noted) that the protagonists and events in folk narrative are "functions" of the tale's overall structure. It has been widely supposed, as for example by Northrop Frye (1957), that there is a highly limited number of such narrative structures, constituting the "genres" of literature. The rich variety of tales in any culture's treasury falls into these limited types. Within any one genre, there are many ways of filling the functions demanded by it. The "hero" of Propp's "wonder tale," for example, is required to be a culturally entitled figure, and for the story to begin appropriately, he must have been left to his own resources by some higher authority. He can be a prince, a young genius, a courageous believer, whatever, so long as he is culturally entitled and left to his own resources. In the wonder-tale genre, he must then go on a canonical quest—for the Grail, for hidden treasure, for an elixir, whatever. It is then required by the genre that he encounter a figure with extraordinary power who offers him some form of supernatural aid in his quest: a tireless horse, an endless golden thread, the gift of tongues, the power of foresight, whatever. To work, the tokens that fill each function must create and preserve the narrative coherence of the whole. The chief protagonist must perform appropriate acts that get him toward proper goals, must deal properly with commitments and persist in overcoming them, must ally himself appropriately and deploy his resources fittingly.

Propp's wonder tales are ancient and smoothed by usage. But new genres emerge that are less smooth and determined in structure. The "inward turn" of the novel (Auerbach, 1953; Bruner, 1990; Heller, 1976) in the last century even produced new genres, as in the novels of Joyce or Proust or Musil. The changes in narrative convention that have resulted may even transform our notions of possible selves. Charles Taylor's magisterial *Sources of the Self* (1989) certainly suggests that it has. All that seems clear is that our conceptions of selfhood, and even our ways of structuring our private experience of Self, get modified to match the changing narrative conventions of the times. The Romantic dictum that life imitates art certainly sounds less upside down than it used to!

VIII

I want to turn finally to a curious question that emerges from what has been said up to now. If selves modelled on the narratives imposed on a life, how do these narratives get into the life? How do the culture's narratives work their way inward to the Self? Few people, surely, ever write or think out their lives in a completed or even a fully organized narrative. Most lives are recounted fitfully and patchily: in excuses for this act or in justifications for that belief or desire. We like to say that such local patches of a life are derived from some more *implicit* life narrative that we have "in memory" or "in imagination" or somewhere. But I must admit that, as a person who has written one, and has read and listened to a good many narrative autobiographies, I doubt that there are stored implicit narratives. Told self-narratives are more typically purpose-built for the occasion. And most lives in the process of being told are, as already noted, rather notable for their uncertainties, with their turning points, their ziggings and zaggings, their isolated episodes and events, their undigested details. Well-wrought self-narratives are rare. When you encounter them, they seem as if rehearsed. Even that broken-boned gifted young poet lost his way once he got into the nitty gritty of his autobiography.

So what stored internal schema guides our self accounts? I think that question obscures the issue. I would like to propose, rather, that self construction is preeminently a *meta*cognitive pursuit—like reconceiving some familiar territory in order to put it into a more general topography. We create the mountain ranges, the plateaus, the continents, in retrospect, by our reflective efforts: We impose bold and imaginative metastructures on local details to achieve coherence. This is not to say that the local details are not experientially real in our memories. It is only that they need to be placed in a wider context. Every clinician listening to his patients, every priest hearing confessions, every attorney working up a "case" with a client for litigation— they each know this compelling truth. What is interesting about these professions is that their practitioners are provided with appropriate models to help their clients fashion overall narratives out of the bits and pieces of their lives to fit the purpose at hand. The clinician has his theories; the priest his doctrines of repentance and redemption; the attorney his adversarial procedures for establishing culpability and counter-culpability. But in fact we don't even need professionals to help us most of the time. Most of the time we help each other in the process of dialogue.

Why metacognitive, and why not stored schemas or skeleton narratives?

There are very few ordinary occasions when we are called upon to reconstruct "larger-scale" versions of ourselves and our lives. Mostly, such occasions come when a physician takes our medical history, or when we apply for admission to a university or club, or fill in forms for a fellowship and are asked our reasons for applying. And, of course, we do the usual self-construction when we offer reasons and excuses, as already noted. We keep these accounts "to the point" to adhere to the Gricean maxims about being brief, perspicuous, relevant, and truthful (Grice, 1989; see particularly the chapter entitled "Logic and Conversation"). But a life story and an extended self in the broader sense are not just about excuses for being late, nor about childhood measles. Whatever they are about, we do not often take much time or trouble constructing them coherently and in detail. We seem to believe, each of us, that if called upon to do it, we have the means readily at hand. There may be another reason for this.

I believe that there is something both culturally adaptive and psychologically comfortable about "keeping one's options open" where one's life story is concerned. For fixing the story of one's life, and with it one's conception of one's Self, may shut down possibilities prematurely. A fixed-in-advance life-story creates, to use Amélie Rorty's expression (1976), a "figure" with no options. In our social world, the more fixed one's self-concept, the more difficult it is to manage change. "Staying loose" makes repair and negotiation possible. Not so surprising, then, that turning points are so characteristic of the autobiographies we finally write or tell.

Why are we so sure we can spell out our lives and Selves if asked to, despite our reluctance to fix our position? I suspect that the illusion of narrative self-constructability inheres in our confidence in the narrative possibilities present in natural languages. Let me say a word about this.

Some colleagues and I had the good fortune of analyzing the bedtime soliloquies of a child, Emmy, between her second and third birthdays—lengthy monologues after lights were out and parents had withdrawn (see particularly Bruner & Lucariello, 1989). Many of these were autobiographic, even by Professor Lejeune's definition. It was a year in which a baby brother was born and in which Emmy entered the noisy, brawling world of nursery school. In her soliloquies she goes over her daily life, seeking to establish what is reliable and canonical, what is steady enough to "should be." She "tries on" stances toward the people and events recounted, expressing them by such locutions as "I wish that . . ." or "I don't really know whether . . ." It became plain to us in the course of this lengthy study that the act of self-accounting—at least, short-term accounting—is acquired almost with the acquisition of language itself.

So something like a "natural language" of artless autobiography seems to be accessible to us from early on in the form of connectives, causals, temporal markers, and the like. But to employ these narratively friendly linguistic forms to create a coherent and extended self-story requires something more than just linguistic skill. It also requires narrative skill and a stock of narratives or narrative components. Giving excuses and reasons for particular acts and justifying our desires does not provide us with such equipment. Such episodic self-accountings do not provide us the means for fitting into a wider cultural surround, or even for becoming acquainted with the cultural affordances on which our existence depends. All of this requires a more extended form of learning, which we seem rather reluctant to do, except under special conditions.

What then leads people to "move up" to a more comprehensive, more temporally extended, more narratively structured, mode of self-accounting? Why do we ever construct more extended versions of Self, even granting our cautious attitude toward them mentioned earlier? One can easily oversimplify answers to these questions by falling back on clichés—like the alleged need of people to justify their lives when they imagine themselves to be under the gun of criticism, as with the accused politician's apologia so familiar in our times; or the cliché that people, seized by guilt, need to expiate their sins. I think we can do better than clichés.

Indeed, the major impetus to more extended autobiographical self-accounting may be suggested by the very nature of the narratives that we choose to use when we do more extended accounting. Many students of narrative—notably, Kenneth Burke (1945), Hayden White (1981), and William Labov (Labov & Waletzky, 1967)—have noted that the very *engine* of narrative is *trouble* (J. Bruner, 1986, 1990), sensed trouble, or what we referred to before as *jeopardy*. Narrative, as we know, begins with an explicit or implicit indication of a stable, canonical state of the world, and then goes on to an account of how it was disrupted, elaborates on the nature and consequences of the disruption, and climaxes with an account of efforts to restore the original canonical state, or to redress its violation. It is specialized for dealing with troubles created by departures from legitimacy—a meta-genre for encompassing the travails of jeopardy.

Trouble, then, may not only be the engine of narrative, but the impetus for extending and elaborating our concepts of Self. Small wonder that it is the chosen medium for dealing not only with Trouble, but for constructing and reconstructing the Self.

James Young reports that many concentration camp inmates during the Holocaust were obsessed with autobiographically recording the horrors they were living through and often risked their lives to do so secretly (Young, 1988). These memories are gripping, but few go beyond mere witness, for to achieve the detachment required for meta-cognition in the daily life of Auschwitz or Ravensbruck was virtually impossible, for it was precisely *detachment* that these *Lagern* were designed to destroy. But some succeeded, such as Primo Levi and a few others. Take this excerpt from Levi (1984), in which he is trying to understand what he is experiencing while attempting to reformulate his sense of Self. (Tragically, he did not fully succeed, for he committed suicide in despair several years after this was written.) But the excerpt tells more about indicators of selfhood than can any scholarly prose. It is about the author's life at a chemical factory close to Auschwitz where he was sent to work as a slave-chemist, and it is told preparatory to an account about stealing cerium rods from the factory, returning each night to trade them (as lighter-flints) with the camp guards for foods and favors at Auschwitz.

> I was a chemist in a chemical plant, in a chemical laboratory (this too has been narrated), and I stole in order to eat. If you do not begin as a child, learning how to steal is not easy; it had taken me several months before I could repress the moral commandments and acquired the necessary techniques, and at a certain point I realized (with a flash of laughter and a pinch of satisfied ambition) that I was reliving—*me*, a respectable little university graduate—the involution–evolution of a famous respectable dog, a Victorian, Darwinian dog who is deported and becomes a thief in order to live in his Klondike *Lager*—the great Buck of *The Call of the Wild*. I stole like him and like the foxes: at every favorable opportunity but with sly cunning and without exposing myself. I stole everything except the bread of my companions. (p. 140)

Perhaps I have chosen too extreme an example. We obviously do not need such extremity to prompt the process of self-reconstruction. Consciousness-raising, which contains a large element of self-reconstruction, is often an accompaniment of being marginalized, placed outside the reassurance of a mainstream. It is when Self is no longer able to function in a fashion that relates us to others and, indeed, to our prior conceptions of ourselves, that we turn to renewed self-construction. If one's self-concept neither serves to give us requisite individuation nor requisite mutuality with the other human beings on whom we depend, it is then that we set out to change Self.

In suggesting that trouble is what impels us to refashion Self, I do not mean to imply that trouble is something decreed by fate, or that it simply comes upon us through bad luck—though there must surely be troubles of that kind, like death itself. Some human beings have a sensibility that disposes or impels them to see troubles where others see only a texture of ordinariness. Whether this sensibility comes by dint of intelligence, temperament, or imagination, it seems to drive those gifted with it to deeper Selfhood, to great instability in holding fast the limits of selfhood, or to both in some uncomfortable mix. The gifted writer, Eudora Welty, calls this sensibility "daring" and she ends her remarkable memoir with these words: "A sheltered life can be a daring life as well. For all serious daring starts from within" (Welty, 1983, p. 104).

It is in facing troubles, real or imagined, that we fashion a Self that extends beyond the here-and-now of immediate encounters, a Self better able to encompass both the culture that shapes those encounters and our memories of how we have coped with them in the past. The anomaly in all this, and perhaps it is the burden of our human species, is that to extend and elaborate our version of selfhood, either for ourself or for others, is to make the task of self-construction the more difficult. Meta-cognition may be the source of our self-making, but it is not an easy skill.

Perhaps as Kierkegaard hinted, the difficulty lies in the fact that life is lived forward, encounter by encounter, but Self is constructed in retrospect, meta-cognitively.

In conclusion, then, the Self is both outer and inner, public and private, innate and acquired, the product of evolution and the offspring of narrative. Our self-concepts are enormously resilient, but as we have learned tragically in our times, they are also vulnerable. Perhaps it is this combination of properties that makes Self such an appropriate if unstable instrument in forming, maintaining, and assuring the adaptability of human culture.

REFERENCES

ASTINGTON, J. (1994). *The child's discovery of the mind*. Cambridge: Harvard University Press.

AUERBACH, E. (1953). *Mimesis: The representation of reality in Western literature*. Princeton, NJ: Princeton University Press.

BENSON, C. (1993). *The absorbed self*. Hemel Hempstead: Harvester Wheatsheaf.

BOURDIEU, P. (1984). *Distinction: A social critique of the judgement of taste*. Cambridge: Harvard University Press.

BRUNER, E. M. (1986). Ethnography as narrative. In V. W. Turner and E. M. Bruner (Eds.), *The anthropology of experience* (pp. 139–155). Urbana, IL: University of Illinois Press.

BRUNER, J. (1986). *Actual minds, possible worlds*. Cambridge: Harvard University Press.

BRUNER, J. (1990). *Acts of meaning*. Cambridge: Harvard University Press.

BRUNER, J. (1992). Another look at New Look 1. *American Psychologist, 47,* 780–783.

BRUNER, J. (1995, June). *Self reconsidered*. Invited address to the annual meeting of the Society for Philosophy and Psychology, the State University of New York, Stony Brook.

BRUNER, J. & KALMAR, D. A. (in press). Toward a narrative model of Self. In M. Ferrari & R. J. Sternberg (Eds.), *Self-awareness: Its nature and development*. New York: Guilford Press.

BRUNER, J. & LUCARIELLO, J. (1989). Monologue as narrative recreation of the world. In K. Nelson (Ed.), *Narratives from the crib* (pp. 73–97). Cambridge: Harvard University Press.

BURKE, K. (1945). *A grammar of motives*. New York: Prentice-Hall.

CAMPBELL, J. (1994). *Past, space, and self*. Cambridge: MIT Press.

EIBL-EIBESFELD, I. (1975). *Ethology*. New York: Holt, Rinehart & Winston.

FERNALD, A. (1989). Intonation and communicative intent in mothers' speech to infants: Is the melody the message? *Child Development, 60,* 1497–1510.

FERNALD, A. (1991). Prosody in speech to children: Prelinguistic and linguistic functions. *Annals of Child Development, 8,* 43–80.

FREUD, S. (1956). *Delusion and dream: An interpretation in the light of psychoanalysis of Gravida, a novel, by Wilhelm Jensen* (P. Rieff, Ed.). Boston: Beacon Press.

FRYE, N. (1957). *Anatomy of criticism.* Princeton: Princeton University Press.

GERGEN, K. J. (1991). *The saturated self: Dilemmas of identity in contemporary life.* New York: Basic Books.

GOODWIN, C. & DURANTI, A. (1992). "Rethinking context: An introduction." In A. Duranti & C. Goodwin (Eds.), *Reading, thinking, context: Language as an interactive phenomenon* (pp. 1–42). Cambridge: Cambridge University Press.

GRICE, P. (1989). *Studies in the way of words.* Cambridge: Harvard University Press.

HELLER, E. (1976). *The artist's journey into the interior, and other essays.* New York: Harcourt Brace Jovanovich.

VON HOLST, E. (1973). *The behavioural physiology of animals and man.* London: Methuen.

HUMPHREY, N. (1983). *Consciousness regained.* Oxford: Oxford University Press.

HUMPHREY, N. (1986). *The inner eye.* London: Faber and Faber.

JAMES, W. (1890). Chapter 10. The consciousness of self. *The principles of psychology.* New York: H. Holt.

JOHANNSON, G. (1973). Visual perception of biological motion and a model for its analysis. *Perception and Psychophysics, 14,* 201–211.

LABOV, W. & WALETZKY, J. (1967). Narrative analysis: Oral versions of personal experience. In J. Helm (Ed.), *Essays on the verbal and visual arts: Proceedings of the 1966 Annual Spring Meeting of the American Ethnological Society* (pp. 12–44). Seattle: University of Washington Press.

LANGER, E. (1989). *Mindfulness.* Reading, MA: Addison Wesley.

LEJEUNE, P. (1989). *On autobiography.* Minneapolis: University of Minnesota Press.

LEVI, P. (1984). *The periodic table.* New York: Shocken Books.

LIFTON, R. (1993). *The protean self.* New York: Basic Books.

MARKUS, H. & KITAYAMA, S. (1991). Culture and the self: Implications for cognition, emotion, and motivation. *Psychological Review, 98,* 224–253.

MAYR, E. (1982). *The growth of biological thought: Diversity, evolution and inheritance.* Cambridge: Harvard University Press.

MERTON, R. K. (1968). *Social theory and social structure* (enlarged ed.). New York: Free Press.

MISCH, G. (1950). *A history of autobiography in antiquity* (2 vols.). London: Routledge & Paul.

NEISSER, U. (1988). Five kinds of self-knowledge. *Philosophical Psychology, 1,* 35–59.

NIEDENTHAL, P. M. & KITAYAMA, S. (EDS.) (1994). *The heart's eye: Emotional influences in perception and attention.* New York: Academic Press.

OCHS, E. (1988). *Culture and language development.* Cambridge: Cambridge University Press.

OCHS, E. & SCHIEFFELIN, B. (1983). *Acquiring conversational competence.* London: Routledge.

PROPP, V. (1968). *Morphology of the folktale* (2nd ed.). Austin: University of Texas Press.

RICOEUR, P. (1984). *Time and narrative* (vol. 1). Chicago: University of Chicago Press.

RICOEUR, P. (1992). *Oneself as another.* Chicago: University of Chicago Press.

RORTY, A. (1976). A literary postscript: Characters, persons, selves, individuals. In *The identities of persons.* Berkeley: University of California Press.

SAVAGE-RUMBAUGH, E. S., MURPHY, J., SEVCIK, R. A., BRAKKE, K. E., WILLIAMS, S. L. &

RUMBAUGH, D. M. (1993). Language comprehension in ape and child. *Monographs of the SRCD, 58,* (Whole Serial No. 233, 3–4).

SHORE, B. (1996). *Culture in mind: Cognition, culture and the problem of meaning.* New York: Oxford University Press.

SPENGEMANN, W. C. (1980). *The forms of autobiography: Episodes in the history of a literary genre.* New Haven, CT: Yale University Press.

TAYLOR, C. (1989). *Sources of the self: The making of modern identity.* Cambridge: Harvard University Press.

TOMASELLO, M. (1992). The social bases of language acquisition. *Social Development, 1*(1), 67–87.

WELTY, E. (1983). *One writer's beginnings: The William E. Massey Sr. Lectures in the History of American Civilization, 1983.* Cambridge: Harvard Unversity Press, p. 104.

WHITE, H. (1981). The value of narrativity in the representation of reality. In W. J. T. Mitchell (Ed.), *On narrative* (pp. 1–23). Chicago: University of Chicago Press.

YOUNG, J. E. (1988). *Writing and rewriting the Holocaust: Narrative and the consequences of interpretation.* Bloomington: Indiana University Press.

*William Hirst (right) is Professor of Psychology at the New School for
Social Research and has published widely on the topic of memory. He
co-edited with Joseph LeDoux* Mind and Brain *and with Robyn
Fivush and Eugene Winograd* Ecological Approaches to Cognition.
*His recent work has been on two quite different topics: amnesia and
conversational remembering. David Manier (left) is a postdoctoral
fellow at the New School and is co-editing a book with William Hirst
and James Miller entitled* Social Remembering. *Ioana Apetroaia
(center) is a graduate student at the New School.*

The Social Construction of the Remembered Self: Family Recounting[a]

WILLIAM HIRST,[b] DAVID MANIER, AND IOANA APETROAIA

Department of Psychology
New School for Social Research
New York, New York 10003

W\ho we are is shaped by what we remember, as well as by the clothes we wear, the people we interact with and our manner of interaction, our professional standing, and the place where we live. We are concerned here with understanding how memory contributes to the self. Some semantic memories have relevance to the self. People offer many generalizations about themselves without recollecting a specific episode to justify the assertion, as when an individual claims that she is a generous person without remembering any specific episode involving generosity. Even implicit memories may contribute to the self. The person who asserted her generosity may have done so because she was described this way by a friend the day before, but she may not be able to remember the conversation when making her assertion. Her assertion may have been primed by her past experience without her having any awareness of its influence. But not all semantic or implicit memories contribute to the self, such as semantic memories of a telephone number, a mathematical formula, or facts about the break-up of Yugoslavia, or implicit memories such as a subject's performance in a stem completion experiment or his improvement at mirror reading.

We focus here not on semantic or implicit memories, but on episodic or explicit memories. We confine ourselves to what has been called autobiographical memory. The exact definition of autobiographical memory has proven elusive (see Brewer, 1986). For us, people recollect autobiographical memories when they remember events from their own past. Thus, a person's claim of generosity can be justified by appeal to specific autobiographical memories—for instance, detailed recollections of dinners in which she

[a]This work was supported by grants from the National Institutes of Health (MH423535) and the McDonnell Foundation.

[b]Address for correspondence: William Hirst, Department of Psychology, New School for Social Research, 65 Fifth Avenue, New York, New York 10003. e-mail: hirst@newschool.edu

treated her friends, including where she dined, what she ate, and how the conversation went.

But when a person makes a claim about her generosity, she is doing more than merely recollecting these dinners. If these memories are to be incorporated into the self, then she must also weave them into a narrative about the self. Whatever their particular theory about the nature of the self, scholars generally agree that the self serves to connect disparate elements of an individual's actions, presentations, and recollections. If someone remembers that she treated four people to dinner, this recollection is open to multiple interpretations. It must be placed in a larger context: that her behavior is a life-long pattern, or that her dinner companions were influential and could be professionally helpful, or that her friends had recently complained about her stinginess. The narrative one would tell about the dinners would differ, depending on what background details one incorporated. What makes the autobiographical recollection important to the self is not the memories *per se,* but the interpretation of the memories, or more specifically, the narrative told around the memories.

Recognition of the importance of narratives to the self has inspired many psychologists to develop a narrative approach to the study of self. Bruner (1990), for instance, has distinguished between paradigmatic and narrative thinking and sees narrative thinking as central to the development of a sense of self. Spence (1982; see also Schafer, 1992) considered psychotherapy in light of the importance of narrative, emphasizing the distinction between historical and narrative truth. According to Spence, psychotherapists need not plumb the historical truth of a past conflict to aid patients. Rather they can assist patients by guiding them in making their narratives of the past more coherent, even if these revised narratives do not conform strictly to historical truth. David White and his colleagues have also taken a narrative approach to family therapy, illustrating how using narrative techniques such as "reframing" can lead to therapeutic change in the family context (White & Epston, 1990).

Some autobiographical narratives seem more central to the self than others. Certain narratives may be considered important or self-defining for almost everyone. Many psychoanalysts, for instance, find narratives around the resolution of the Oedipal complex to be of universal importance. And common sense suggests that most people would consider a narrative about the death of a loved one as more important to an individual's sense of self than a narrative about the events of a day of no particular note. The importance of autobiographical recollections to one's sense of self may also depend on culturally specific factors or the idiosyncrasies of an individual. Two narratives could contain the same event: for instance, eating pork. In one culture, this might represent an ordinary meal, while in another, it might be construed as a sin or a declaration of rebellion.

But even the mundane autobiographical narratives that make up most of our reminiscences may contain gems of self-definition. For instance, in the research described below, we solicited from a family narratives about a trip to Coney Island. In the course of telling the narrative, the mother noted with pride that they did not buy food on the trip. Rather she prepared it ahead of time and brought it along, asserting her caretaker role and her frugality. In the same conversation, the daughter talked about how her family made fun of her fear of the bumper cars, providing an implicit account of her standing in the family. Even something as ordinary as a family outing offers rich narrative veins from which to mine the material needed for the construction of the self.

One final point: As any therapist can attest, people do not have to include in their narratives an explicit account of how the recollected events help define themselves, or even be consciously aware of the meaning of their narrative. But whether explicitly stated, implicitly understood, or unappreciated, most narratives of the past can contain building blocks from which one can construct a sense of self.

Yet even if we acknowledge the importance of autobiographical memories to the construction of the self, we have only made one of several necessary steps towards understanding the remembered self. Much work on autobiographical memory and life narrative treats autobiographical narrative telling as an individual act, uninfluenced by the social context in which the telling occurs, but occasionally the conversational character of autobiographical remembering is acknowledged. In recent decades, psychoanalysts interested in building a narrative approach to therapy have stressed the conversational character of autobiographical narrative telling as they seek to transform life stories through conversations within the therapy session (Schafer, 1992; Spence, 1982; Labov & Fanshel, 1977). Bruner (1990) has sought to understand how membership in groups as diverse as families or drama collectives can shape autobiographical telling. Linguists and sociolinguists specializing in discourse analysis have examined the interaction between narrative telling and conversation (see Brown & Yule, 1983), but discourse analysis is rarely connected with extant theories of memory, autobiographical narrative telling, or the social psychology of the group (see, however, Linde, 1988).

Cognitive psychologists interested in autobiographical memory generally have not focused on the conversational nature of autobiographical remembering. Although the study of autobiographical memory grew out of the ecological validity movement, it does not as a rule reflect the conversational origins of much autobiographical remembering. Rather, it often mirrors more traditional studies of memory by asking subjects to remember autobiographical material individually (cf. Rubin, 1986, *passim*). For instance, a common technique for studying autobiographical memory asks subjects to remember events associated with a particular activity or action, the so-called Crovitz technique. Subjects recall the elicited event in a monologue, telling the story as the experimenters remain silent and aloof. A few cognitively oriented psychologists have examined what they call "group memory," but they do not analyze the conversations members of the group have as they remember collectively, concentrating instead on the product of the group interaction. Intensive investigation of conversational remembering is more likely to be found in a department of communication than in a cognitive psychological laboratory. The best example of such research is the work of Edwards and Middleton (Edwards & Middleton, 1986, 1988; Middleton & Edwards, 1990), but it was not designed to yield a cognitive model.

The relative absence of research on the conversational aspects of autobiographical remembering is unfortunate because such research could provide a means of understanding how the self is influenced by social interactions. We essentially want to take up this theme in this paper. We want to develop here what we construe as a cognitive psychological model. This model will trace in detail the connection between the social dynamics in conversational acts of autobiographical remembering and the life stories people tell. In this way, we hope to explore the role played by conversations within the family in the social construction of the remembered self.

Many cognitive psychologists may neglect the study of the conversational aspects of autobiographical remembering, not because they are unaware of them, but because they think that they are of little importance. Conversational dynamics may shape what the participants in the conversation recount, the argument goes, but they do not have any lasting effect on the memory of the participants. A participant may be inclined to talk about the positive aspects of his college days at a reunion, because it is a time for him to celebrate with his former classmates. This upbeat rendering of this college experience, however, does not reshape his more nuanced memories of college. On another occasion, when he wants to convey the limitation of college, he will be capable of offering quite a different recounting of his college experiences.

We want to argue here that this received view is mistaken. The social dynamics governing a conversation not only determine what is recounted within the conversation, but also what is subsequently recounted. To the extent that this is true, then a full understanding of any act of conversational remembering must reach back to conversations previously had about the topic and the social dynamics governing these conversations. We want here to sketch a model that proceeds from the social dynamics of the group, to the conversational dynamics governing the recounting, to the recounting itself, and finally to subsequent acts of recounting.

The model is developed in the context of family recounting. If we are to discuss the social dynamics of a group, then it is probably best to start with a particular kind of group. Families represent an ideal case, because of the generally acknowledged impact the family has on individual development and in particular, the self. Moreover, psychologists and sociologists have intensely studied the social dynamics underlying family interaction (e.g., see Boss, Doherty, LaRossa, Schumm & Steinmutz, 1993). There has even been extensive study of the conversational patterns of families (see Fitzpatrick & Ritchie, 1993).

Thus, in the present model, we want to trace the relation between family dynamics and autobiographical memory. The model is preliminary. We have only begun to collect the necessary empirical evidence needed to make our model credible. We outline the model here in its preliminary stage because we hope to show how it may be possible to chart the influence of social interactions within a group on the ways in which the group—in this case, the family—shapes individual members' autobiographical narratives.

THE MODEL

The relation between family dynamics and family members' memories is probably not direct. Rather the link from family dynamics to the memories family members have of their shared past is mediated by several distinct steps (FIGURE 1.) Our claim is that family dynamics affect what roles family members hold as the family, as a group, recounts its shared past (for details, see Manier, 1996). We suggest that family members may hold three important, mnemonically relevant roles: *narrator, monitor,* and *mentor.* These roles engender specific activities that influence what family members recount collec-

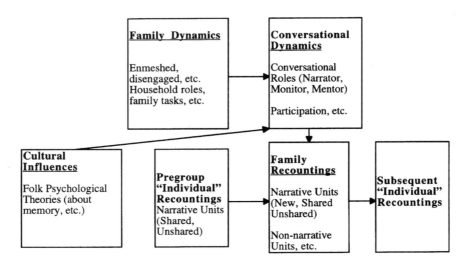

FIGURE 1. Model tracing the influence of family dynamics on the memories of family members.

tively. The resulting recounting in turn can reshape what family members might subsequently remember. We claim that each step—from family dynamics to conversational dynamics, from conversational dynamics to family recounting, from family recounting to subsequent recollection—is guided by its own set of principles. Nevertheless, taken as a whole, these principles can guide one in tracing the relation of family dynamics to the individual recollections of family members. One can predict, for instance, whether family conversations differentially affect subsequent memory in enmeshed and disengaged families by tracing through the three steps in FIGURE 1, determining first the effect of, for instance, being enmeshed on the distribution of roles, then the effect this distribution has on what is recounted, and finally the effect of the recounting on subsequent recollection. This three-step model, then, provides a framework for understanding how one might map one facet of family dynamics—whether the family is enmeshed or disengaged—onto what family members remember about their shared past.

We are chiefly concerned here with articulating the subtasks a family might distribute across members as it collectively recounts a shared past. Other researchers have studied how groups of unrelated people arrive at a consensus memory, that is, a memory on which subjects agree (Benjamin, 1992; Eisenberg, 1985; Stephenson, Clark & Wade, 1986; see Clark & Stephenson, 1989, for a review). This research has been chiefly interested in analyzing *what* is remembered rather than *how* it is remembered. We are concerned with articulating the subtasks a family might distribute across members as it collectively recounts a shared past. For anything as complex as a conversation, a family has a variety of different tasks to accomplish: to remember the past, to tell the story in a coherent manner, to make sure the story is told without too much disruption in the relationships among family members. Families, either collectively or as individuals, no doubt have theories of how the process of remembering works. We contend that they use these "folk psychological" theories to break the act of remembering into component processes or subtasks. They then distribute these mnemonically relevant subtasks across the family. To the extent that the family's folk psychological theories actually correspond to what "occurs in the head," then one can speak of the family externalizing and distributing what an individual might do when remembering singly (see Fivush, 1991; Fivush & Fromhoff, 1988; Fivush & Hudson, 1990; Nelson, 1993; Vygotsky, 1978; Wertsch, 1991; also see work on distributed acts of committing material to memory, e.g., Wegener, 1986; Wegener, Erber & Raymond, 1991). Similar claims have been made for other collective acts of cognition (Lave, 1991; Reiss, 1981; Schuman, 1990; Vygotsky, 1978). We want to claim that the same principle holds for family recounting.

Of course, in an act of conversational remembering, participants could fail to appreciate that remembering can be broken down into component processes and that these component processes could be distributed across individuals. Rather, each individual could accept the full burden of telling his or her story, one person telling his recollection without comment on what is said by other family members. The recounting could unfold serially, one story following another. Or, the stories could all be told simultaneously. Alternatively, one person could offer his or her recollection, while the others remain silent. This assignment of storytelling could arise out of the family "power structure" or from the place in the family (mother, father, sister, brother).

Our claim here is that such scenarios rarely if ever occur. Rather, family members appear to adopt specific and well-defined mnemonically relevant roles based on their (often implicit) folk psychological theories about the processes of remembering. The division of recounting into subtasks and the distribution of these subtasks need not occur consciously. It may simply grow out of the family's interactional patterns, without family members being aware that they have selected, or even that they hold, different roles. Moreover, the development of folk psychological theories of memory, the division of the process of remembering into its components, and even the appropriate distribution of these processes across a family may occur not at the beginning of a particular act of recounting, but may result from a complex sociohistorical process. For many families, who occupies what role may reflect a long-standing pattern of conversational interaction. At some point, the family fell into a pattern in which roles were fairly well specified, and it has adhered to this pattern ever since. In other cases, the roles were fairly well specified, and it has adhered to this pattern ever since. In other cases, the roles held by family members may be determined by cultural conventions. Whatever the scenario, the "externalization and distribution" of mnemonically relevant conversational roles may be best viewed in sociohistorical terms, following Vygotsky, rather than as an individual or group effort occurring as each act of recounting begins. Clearly, a full understanding of the dynamics of role specification and role distribution would entail a multidisciplinary exploration outside the scope of this paper.

What might the mnemonically relevant roles be? One way to gain insight into this question is to examine what people say they are doing when trying to remember. In their analysis of just such protocols (e.g., Williams, 1977), Norman & Bobrow (1979) discerned three aspects to remembering: (1) *retrieval specification*, an activity in which people specified what had to be remembered, gave partial descriptions of the target, and outlined the acceptable format of a recollection; (2) *match*, an activity in which the retrieval specification was matched with the encoded information and a memory was produced (or in our case, a narrative); and (3) *evaluation*, an activity in which the retrieved information was verified.

We recognize that there is more to remembering than is captured by these three processes. Nevertheless, we assert that, from a folk psychological perspective (or, at least, from the folk psychological perspective of people like those of Norman & Bobrow's sample) a core, if not *the* core activity, or any act of autobiographical narrative remembering is the act of recounting the memory in narrative form. (Norman and Bobrow's *matching* component corresponds in a loose way to this activity. Matching, for Norman and Bobrow, involves the act of retrieving. We are speaking here of retrieving in narrative form.) We call this activity *narrating*. We also posit that people evaluate whether what they have retrieved and narrated is valid (Norman and Bobrow's third element). We will call this activity *monitoring*. Finally, we will refer to Norman and Bobrow's "retrieval specification" as *mentoring*, the process of guiding or facilitating an act of remembering. Mentoring involves such things as *(a)* supplying retrieval cues to guide further remembering, for instance prompts such as "We ate something while we were there—what was it?" or *(b)* offering guidelines as to what should be remembered and what needs to be expanded upon, for instance, when a person says, "You are getting off the track," or "You should be trying to remember what you did last summer, not three summers ago."

A central claim here is that family members adopt roles of *narrator, monitor*, and *mentor* when recounting. As the research described in the section below suggests (see also Hirst & Manier, 1996a, 1996b; Manier & Hirst, 1996; Manier, Pinner & Hirst, 1996), there is little doubt that this occurs. Using an elaborate coding scheme we developed, we discerned the roles of Narrator, Monitor, and Mentor in the recountings of two families. But our observations would be of limited importance if this distribution of mnemonic tasks did not have some functional consequences.

According to the perspective being developed here, what a family recounts and what family members subsequently recollect are the result of the mnemonic potential of the individual family members and the mnemonically relevant activities engendered by the roles of Narrator, Monitor, and Mentor in the family recounting. The place of family members in the family, their power, their economic prowess, or their expertise may guide families as they distribute conversational roles across the family. The role held by a family member will in turn determine what mnemonically relevant activity he or she will undertake. And it is this activity that in the end determines what is recounted.

Thus, Narrators, as the persons telling the story, should have a better chance of imposing their version of the past onto the family recounting than would Monitors or Mentors. Mentors, on the other hand, may have more of a chance of directing the telling toward their perspective than would Monitors. Mentors, after all, guide the narrating, whereas Monitors only assess it.

What family members recount, then, is directly determined by whether they act as a Narrator, Monitor, or Mentor, and only indirectly by their place in the family, their power, their economic prowess, or their expertise. Memory theorists adopting a processing perspective have made a similar point in other contexts (for a discussion of this point, see Hirst, 1988). For instance, process theorists have noted that the motivation of an individual may affect memory performance, but only through motivated mnemonic activity. A person may be strongly motivated to remember, for instance, a list of concrete words, but he will remember the list less well than an unmotivated individual if the unmotivated individual images the words and the motivated individual does not. It is what the person does—image or fail to image—that matters, not the motivation (Bower, 1972).

Along the same lines, in some families the most powerful person may narrate; in others, someone with less power may narrate. What ultimately shapes the recounting is who adopts the Narrator role and how strong a Narrator he or she is, not who is most powerful. Power and other family characteristics no doubt contribute to the role assignment, but it is what family members do while recounting—whether they narrate, monitor, or mentor—that matters.

We have now a more detailed version of the model (again, see FIGURE 1). The family divides the task of recounting into subcomponents and its members assume various conversational roles, each designed to perform one or more of these component tasks. (This can be done at the beginning of an act of conversational remembering, consciously or unconsciously, or it may follow a pre-established pattern, formed over time as family members learn to interact with each other.) Family dynamics influence the distribution of roles among family members; this will be discussed in the next section of this paper. Once roles are established, each member contributes to the act of recounting according to his or her assumed role. The resulting activity affects what is recounted and subsequently recollected.

One final comment: Although we view the collective act of recounting as the externalization and distribution of internal processing, the recounting of a family is not the same thing as the recollections of an individual family member. What individuals remember singly depends on their perspective toward the remembered material (what Bartlett, 1932, called "attitude" and others have referred to as "schema") and their "mnemonic potential" (i.e., the information stored in memory). But in an act of conversational remembering, participants will have different perspectives and differing mnemonic potentials. How an individual's perspective and mnemonic potential influence the collective act of remembering will depend on his or her role in the conversation. The resulting recounting, then, will in most cases differ from what an individual would recollect singly. It is reconstructed through social interaction mediated by the conversation rather than solely through the internal processing of the individual participants in the conversation. Moreover, the recounting can alter the individual's potential to remember and his or her attitude toward the material. Subsequent acts of recollection, then, could be expected to reflect the social interaction shaping previous acts of recounting.

EMPIRICAL SUPPORT

Conversational Roles

Four core claims in the model sketched in Figure 1 are: (1) that conversational dynamics involved in an act of recounting can be characterized by the roles of Narrator, Monitor and Mentor; (2) that the roles family members adopt shape what the family remembers; (3) that acts of group remembering in turn shape subsequent individual memories; and (4) that family dynamics determine what roles family members adopt. We sought to address all four of these claims. With the assistance of Stephen Hartman and Elizabeth Pinner, we therefore began our research with the examination of two quite distinct families to determine whether we could detect the conversational roles family members adopted throughout a conversation.

The first family, the Patels, immigrated to New York from India two years prior to our study. They were Roman Catholics, and attended Mass regularly. The father, 44 years old, was studying for a Ph.D. in engineering; the 36-year-old mother worked as an administrative assistant to support the family. A 17-year-old son had just graduated from a Catholic high school and was planning to start college soon, and a 15-year-old daughter had just finished her sophomore year in high school. Everyone in the family was thoroughly bilingual, with both Telegu and English spoken at home.

The second family, the Ionescus, live in a small town in the northeast of Romania, in a region known as Moldavia. They were interviewed in Romanian, and the transcription and coding of their interviews was done by native speakers of Romanian trained in the methods described in this paper. The 46-year-old mother is a secretary in a junior high school, and the 51-year-old father is a teacher of history at the same school. The 19-year-old daughter had just finished high school and was applying for college, and the 17-year-old son was a junior in high school.

Method

We asked our families to recount certain past events experienced by the family. Through administering a questionnaire and interviewing family members, we ensured that each family member had participated in the events and could remember them clearly. After a careful selection process, we decided upon which events the families would discuss. The events described here were selected in part because of their autobiographical significance and possible relevance to the construction of the self of each family member.

For each family, we individually asked each member, outside the presence of the other members, to tell an interviewer unknown to them a narrative about the events—we will refer to this as the "pregroup recounting." A week later, we asked the family to recall the events in a group conversation in which all were encouraged to take part freely. In this "group recounting," the family assembled in their living room and recounted to a different interviewer, also unknown to them, their recollections. In both the pregroup and group recounting, we did not impose time constraints and encouraged the family to recall as much as they could. The interviewers were instructed to contribute as little as possible to the discussions—simply to say "Tell me everything you can remember about . . . ," then to listen quietly, and finally to ask "Is that all?" until the interviewees responded affirmatively.

As mentioned above, the stories we elicited contained elements that could contribute to the construction of the self of each family member. We have already noted how one story, about a trip to Coney Island, contained elements relevant to the construction of the self. For the elements we discussed, we focused on the mother and the daughter in the Patel family. Other examples will reinforce the point. For example, the Ionescus told a story about a wedding, which centered around the children's attempt to avoid the ceremony, and the parents' effort to get their children to come—a typical scenario touching on both the children's need for independence and the parents' attention to family responsibility. The Ionescus told another story about a trip to the mountains, which allowed each member of the family to discuss, through a concrete instance, their romance with the countryside and their love of the mountains. The narratives analyzed here all concerned events of personal significance to each of the family members, and all were recounted in a way that demonstrated their relevance to the construction of self (see Manier and Apetroaia, 1996).

Uncovering the Roles

We videotaped and transcribed both the pregroup and group recountings. We divided the transcribed text into what we will call narrative units. A *narrative unit*, consisting of a subject (perhaps implicit) and predicate, describes a single "state," "action," or "event." They may include temporal tags and other descriptive phrases, but these phrases cannot describe an *additional* state, event, or action. The sentences "I enjoyed the amusement rides" and "We saw the polar bear," which describe, respectively, a state and an event, are narrative units. The sentence "We went to Coney Island the year we came to the United States" would also be coded as a single narrative unit, inasmuch as the temporal tag "the year we came to the United States" does not describe an additional action. On the other hand, "We went to the amusement park and to the beach" would be coded as two narrative units because it entails two actions. Narrative units are similar to the "terminal nodes" of the story grammar devised by Mandler and Johnson (1977; see also Kintsch, 1974; Stein & Glenn, 1979).

Not every utterance in the transcribed discourse could be called a narrative unit. Meta-memory statements, such as "I can't remember," or overt requests for assistance, such as "Was last Christmas the one we spent at home?" do not describe either an event or a state. We treated such utterances as *non-narrative units*. Thus, we divided the text into narrative and non-narrative units.

Both narrative and non-narrative units were divided into more specific categories—"structural units," which were adapted from Middleton and Edwards (1990). Narrative units were subdivided into *narrative tellings, contextualizing statements*, and *affective-evaluative remarks*. Non-narrative units were specified further as *meta-memory statements, meta-narrative statements, facilitating remarks, overt requests for assistance, responses to overt requests*, and *assessing statements*. We were chiefly interested in narrative tellings, facilitating remarks, and assessing statements, which are defined as follows:

Narrative Tellings	Describe states or events that are linked together (casually, temporally, or spatially) and that relate to a central topic or theme. *Examples:* "We went to all these other places and then we went to Coney Island, and we went to the aquarium. We went to the amusement park and we went to the beach."
Facilitating Remarks	Attempt to spur someone else to further the narrative, provide more details, or "search their memory." Also, may evaluate someone else's narrative with (implicit or explicit) reference to standards of narrative structure. *Examples:* "What did we eat there?" "What did you, what else do you remember?" "Keep to the point." "That's irrelevant."
Assessing Statements	Agree, disagree, or in some other way judge the validity of a previous statement that is not an overt request for assistance. Includes a repetition of a phrase just spoken by someone else, as well as responsive utterances like, "oh," "okay," and "sure" (but not responses to overt questions). *Examples:* "Yeah, that's right." "No, you're wrong."

Two coders went through the transcripts of both the pregroup and the group recountings jointly. The coders divided the text of the group recountings into narrative and non-narrative units and then further into structural units, resolving any disagreements that arose (out of a total of 744 narrative units in all the analyzed stories, there were 78 disagreements to be resolved). We also coded in the same manner the pregroup recountings. These consisted almost entirely of narrative units, except for a few meta-memory statements and contextualizing statements that were not relevant to our present analysis. They were coded in the same manner.

We defined the roles of Narrator, Monitor, and Mentor as follows:

> NARRATORS: assume the function of telling the story. Their utterances are meant in some fashion to "further the narrative." Generally speaking, a Narrator's utterances preserve "narrative continuity" (cf. Middleton and Edward's "default continuity"), that is, any given narrative telling is interlinked (either causally, spatially, temporally, or thematically) with narrative tellings that precede or follow it. Characteristically, they might be expected to: utter a large share of the group's meta-narrative statements (e.g., "I'm getting off the point"); seek outside confirmation, perhaps by making overt requests for assistance; and endeavor to "contextualize" the narrative.

> MENTORS: assume the function of prompting Narrators to further their narratives and provide more details. They encourage Narrators to adhere to standards of narrative form and content, spurring Narrators on by providing criticisms, directions, helpful remarks, substantial queries, and memory probes. Rather than furthering the narrative directly through their own utterances. Mentors guide the narrative telling, often by providing retrieval cues to Narrators in order to elicit further recollections from them.

> MONITORS: assume the function of explicitly agreeing or disagreeing with the utterances of the Narrator, without taking personal responsibility for constructing the narrative. They attempt to ensure that the narrative, as told by the Narrator, correctly and completely describes the episode, as remembered by the Monitor.

Working with these intuitive definitions of conversational roles, we developed the following more rigorous definitions:

> NARRATORS: Narrative tellings are among the two most frequent structural units within their contributions to the group conversation. Also, they must utter at least a chance share of all the narrative tellings uttered by all family members within the conversation. For a family of four, this means that they must utter at least 25% of the narrative tellings uttered by all participants in the conversation.

MENTORS: Facilitating remarks are among the two most frequent structural units within their contributions to the group conversation. Also, they must utter at least a chance share of all the facilitating remarks uttered by all family members within the conversation.

MONITORS: Assessing statements are among the two most frequent structural units within their contributions to the group conversation. Also, they must utter at least a chance share of all the assessing statements uttered by all family members within the conversation.

These definitions lead to the concept of the *strength of a conversational role*, which captures the degree to which a family member appears to adopt that role throughout a conversation.

NARRATOR: strength of Narrator role = $N/2$, where N = the percentage of the Narrator's tellings out of the total number of structural units he or she contributed + the percentage of the Narrator's narrative tellings out of the total uttered in the conversation.

MENTOR: strength of Mentor role = $F/2$, where F = the percentage of the Mentor's facilitating remarks out of the total number of structural units he or she contributed + the percentage of the Mentor's facilitating remarks out of the total in the conversation.

MONITOR: strength of Monitor role = $A/2$, where A = the percentage of the Monitor's assessing statements out of the total number of structural units he or she contributed + percentage of Mentor's assessing statements out of the total in the conversation.

Results

We confine our analysis here to two stories recounted by the Patels and four stories recounted by the Ionescus. TABLE 1 contains the strength of the roles for each family member averaged over the recounted stories. As TABLE 1 indicates, for the Patels, the daughter served as Narrator, showing strength that far exceeded that of any other family member. The father held the role of Mentor.

As for the Ionescus, the family seemed less inclined to assign to a single member the role of Narrator. All four family members were fairly strong Narrators. The daughter was clearly the weakest Narrator, but even she was fairly strong (at least if we compare her strength with the non-Narrators in the Patel family). As for the other conversational roles, the daughter was a strong Mentor. For the Ionescus, family dynamics did not lead to the assignment of a single family member as the Narrator. Rather the task was shared. The task of Mentor, however, was not. Here the family dynamics led

TABLE 1. Average Strength of the Family Members for Three Roles

	Narrator	Monitor	Mentor
Patels			
Daughter	.60	.17	.07
Father	.19	.22	.51
Mother	.34	.27	.40
Son	.23	.15	.00
Ionescus			
Daughter	.33	.18	.43
Father	.46	.04	.00
Mother	.59	.25	.13
Son	.42	.17	.00

the daughter to serve as the Mentor with greater strength than any other family member.

The results clearly indicated that families do not recount their past jointly in the same manner. In all cases we could clearly discern at least one Narrator. That narration occurs is not surprising. After all, the instructions essentially ask the families to tell a narrative. On the other hand, there was no *a priori* reason to expect that one family member would alone adopt the role of Narrator in a recounting while other family members deferred to him or her. The degree to which a family deferred to a single member and allowed him or her to occupy the Narrator role alone varied. For the Patels, the daughter strongly held the role of Narrator in both analyzed stores. For the Ionescus, the mother was a strong Narrator, but other family members occasionally also strongly held the role of Narrator. Indeed, in one story recounted by the Ionescus, at least three of the four members strongly occupied the role of Narrator.

THE FUNCTIONAL CONSEQUENCES OF ADOPTING A CONVERSATIONAL ROLE

Of course, the concept of conversational roles is of interest only if it has functional consequences, that is, only if it affects what a family recounts. We concentrate here on the relation between what a family remembers jointly and what family members recollect individually (as probed by the pregroup recollection).

According to the model presented in FIGURE 1, family members may adopt distinct conversational roles, some of which could contribute more to the construction of a memory than others. If conversational roles shape family recountings in the way that we claim in FIGURE 1, then we would expect that the recounting should reflect the distribution of conversational roles across the family. For some situations, each family member might accept the responsibility of narrating the story, as family members did in the Ionescu family. As a consequence, the recounting should reflect the joint and equal contribution of all family members. In other situations, when there is only one strong Narrator, as was the case for the Patels, the family recounting should reflect in the main the version of the past expressed by this Narrator. More specifically, if the pregroup recountings of the family members differ substantially from each other, and the group recountings are sufficiently long, then when there is only one strong Narrator in the recounting, the details the Narrator uniquely produced in her pregroup recall (what we call unshared narrative units) should be more likely to surface in the family recounting than would the unshared pregroup narrative units of any other family member.

Thus, one would expect that the relation between pregroup and group recountings will differ for our two families. For the Patels, where the daughter served as a strong Narrator, the family recounting should reflect the version of the past told in the Narrator's pregroup recounting. For the Ionescus, where all family members shared the role of Narrator, the family recounting should be a consensus of the pregroup recountings of the four family members.

In order to test this claim, we asked the two coders to compare the narrative units produced in the pregroup recollections of each family member to those of every other member, assessing whether the narrative units shared the same meaning. The following example illustrates the method we followed. One of the narrative units in the Patel family's recollection of the most recent Christmas related to the time of day of the Christmas Mass they attended. In the group recounting, the daughter simply made the following statement: "As usual we went to, um, midnight Mass." In the pregroup recountings family members differed on this matter somewhat. The son gave the following statement: "uh, it's like just we went to a Christmas Mass, like th- the night Mass." The daughter made two statements on this issue: First, "um, last Christmas was, um, we went for an, uh, late Mass." Later she is more specific: "We went, I think, at eleven thirty [p.m.] or something to church." The mother states what happened a bit indirectly: "So we wanted to experience the night Mass, in, uh, the church. So we went, um, all decked up in Indian clothes." The father's account disagrees with those of the other family members: "Uh, the only thing I can remember is we all went together to church in the, m-, morning, I don't know if it is nine o'-clock or ten o'clock."

As this example illustrates, the individual pregroup recounting of each family member contained some narrative units that were also uttered by other family members ("shared pregroup narrative units"), as well as some narrative units that were uttered by no other family members ("unshared pregroup narrative units"). The son, mother, and daughter all expressed the shared pregroup narrative unit, "we went to late night Mass." The daughter expressed an unshared pregroup narrative unit specifying that they went at eleven thirty. The mother, in addition to the shared pregroup narrative unit about attending late night Mass, also expressed two unshared pregroup narrative units, relating to what the family wore to church and what they "wanted to experience." The father's account of when they went to Mass contained only unshared pregroup narrative units, that is, his account substantially disagreed with that of everyone else.

Our analysis showed that the pregroup recountings of the four family members differed substantially from each other. For the two stories recounted by the Patels, 56% of the narrative units in the pregroup recountings of the four family members were recounted by only one family member. Only 2% of the narrative units were recounted by all four family members. For the Ionescus, 71% of the pregroup narrative units were unshared, while only 8% of the narrative units were recounted by all four family members. Clearly, the family members were not recounting the same events in their pregroup recollections.

In the present instances of conversational remembering, a large proportion of the narrative units appearing in the group did not match narrative units in any pregroup recounting, that is, they were "new" to the group recountings. For the Patels, on average, 46% of the narrative units were "new"; for the Ionescus, a surprising 67% of the narrative units were "new." Nevertheless, in all instances, a substantial number of the narrative units in the group recountings were determined by two judges to match narrative units in at least one family member's pregroup recounting. Does our prediction about the relation between unshared pregroup narrative units and group recountings hold for these items?

Let us first look at the Patels. When the pregroup recollections of the family members differ substantially, as they do here, there should be few shared narrative units to recount. As a result, when only one family member has the responsibility of narrating, the Narrator should be forced, by the arithmetic of the situation, to contribute more of her unique narrative units to the story than would other family members. For the Patels, the strength of the daughter as a Narrator was substantially greater than that of any other family member (.60 versus an average of .25 for the rest of the family). And as the only Narrator, she introduced more of her unique narrative units than did anyone else, as TABLE 2 indicates.

The daughter not only introduced a larger proportion of her unique narrative units into the recounting than did anyone else, but also contributed more such narrative units to the recounting than did any other family member. TABLE 3, which illustrates this point, examines the distribution among family members of three types of narrative units expressed in the group recounting: (1) new group narrative units: i.e., narrative units not appearing

TABLE 2. Effectiveness of Family Members at Introducing Into the Group Recountings Unshared Pregroup Narrative Units From Their Own Pregroup Recountings

	Totals for Both Group Recountings	
	Proportions[a]	Percentages
Patels		
Daughter	19/58	33%
Father	2/8	25%
Mother	2/22	9%
Son	2/40	5%
Ionescus		
Daughter	196/420	47%
Father	70/105	67%
Mother	50/96	58%
Son	251/390	76%

[a]Denominator represents number of unshared pregroup narrative units in each member's pregroup recountings. Numerator represents number of narrative units in each member's contribution to the group recounting that match unshared pregroup narrative units from that member's pregroup recounting.

in any pregroup recounting; (2) unshared group narrative units: i.e., those narrative units in the group recounting that match narrative units appearing in the pregroup recounting of only one family member, i.e., the "unshared pregroup narrative units," and that are expressed in the group recounting by that same family member; and (3) shared group narrative units: i.e.,

TABLE 3. Distribution Among Family Members of New, Unshared, and Shared Group Narrative Units (Includes Both Group Recountings)

	Types of Narrative Units			
	New	Unshared	Shared	All
Patels				
Daughter	51%	76%	51%	58%
Father	25%	8%	24%	20%
Mother	11%	8%	14%	11%
Son	13%	8%	11%	11%
Ionescus				
Daughter	10%	16%	19%	13%
Father	26%	27%	13%	24%
Mother	48%	35%	49%	47%
Son	15%	22%	20%	17%

those narrative units in the group recounting either matching the pregroup recountings of more than one family member, the "shared pregroup narrative units," or else expressed during the pregroup recountings by only one family member but expressed in the group recounting by a different family member. It is apparent that the daughter dominated in all three categories, especially for the unshared units. Moreover, she contributed more such units than would be expected from her overall contribution to the story. The recounting, then, reflected her version of the past.

Let us now turn to the Ionescus. Although the Ionescus introduced fewer unshared pregroup narrative units into the family recounting than did the Patels, they still were remarkably effective at finding a place for them in the family recounting, with 59% of the unshared pregroup narrative units appearing in the group recounting. Unlike the Patels, however, no single family member had a clear advantage (see TABLE 2). To be sure, the daughter, as the weakest Narrator, was the least successful in introducing her pregroup narrative units into the group recounting. But even the daughter, who still acted fairly strongly as a Narrator (with a strength of .33), introduced 47% of her unshared pregroup narrative units into the group recounting. If we look more carefully at the composition of the recounting, as we do in TABLE 3, we find that the equal distribution of the role of Narrator across the Ionescus also prevented any one family member from imposing his or her version of the past onto the narrative: Family members were no more likely to contribute an unshared pregroup narrative unit to the family recounting than would be expected from their overall contribution to the conversation. The mother, as the strongest Narrator, may have contributed more to getting these units introduced into the family conversations than anyone else, but her strength as Narrator was not sufficiently different from other family members to allow her to impose her version of the past onto the story.

Conversational roles can help explain what gets included in group recountings. What the group recounts will depend not only on the internal memory processing of the individuals in the family, but also on the conversational roles family members occupy. By making clear an advantage of functioning as a strong Narrator, attending to conversational roles helps us to understand why groups remember what they do. Our study produced several interesting findings:

First, three different conversational roles were characteristic of the family's group recountings, but the distribution of these roles differed from family to family. For the Patels, the daughter was primarily a Narrator, and the father was a Mentor. For the Ionescus, everyone was a fairly strong Narrator, and the daughter took on the additional role of Mentor.

Second, there were identifiable consequences of the conversational roles family members occupied. The relation between the pregroup recounting and the group recounting depended on the distribution of the role of Narrator across a family. There was one strong Narrator in the Patels' recountings and this Narrator's version of the past (as probed by the pregroup recollection) dominated the group recounting. Everyone strongly narrated in the Ionescus' recounting, and the family recountings could be considered more of a consensus or an average of the pregroup recountings than could those of the Patels. For both families, the story they told emerged out of the conversational dynamics of the recounting and can be understood only in those terms.

Finally, close to half the narrative units in the group recountings did not occur in any of the pregroup recountings. The group recountings contained more narrative units than any single pregroup recounting, though less than the sum total of the narrative units in all the pregroup recountings. These findings mean that the story told collectively by this family differed substantially from that told by the family members individually. Group dynamics presumably were also responsible for this difference.

THE EFFECT OF RECOUNTING ON SUBSEQUENT RECOLLECTION

The work with the Patels and the Ionescus suggests that conversational roles structure the way a family talks about a past event and what they recount about this event. But, as the model in FIGURE 1 suggests, the adoption of a conversational role may have an impact beyond the immediate conversation. It may have an impact on an individual's subsequent recountings, with his or her family, with others, and by him/herself alone (Wilkes-Gibbs & Kim, 1991). Group recountings may remind participants of forgotten events and details, provide links and organization that they had not appreciated previously, or imbue the episode with an emotional or social nuance that it previously lacked. These activities should facilitate subsequent recountings. We began to address this issue by looking, at least at first, at groups of unrelated subjects, not families (see Pinner & Hirst, 1994; Manier, Pinner & Hirst, 1996). We contrasted the effect of an intervening group recounting with the effect of an intervening individual recounting on subsequent individual recountings.

We asked each member of a group to read an article of 247 words through once and with care. The article described several community service projects in the Bronx and the personalities associated with these projects. Immediately after finishing the reading, subjects wrote down the article in "as much detail as possible." In the experimental condition, they watched the film *Babes in Arms* for 10 minutes before joining the others in the group in a joint effort to recall the story. In this group recall, subjects were asked to tell the experimenter the content of the article, again "in as much detail as possible." In the control condition, subjects individually told the experimenter about the article. Twenty more minutes of watching the film *Babes in Arms* followed this part of the study. Finally, subjects were again asked to write down the article in "as much detail as possible." The initial reading of the passage and the three recall sessions were self-paced, but an experimenter noted the duration of each part of the study for each individual.

We divided the individual and group recalls in "idea units," in a manner similar to the studies discussed above. Individuals in both the pregroup and postgroup recounting offered fewer idea units than the group as a whole offered. In this respect, this study replicated others in the literature (Clark & Stephenson, 1989). Control subjects remembered the same amount in the postgroup recounting (38.0% of the idea units) as they did in the pregroup recounting (37.9%). On the other hand, experimental subjects recounted significantly more in the postgroup recounting (44.9%) than in the pregroup recounting (37.8%). We concluded that, at least for our subjects, participating in recounting a story in a group improves subsequent recountings.

What about the conversations led to this facilitation? We posited that a speaker's utterances can evoke fresh memories from the listener. An item absent from a group member's pretest recall could surface in her post-test recall, "jogged" by its introduction by another group member in the test phase. We were interested in a refinement of this hypothesis. We did not doubt that the mere mention of new information during the test can affect post-test memory, either by facilitating or interfering with subsequent remembering. Nevertheless, there may be conditions that make it more likely that the introduction of new information in the test phase will facilitate subsequent remembering. We can rephrase the familiar levels-of-processing maxim into: the more effectively something is communicated, the better it is remembered. All things being equal, new information introduced in the test phase should be more likely to find its way into the post-test recall as it is more effectively communicated. Although most discussions of "communicative effectiveness" concentrate on the effectiveness of the speaker, recent treatments of conversations have treated communicative effectiveness in terms of the interaction between speaker and listener. For instance, Schober and Clark (1989) have documented that participation is an important factor for imparting meaning to a conversation. They found that partners in a conversation showed a greater understanding of the content of the conversation if they actively participated in the conversation than if they merely listened to others conversing. Thus, an idea is communicated effectively not only because the speaker has said it well, but also because the listener has participated in the speech act.

The implication for the effect of conversation on subsequent remembering is clear: If memory improves with increased communicative effectiveness, new information introduced in a conversation should be more likely to find its way into subsequent recollection if partners in the conversation adopt a more active role and participate in the construction of the information than if they hold a passive role and merely listen. For Clark and his colleagues (Clark & Schaefer, 1989; Schober & Clark, 1989), "participation" refers to either the initiation or the continuation of that idea unit or a verbal acknowledgment of or disagreement with the idea unit being presented, e.g., a person saying "yeah," "right" or "no way." Or to use our terminology, a person "participates" in the construction of an idea unit if they either narrate it or monitor it.

We focused our analyses on those idea units that were not recalled in the pretest of a given Subject A, but emerged in the test phase, our *baseline* set. We were interested in determining whether Subject A's participation in the construction of a new idea unit in the test phase influenced the likelihood of the idea unit's appearing in the post-test of Subject A. There are many ways one could frame this comparison. We chose two (see Manier, Pinner & Hirst, 1996, for details). We found that those items in the baseline set that Subject A participated in constructing during the test phase had a probability of appearing in the post-test phase that was greater than both (a) the probability of any item in the baseline appearing in the post-test of Subject A and (b) the probability of an idea unit appearing in the post-test phase when Subject A DID NOT participate in its construction during the test phase. Whichever measure we used, we found that participation in the construction of an idea unit improved the subsequent recollection of a new unit.

Thus, when individuals recount an article in a group, the group as a whole shows an enhancement when compared to the individual recollections of a group member. This enhancement has a lasting mnemonic effect on the members of the group. Not only is memory improved with a conversation, but subsequent memory also improves. This effect on subsequent memory is more powerful when listeners adopt an active role in the construction of the idea unit. In other words, a broad measure of social dynamics—the active participation of members of the group—predicts in part what is subsequently remembered. Our findings provide insight into what we might expect to find as we undertake more thorough analyses with families and conversational roles. Specifically, persons assuming some roles, such as Narrator, are more likely to participate actively in the construction of the narrative than are others, such as Mentor. As a consequence, one might expect subsequent recountings of Narrators to be more influenced by their acts of conversational remembering than would be the case for subsequent recountings of Mentors.

CONCLUSION

Obviously, we are only beginning to obtain the kind of support we need to advance the model in FIGURE 1. First, we found that the distribution of family roles across the family differed for the Patels and the Ionescus. Although we are not able to present here the data to support our opinion, we believe that this difference in the distributional pattern has its root in the dynamics of the family (see Manier, 1996; Manier & Apetroaia, 1996). There was a disparity in education in the Ionescu family that did not exist for the Patels. The Ionescu parents were not as well educated as their children, and hence may have felt that they had to defer to them in many instances. This may have accounted for why the daughter in this family served the role of Mentor. As for the Patels, the father was well-educated, viz., studying for a Ph.D. His superior educational achievements may account in part for his adoption of a mentoring role.

Whatever the reason, the difference in distribution led to differences in family recounting. We have only begun the requisite analysis, but the mere presence of a strong lone Narrator in a recounting, as was the case for the Patels, makes it difficult for the family to build a consensus or "averaged" memory. The lone Narrator not only recounts more narrative tellings than anyone else, but he or she also has the advantage of introducing more new narrative tellings and more unshared pregroup narrative tellings than anyone else. Thus, to a large extent, when the distribution of roles is similar to that of the Patels, the family recounting is the version of the past held by the Narrator. Other family members presumably can influence the recounting by monitoring and mentoring. But we maintain that whatever the influence of the other family members might be, it is less consequential than that of the Narrator (see Manier, 1996, for details).

Of course, not all family recountings are merely the version told by a lone Narrator, because not all families assign to a single individual the role of Narrator. The Ionescus, for instance, shared the chore of narrating. Consequently, their family recounting was more a sum of the individual recollections of the family members than a version of the past as told by a single family member.

Thus, we have preliminary evidence that family members adopt the conversational roles of Narrator, Monitor, and Mentor and, more importantly, in acting out these roles, family members shape the family recounting into a form that may differ markedly from what any family member would recall individually. We also obtained preliminary evidence suggesting that the reshaped family recounting may have a lasting effect on subsequent individual memory. The relevant study did not examine families, nor did it specifically look at conversational roles, but it did establish that elements emerging in a group recounting reappear in the post-group recountings under specific circumstances. Specifically, for a group member A, a narrative element that appeared in the group recounting of A, but not in his pregroup recounting, is more likely to surface in the post-group recounting if A participated in its construction in the group. This principle is particularly interesting for us, because we suspect that the level of participation in a construction of a narrative element will vary with the conversational role. The Narrator would be more participatory, then Mentors, and finally Monitors. Future empirical work should help determine whether this prediction is correct.

We began this paper by arguing that psychologists need to recognize that persons often construct their autobiographical memories in the context of a conversation. The conversational nature of autobiographical remembering makes any model of autobiographical memory that fails to account for conversational dynamics and social dynamics incomplete. The model set forth in FIGURE 1 does not trace the sole means by which social dynamics influence autobiographical memory, but it does depict a route of possible influence that we have found useful in guiding our research. It is offered here as a suggestion, one with at present only preliminary empirical support, of how we might begin to incorporate social factors into the study of autobiographical memory. As we do so, we will begin to lay the foundations for understanding the social construction of the remembered self.

ACKNOWLEDGMENTS

We would like to thank Elizabeth Pinner, Alex Cuc, David Gluck, Nimali Jayasinghe, and Richard Stern for their assistance and advice.

REFERENCES

BARTLETT, F. (1932). *Remembering: A Study in Experimental and Social Psychology.* Cambridge, England: Cambridge University Press.

BENJAMIN, K. (1992). *Group Versus Individual Memory for Dynamic and Static Stimuli.* Doctoral dissertation. New School for Social Research, New York, NY.

BOWER, G. H. (1972). Mental imagery and associative learning. In L. W. Gregg (Ed.), *Cognition in Learning and Memory.* pp. 51–88. New York: Wiley.

BREWER, W. F. (1986). What is autobiographical memory? In D. C. Rubin (Ed.), *Autobiographical Memory.* pp. 25–49. New York: Cambridge University Press.

BROWN, G. & YULE, G. (1983). *Discourse analysis.* New York: Cambridge University Press.

BRUNER, J. (1990). *Acts of meaning.* Cambridge, MA: Harvard University Press.

CLARK, H. H. & SCHAEFER, E. F. (1989). Referring as a collaborative process. *Cognition, 22,* 1–39.

CLARK, N. K. & STEPHENSON, G. M. (1989). Group remembering. In P. B. Paulus (Ed.), *Psychology of group influence.* pp. 357–391. Hillsdale, NJ: Lawrence Erlbaum.

EDWARDS, D. & MIDDLETON, D. (1988). Conversational remembering and family relationships: How children learn to remember. *Journal of Social and Personal Relationships, 5,* 3–25.

(1986). Joint remembering: Constructing an account of shared experience through conversational discourse. *Discourse Processes, 11:* 337–355.

FIVUSH, R. & HUDSON, J. A., (EDS.). (1990). *Knowing and remembering in young children.* New York: Cambridge University Press.

GERGEN, K. J. (1991). *The saturated self: Dilemmas of identity in contemporary life.* New York: Basic Books.

HIRST, W. (1988). Improving memory. In M. S. Gazzaniga, (Ed.), *Perspectives on memory research*. Cambridge, MA: MIT Press.

HIRST, W. & MANIER, D. (1996). Remembering as communication. In D. Rubin (Ed.), *Remembering our past*. New York: Cambridge University Press.

(1995). Opening vistas for cognitive psychology. In L. Martin, B. Rogoff, K. Nelson & E. Tobach (Eds.), *Sociocultural psychology*. New York: Cambridge University Press.

KINTSCH, W. (1974). *The representation of meaning in memory*. Hillsdale, NJ: Erlbaum.

LABOV, W. & FANSHEL, D. (1977). *Therapeutic discourse: Psychotherapy as conversation*. New York: Academic Press.

LAVE, J. (1991). *Situated learning*. New York: Cambridge University Press.

LINDE, C. (1988). Who's in charge here? Cooperative work and authority negotiation in police helicopter missions. In *CSCW 88: Proceedings of the conference on computer-supported cooperative work*. pp. 52–64. New York: Association for Computing Machinery.

MANDLER, J. & JOHNSON, N. (1977). Remembrance of things parsed: Story structure and recall. *Cognitive Psychology, 9*, 111–151.

MANIER, D. (1996). Family remembering: Autobiographical remembering in the context of family conversations. Doctoral dissertation. New School for Social Research, New York, NY.

MANIER, D. & APETROAIA, I. (1996). The impact of culture on family remembering. In E. & D. Manier (Eds.), *Neurobiology and narrative*. Notre Dame, IN: University of Notre Dame Press.

MANIER, D. & HIRST, W. (1996). The brain doesn't tell the whole story. In E. & D. Manier (Eds.), *Neurobiology and narrative*. Notre Dame, IN: University of Notre Dame Press.

MANIER, D., PINNER, E. & HIRST, W. (1996). Conversational remembering. In D. Hermann, M. K. Johnson, C. McEvoy & P. Hertzel (Eds.), *Research on practical aspects of memory. Vol. 2*. Hillsdale, NJ: Erlbaum.

MIDDLETON, D. & EDWARDS, D. (1990). Conversational remembering: A social psychological approach. In *Collective remembering*. pp. 23–45. D. Middleton & D. Edwards (Eds.). London: Sage Publications.

MINUCHIN, S. (1974). *Families and family therapy*. Cambridge, MA: Harvard University Press.

NELSON, K. (1993). The psychological and social origins of autobiographical memory. *Psychological Science, 4*(1): 7–14.

NORMAN, D. A. & BOBROW, D. G. (1979). Descriptions: An intermediate stage of retrieval. *Cognitive Psychology, 11*: 107–123.

OLSON, D., PORTNER, J. & LAVEE, Y. (1985). *FACES III*. St. Paul, MN: Department of Family Social Science, University of Minnesota.

PINNER, E. & HIRST, W. (1994). Effects of group recounting on subsequent individual memories. Paper presented at the Third Conference on Practical Aspects of Memory, College Park, Maryland.

REISS, D. (1981). *The family's construction of reality*. Cambridge, MA: Harvard University Press.

RUBIN, D. (ED.). (1986). *Autobiographical memory*. New York: Cambridge University Press.

SCHAFER, R. (1992). *Retelling a life*. New York: Basic Books.

SCHOBER, M. F. & CLARK, H. H. (1989). Understanding by addressees and overhearers. *Cognition, 21*, 211–232.

SPENCE, D. (1982). *Narrative truth and historical truth*. New York: Norton.

STEIN, N. & GLENN, C. (1979). An analysis of story comprehension in elementary school children. In R.O. Freedle (Ed.), *Discourse production and comprehension.* Norwood, NJ: Ablex.

STEPHENSON, G. M., CLARK, N. K. & WADE, G. S. (1986). Meetings make evidence: An experimental study of collaborate and individual recall of a simulated police interrogation. *Journal of Personality and Social Psychology, 50:* 1113–1122.

SUCHMAN, L. (1990). *Plans and situated actions: The problem of human–machine communication.* New York: Cambridge University Press.

VYGOTSKY, L. (1978). *Mind in society.* Cambridge, MA: Harvard University Press.

WEGENER, D. (1986). Transactive memory: A contemporary analysis of the group mind. In B. Mullen & G. Goethals (Eds.), *Theories of group behavior.* pp. 185–208. New York: Springer-Verlag.

WEGENER, D., ERBER, R. & RAYMOND, P. (1991). Transactive memory in close relationships. *Journal of Personality and Social Psychology. 61*(6): 923–929.

WERTSCH, J. (ED.). (1991). *Voices of the mind: A sociocultural approach to mediated action.* Cambridge, MA: Harvard University Press.

WHITE, M. & EPSTON, D. (1990). *Narrative means to therapeutic ends.* New York: Norton.

WILKES-GIBBS, D. & KIM, P. H. (1991). Discourse influences on memory for visual forms. Paper presented to the 1991 meeting of the Psychnomic Society. San Francisco, CA.

WILLIAMS, M. D. (1977). Some observations on the process of retrieval from very long term memory. Doctoral dissertation. University of California, San Diego.

Part V: Social and Cultural Aspects of the Self

Introduction

JOAN GAY SNODGRASS

Department of Psychology
New York University
New York, New York 10003

This section considers social and cultural aspects of the self. In their contribution, Wendi Walsh and Mahzarin Banaji consider how an individual's membership in social groups comes to influence that individual's self-concept. They focus on two aspects of the relationship between the group and the individual: how the social group affects self-enhancement and how the social group affects self-knowledge. They review literature that shows that enhanced self-esteem derives from viewing one's own group (the in-group) as more favorable than another's group (the out-group), and consider ways in which individuals cope when they view their in-group as stigmatized. In their review of the effect of group membership on self-knowledge, Walsh and Banaji cite McGuire's distinctiveness theory as providing an explanation for which characteristics of a social group will be salient in defining one's self. Distinctiveness theory proposes that when a self-characteristic is distinctive in a larger group (e.g., being black in a predominantly white school) that characteristic will be emphasized in self-descriptions.

In the second paper in this section, Joan Miller considers how culture affects the development of the self-concept in the area of interpersonal morality. Miller takes as her starting point Gilligan's morality-of-caring framework. While existing conceptions of morality have typically included only justice and individual rights, Gilligan adds the moral responsibility to attend to the needs of others. Miller then reviews her own research on cultural differences in morality of caring between European-Americans living in the United States and Hindu Indians living in southern India. She hypothesized that the two cultures would differ in the degree to which individualism and collectivism would dominate, with the individualistic U.S. culture responding less to the moral imperative of caring for others than the more collective Hindu Indian culture. Miller's research methodology included presenting scenarios which portrayed an agent either helping or failing to help someone in need (e.g., a son who failed to care for elderly parents in his own home), and asking her respondents to make moral judgments of the agent. As expected, Hindu Indians placed highest priority on the collective values and judged harshly a son who failed to keep his parents with him, whereas

European-Americans placed greatest weight on the freedom of the individual to live life as he or she wished. Miller concludes that the morality-of-caring model is, in contrast to Gilligan's claims, culturally bound, and she urges that cultural perspectives be more generally adopted in evaluating other genres of psychological theory.

In the final paper of this section, Susan Andersen, Inga Reznik, and Serena Chen focus on the importance of interpersonal relationships in the self-concept. Beginning with the assumption that a basic human motivation is the need for connection to others, the authors argue that information about significant others in one's life become connected in memory to information about one's self. The information about significant others is used routinely to evaluate new persons. To the extent that a new person resembles a significant other, that person will be seen to possess some of the traits and characteristics of the significant other, whether the traits are positive or negative. The perceiver, then, will expect similar actions and attitudes from the new person that have been experienced before from the significant other.

Andersen *et al.* relate their view of the role of the significant other in guiding new interpersonal relationships to the concept of transerference. Transference was originally defined by Freud as the process whereby a patient superimposes his or her fantasies and conflicts about a parent onto the analyst. Andersen and her colleges have extended this notion of transference to interpersonal relationships in general, in which characteristics of one of several significant others may be attributed to a new person according to his or her similarity to a significant other. The assumption that information about a significant other and the self are linked in memory comes from evidence that expectations and inferences are bidirectional—not only does the perceiver ascribe qualities of the significant other to a similar new person that were not given, but the perceiver expects the similar new person to act towards him/herself in ways similar to that of the significant other.

Wendi A. Walsh is a doctoral student in the Psychology Department at Yale University. She is currently completing her dissertation entitled When stereotypes get applied to the self: The role of perceived ingroup variability in self-stereotyping. *In this research, she explores the influence of gender stereotypes about women's inferior math ability on students' math performance and self-perceptions.*

Mahzarin R. Banaji is an Associate Professor of Psychology at Yale University. She received her Ph.D. at Ohio State University and was an NIAAA postdoctoral fellow at the University of Washington. Her research on social cognition has focused on unconscious beliefs and attitudes, on the role of emotion in memory, and on the development of self in social contexts. She recently completed a term as Associate Editor of the Journal of Social Psychology, *and currently serves as Associate Editor of* Psychological Review.

The Collective Self[a]

WENDI A. WALSH AND MAHZARIN R. BANAJI[b]

Department of Psychology
Yale University
New Haven, Connecticut 06520-8205

In the hands of sociologists and increasingly of social psychologists as well, the analysis of self reveals a paradox. At its very essence, the construct of self is meant to capture the most unique and individualized aspect of personality. Even so, the thrust of many arguments has repeatedly been that this unique and individual core of personality may be fundamentally determined by shared membership in larger collectives. The notion that the individual self (James' empirical self or "me") is born of the collective, that social forces of culture and society as well as social microenvironments shape it in indelible ways is, in one sense, quite radical. Yet, at least to those who are broadly educated regarding the last several decades of thinking about self, the notion that a sense of self is socially determined seems quite acceptable. The ease with which the link between self and larger social units has come to be assumed is the result of a longstanding and recurrent theme in social science emphasizing the social construction of identity. Whether it be in classic books such as *Mind, Self, and Society* (1934), in constructs such as the "looking-glass self" (Cooley, 1922), in notions of self as managed in presentation to others (Goffman, 1956), in collections of ideas in volumes such as *Self in Social Interaction* (Gordon & Gergen, 1968), or more recent psychological treatments of self (see Banaji & Prentice, 1994; Deaux & Major, 1987; Markus & Kitayama, 1991; Tajfel & Turner, 1986) the idea is forcefully driven home that a sense of self exists and even comes to be because of and in response to a social world of many others.

Although recent social constructionist critiques, allied with postmodernist and deconstructionist views of the individual self (Gergen, 1987; see Kitzinger, 1992), have offered new opinions about the social construction of self and identity, we find our kindred spirits in the classical writings of Mead, Cooley, Goffman, Parsons, Freud, and Turner among others, and in contemporary empirical research that examines the extent to which self and identity are socially determined. Of the many facets of social influences on self, we attend to those that show, as directly as possible, the influence of so-

[a]This work was supported in part by Grant SBR 9422291 from the National Science Foundation.
[b]Address for correspondence: Wendi Walsh or Mahzarin Banaji, Department of Psychology, Yale University, P. O. Box 208205, New Haven, CT 06520-8205.

cial groups on individual constructions of self. Perhaps most closely to our own thinking, George Herbert Mead (1934) pointed out the relation between the individual and the collective: "So the self reaches its full development by organizing these individual attitudes of others into the organized social or group attitudes, and by thus becoming an individual reflection of the general systematic pattern of social or group behavior in which it and the others are all involved—a pattern which enters as a whole into the individual's experience in terms of these organized group attitudes which, through the mechanism of his central nervous system, he takes toward himself, just as he takes the individual attitudes of others" (p. 156–158). Mead's point is a most general one, of how social groups influence attitudes and beliefs about the world at large. Our focus will be to examine the empirical literature regarding how social groups come to influence a subset of such views, e.g., attitudes and beliefs about oneself. The line between what constitutes self and non-self beliefs and attitudes can become quite blurry, and our demarcation will be largely pragmatic.

The question we seek to address here concerns a specific thread of the general assumption regarding the social nature of the self. In particular, our concern lies with the question of how we come to be who we are because of the social groups of which we are members. In other words, how and to what extent are the most unique aspects of personality, our descriptive and evaluative views of our self, shaped by the collectives to which we belong. Our focus will be rather narrowly circumscribed. We attend specifically to the extent to which an individual self emerges as a function of one's social identity, that is, through one's belonging in social groups. Such groups may be ones into which one is born (e.g., gender, race, religion, nationality) or groups into which one is elected (Republican, NYAS). The latter condition muddies the research question of how social groups shape an individual self by creating the problem of self-selection, but it nevertheless represents an important type of group membership to which attention must be paid.

Although early views regarding self such as Mead's are emphatic about the fundamental nature of the link between self and collective, it is only recently that empirically testable social psychological theories and evidence have come to be available, at least on this side of the Atlantic. For this reason, the literature is not vast, and it only scratches the surface of the multiplicity of issues regarding the self and the collective. In the main portion of the chapter, we focus on only two aspects of this relationship. First, what is the nature of the influence of collectives on self-enhancement? How and to what extent do the groups of which we are members create and enhance our feelings of self-worth and esteem? Second, what is the nature of the influence of collectives on self-knowledge? How and to what extent do the groups of which we are members define the contents of our self definitions and self images? Obviously the two questions are related, that is, self-knowledge can be positive or negative and therefore with clear consequences for self-enhancement, but we discuss them separately to maintain the traditionally separate theoretical and methodological focus on self-enhancement and self-knowledge.

An interesting aspect of the individual/collective self is the apparent inconsistency that exists between perceptions of self-uniqueness and actual self-sharedness with members of one's social groups. Individuals, especially those raised in cultures that emphasize individualism, express a strong sense of their uniqueness and the belief that their individuality is a function of personal choices they freely make. One might easily examine this in statements such as "I am a talented basketball player" or "I am choosing motherhood over a career" or "I don't like math" or "I like spicy food." Among the goals of the review is to assess the extent to which individuals' belief in self-autonomy, uniqueness of preferences, and control over life choices may be illusory. Insofar as prominent components of one's self-concept show the influence of collectives (even when one may be unaware of such influences or even actively rejects them), we may be able to speculate about the unconscious influence of social group membership on self. To this end, we present data that indicate the extent to which self-esteem and self-knowledge are shaped by the collectives to which we belong.

SELF-ENHANCEMENT

The desire for self-enhancement, or a positive view of oneself, has traditionally been considered a fundamental motive of the self (e.g., Allport, 1937; James, 1890; Greenwald, 1980; Steele, 1988; Swann, 1990; Taylor & Brown, 1988; Tesser, 1988; Wylie, 1979). More than a century ago, James (1890), who described a multiply-defined self consisting of spiritual, material, and social components, asserted that individuals actively choose those aspects of self "on which to stake one's salvation" (p. 310), in order to maximize positive self-evaluation. Search for the roots of self-enhancement continues in contemporary empirical research as well, such as Steele's self-affirmation theory (1988) and Tesser's self-esteem maintenance theory (1988). Whatever the particular form of self-enhancement, individuals are expected to strive to maximize psychological well-being by seeking out and attending to experiences that reflect positively on the self, while avoiding those that reflect poorly on the self. It appears that such a strategy is not without its rewards. In the past decade, a growing consensus has emerged that maintaining a positive view of self has many benefits. For example, individuals with relatively positive self-views tend to be at lower risk for depression (Crandall, 1973; Wylie, 1979) and hopelessness (Abramsom, Metalsky & Alloy, 1989), to experience more positive affect (Pelham & Swann, 1989) and greater life satisfaction (Diener, 1984), and to be at lower risk for negative health outcomes (Taylor & Brown, 1988). Thus, a positive self-view appears to play an important role in individuals' psychological and physical well-being.

A robust body of research now exists documenting the strategies individuals employ to achieve and maintain a positive self-view (see Banaji & Prentice, 1994 for a review). For example, individuals routinely engage in a variety of social-reasoning strategies including biased memory retrieval (Kunda & Sanitioso, 1989), self-serving attributional processes (Tennen & Herzberger, 1987), and the use of self-serving definitions of success and goodness (e.g., Dunning & Cohen, 1992; Dunning, Perie & Story, 1991). However, most of this research has focused exclusively on the ways that self-enhancement is derived from individualistic aspects of the self such as one's competencies, attractiveness, or personal accomplishments. For our purposes, a less traditional literature bearing on the issue of self-enhancement must be considered. This literature needs to inform us about the ways, if any, that self-enhancement can be achieved through identification with collectives.

Much research on the collective aspects of self has been guided by *social identity theory* and its later incarnation, *self-categorization theory*. The advantage of the presence of a single major theoretical account is that it has provided research focused on a prescribed set of hypotheses that are central to the theory. The two theories are embedded in what Abrams and Hogg (1988) labeled "the self-esteem hypothesis," that individuals are motivated by a desire for a positive self-view. The theories' most relevant contribution from our perspective is that one's views of self can be derived not only from individual aspirations and accomplishments but also from membership in and identification with social groups. Specifically, social identity theory asserts that through processes of categorization of the self as a group member and subsequent depersonalization, one maintains or enhances self-esteem through intergroup social comparisons (for reviews, see Tajfel, 1978, 1981, 1982, 1984; Tajfel & Turner, 1986; Turner & Giles, 1981). That is, an individual's motivation for a positive self-view provides a basis for viewing ingroups, and thus the self, in a positive light relative to outgroups and their members. In order to achieve these goals, individuals may employ a number of biased reasoning strategies including intergroup differentiation and discrimination, and ingroup favoritism. Thus, these theories provide an explanation not only for how self-concepts are shaped by social groups, but also for how individuals achieve positive views of the self through intergroup processes.

A favorite among social psychologists, the classic study by Hastorf and Cantril (1954), demonstrated how group members will employ biased reasoning strategies that result in favorable perceptions of one's ingroup. Following a Princeton-Dartmouth football game, Hastorf and Cantril had students from both schools view a film of the game, and asked them to make note of all the illegal plays. Even after being explicitly instructed to put aside school loyalties when making their judgments, students from both schools perceived their team as less infractious than reflected by the officials' assessments. Regardless of the fact that most of the students in the study were unlikely to personally know any of the football players, they appear to have demonstrated an ingroup bias which quite possibly may have resulted from a desire to derive positive feelings from sharing social category membership with the football team from one's own school. While this study shows that group membership did influence judgments of one's group (a group-enhancement effect), and other research shows that individuals do indeed bask in the reflected glory of group achievement (Cialdini, Borden, Thorne, Walker, Freeman & Sloan, 1976), these studies do not directly demonstrate whether one's own self-image is enhanced by membership in a group. However, it is possible that by viewing one's team in a positive light, one could simultaneously enhance or at least maintain a positive self-view as well.

A recent collection of studies has explored the direct effects of ingroup bias on individual self-esteem (see Abrams, 1992 for a review). For example, Oakes and Turner (1980) employed the minimal group paradigm in which subjects were randomly assigned to one of two groups, ostensibly on the basis of preference for a painting. Despite the minimal basis for group membership (group members had no contact and did not know one another), when given the opportunity to allocate resources, experimental subjects showed an ingroup bias. That is, they assigned greater resources to members of their ingroup than to members of the outgroup. Social identity theory asserts that such ingroup biases derive from individuals' desire for a positive self-view, which is largely based on favorable evaluations of one's ingroup relative to outgroups. In other words, because individuals derive meaningful information about the self from the groups to which they belong, it is desirable to achieve favorable intergroup comparisons, thereby achieving a positive view of the self. Oakes and Turner (1980) indeed found that experimental subjects who had just demonstrated the ingroup bias reported higher self-esteem than subjects who did not engage in the allocation task and thus had not discriminated against the outgroup. Consistent with this finding, Lemyre and Smith (1985) later demonstrated that group membership alone did not provide a basis for enhanced self-esteem. Instead, only after engaging in intergroup discrimination (and hence, ingroup favoritism) did subjects achieve higher self-esteem. Other studies have also provided direct evidence that ingroup favoritism elevates self-esteem, even when subjects were explicitly instructed to cooperate with outgroup members (Hogg, Turner, Nascimento-Schulz, & Spriggs, 1986). Thus, these studies support social identity theory's assertion that enhancement in self-esteem is accomplished through positive intergroup comparisons.

Although originally formulated to explain intergroup behavior, social identity theory provides a basis for understanding the development of a "collective self." Derived from social identity theory, self-categorization theory asserts that the self is a cognitive structure containing two subsystems:

an individual self ("I") and a social self ("we") (Turner, 1985; Turner, Hogg, Oakes, Reichter & Wetherell, 1987; Turner, Oakes, Haslam & Mc-Garty, 1994), and situations vary in the degree to which they regulate the salience of these different selves. For example, viewing oneself as a "Princeton student" will be much more likely when attending a university football game than when taking a final exam. The intergroup nature of the football game makes salient one's group (or social) identity, while the exam-taking situation is likely to invoke thoughts about one's unique attributes and personal identity such as being a good student. Salience of group membership (or social identity) can be triggered by several factors inherent in either the self, in others, or in the situation (see Deaux & Major, 1987 for a discussion of these factors).

When the social aspects of self become salient, one presumably de-emphasizes unique, idiosyncratic attributes in deference to "perceptions of self as an interchangeable exemplar of some social category . . ." (Turner *et al.*, 1987, p. 50). Once this shift to a collective identity occurs, self-perceptions are systematically biased to render the self more closely aligned with stereotypic ingroup characteristics. Thus, where group identity is salient, individuals behave and perceive themselves in accord with characteristics of their group. Because self-evaluations will be derived from evaluations of the group when group identity is salient, individuals are motivated to view the group, and consequently the self, as positively distinctive (Oakes & Turner, 1980; Turner, 1981).

Several empirical studies support the assertion that an individual's behavior and self-conceptions are more likely to reflect characteristics of the group when social group membership is salient. For example, Hogg and Turner (1987) demonstrated that when the salience of gender is enhanced, men and women define themselves according to gender by endorsing gender-stereotypic attributes as true of the self, as will be discussed further in the later section on the social bases of self-knowledge. However, an increasing number of studies have begun to demonstrate that collective identification does not always lead to enhanced self-esteem. For example, Hogg and Turner found that collective identification had positive consequences for the self-esteem of men, but had a negative effect on women's self-esteem. Despite the fact that women showed more ethnocentrism (ingroup favoritism) than men, their self-esteem nonetheless suffered when gender was made salient. Hogg and Turner (1987) acknowledged that due to social status differences between groups, identification with a low-status group could sometimes lead to a negative social identity and a negative self-view (see also Tajfel & Turner, 1979). Lorenzi-Cioldi (1991) found similar evidence for the negative effects of self-categorization on members of low-status groups. In this study as well, self-categorization was examined as a function of gender salience, and by the nature of the social intergroup context, women were *a priori* identified to be the low-status group. Results from this study supported the previous finding by showing that negative attributes were more likely to be endorsed by women when gender was salient, thus providing a more negative self-view.

Consistent with the idea that perception of low status of the ingroup results in negative effects on self-esteem, Frable, Wortman, Joseph, Kirscht and Kessler (1994) found that gay men who perceived their group as stigmatized had lower self-esteem. Several other studies have provided similar evidence for the negative self-evaluative consequences of identifying with a low-status group (e.g., Brewer & Weber, 1994; Simon & Hamilton, 1994; Simon, Pantaleo & Mummendey, 1995). Together, these studies suggest that group membership may actually pose a threat to self-esteem under some conditions, which is problematic for a self-esteem explanation for collective identification (see Abrams, 1992; Abrams & Hogg, 1988). According to social identity and self-categorization theories, because the individual is assumed to be always striving for a positive self-view, members of low-status groups should either attempt to leave or dissociate themselves from such groups or to reconceptualize the ingroup's status in such a way as to achieve a positive ingroup perception. However, observation and research has not supported the idea that members of low-status groups consistently engage in these strategies, nor that these strategies are always successful in enhancing self-esteem. Instead, members of low-status groups appear to sometimes continue to identify with and define themselves in terms of their group membership, despite its negative status. Furthermore, individuals who belong to disadvantaged groups do not appear to suffer from low self-esteem (Crocker & Major, 1989). In a recent review of empirical work on stigma and self-esteem, Crocker and Major (1989) concluded that the empirical evidence does not support the claim that membership in a low-status (or stigmatized) group negatively affects the self-concepts of its members. These authors review twenty years of self-esteem research showing that stigmatized individuals maintain feelings of global self-esteem equal to (and in some cases, higher than) nonstigmatized individuals.

Several explanations have been offered to account for the lack of a consistent correlation between group status and self-esteem. For example, Abrams (1992) suggests that global self-esteem measures may be insensitive to the momentary changes brought about by the situational salience of group membership. Following the advice of Fishbein (1967), Abrams and Hogg (1988) also suggest that self-esteem measures must account for the appropriate level of specificity, which would entail measures of collective rather than personal self-esteem. Only recently has research begun to assess the collective self-esteem of group members, using a measure developed by Crocker and Luhtanen (1990). In a recent study by Crocker, Luhtanen, Blaine and Broadnax (1994), white, black and Asian subjects completed Collective Self-Esteem scales specific to their race. The results demonstrate that there is not always a clear and direct relationship between the perceived status of one's group and collective self-esteem. For example, among black subjects, there was a near-zero correlation between perceptions of how others viewed their group and their own collective self-esteem. Black subjects, at least those who participated in this study, chose to identify strongly with their group and to positively evaluate their group regardless of perceived devaluation from the outgroup. This finding is in stark contrast to the results for white and Asian subjects from the same population, who showed a relatively strong correlation between how they believe others evaluate their group and their own collective self-esteem. Thus, the findings for white and Asian subjects provide support for the symbolic interactionist concept of "reflected appraisals" or the "looking-glass self" (Cooley, 1922), while the findings from black subjects suggest that individuals may develop strategies for dissociating themselves from the negative evaluations of a dominant group.

In fact, Crocker & Major (1989) suggest several ways in which membership in a stigmatized group may actually protect self-esteem (see also Myrdal, 1944; Taylor & Walsh, 1979). They propose three self-protective mechanisms which may be employed by members of low-status groups. Specifically, they propose that low-status individuals protect the self by (*a*) attributing negative feedback to prejudice against one's group, (*b*) selectively comparing outcomes with members of one's own group rather than with nonstigmatized outgroup members, and (*c*) selectively devaluing domains in which one's own group performs poorly or valuing domains in which one's group excels. Recent empirical research supports the viability of each of these strategies.

Several studies have begun to explore the effectiveness of the first strategy, attributing negative feedback to prejudice, for maintaining self-esteem. For example, Jensen, White & Galliher (1982) found that subjects who attributed the negative treatment of others to their race, religion, or nationality maintained self-esteem, while subjects who attributed negative treatment to personal attributes such as appearance or intelligence showed decrements in self-esteem. Recent experimental studies by Crocker, Major and colleagues (Crocker, Cornwell & Major, 1993; Crocker, Voelkl, Testa & Major, 1991; Major & Crocker, 1993) provide further and more direct evidence for the conditions under which individuals are likely to attribute negative feedback to prejudice and its implications for self-esteem. This line of research demonstrates that under conditions of attributional ambiguity, individuals may engage in a self-protective strategy to contend with the self-evaluative implications of having a stigmatized identity. Attributional ambiguity arises when individuals who belong to stigmatized groups experience ambiguity with regard to the causes of the behavior of others toward them. For example, in one set of experiments, overweight subjects who were aware that the experimenter could see them attributed negative feedback to the experimenter's prejudice against overweight people. When subjects were able to make this external attribution, they maintained high self-esteem despite the negative feedback. However, when they received positive feedback under these circumstances, they also attributed this to experimenter bias and thus, this attribution too had a negative effect on self-esteem (Crocker, Cornwell & Major, 1993). Studies by Dion and his colleagues similarly demonstrate the self-protective effects of attributions of prejudice on self-esteem (Dion & Earn, 1975; Dion, Earn & Yee, 1978). However, both of these lines of research also demonstrated that when subjects were unable to attribute feedback to prejudice, self-esteem suffered at the hand of negative feedback and increased following positive feedback.

The second self-protective strategy suggested by Crocker and Major (1989), the tendency to make intragroup rather than intergroup comparisons, is also empirically supported. Studies of social comparison processes demonstrate that people often choose to compare themselves with similar others (Suls & Wills, 1991), and especially with other ingroup members (e.g., Major & Forcey, 1985). Ingroup comparisons appear not only to be informative, but also to provide opportunities for downward comparison as a self-esteem enhancing strategy (see Wood, 1989). For example, several empirical studies have repeatedly demonstrated that members of stigmatized groups perceive their ingroup as receiving more negative outcomes (e.g., salaries) and treatment (e.g., discrimination) than they receive personally, a phenomenon called the personal/group discrimination discrepancy (for a review, see Taylor, Wright & Porter, 1994). Many explanations have been offered to account for this phenomenon which are beyond the scope of this chapter. For our purpose, these findings provide evidence for the ways that low-status group members may be able to maintain or even enhance self-esteem through within-group comparisons. Unfortunately, little if any of this research has directly explored the effects of ingroup comparisons on self-esteem.

Finally, Crocker & Major (1989) suggest that members of low-status groups may selectively devalue domains in which their group, and by implication the self, compares negatively with outgroups. Selective attention to dimensions on which one excels was first suggested by James (1890) and is illustrated in the following quote: "I, who for the time have staked my all on being a psychologist, am mortified if others know much more psychology than I. But I am contented to wallow in the grossest ignorance of Greek. My deficiencies there give me no sense of personal humiliation at all" (p. 310). A similar perspective has recently been put forth in Steele's self-affirmation theory (Steele, 1988). Steele argues that individuals will disidentify with domains in which they experience repeated disappointment. Because members of stigmatized groups experience chronic negative expectations and feedback in specific domains, members of these groups may choose to "disidentify" with these domains. Empirical support for this proposition comes from studies of African-American adolescents' disidentification with academic achievement (Ogbu, 1986) as well as physically disabled individuals' disidentification with normative definitions of physical attractiveness (Taylor, 1983).

A tacit assumption underlying much of the research reviewed thus far is that individuals are motivated to think and act in ways that are beneficial to their personal interests, or to their personal self-esteem. While there is ample evidence that individuals employ self-protective as well as self-enhancing strategies under many conditions, current theories are less well-equipped to address conditions under which individuals endorse negative attributes of the group as true of the self, yet as we have already discussed, such effects have been frequently documented (e.g., Frable *et al.*, 1994; Lorenzi-Cioldi, 1991; Simon, Glässner-Bayerl & Stratenwerth, 1991). To explain why individuals would endorse negative views of their own groups as well as of themselves, Jost and Banaji (1994) offered the concept of system justification. Jost and Banaji argue that negative images (or stereotypes) of social groups serve ideological functions, that is, they maintain and explain the *status quo*. Because the dominant ideology tends to be endorsed by the dominated, negative stereotypes about disadvantaged social groups may come to be endorsed even by members of the stigmatized group in order to explain or understand the existing social arrangement. Consistent with social identity theory, the system justification approach suggests that negative stereotypes are most likely to be endorsed by the ingroup when the prevailing social order appears legitimate and stable. Further, Jost and Banaji (1994) suggest that ideology often operates outside of conscious awareness, which would further limit the targets' ability to engage in the self-protective strategies outlined earlier. In other words, the dominant group's negative portrayals of low-status groups may have implicit negative effects on their targets.

While research demonstrates that group membership may be one means by which to achieve a positive self-image, the inconsistency in the data of the relationship between identification with social groups and self-esteem brings into question the appropriateness of the nearly exclusive emphasis on self-esteem as the primary motive for collective identification and suggests that there may be reasons to identify with social groups aside from personal enhancement. The system justification approach suggests one such alternative: individuals may be motivated to justify the social system, rather than to enhance the self or social group. Underlying the system-justification perspective is the notion that social groups provide meaningful information about the self and one's place in the larger social structure. In other words, social groups provide self-knowledge. Recent research on the collective self has explored the ways in which individuals derive self-knowledge through group memberships. In other words, research has shifted away from the evaluative question "How good am I?" to the more cognitively based question, "Who am I?". In the following section, we will review research exploring the ways in which self-knowledge, rather than self-esteem, is derived from group membership.

SELF-KNOWLEDGE

Motivation for self-knowledge refers to the desire to define and comprehend one's attributes, abilities, opinions, and accomplishments as well one's social role and social status. In other words, individuals strive to construct a coherent self-definition among the otherwise "booming, buzzing confusion." Several related motives have come to be associated with the desire for self-knowledge, including the desire for balance or consistency (Backman, 1988; Pittman & Heller, 1987), for uncertainty reduction (Trope, 1986), for competence (White, 1959), for the ability know the environment (Cofer & Appley, 1964; Swann, 1990), and even for self-actualization (Maslow, 1954) or self-enlightenment (Rogers, 1951). Common among all of these motives is a fundamental desire to construct a meaningful subjective reality (Bartlett, 1932).

Numerous theoretical perspectives have been proffered to explain how individuals acquire self-knowledge, and surprisingly, these accounts have engaged the question of the role of social groups in producing self-knowledge. Common to such well-established theories as social learning theory (Bandura & Walters, 1963), reflected appraisals (Cooley, 1922; Mead, 1934), social comparison theory (Festinger, 1954), social identity theory (Tajfel & Turner, 1986), self-categorization theory (Turner et al., 1987), and impression management (Goffman, 1956) is the assertion that the beliefs of significant others as well as societally held beliefs about an individual's social category memberships shape the self-concept and provide critical information in the self-assessment process. It is relatively well-accepted among self-theorists that self-knowledge, at least to some extent, stems from the relationship between self and the social groups to which one belongs.

A theory that has produced some of the most elegant demonstrations of the ways that self-knowledge is derived from social groups is McGuire's distinctiveness theory (McGuire, 1984; McGuire & McGuire, 1988). According to distinctiveness theory, the features of the self that will be most salient in the self-concept are those that distinguish the self from others. Often, the distinctiveness of self-characteristics will be determined by the numerical composition of individuals in the immediate social situation. In other words, the social context can prime an individual to think of him/herself in terms of group membership. For example, in a study of children's responses to the open-ended prompt, "Tell us about yourself," McGuire and McGuire (1988) found that children describe themselves in terms of characteristics that are distinctive, and therefore salient, in a particular social context. For instance, in a school where the majority of students were white, only 1% of the white students, but 17% of the African-American students mentioned their race in their spontaneous self-descriptions. Because of African-Americans' minority status in the school, race became a more meaningful self-descriptor for African-American students than for white students. Further, the salience of ethnicity in the self-concept was a function of the ethnic representation in particular classrooms. For example, the percentage of white students who mentioned ethnicity rose significantly when the representation of whites in the classroom dropped below the school average of 80%. These findings not only demonstrate that the size of one's group enlarges and minimizes particular dimensions of self-descriptions, but they also suggest that the self-concept may be quite malleable, changing as a function of the properties of one's social group. Distinctiveness theory has been employed to demonstrate the importance of contextually determined gender salience (Cota & Dion, 1986), age salience (Gfellner, 1986), race salience (Bochner & Ohsako, 1977), and the salience of religious affiliation (Charters & Newcomb, 1952) for self-identification.

Although much of the research has focused on the ways that numerical distinctiveness leads to the salience of group membership, other factors have also been identified. For example, the salience of group membership may be enhanced in situations where the task, rather than the composition of the group, promotes conflict or confrontation with an outgroup (Dion, Earn & Yee, 1978) or enhances group differences (e.g., Brown & Deschamps, 1980), or where the situation places emphasis on important ingroup norms (Boyanowsky & Allen, 1973; Minard, 1952).

A related theory addressing the ways that the contextual salience of group membership can affect the self has already been discussed, that is, self-categorization theory. While research on social identity was ultimately interested in the consequences of self-categorization for self-esteem, this research provided a basis for later work on the cognitive processes involved in conferring a self-definition that is consistent with perceptions of one's group. Self-categorization theory goes beyond distinctiveness theory in that it suggests that not only will group members define themselves in terms of the group (e.g., "I am a woman"), but will also describe the self in terms of group characteristics (e.g., "I am nurturant" or "I am not aggressive"). The idea that increased salience of group membership will produce self-descriptions consistent with the group is not a new notion. In 1943, Lewin suggested that in certain situations where group identity is enhanced, individuals behave and perceive themselves in accord with characteristics of their group. Similarly, self-categorization theory asserts that through self-categorization processes, individuals acquire meaningful information about the self by defining the self as prototypical of the ingroup and differentiated from outgroups. For example, Hogg and Turner (1987) reviewed empirical research that provided indirect evidence for "self-stereotyping." By self-stereotyping, we refer to the systematic conscious or unconscious influence of beliefs about the attributes of one's own groups on judgments of the self. In their own work, Hogg and Turner (1987) demonstrated that self-stereo-typing is most likely to occur when a particular group membership is contextually salient. That is, when group membership (e.g., gender) was highly salient, subjects' self-descriptions were consistent with ingroup stereotypes. Several other studies have since demonstrated the role of contextual salience in self-stereotyping (e.g., Lorenzi-Cioldi, 1991; Simon, Glässner-Bayerl & Stratenwerth, 1991; Simon & Hamilton, 1994). Using both minimal and existing groups, these studies provide evidence for ways that the social context affects conceptions of the self. When one's group membership becomes salient in the social context, often due to relative distinctiveness, one's conception of the self shifts from a unique individual to a stereotypical representation of the social group.

More recently, Brewer (1991, 1993; Brewer, Manzi & Shaw, 1993) has also discussed the importance of relative distinctiveness as a determinant of collective identification, but with a different focus. Brewer maintains that individuals do not strive to be synonymous with the social groups to which they belong. Instead, she asserts that individuals strive to attain a balance between desires for validation and inclusion of the self in larger social collectives and desires for uniqueness and differentiation between the self and others. In other words, individuals are motivated to achieve some level of optimal distinctiveness. In support of optimal distinctiveness theory, Brewer (1991) reviewed research showing that individuals often act in accordance with social identity rather than their personal identity, even when the context is not explicitly depersonalizing. That is, individuals may choose to identify with their group even in the absence of contextual salience. According to optimal distinctiveness theory, such collective identification should be most likely when one is a member of a distinctive or minority group. Minority groups meet individuals' proposed need for inclusion of the self in a larger collective while allowing individuals' to maintain feelings of distinctiveness (by virtue of their minority status).

Because minority status is often confounded with low status, the desire for enhanced self-esteem (as described by social identity theory), may often come into conflict with the desire for distinctiveness. However, in a study examining the effects of ingroup status, ingroup size and depersonalization, Brewer et al. (1993) found that both ingroup status and size contributed to positive valuation of the ingroup. That is, high-status majority group members and low-status minority group members evaluated their groups most positively. However, under depersonalized conditions, subjects valued minority group membership over majority group status, regardless of size. Similarly, Simon & Hamilton (1994) report interactive effects of group status and group size. In their study, high-status minority members were more likely to describe themselves in terms of group characteristics than were low-status minority members. However, majority group members were equally likely to describe group attributes as self-relevant, regardless of group status. Thus, while individuals may look to salient or distinctive group memberships to derive meaningful information about the self, the influence of these groups appears to be qualified by their potential for providing self-enhancing information. These studies suggest that collective identification may be affected by a more complex interplay of motivations for both self-enhancement and self-knowledge than may have been previously suggested.

The knowledge acquired through collective identification extends beyond one's attributes and abilities. For example, social groups appear to provide individuals with guides for behavior (Turner, 1985, 1991; Hogg & Abrams, 1990), attitudes (Turner, 1991), and goals (Geis, Brown, Jennings & Porter, 1984). For example, Geis et al. (1984) demonstrated that the salience of gender-stereotypic images affected women's achievement expectations. After exposure to stereotype-consistent images, where women were portrayed in traditional female roles, female subjects were more likely to de-emphasize career themes and to emphasize homemaking themes in their own goals for the future. In other words, group stereotypes can be viewed as scripts that contain a host of information not only about what is appropriate to present to the world, but also about how to think and feel about the self.

More recent evidence suggests that self-stereotyping can occur without conscious awareness. Influenced by several lines of research that have now demonstrated that a person's perception can be influenced by stereotypes which are cognitively available but not consciously accessible (see Greenwald & Banaji, 1995 for a review), research on self-stereotyping has explored the ways that stereotypes can implicitly affect self-conceptions and behavior. In a recent study, Levy (1996) explored the implicit effects of stereotypes about old age on memory performance. In this research, elderly subjects were assigned to one of two implicit stereotype conditions. In one condition, subjects were briefly exposed to stereotypes paired with an image of a wise elder or a senile elder. Elderly subjects who had seen the "wise elder" paired with stereotypes showed a subsequent improvement in memory, whereas subjects in the "senile elder" condition experienced a decline in memory. Consistent with previous work on implicit stereotyping, this research supports the hypothesis that stereotypes about one's group can operate without the target's awareness to influence not only self-description but performance as well. In fact, Levy suggests that negative self-stereotyping might be most likely to occur under such implicit conditions where explicit self-protective strategies are unlikely to be employed.

It is possible that performance measures such as those used by Levy (1996) provide some of the strongest evidence for the implicit influence of collectives on the self, since performance may be less susceptible to self-presentation than descriptions of the self. Compelling evidence for the effects of group stereotypes on targets' performance comes from a recent set of studies by Steele and Aronson (1995). Steele and Aronson (1995) varied the vulnerability of African-American subjects to a racial stereotype about academic achievement (e.g., by asking subjects to record their race on a questionnaire) just prior to taking a difficult academic test. When race was made salient, African-American subjects underperformed white subjects on the test, but performed equally well when the racial stereotype was not invoked. Because the manipulation of racial salience was so subtle, these experiments provide powerful evidence for the subtle influence of groups on the behavior of their members.

The work reviewed up to this point might leave one with the impression that the self is a pliant grouping of fleeting collective identifications, varying from one context to another and influenced by the transient salience of particular group memberships. While these demonstrations are of utmost importance in leading the way away from a static view of the self in favor of a more dynamic and contextually dependent view (see Simon & Hamilton, 1994), it is also likely that there are particular group memberships that have more global, enduring effects on the self. In other words, there may be specific collective identifications that are chronically accessible across situations. The collective aspects of self that have most generally been discussed as chronically accessible are the so-called "master statuses" (Stryker, 1987), such as sex and ethnicity. These ascribed, as opposed to achieved, group memberships may play a more dominant role in shaping self-knowledge as they are enduring aspects of self-knowledge used to categorize oneself, and also ones by which individuals are continually categorized by others. For these reasons, an individual's identification with a central core of group memberships may overshadow the multitude of groups to which she belongs, regardless of the situational salience of less central identities (Breakwell, 1986; Rosenberg, 1981).

In the 1980s, a body of work emerged viewing gender as a personality variable, with individuals assumed to vary in the degree to which they used gender in the way in which they viewed the world. "Gender schemas" were offered as hypothetical cognitive structures which predisposed the individual to process information in gender-related terms and also to shape goals and guide behaviors (see also Markus, Crane, Bernstein & Siladi, 1982). In other words, the pervasive importance of gender in a society can lead individuals to perceive and understand incoming information in terms of this demarcation and to determine appropriate behaviors for the self (as well as for others). This view of the influence of group membership on self-knowledge and behavior may result in the conclusion that such influences are the result of a rather passive process. However, other research suggests that men and women are not passive recipients of social definitions of gender. Instead, the development of a gender identity is an active process which is continually shaped by both personal experience, culturally held (as well as subculturally held) beliefs, and the immediate social context (Ashmore,

1990). Similar arguments have been offered by researchers exploring the development of an ethnic identity (e.g., Cross, 1991; Liebkind, 1992), deaf identity (Bat-Chava, 1992), and gay identity (Coyle, 1992). For example, Ethier & Deaux (1994) demonstrate that not all members of a social category respond identically to a sudden change in the numerical distinctiveness of their group. In their study, Hispanic students who initially had strong ethnic identities responded to entering an Ivy league (predominantly white) university by strengthening their ethnic identification through involvement in cultural activities. However, Hispanic students who initially had weak ethnic identification tended to perceive greater self-related threat in the environment and subsequently further weakened their ethnic identity. This study demonstrates that commitment to a group membership develops over a period of time and that the strength of this commitment will influence perceptions and behaviors in specific social contexts. For some individuals, one group membership may come to be highly influential across situations in determining goals, values, and behaviors while other individuals may not associate strongly with any single identity. The factors that lead to these outcomes are simply not well understood at this time.

Clearly, individuals derive self-knowledge from the social groups to which they belong. However, it is less clear whether this is a primary motivation for collective identification. Further research must address this issue directly. While several studies of the personal (rather than collective) self-concept have attempted to test a self-esteem hypothesis against a self-knowledge hypothesis (e.g., Swann, Griffin, Predmore & Gaines, 1987; Swann, Hixon, Stein-Seroussi & Gilbert, 1990; Swann, Pelham & Krull, 1989), very little research has attempted a similar critical test of the collective self (although see Lorenzi-Cioldi, 1991). Further research is also needed to delineate the conditions under which the collective self is likely to serve these varied motives. In reality, it is likely that collective identifications are useful for both self-enhancement and for gaining self-knowledge. As well, there may be a host of other motives that are served by collective identification. For example, Hogg and Abrams (1993) suggest that individuals are motivated to attain power and control, affiliation, and self-efficacy. Very little, if any research has explored the ways in which identifying with social groups might satisfy these goals.

CONCLUSION

In recent years, social psychologists have taken quite seriously the task of empirically demonstrating the ways in which collectives create or influence a sense of self. The formidable challenge lay in the creation of experiments to observe the relationship that psychologists and sociologists from an earlier generation had proposed but not tested. Focusing attention on two related processes where such an influence may be observed, we found that a substantial and growing literature now exists in response to this challenge. Research on self-enhancement and self-knowledge shows that relatively straightforward notions of how social groups come to influence and create a sense of self are rapidly rendered complex by demonstrations that group membership does not have a simple and, as yet, fully predictable influence on self and identity.

Research using experimentally created groups confirms that group status can and does produce self-enhancement and may indeed be one of the bases for group affiliation. Research using existing group memberships, however, also suggests that the relationship may be more complex. In particular, future research must look to the counterintuitive finding that membership in low-status groups does not necessarily lead to reduced self-esteem, at least as it is typically measured using scales that assess consciously accessible esteem. Regarding self-knowledge, the findings also show how collectives influence the way in which one comes to describe and view oneself. Here too, the evidence suggests that the group to which one belongs can significantly influence the self-descriptions that emerge and the choices and preferences that come to be adopted, with or without awareness of such influences. On the other hand, this research also suggests that the manner in which one negotiates a sense of self and identity is an active process that involves adopting as well as distancing from the attributes of one's social group. The relationship is unlikely to be a simple one where self comes to mirror the collective, and future research will need to probe more deeply into both the conscious and unconscious ways in which the collective shapes the individual.

REFERENCES

ABRAMS, D. (1992). Processes in social identification. In G. M. Breakwell (Ed.), *Social psychology of identity and the self concept* (pp. 57–99). London: Surrey University Press.

ABRAMS, D. & HOGG, M. A. (1988). Comments on the motivational status of self-esteem in social identity and intergroup discrimination. *European Journal of Social Psychology, 18,* 317–334.

ABRAMSON, L. Y., METALSKY, G. I. & ALLOY, L. B. (1989). Hopelessness depression: A theory-based subtype of depression. *Psychological Review, 96,* 358–378.

ALLPORT, G. W. (1937). *Personality: A psychological interpretation.* New York: Holt.

ASHMORE, R. D. (1990). Sex, gender, and the individual. In L. A. Pervin (Ed.), *Handbook of personality: Theory and research* (pp. 486–526). New York: Guilford Press.

BACKMAN, C. (1988). The self: A dialectical approach. *Advances in Experimental Social Psychology, 21,* 229–260.

BANAJI, M. R. & PRENTICE, D. A. (1994). The self in social contexts. *Annual Review of Psychology, 45,* 297–332.

BANDURA, A. & WALTERS, R. H. (1963). *Social learning and personality development.* New York: Holt, Rinehart & Winston.

BARTLETT, F. C. (1932). *Remembering*. Cambridge, England: Cambridge University Press.

BAT-CHAVA, Y. (1994). Group identification and self-esteem of deaf adults. *Personality and Social Psychology Bulletin, 20,* 494–502.

BOCHNER, S. & OHSAKO, T. (1977). Ethnic role salience in racially homogeneous and heterogeneous societies. *Journal of Cross-Cultural Psychology, 8,* 477–492.

BOYANOWSKY, E. O. & ALLEN, V. L. (1973). Ingroup norms and self-identity as determinants of discriminatory behavior. *Journal of Personality and Social Psychology, 25,* 408–418.

BREAKWELL, G. (1986). *Coping with threatened identities.* London: Methuen.

BREWER, M. B. (1991). The social self: On being the same and different at the same time. *Personality and Social Psychology Bulletin, 17,* 475–482.

BREWER, M. B. (1993). Social identity, distinctiveness, and in-group homogeneity. *Social Cognition, 11,* 150–164.

BREWER, M. B. (1994). Self-evaluation effects of interpersonal versus intergroup social comparison. *Journal of Personality and Social Psychology, 66,* 268–275.

BREWER, M. B., MANZI, J. M. & SHAW, J. S. (1993). In-group identification as a function of depersonalization, distinctiveness, and status. *Psychological Science, 4,* 88–92.

BREWER, M. B. & WEBER, J. G. (1994). Self-evaluation effects of interpersonal versus intergroup social comparison. *Journal of Personality and Social Psychology, 66,* 268–275.

BROWN, R. & DESCHAMPS, J.-C. (1980). Discrimination between individuals and between groups. *Bulletin de Psychologie, 34,* 185–195.

CHARTERS, W. W. & NEWCOMB, T. M. (1952). Some attitudinal effects of experimentally increased salience of a membership group. In G. E. Swanson, T. M. Newcomb & E. L. Hartley (Eds.), *Readings in Social Psychology.* New York: Holt.

Cialdini, R. B., Borden, R. J., Thorne, A., Walker, M. R., Freeman, S. & Sloan, L. R. (1976). Basking in reflected glory: Three (football) field studies. *Journal of Personality and Social Psychology, 34,* 366–375.

COFER, C. N. & APPLEY, M. H. (1964). *Motivation: Theory and Research.* New York: Wiley.

COOLEY, C. H. (1922). *Human nature and the social order.* New York: Scribners.

COTA, A. A. & DION, K. L. (1986). Salience of gender and sex composition of ad hoc groups: An experimental test of distinctiveness theory. *Journal of Personality and Social Psychology, 50,* 770–776.

COYLE, A. (1992). "My own special creation"? The construction of gay identity. In G. M. Breakwell (Ed.), *Social psychology of identity and the self concept* (pp. 187–220). London: Surrey University Press.

CRANDALL, R. (1973). The measurement of self-esteem and related constructs. In J. Robinson & P. Shaver (Eds.), *Measures of social psychological attitudes.* Ann Arbor: University of Michigan.

CROCKER, J., CORNWELL, B. & MAJOR, B. (1993). The stigma of overweight: Affective consequences of attributional ambiguity. *Journal of Personality and Social Psychology, 64,* 60–70.

CROCKER, J. & LUHTANEN, R. (1990). Collective self-esteem and ingroup bias. *Journal of Personality and Social Psychology, 58,* 60–67.

CROCKER, J., LUHTANEN, R., BLAINE, B. & BROADNAX, S. (1994). Collective self-esteem and psychological well-being among white, black, and Asian college students. *Personality and Social Psychology Bulletin, 20,* 503–513.

CROCKER, J. & MAJOR, B. (1989). Social stigma and self-esteem: The self-protective properties of stigma. *Psychological Review, 96,* 608–630.

CROCKER, J., VOEKL, K., TESTA, M. & MAJOR, B. (1991). Social stigma: The affective consequences of attributional ambiguity. *Journal of Personality and Social Psychology, 60,* 218–228.

CROSS, W. E. (1991). *Shades of black: Diversity in African-American identity.* Philadelphia: Temple University Press.

DEAUX, K. & Major, B. (1987). Putting gender into context: An interactive model of gender-related behavior. *Psychological Review, 94,* 369–389.

DIENER, E. (1984). Subjective well-being. *Psychological Bulletin, 95,* 542–575.

DION, K. L. & EARN, B. M. (1975). The phenomenology of being a target of prejudice. *Journal of Personality and Social Psychology, 32,* 944–950.

DION, K. L., EARN, B. N. & YEE, P. H. N. (1978). The experience of being a victim of prejudice. An experimental approach. *International Journal of Psychology, 13,* 197–294.

DUNNING, D. & COHEN, G. L. (1992). Egocentric definitions of traits and abilities in social judgment. *Journal of Personality and Social Psychology, 63,* 341–355.

Dunning, D., Perie, M. & Story, A. L. (1991). Self-serving prototypes of social categories. *Journal of Personality and Social Psychology, 61,* 957–968.

ETHIER, K. A. & DEAUX, K. (1994). Negotiating social identity when contexts change: Maintaining identification and responding to threat. *Journal of Personality and Social Psychology, 67,* 243–251.

FESTINGER, L. (1954). A theory of social comparison processes. *Human Relations, 7,* 71–82.

FISHBEIN, M. (1967). Attitudes and the prediction of behavior. In M. Fishbein (Ed.), *Readings in attitude theory and measurement* (pp. 477–492). New York: Wiley.

FRABLE, D. E. S., WORTMAN, C., JOSEPH, J., KIRSCHT, J. & KESSLER, R. (1994). Predicting self-esteem, well-being, and distress in a cohort of gay men: The importance of cultural stigma and personal visibility. Unpublished manuscript.

GEIS, F. L., BROWN, V., JENNINGS, J. & PORTER, N. (1984). TV commercials as achievement scripts for women. *Sex Roles, 10,* 513–525.

GERGEN, K. J. (1987). Toward self as relationship. In K. Yardley & T. Honess (Eds.), *Self and identity: Psychosocial perspectives.* New York: Wiley.

GFELLNER, B. M. (1986). Age salience in order adults' spontaneous self-concept. *Perceptual and Motor Skills, 63,* 1196–1198.

GOFFMAN, E. (1956). *The presentation of self in everyday life.* Edinburgh: University of Edinburgh.

GORDON, C. & GERGEN, K. J. (1968). *The self in social interaction.* New York: Wiley.

GREENWALD, A. G. (1980). The totalitarian ego: Fabrication and revision of personal history. *American Psychologist, 35,* 603–618.

GREENWALD, A. G. & BANAJI, M. R. (1995). Implicit social cognition: Attitudes, self-esteem, and stereotypes. *Psychological Review, 1,* 4–27.

HASTORF, A. & CANTRIL, H. (1954). They saw a game: A case study. *Journal of Abnormal and Social Psychology, 49,* 129–134.

HOGG, M. A. & ABRAMS, D. (1988). *Social identifications: A psychology of intergroup relations and group processes.* New York: Routledge.

HOGG, M. A. & ABRAMS, D. (1990). Social motivation, self-esteem, and social identity. In D. Abrams & M. A. Hogg (Eds.), *Social identity theory: Constructive and critical advances* (pp. 28–47). New York: Harvester Wheatsheaf and Springer.

HOGG, M. A. & ABRAMS, D. (1993). *Group motivation.* New York: Harvester Wheatsheaf.

HOGG, M. A. & TURNER, J. C. (1987). Intergroup behaviour, self-stereotyping and the salience of social categories. *British Journal of Social Psychology, 26,* 325–340.

HOGG, M. A., TURNER, J. C., NASCIMENTO-SCHULZ, C. & SPRIGGS, D. (1986). Social categorization, intergroup behaviour and self-esteem: Two experiments. *Revista de Psicología Social, 1,* 23–37.

JAMES, W. (1890). *Principles of psychology.* New York: Holt.

JENSEN, G. F., WHITE, C. S. & GALLIHER, J. M. (1982). Ethnic status and adolescent self-evaluations: An extension of research on minority self-esteem. *Social Problems, 30,* 226–239.

JOST, J. T. & BANAJI, M. R. (1994). The role of stereotyping in system-justification and the production of false consciousness. *British Journal of Social Psychology, 33,* 1–27.

KITZINGER, C. (1992). The individuated self concept: A critical analysis of social-constructionist writing on individualism. In G. M. Breakwell (Ed.), *Social psychology of identity and the self concept* (pp. 221–250). London: Surrey University Press.

KUNDA, Z. & SANITIOSO, R. (1989). Motivated changes in the self-concept. *Journal of Experimental Social Psychology, 25,* 272–285.

LEMYRE, L. & SMITH, P. (1985). Intergroup discrimination and self-esteem in the minimal group paradigm. *Journal of Personality and Social Psychology, 49,* 660–670.

LEWIN, K. (1943). Defining the "field at a given time." *Psychological Review, 50,* 292–310.

LEVY, B. (1996). Improving memory in old age through implicit self-stereotyping. *Journal of Personality and Social Psychology, 71,* 1092–1107.

LIEBKIND, K. (1991). Ethnic identity—Challenging the boundaries of social psychology. In G. M. Breakwell (Ed.), *Social psychology of identity and the self concept* (pp. 147–185). London: Surrey University Press.

LORENZI-COLDI, F. (1991). Self-stereotyping and self-enhancement in gender groups. *European Journal of Social Psychology, 21,* 403–417.

MAJOR, B. & CROCKER, J. (1993). Social stigma: The consequences of attributional ambiguity. In D. M. Mackie & D. L. Hamilton (Eds.), *Affect, cognition and stereotyping: Interactive processes in group perception* (pp. 345–370). San Diego, CA: Academic Press.

MAJOR, B. & FORCEY, B. (1985). Social comparisons and pay evaluations: Preferences for same-sex and same-job wage comparisons. *Journal of Experimental Social Psychology, 21,* 393–405.

MARKUS, H., CRANE, M., BERNSTEIN, S. & SILADI, M. (1982). Self-schemas and gender. *Journal of Personality and Social Psychology, 42,* 38–50.

MARKUS, H. & KITAYAMA, S. (1991). Culture and the self: Implications for cognition, emotion, and motivation. *Psychological Review, 98,* 224–253.

MASLOW, A. H. (1954). *Motivation and personality.* New York: Harper.

MCGUIRE, W. J. (1984). Search for the self: Going beyond self-esteem and the reactive self. In R. A. Zucker, J. Arnoff & A. I. Rabin (Eds.), *Personality and the prediction of behavior* (pp. 73–120). New York: Academic Press.

MCGUIRE, W. J. & MCGUIRE, C. V. (1988). Content and process in the experience of self. *Advances in Experimental Social Psychology, 21,* 97–144.

MEAD, G. H. (1934). *Mind, self, and society.* Chicago: University of Chicago Press.

MINARD, R. D. (1952). Race relationships in the Pocahontas coalfield. *Journal of Social Issues, 8,* 29–44.

MYRDAL, G. (1944). *An American Dilemma.* New York: Harper & Row.

OAKES, P. J. & TURNER, J. C. (1980). Social categorization and intergroup behaviour: Does minimal intergroup discrimination make social identity more positive? *European Journal of Social Psychology, 10,* 295–301.

OGBU, J. (1986). The consequences of the American caste system. In U. Neisser (Ed.), *The school achievement of minority children: New perspectives.* Hillsdale, NJ: Erlbaum.

PELHAM, B. W. & SWANN, W. B. (1989). From self-conceptions to self-worth: On the sources and structure of global self-esteem. *Journal of Personality and Social Psychology, 57,* 672–680.

PITTMAN, T. S. & HELLER, J. F. (1987). Social motivation. *Annual Review of Psychology, 38,* 461–489.

ROGERS, C. R. (1951). *Client-centered therapy.* Boston: Houghton Mifflin.

ROSENBERG, M. (1981). The self-concept: Social product and social force. In M. Rosenberg & R. H. Turner (Eds.), *Social psychology. Sociological perspectives.* New York: Basic Books.

SIMON, B., GLÄSSNER-BAYERL, B. & STRATENWERTH, I. (1991). Stereotyping and self-stereotyping in a natural intergroup context: The case of heterosexual and homosexual men. *Social Psychology Quarterly, 54,* 252–266.

SIMON, B. & HAMILTON, D. L. (1994). Self-stereotyping and social context: The effects of relative in-group size and in-group status. *Journal of Personality and Social Psychology, 66,* 699–711.

SIMON, B., PANTALEO, G. & MUMMENDEY, A. (1995). Unique individual or interchangeable group member? The accentuation of intragroup differences versus similarities as an indicator of the individual self versus the collective self. *Journal of Personality and Social Psychology, 69,* 106–119.

STEELE, C. M. (1988). The psychology of self-affirmation: sustaining the integrity of the self. *Advances in Experimental Social Psychology, 21,* 93–159.

STEELE, C. M. & ARONSON, J. (1995). Stereotype threat and the intellectual test performance of African Americans. *Journal of Personality and Social Psychology, 69,* 797–811.

STRYKER, S. (1987). Identity theory: Development and extensions. In K. Yardley & T. Honess (Eds.), *Self and identity: Psychological perspectives* (pp. 89–104). Chichester, England: Wiley.

SULS, J. & WILLS, T. A. (Eds.) (1991). *Social comparison.* Hillsdale, NJ: Erlbaum.

SWANN, W. B. (1990). To be adored or to be known: The interplay of self-enhancement and self-verification. In R. M. Sorrentino & E. T. Higgins (Eds.), *Handbook of motivation and cognition* (pp. 408–450). New York: Guilford.

SWANN, W. B., GRIFFIN, J. J., PREDMORE, S. X. & GAINES, B. (1987). The cognitive-affective crossfire: When self-consistency confronts self-enhancement. *Journal of Personality and Social Psychology, 52,* 881–889.

SWANN, W. B., HIXON, J. G., STEIN-SEROUSSI, A. & GILBERT, D. T. (1990). The fleeting gleam of praise: Cognitive processes underlying behavioral reactions to feedback. Embracing the bitter "truth": Negative self-concepts and marital commitment. *Journal of Personality and Social Psychology, 59,* 17–26.

SWANN, W. B., PELHAM, B. W. & KRULL, D. S. (1989). Agreeable fancy or disagreeable truth? Reconciling self-enhancement and self-verification. *Journal of Personality and Social Psychology, 57,* 782–791.

TAJFEL, H. (Ed.) (1978). *Differentiation between social groups: Studies in the social psychology of intergroup relations.* London: Academic Press.

TAJFEL, H. (1981). Social stereotypes and social groups. In J. C. Turner & H. Giles (Eds.), *Intergroup Behavior.* Oxford: Blackwell.

TAJFEL, H. (1982). *Social identity and intergroup relations.* Cambridge: Cambridge University Press.

TAJFEL, H. (Ed.) (1984). *The social dimension: European developments in social psychology (Vols. 1, 2).* Cambridge, England: Cambridge University Press.

TAJFEL, H. & TURNER, J. C. (1979). An integrative theory of intergroup conflict. In W. G. Austin & S. Worchel (Eds.), *The social psychology of intergroup relations* (pp. 33–47). Monterey, CA: Brooks-Cole.

TAJFEL, H. & TURNER, J. C. (1986). The social identity theory of intergroup behaviour.

In S. Worchel & W. G. Austin (Eds.), *Psychology of intergroup relations* (pp. 7–24). Chicago: Nelson-Hall.

TAYLOR, M. C. & WALSH, E. J. (1979). Explanations of black self-esteem: Some empirical tests. *Social Psychology Quarterly, 42,* 242–253.

TAYLOR, S. E. (1983). Adjustment to threatening events: A theory of cognitive adaptation. *American Psychologist, 38,* 1161–1173.

TAYLOR, S. E. & BROWN, J. D. (1988). Illusion and well-being: a social psychological perspective on mental health. *Psychological Bulletin, 15,* 337–348.

TAYLOR, D. M., WRIGHT, S. C. & PORTER, L. E. (1994). Dimensions of perceived discrimination: The personal/group discrimination discrepancy. In M. P. Zanna & J. M. Olson (Eds.), *The psychology of prejudice: The Ontario symposium, Vol. 7* (pp. 233–255). Hillsdale, NJ: Erlbaum.

TENNEN, H. & HERZBERGER, S. (1987). Depression, self-esteem, and the absence of self-protective attributional biases. *Journal of Personality and Social Psychology, 52,* 72–80.

TESSER, A. (1988). Toward a self-evaluation maintenance model of social behavior. *Advances in Experimental Social Psychology, 21,* 181–227.

TROPE, Y. (1986). Self-enhancement and self-assessment in achievement behavior. In R. M. Sorrentino & E. T. Higgins (Eds.), *Handbook of motivation and cognition: Foundations of social behavior* (pp. 350–378). New York: Guilford.

TURNER, J. C. (1981). The experimental social psychology of intergroup behavior. In J. C. Turner & H. Giles (Eds.), *Intergroup behavior.* Oxford, England: Blackwell.

TURNER, J. C. (1985). Social categorization and the self-concept: A social-cognitive theory of group behavior. In E. J. Lawler (Ed.), *Advances in group processes: Theory and research, Vol. 2.* Greenwich, CT: JAI Press.

TURNER, J. C. (1991). Social influence. Milton Keynes, England: Open University Press.

TURNER, J. C. & GILES, H. (Eds.) (1981). *Intergroup behaviour.* Oxford, England: Blackwell.

TURNER, J. C., HOGG, M. A., OAKES, P. J., REICHER, S. D. & WETHERELL, M. S. (1987). *Rediscovering the social group: A self-categorization theory.* Oxford, England: Blackwell.

TURNER, J. C., OAKES, P. J., HASLAM, S. A. & McGARTY, C. (1994). Self and collective: Cognition and social context. *Personality and Social Psychology Bulletin, 20,* 454–463.

WHITE, R. W. (1959). Motivation reconsidered: The concept of competence. *Psychological Review, 66,* 297–333.

WOOD, J. V. (1989). Theory and research concerning social comparisons of personal attributes. *Psychological Bulletin, 106,* 231–248.

WYLIE, R. C. (1979). *The self concept: Theory and research on selected topics,* (vol. 2). Lincoln, NE: University of Nebraska Press.

Joan G. Miller is a research scientist in the Department of Psychology at Yale University, where she has been on the faculty since 1984. She received her Ph.D. in human development from the University of Chicago. Her research interests are in the area of cultural psychology. Her ongoing cross-cultural research among European-American and Hindu Indian adults and children is uncovering the existence of cultural variability both in the morality of caring and in interpersonal motivation.

Culture and the Self:
Uncovering the Cultural Grounding
of Psychological Theory

JOAN G. MILLER

Department of Psychology
Yale University
P.O. Box 208205
New Haven, Connecticut 06520-8205

For most of its history, psychology has been a culturally grounded discipline that has recognized the constitutive role of collective meanings and practices on the development of self. Yet, as Jahoda's insightful account reveals, this sensitivity to culture has been muted during most of the twentieth century, as psychology has tended to be dominated by an idealized physical science model of explanation (Jahoda, 1993). The behaviorist emphasis in psychology that prevailed during the first half of the century—challenged as it was both by a recognition of the role of biology and of agency in behavior—gave way to the Cognitive Revolution without taking into account the cultural grounding of meanings (Bruner, 1990).

During the twentieth century, the predominant goal of psychological explanation has been that of formulating generalizations that apply across cultural groups and historical contexts—generalizations that are analogous to the covering laws of physical science. Just as there is absolute prediction of physical phenomena within a vacuum, psychology has sought to remove or to control the effects of culture in order to isolate the processes and properties that are assumed to be responsible for observed regularities in behavior. This stance was not called into question by early research in cross-cultural psychology (Triandis & Lambert, 1980). Rather, early research in cross-cultural psychology was oriented primarily toward hypothesis testing, that is, toward applying existing psychological theories in diverse cultural contexts in an attempt to test their generality. It tended not to be involved in the formation of basic theory and did not fundamentally challenge the assumption that psychological structures and processes can be understood independently of the cultural contexts in which they operate.

This view of psychological processes as culture-free is being seriously challenged by recent theory and research associated with the interdisciplinary perspective of cultural psychology (Cole, 1990; Miller, 1996; Shweder, 1990). This latter perspective conceptualizes culture and psychology as mutually constitutive. Consonant with the insights of the Cognitive Revolution, individuals are viewed as agents whose active interpretations of their experiences are fundamental to their psychological functioning. However, it is further recognized that individuals inhabit social environments that are structured by preexisting cultural meanings and practices. In affecting individual understandings and intentions, these meanings and practices are seen as having a qualitative impact on the development of psychological phenomena.

The goal of the present chapter is to highlight some of the insights for understanding the self and for the formation of psychological theory which emerge from attention to the cultural grounding of behavior. The first section addresses the changing conceptions of culture that have contributed to the recent increased interest in culture within psychology, and to the major premises associated with the perspective of cultural psychology. In the second section, a program of cross-cultural research, which I and my colleagues have undertaken on interpersonal morality, is discussed to document ways in which cultural research has value in uncovering the implicit cultural grounding of psychological theories and of the research enterprise. In conclusion, consideration is given to the multiple contributions of a cultural perspective in psychology.

THE RE-EMERGENCE OF CULTURE IN PSYCHOLOGY

Semiotic Views of Culture

One of the key conceptual shifts that has contributed to the recent increased interest in culture in psychology is the emergence of semiotic conceptions of culture. For many years, culture was ignored in psychological explanation or treated exclusively as an ecological context (Bronfenbrenner, 1979). From this ecological perspective, cultural beliefs and practices are understood in functional terms as accommodations to the objective adaptive constraints that are presented by aspects of the physical setting and social structure and that make certain forms of behavior more or less adaptive.

This perspective is applied, for example, in behavioral genetic research on intelligence, in which environments are understood as presenting more or less cognitive complexity and accordingly as more or less facilitating of cognitive development (Scarr, 1992). Thus, it is maintained, for example, that homes which provide children with more varied and complex cognitive stimulation in the form of books, toys, modes of verbal interaction, etc. are more successful in enabling children to realize their inborn cognitive potentials than are homes which lack this environmental richness. An ecological view of culture has also informed much work within the field of cross-cultural psychology. For example, much of the early work on culture and personality assumed that cultural variation in personality arose as a function of the contrasting ecological demands found in different societies (Whiting & Whiting, 1975).

An ecological view of culture understandably has considerable appeal within psychology. A concern with adaption is fundamental to human survival and thus is a crucial consideration to take into account in explaining behavior. At least some of the attraction of an ecological view of culture also lies in its consonance with the dominant concepts and methodologies of psychology. The ecological parameters of environments are seen as objective features that may be inductively assessed, with their effects on behavior understood in causal terms.

Ironically, however, the ecological conception of culture which has prevailed in both mainstream and cross-cultural psychology has contributed to the construct of culture's adding little or no explanatory force to psychological explanation. This view of culture does not call into question the dualistic form of most psychological theories, which focus either on objective features of the context (e.g., information, adaptive constraints, etc.) and/or on subjective features of the person (e.g., information processing, genetic potential, etc.). To the extent that culture is conceptualized as the objective environment to which behavior is adapted it is already a consideration that is accounted for within psychological explanation.

A qualitative shift in how culture is understood and in its role in psychological theory has emerged in recent years with the development of semiotic conceptions of culture. This stance may be seen, for example, in Geertz's classic definition of culture as "an historically transmitted pattern of meanings embodied in symbols" (Geertz, 1973, p.89). Culture in this and other recent views is regarded, at least in part, as an ideational lens through which experience is both known and created. It is neither the objective world of brute facts nor the subjective world of individual psychological experience, but rather an intersubjective world of shared meanings and practices that provides a medium through which these other worlds are known, experienced, and, in part, formed (Cole, 1995).

From a semiotic perspective, cultural meanings are viewed as including representational information, such as shared knowledge about the covariational structure of experience, as well as directive information, such as normative expectations. What is most significant about a semiotic perspective, however, is its recognition that culture includes as well constitutive meanings that serve to define and thereby to create realities. These constitutive meanings encompass not only social categories, as familiarized in Searle's well-known example of the constitutive entity of a "bride" and of a "marriage", but also primary categories of epistemological knowledge (Searle, 1969). Thus, it is recognized that such fundamental constructs in psychology as self, mind, and emotion depend, at least in part, on conventional cultural definitions for their existence and form.

Premises and Goals of Cultural Psychology

Cultural psychology represents a newly emerging perspective that embodies this qualitatively different view of culture and of its role in psychology. From the perspective of cultural psychology, psychological processes are understood to be patterned, in part, by cultural meanings and practices just as these meanings and practices are understood to be dependent, in part, on the involvement of specific communities of intentional agents. As reflected in the label of "cultural psychology," it is assumed that culture and psychology represent integral rather than isolable units.

The perspective of cultural psychology rejects the stance, associated with the tradition of cross-cultural psychology, of viewing culture as an independent variable whose effects may be observed on the dependent variable of individual psychological processes. This latter stance is seen as treating psychological processes as outside of culture rather than as dependent on culture for their form and structure. Equally, it rejects the stance associated with social constructionism of treating psychological processes as purely discursive phenomena (Gergen, 1992). From the viewpoint of cultural psychology, such a position is considered to be reductionist, in its stance of treating psychological phenomena as isomorphic with cultural phenomena, and in its limited attention to individual agency.

Within cultural psychology, the assumption is made that psychology is inherently a cultural enterprise in that its subject matter is enculturated agents whose understandings and motivations are always patterned, in part, by the meanings and practices of their communities. A major goal of cultural psychology is to make overt the implicit cultural dependence of psychological theories. From the perspective of cultural psychology, culture is treated not as an unwanted source of bias, but as a primary explanatory consideration that must form an integral part of all psychological explanations.

INTERPERSONAL MORALITY AND CULTURE

In this section, a cultural psychology perspective will be applied in examination of interpersonal morality. The point of this discussion is to illustrate ways in which a cultural perspective may provide insight not only into the nature of psychological processes but more broadly into the research enterprise and its larger cultural context.

The centrality of interpersonal morality to social life makes it an important domain of the self. Interpersonal morality focuses on the commitments which individuals feel to be responsive to the needs of family, friends, and others in special relationships. It then bears on a view of the self not merely as a solitary agent, with personal preferences and needs, but also as a social agent, in interdependent relationship with others. Conceptions of interpersonal morality are closely linked not only to personal identity but also to attachment expectations and experiences, behavior in close relationships, and interpersonal motivation.

Contributions and Promise of Morality-of-Caring Framework

In examination of interpersonal morality, initial attention will be directed to the morality-of-caring framework forwarded by Gilligan and her colleagues (Gilligan, 1982; Gilligan & Wiggins, 1988). Beyond its impact on the field of moral development, Gilligan's theory has stimulated the interest of feminist theorists, has been embraced as a cultural critique of psychology, and has informed anthropological research, as well as provided impetus for educational reform. The model has also been well received by the lay public, as evidenced, for example, in the widespread interest in Gilligan's book, *In a Different Voice: Psychological Theory and Women's Development.*

In terms of moral theory, the foremost contribution of Gilligan's morality-of-caring framework has been in broadening existing conceptions of the content of morality. As Kohlberg himself acknowledged, Gilligan successfully identified an important concern that was missing in his theory (Kohlberg, Levine & Hewer, 1983). Whereas the Kohlbergian scheme treats morality as limited to issues of justice and individual rights, Gilligan demonstrates that morality additionally includes responsibilities to meet the needs of others.

A second major contribution of Gilligan's model has been in highlighting the need for attention to subgroup diversity in morality. Part of the great initial interest in Gilligan's model lay in its claim that morality is gender-related, with the morality of justice emphasized particularly by males and the morality of caring emphasized particularly by females. Although subsequent research has provided only weak support for either assertion (Walker, 1984), the charges have sensitized researchers to the possibility of gender variation in morality as well as spurred interest in gender differences that may exist in other related areas.

Arguably, however, the most central reason for the broad interest generated by Gilligan's approach lies in neither of these contributions, but rather in the model's speaking to concerns with community, which are held by psychologists and the broader culture. As numerous commentators have observed, with the rise of modernity there appears to have been a loss of community that is reflected in personal feelings of isolation, the devaluation of relationships, and other related social stresses (Bellah, Madsen, Sullivan, Swidler & Tipton, 1985; Conger, 1981). It is argued that the solution to this problem cannot be found in a return to the forms of community found in the pre-industrial West or in non-Western collectivist cultures. These latter approaches are regarded as oppressing the individual, in their rigid role requirements and restriction of personal autonomy. Rather, social theorists tend to portray the ideal as a form that retains the respective strengths of the individualistic and collectivist approaches, while avoiding their shortcomings (Guisinger & Blatt, 1994; Sandel, 1982). As portrayed by these theorists, the ideal system is one which embodies a strong sense of community yet which avoids subordinating the individual to the group.

One of the attractions of Gilligan's theory is that it provides a model of community that not only fits this ideal but that also forwards an empirical claim. The assertion is made that this type of robust yet non-oppressive sense of community is not merely a hypothetical form, but is an orientation that actually exists among individuals who maintain a morality of caring. The theory then offers the hopeful news that a strong sense of community may actually be present at least among certain subgroups of Americans.

As described in Gilligan's model, the morality of caring represents an orientation in which individuals feel a responsibility to care for needy individuals when they become aware of the others' needs and are able to help. This sense of moral responsibility is based on individuals' development of a connected view of self, in which they consider meeting the other's needs as integral to their personal identity. Such perceived interpersonal responsibilities are assumed to be enduring in time, far reaching in scope, and non-contingent on purely egoistic considerations, such as trivial matters of taste or liking.

Importantly, the morality of caring avoids the perceived coercion associated with traditional collectivist approaches to interpersonal responsibilities. Moral responsibilities of caring are assumed to arise as freely given commitments rather than in conformity to role expectations or to other external pressures. Emphasis is also placed on effecting a balance between the individual's personal needs and those of others, as well as on avoiding an overly selfless stance. In sum, the morality of caring represents an orientation that promotes individuality and choice, at the same time that it also achieves a system of interdependence in which support from others can be taken for granted. As one of Gilligan's informants expresses this type of view, it represents a system ". . . where everyone is encouraged to become an individual and at the same time everybody helps others and receives help from them" (Gilligan, 1982, p. 54).

A Cultural Psychology Approach to Interpersonal Morality

From a perspective of cultural psychology, the morality of caring may be criticized as giving little attention to aspects of culture besides those associated with gender differentiation. In the morality of caring model, the morality of justice is portrayed as being supported by the individualistic values of the culture, whereas the morality of caring is portrayed as developing outside of and exclusively in opposition to such individualism. This view, it may be argued, fails to recognize the extent to which all experience is culturally mediated.

Taking this cultural grounding into account, it would be expected that any morality of caring which develops in an individualistic culture, such as that of the United States, would reflect aspects of the cultural individualism, just as does any morality of justice. Furthermore, it would be anticipated that certain contradictions might exist between realizing these individualistic concerns and meeting responsibilities of community. Such contradictions would result in a weaker sense of community developing than that which would occur in a culture that maintained a less individualistic view of self.

Summarized below are findings from a program of cross-cultural research which I and my colleagues have undertaken that explore these questions regarding both the universality of the morality of caring and the possibility of achieving a form of interpersonal morality that gives full weight both to community and to individuality. The research to be described was undertaken among samples of European-American adults and children from New Haven, Connecticut and among samples of Hindu Indian adults and children from Mysore City, in southern India. No effects of gender and few effects, if any, of socioeconomic status were observed in any of the results.

Hindu Indian culture provides an informative case to compare with European-American culture because of its contrasting conceptions of the person and of the social order. The view of self emphasized in European-American culture is one that treats the individual as prior to and more fundamental than society (Dumont, 1970). In this cultural conception, social expectations tend to be seen as external forms that constrain the true underlying self. In contrast, in Hindu Indian culture, the person tends to be conceptualized as inherently part of a social body. Central to this view of self is the concept of *dharma,* which denotes simultaneously moral duty, code for conduct, right action, and inherent character (O'Flaherty & Derrett, 1978). Unlike Western conceptions of self, which tend to portray individuals as naturally autonomous and duty as a restriction on this freedom, Hindu Indian conceptions tend to portray individuals as naturally social and duty as an aspect of individual nature.

The methodology employed in the studies involved either (*a*) asking subjects to generate examples of real-life helping behavior; or (*b*) presenting subjects with hypothetical scenarios which portrayed an agent helping or failing to help someone in need. In the latter type of studies, a combination of both between-subjects and within-subjects manipulations were employed to vary aspects of the scenarios, such as the magnitude of the unmet need, the cost to the agent of helping, the role relationship between the agent and the needy party, and the presence of potentially extenuating circumstances. Subjects were asked both open-ended and short-answer questions about their moral assessments and other evaluations of the behaviors.

To ensure the cultural appropriateness of the research materials in the Indian context, the study protocols were examined for cultural suitability by Indian scholars and modified, as necessary, on the basis of their comments. American and Indian forms of the research protocols were prepared, with these forms differing only in minor details, such as in their use of proper names. Standard back-translation techniques were employed in translating the American versions of the research protocols into Kannada. Interviews with Americans were conducted in English by Yale University research assistants, whereas interviews with Indians were conducted in the local language of Kannada by researchers from the Mysore area who were native Kannada speakers.

The Scope and Stringency of Interpersonal Responsibilities

Studies which I and my colleagues have undertaken demonstrate that Indians perceive interpersonal responsibilities in in-group relationships as broader in scope and more stringent than do Americans (Miller & Bersoff, 1982; Miller, Bersoff & Harwood, 1990). Thus, we have shown that in "low cost" situations, Indians maintain that agents' responsibilities to meet the needs of others extend even to cases involving minor need and in which the needy party is a stranger. In contrast, Americans less frequently judge that there is a responsibility to help in these types of cases. We have also demonstrated that Americans approach interpersonal responsibilities in more discretionary terms than do Indians. Thus, whereas Indians tend to consider an agent's failure to help as legitimately subject to social censure, Americans tend to treat it as the agent's own business.

This cross-cultural difference in the scope and stringency of interpersonal responsibilities is illustrated in the following responses offered by subjects to a case involving a grown son who failed to care for his elderly parents in his own home and instead arranged for them to be cared for elsewhere. In appraising the act as a moral breach, an Indian adult referred to the son's duty to care for his parents:

> . . . because it's a son's duty—a birth duty—to take care of his parents. It's not only money that matters. It's being near your dear ones which counts more. So even though they were being looked after elsewhere, they were not with their own children. Secondly, even from the simple philosophy of give and take, the son has no business to ask his father to go away. Even if the parents had not exerted so much for the son, still he is expected to have a certain responsibility towards his parents.

In contrast, an American adult, who categorized the agent's behavior as a matter of personal choice, cited the importance of every individual's being free to work out for him- or herself an appropriate balance between responsibilities to others and to themselves:

It's up to the individual to decide. It's duty to the parents versus one's own independence and, I guess, one's self interest. He's fulfilling the minimal obligations to his parent. It wasn't a life and death situation and their needs were being taken care of. Beyond that it's a personal choice. Whether he wants to live with them has more to do with their emotional and personal relationship. Gratitude is something that's either there or it's not. You can't look at the parent–child relationship as a contractual one—or as a tit for tat (Miller & Luther, 1989, p. 253).

Contextual Sensitivity

Our cross-cultural research has also demonstrated that Indians maintain a more contextually sensitive and less rule-based approach to moral reasoning than do Americans. Thus, we have shown that Indians are more prone than are Americans to absolve agents of accountability for breaches of justice which result from extenuating circumstances, such as emotional duress or developmental immaturity (Bersoff & Miller, 1993). This cross-cultural difference arises from the tendency of Indians to view the self as a relatively open entity that is highly vulnerable to contextual influences, as contrasted with the tendency of Americans to view the self as a relatively bounded entity that is capable of resisting situational pressures.

These contrasting assumptions are reflected in the following responses made by subjects to a case that involved a man who defaulted on a loan. An Indian justified why the agent should not be held morally accountable for this breach by reference to the agent's vulnerability to contextual influences:

I feel he should not be held accountable because he was facing a bad financial situation. The friend should not have expected that he repay. The friend should have told him "well you are not in a position to pay me now. You pay me when you are in a position to pay me." Then this man would not have left the city. The friend expected him to pay money which he could not do, so he had no choice but to leave the city.

In arguing that the man should be held accountable for this breach, an American subject, in contrast, stressed the importance of personal responsibility:

I think it's basically an ethical issue—that if you take something from someone that you try and repay it. They entered into a contract—it's a breach of contract. People should be expected to respect that principle. I think that this is certainly a big character defect. People like this are just not very realistic and they're probably generally not very responsible (Miller & Luther, 1989, p. 254).

Relationship of the Individual to the Group

Our cross-cultural research also indicates that qualitatively distinct views of duty and of the relationship of the individual to the group are held in each culture. Americans tend to maintain a hydraulic view, in which acting out of duty is seen as opposed to individual inclinations, whereas Indians tend to maintain a monistic view, in which acting out of duty is seen as congruent with individual inclinations. In particular, we have demonstrated that Americans infer that agents are less endogenously motivated and derive less satisfaction if they are helping someone in response to social expectations, as contrasted with spontaneously (Miller & Bersoff, 1994). Indians, on the other hand, tend to infer that agents are equally endogenously motivated and derive equal satisfaction whether their helping is constrained by social expectations or is given more freely.

Studies that we have conducted demonstrate that whereas selflessness is viewed by Americans as having deleterious individual and interpersonal implications, it is regarded in positive terms by Indians (Miller & Bersoff, 1995). Thus, as compared with Americans, Indians judge that agents experience greater personal satisfaction in behaving in selfless ways (e.g., in remaining loyal to a spouse who has become severely disabled). Indians also tend to regard extreme selfless behavior as a sign of strength in the agent's character and as an act which deepens the bonds in special relationships (Miller, 1995). In contrast, Americans tend to regard extreme selfless behavior as a sign of weaknesses in the agent's character and as an act which may strain special relationships through the sense of debt and obligation which it creates.

Achieving a Non-Egoistic Sense of Community

Most importantly, our research has demonstrated that the view of interpersonal responsibilities within in-group relationships maintained by Indians appears to be less contingent on certain self-serving considerations than that maintained by Americans (Miller & Bersoff, 1996). We have shown that Indians tend to treat interpersonal responsibilities in special relationships as unaffected by considerations of personal affinity and liking. In contrast, with the exception of parent/young child relationships, Americans tend to maintain that an agent has less responsibility to help someone in a special relationship if he or she does not like the person and does not share common tastes and interests with them than he or she would if such personal liking and affinity is present.

This cross-cultural difference reflects the priority given to individuality and choice in each system. In treating interpersonal responsibilities as matters of duty, Indians judge that interpersonal responsibilities should not be dependent on the personal tastes and preferences of the agent. In contrast, in treating interpersonal responsibilities in voluntaristic terms, Americans give considerable weight to the agent's personal tastes and preferences in determining interpersonal responsibilities.

Implications

Our findings imply that the morality-of-caring model is both culturally bound and incomplete. Such a morality appears to represent an orientation that characterizes, at least in part, the approach to interpersonal morality found among European-Americans, if not also among other populations that maintain an individualistic cultural view of self. However, it does not characterize the approach to interpersonal morality that is emphasized among Hindu Indians and possibly among other populations that maintain a more collectivist cultural view of self. The results also imply that the morality-of-caring model does not pay adequate attention to some of the self-interested individualistic assumptions that have an impact on the type of interpersonal morality found among Americans. Our findings then challenge not only the generality of the morality-of-caring framework, but also its explanatory adequacy (Miller, 1994). It must be concluded that even among European-Americans, the development of the morality of caring cannot be fully explained by reference to gender-related socialization practices, or to issues in attachment and in identity formation, but requires attention as well to cultural meanings and practices.

Our findings also suggest that there may be a perceived contradiction between the goals of community and of individual freedom of choice that results in a certain compromise being effected between the two, rather than in their both being fully realized simultaneously. Among Indians, relatively little emphasis is placed on the considerations of personal autonomy and choice that are promoted among European-Americans. However, there appears to exist, at least in ingroup relationships, a sense of community that is broader in scope and less contingent on egoistic considerations than that present among European-Americans.

Certain implications for future theory and research in related domains of the self may be seen to follow from the present results. For example, it would be anticipated that contrasting models of attachment are needed to account for development in a culture such as Hindu India. Present models of attachment (Ainsworth, Blehar, Waters & Wall, 1978), for example, are premised on a tension between too much autonomy, with its threat of isolation, and too much connection, with its threat of loss of self. However, such models are unlikely to be adequate to account for attachment in a culture such as Hindu India, in which the threat of isolation may be less salient, and selflessness perceived as less problematic. Equally, it may be expected that present theories of communal relationships (Mills & Clark, 1982) may need to be modified to accommodate the less voluntaristic views of interpersonal bonds maintained in a culture such as India. For example, the tendency found among Americans for exchange considerations to corrupt communal bonds might be expected to be less marked among Indians, with their tendencies to view interpersonal responsibilities as less dependent on self-serving considerations. In another example, present internalization models of motivation (Deci & Ryan, 1985) are premised on a dichotomy in which perceived extrinsic motivation is viewed as opposed to perceived endogenous motivation. However, such models are also unlikely to be adequate to account for social motivation in a culture such as Hindu India, in which there is a tendency to treat social duties as simultaneously reflecting external constraints and endogenous inclinations.

Our research also highlights certain respective strengths and weaknesses of European-American and of Hindu Indian cultural approaches to interpersonal responsibilities. We have shown that the dominant European-American approach to interpersonal responsibilities is one that affords considerable freedom of choice. However, our research also indicates that there is a perceived precariousness of interpersonal ties in this type of system that is not present to the same degree in a culture such as Hindu India. For example, it is likely that Americans tend to experience more insecurity about interpersonal relationships and feel more pressure to work to maintain the other's positive regard than do Indians for whom interpersonal responsibilities are less voluntaristic.

More generally, I would argue that our research calls attention to cultural biases that may have contributed not only to the widespread enthusiasm for the morality-of-caring framework but that also may have skewed research undertaken to date on this model. Part of what our comparative research has brought to light may be considered to represent negative aspects of European-American approaches to interpersonal responsibilities, that is, a certain shallowness and self-serving quality that exists in interpersonal commitments as a result of the weight given to personal autonomy and choice. I would argue, however, that the failure of previous research in this area to uncover such trends may have arisen, at least in part, because of a certain confirmatory bias. Partly because of the readiness to believe that a strong sense of community can coexist with individualistic beliefs and values, there may have been a tendency not to undertake research that could seriously challenge this claim. Thus, for example, it is striking that whereas one of the major original claims made by Gilligan was that a morality of caring is not vulnerable to the egoistic considerations thought to be present in relationship-based moralities, there is no known research, other than the studies that we have conducted, which directly addresses this assertion. Extensive research has been conducted in what might be considered a hypothesis confirmatory mode, for example, demonstrating ways in which caring can lead to perceived interpersonal responsibilities and to helping behavior. However, no known research has been undertaken previously in what might be considered a hypothesis disconfirmatory mode, for example, examining whether, contrary to the claims of the model, perceived interpersonal responsibilities may be diminished by self-serving considerations.

CONCLUSIONS

Despite the recent increased attention to culture, cultural considerations presently remain in a peripheral role in psychology. As the anthropologist T. Schwartz observes, the dominant tendency is for psychologists to ". . . fail entirely to see the relevance of culture. It is as if others have culture while we have human nature" (Schwartz, 1992, p. 329). A sign of this type of stance is found in psychology textbooks, where the norm is for cultural considerations to be raised, if at all, only in a diversity sense. Cultural considerations are mentioned as a qualification regarding the generality of existing theories and findings. However, they are rarely integrated into textbooks as explanatory considerations that are taken into account in the constructs and theories themselves.

The theory and research discussed in this paper highlights the need to recognize the multiple contributions of a cultural perspective in the formation of psychological theory. Culture is relevant in a diversity sense in pointing to limitations in the generality of existing theories and in highlighting the need to formulate less-parochial theories to account for psychological functioning in contrasting cultural populations. However, beyond this diversity sense, it has been seen that a cultural perspective is critical in understanding ourselves. As has been shown, a cultural perspective provides insight into the processes underlying psychological effects observed among the European-American cultural populations on which psychology, at present, is largely based. It is also relevant in applied respects, in suggesting strengths and weaknesses of alternative patterns of psychological functioning. Finally, a cultural perspective is informative in a sociology-of-knowledge sense, in providing insight into the origins of our constructs and theories and into the subtle cultural biases that may influence the research process.

A vision for the future is of a field in which cultural considerations, like biological considerations, are taken into account overtly in all theory and research. Arguably, we already have a cultural psychology, in that our theories reflect even now the particular cultural assumptions of the sociohistorical contexts in which they have been formulated. The challenge is to uncover this cultural grounding.

REFERENCES

AINSWORTH, M. D., BLEHAR, M. C., WATERS, E. & WALL, S. (1978). *Patterns of attachment: A Psychological study of the strange situation.* Hillsdale, NJ: Erlbaum.

BELLAH, R. N., MADSEN, R., SULLIVAN, W. M., SWIDLER, A. & TIPTON, S. M. (1985). *Habits of the heart: Individualism and commitment in American life.* New York: Harper & Row.

BERSOFF, D. M. & MILLER, J. G. (1993). Culture, context, and the development of moral accountability judgments. *Developmental Psychology, 29(4),* 664–676.

BRONFENBRENNER, U. (1979). *The ecology of human development: Experiments by nature and design.* Cambridge, MA: Harvard University Press.

BRUNER, J. (1990). *Acts of meaning.* Cambridge, MA: Harvard University Press.

COLE, M. (1990). Cultural psychology: A once and future discipline? In R. A. Dienstbier & J.Berman (Eds.), *Nebraska Symposium on Motivation,* (pp. 279–335). Lincoln: University of Nebraska Press.

COLE, M. (1995). Culture and cognitive development: From cross-cultural research to creating systems of cultural mediation. *Culture and Psychology,1,* 25–54.

CONGER, J. J. (1981). Freedom and commitment: Families, youth, and social change. *American Psychology, 36,* 1475–1484.

DECI, E. L. & RYAN, R. M. (1985). *Intrinsic motivation and self-determination in human behavior.* New York: Plenum.

DUMONT, L. (1970). *Homo hierarchicus.* Chicago: University of Chicago Press.

GEERTZ, C. (1973). *The interpretation of cultures.* New York: Basic Books.

GERGEN, K. J. (1992). Psychology in the postmodern era. *The General Psychologist, 28,* 10–15.

GILLIGAN, C. (1982). *In a different voice: Psychological theory and women's development.* Cambridge, MA: Harvard University Press.

GILLIGAN, C. & WIGGINS, G. (1988). The origins of morality in early childhood relationships. In C. Gilligan, J.Ward & J. Taylor (Eds.), *Mapping the moral domain: A contribution of women's thinking to psychological theory and education,* (pp. 110–138). Cambridge, MA: Harvard University Press.

GUISINGER, S. & BLATT, S. J. (1994). Individuality and relatedness: Evolution of a fundamental debate. *American Psychologist, 49,* 104–111.

JAHODA, G. (1993). *Crossroads between culture and mind: Continuities and change in theories of human nature.* Cambridge, MA: Harvard University Press.

KOHLBERG, L., LEVINE, C. & HEWER, A. (1983). Moral stages: A current formulation and a response to critics. In J.A. Meacham (Ed.), *Contributions to Human Development, Vol.10,* (pp. 1–178). Basel, Switzerland: Karger.

MILLER, J. G. (1994). Cultural diversity in the morality of caring: Individually oriented versus duty-based interpersonal moral codes. *Cross-Cultural Research,28,* 3–39.

MILLER, J. G. (1995). Cultural views of the self and their implications for moral judgment. Paper presented at the meeting of the American Psychological Association, New York.

MILLER, J. G. (1996). Theoretical issues in cultural psychology. In J. W. Berry, Y. Poortinga, & J. Pandey (Eds.), *Handbook of cross-cultural psychology: Theoretical and methodological perspectives. Revised edition, Vol. 1.* Boston: Allyn & Bacon.

MILLER, J. G. & BERSOFF, D. M. (1992). Culture and moral judgment: How are conflicts between justice and friendship resolved? *Journal of Personality & Social Psychology, 62,* 541–554.

MILLER, J. G. & BERSOFF, D. M. (1994). Cultural influences on the moral status of reciprocity and the discounting of endogenous motivation. *Personality & Social Psychology Bulletin, 20,* 592–602.

MILLER, J. G. & BERSOFF, D. M. (1995). Development in the context of everyday family relationships: Culture, interpersonal morality and adaptation. In M. Killen & D. Hart (Eds.), *Morality in everyday life: Developmental perspectives* (pp. 259–282). New York: Cambridge University Press.

MILLER, J. G. & BERSOFF, D. M. (1996). Culture and the role of personal affinity and liking in perceptions of interpersonal responsibilities. Manuscript submitted for publication.

MILLER, J. G., BERSOFF, D. M. & HARWOOD, R. L. (1990). Perceptions of social responsibilities in India and in the United States: Moral imperatives or personal decisions? *Journal of Personality and Social Psychology, 58,* 33–47.

MILLER, J. G. & LUTHER, S. (1989). Issues of interpersonal responsibility and accountability: A comparison of Indians' and Americans' moral judgments. *Social Cognition, 3,* 237–261.

MILLS, J. & CLARK, M. S. (1982). Communal and exchange relationships. *Review of Personality & Social Psychology, 3,* 121–144.

O'FLAHERTY, W. & DERRETT, J. (1978). *The concept of duty in south Asia.* Delhi: Vikas.

SCARR, S. (1992). Developmental theories for the 1990's: Development and individual differences. *Child Development, 63,* 1–19.

SCHWARTZ, T. (1992). Anthropology and psychology: An unrequited relationship. In T. Schwartz, G. White & C. Lutz (Eds.), *New directions in psychological anthropology,* (pp. 324–349). New York: Cambridge University Press.

SEARLE, J. R. (1969). *Speech acts: An essay in the philosophy of language.* Cambridge, MA: Cambridge University Press.

SHWEDER, R. A. (1990). Cultural psychology—what is it? In R. A. Shweder & G. Herdt (Eds.), *Essays on comparative human development,* (pp. vii–ix). New York: Cambridge University Press.

TRIANDIS, H. C. & LAMBERT, W. W. (EDS.). (1980). *Handbook of cross-cultural psychology, Vol.2,* (pp. 1–14). Boston: Allyn & Bacon.

WALKER, L. J. (1984). Sex differences in the development of moral reasoning: A critical review. *Child Development, 55,* 677–691.

WHITING, B. B. & WHITING, J. W. (1975). *Children of six cultures: A psycho-cultural analysis.* Cambridge, MA: Harvard University Press.

Susan Andersen received her Ph.D. from Stanford University in 1981 and is presently Professor of Psychology at New York University. She specializes in both social and clinical psychology, and has published extensively on her research in the domain of interpersonal relationships—specifically, how people's representations of their significant others affects their reactions to new others. She has served as Associate Editor of the Journal of Personality and Social Psychology, Social Cognition, *and the* Journal of Social and Clinical Psychology, *and as a member of review panels of NIMH.*

Serena Chen is a Ph.D. candidate in social/ personality psychology at New York University and will receive her Ph.D. in the spring of 1997. She has accepted a position as Assistant Professor of Psychology at the University of Michigan for the fall of 1997. Her research interests are in attitudes and social cognition, and she has published a number of journal articles and chapters. She is a recipient of a National Science Foundation Graduate Research Fellowship, an APA Dissertation Research Award, and NYU's Stuart Cook Award.

Inga Reznik is a Ph.D. candidate in clinical psychology at New York University. She graduated magna cum laude *with honors from New York University in 1994, where she was awarded the Hillary Citrin Award for the most outstanding honors thesis. Her research concerns the social-cognitive study of transference, and she recently co-authored a paper that appeared in the* Journal of Personality and Social Psychology.

The Self in Relation to Others: Cognitive and Motivational Underpinnings[a]

SUSAN M. ANDERSEN,[b] INGA REZNIK,
AND SERENA CHEN

Department of Psychology
New York University
New York, New York 10003

Many theories about the self hold that one's sense of who one is, or one's conception of self, emerges in the context of the interpersonal relations experienced in one's family, social networks, and culture. It is often assumed that early relationships with significant persons in one's life may form patterns of responding that provide, to some degree, a framework for future interpersonal relations. Indeed, in a long history of clinical theory, significant others from one's childhood and later years are thought to be central both to self-definition and to interpersonal life (e.g., Bowlby, 1969, 1973, 1980; Freud, 1912/1958; Greenberg & Mitchell, 1983; Guidano & Liotti, 1983; Horney, 1939; Horowitz, 1991; Kelly, 1955; Luborsky & Crits-Christoph, 1990; Ogilvie & Ashmore, 1991; Rogers, 1951; Safran & Segal, 1990; Shaver & Rubenstein, 1980; Sullivan, 1953; Wachtel, 1981). Whether early interpersonal patterns and self-identities are stable over time, or continuously evolving, such patterns are widely considered to reflect how the self is bound up with others in daily living. Indeed, the notion that relations with specific significant others are crucial in self-definition is increasingly discussed in contemporary interpersonal models in social and personality psychology (e.g., Andersen & Glassman, 1996; Baldwin, 1992; Bugental, 1992; Markus & Cross, 1990).

We begin this paper with a brief consideration of our own work, which highlights the notion that the self is intertwined with significant others. In particular, we present our model of *transference* in everyday social relations that is situated in the general domain of social cognition (for reviews, see Andersen & Chen, in press; Andersen & Glassman, 1996). We then focus on the cognitive underpinnings of the self in relation to others, contending that parts of the self that are most connected with a given significant other

[a]Preparation of this manuscript was supported by Grant R01-MH48789 from the National Institute of Health to S.M.A.

[b]Address for correspondence: Susan M. Andersen, Department of Psychology, New York University, 6 Washington Place, 4th floor, New York, New York 10003.

can be activated along with the representation of the significant other by virtue of linkages stored in memory between knowledge about the significant other and about the self.

Recognizing the potential complexity of the interpersonal self, we then discuss briefly theorizing and research concerned with the different ways in which the self may be connected to others, considering as an example the notion that the self may be related to various societal groupings (based on ethnicity, gender, profession, or other factors, rather than on particular personal relationships). We address this broader social identification even though our work focuses on the self in relation to specific, significant individuals in one's life, so as to acknowledge that the interpersonal self may exist at many levels of analysis, including the group and cultural level.

Having addressed the cognitive underpinnings of the self and the various ways the self may be connected to others, we turn our attention to the motivational underpinnings implied by the notion that the self is defined and experienced in part *in relation* to others. Specifically, we discuss how what is known about basic human motivations speaks to the interpersonal nature of the self. In so doing, we highlight the basic need to attach to or to feel some sense of personal emotional connection with others as particularly pertinent to the notion of the interpersonal self. Although we recognize that numerous other basic human motivations exist, and even present an abbreviated compendium of them, we contend that the need for human connection is fundamental both to overall development and to the formation of the self *in relation to* others.

Finally, we describe our most recent research on transference in some detail. In the process, we highlight how our research speaks to basic motivations in self/significant-other relations and to the very nature of the inextricable ties that link the self with particular important others.

SYNOPSIS OF OUR SOCIAL-COGNITIVE WORK ON TRANSFERENCE WITH ITS IMPLICATIONS FOR THE SELF

Transference refers to the process whereby past relations and experiences with significant others play out in present relations with new persons (Freud, 1912/1958; see also Sullivan, 1953). In our work, we conceptualize transference in social-cognitive terms, arguing specifically that *mental representations of significant others* are stored in memory in some form and then activated and applied to newly encountered individuals, so that these new persons are perceived and responded to in "old" ways. Our research on transference addresses the interpersonal nature of the self. Specifically, evidence emerging from this research supports the notion that self and significant-other representations are linked in memory, influencing each other in bi-directional ways. Thus, our work on transference in everyday social relations touches upon the self in relation to others by postulating some of the social-cognitive mechanisms by which the self emerges interpersonally.

Research examining our social-cognitive model of transference shows that significant-other representations are brought to bear on interpreting new persons, as evidenced by the emergence of inference, memory, feeling, motivation, and self-definition based on these representations—overall, making it quite clear that the self is related to significant others in memory (Andersen & Baum, 1994; Andersen & Cole, 1990; Andersen, Glassman, Chen & Cole, 1995; Andersen, Reznik & Manzella, 1996; Hinkley & Andersen, 1996). More precisely, the activation and application of a significant-other representation to a newly encountered person—that is, transference—is reflected in inferences made based on the representation and in one's memory as well. Moreover, affective reactions expressed facially can be predicted from the representation, as can the tendency to like or dislike the new person, to be motivated to emotionally approach or avoid him or her, and to expect acceptance versus rejection from him or her (Andersen *et al.*, 1996). We view the latter two findings as indicating that the basic need for human connection is reflected in transference. When significant-other activation and application to a new person occurs, it leads the person to experience representation-consistent motivational responses toward, and expectancies about, the new other. Motivational responses and expectancies should emerge in transference by virtue of the stored relations between the self and the significant other that, according to our model, include motivational and expectancy-based content. As more explicit evidence for the notion that the self exists in part in relation to the significant individuals in one's life, we describe other research that demonstrates that the activation and application of a significant-other representation to a new other leads to changes in the "working self-concept," one's current and immediate sense of self. Specifically, one experiences oneself in transference as one is when with the significant other (Hinkley & Andersen, 1996; see also Baldwin & Holmes, 1987). Hence, significant-other activation spreads to the activation of relevant self aspects, showing the relevance of the linkages between significant others and the self in transference. Taken as a whole, then, our data make clear that significant-other representations are pertinent to how the self is experienced in transference, and there are crucial motivational, expectancy-based, and affective elements in this process—all of which speak to the importance of the interpersonal self.

MENTAL REPRESENTATIONS OF THE SELF IN RELATION TO TRANSFERENCE

Although models of self differ widely, they tend to share the notion that knowledge about the self is stored and organized in memory in some form (e.g., Cantor & Kihlstrom, 1987; Linville & Carlston, 1994), though not necessarily a monolithic one (Higgins & Bargh, 1987; Higgins, Van Hook & Dorfman, 1988). Although the exact content and structure of self-knowledge is a matter of considerable debate (e.g., Banaji & Prentice, 1994; Prentice, 1990), most social-cognitive models assume that self-knowledge is stored in memory in ways that make possible both continuity and malleability in the self (e.g., Markus & Kunda, 1986). In particular, most allow for multiple selves—in that different versions of who one is may emerge as a function of the social context (e.g., Deaux, 1991), motivation (e.g., Cantor, Markus, Niedenthal & Nurius, 1986; Higgins, 1989b), social role (e.g., Linville, 1985, 1987; Markus & Nurius, 1986), relationship (e.g., Baldwin, 1992; Ogilvie & Ashmore, 1991), and situation (Mischel & Shoda, 1995). Hence, multiple aspects of the self are widely discussed, involving present, actual, possible, and future selves (e.g., Higgins, 1987, 1989b). Of great pertinence here is the notion that long-standing representations may exist that are chronically accessible, that is, that readily come to mind and are frequently used. Indeed, significant-other representations have been shown to be chronically accessible, and they may thus provide some continuity in patterns of interpretation and responding over time (see also Higgins, 1990). Yet, the fact that not everything that is known and stored about the self is called to the fore in every situation leaves room for malleability as well, as may occur, for example, when different elements of a situation or a person trigger a particular significant-other representation.

The Working Self-Concept

The general notion that only a subset of an individual's entire pool of stored knowledge is active and in use at any given point in time is widely accepted in cognitive psychology and forms the basis of the concept of "working memory" (Cantor & Engle, 1993; Engle, Cantor & Carullo, 1992; Just & Carpenter, 1992). Working memory contains the subset of stored knowledge which is "ready" for use. Stored knowledge is brought into working memory when its activation level has reached a critical threshold. Working memory, then, can be viewed as the window in which particular memory representations influence, either consciously or nonconsciously, perception, interpretation, and inference (Kihlstrom, 1987; see Bargh, 1989).

Emerging directly from notions of working memory, the *"working self-concept"* refers to the subset of one's entire pool of self-knowledge that is accessible and active in working memory at a given time and in a given context (e.g., Cantor & Kihlstrom, 1987; Linville & Carlston, 1994). The working self-concept is both theoretically compelling and increasingly supported by empirical evidence. Indeed, the notion that the working self-concept influences perceptions and feelings by changing the aspects of the self that are currently active is consistent with the notion that certain core self-conceptions may be chronically active, lending stability to the self, while less central self-conceptions may be less chronically accessible, varying contextually and motivationally across situations (Andersen & Chen, in press). The notion of the working self-concept is broadly consistent with both social construct theory in social cognition (Higgins, 1989a; Higgins & King, 1981; Sedikides & Skowronski, 1990, 1991), which focuses on principles of knowledge activation and use, and with connectionistic models of knowledge representation and use (e.g., Read, 1984, 1987; Smith, 1995). Indeed, it is also compatible with work on individual-person exemplars (Smith & Zarate, 1990, 1992). Thus, it appears that the idea that a "working" set of ideas and associations can be constructed relatively anew in each stimulus context (or at each new moment), based in part on frequency of prior use and in part on present cues (Andersen *et al.*, 1995; Barsalou, 1993; Higgins & Brendl, 1995), is quite basic.

Our understanding of the working self-concept in transference is based on a network model of knowledge activation. As with various social-cognitive (e.g., Higgins, 1989a, 1996; Sedikides & Skowronski, 1991) and cognitive models of working memory (e.g., Cantor & Engle, 1993, Engle *et al.*, 1992), we assume that activation spreads among related pieces of knowledge stored in long-term memory. Such spreading activation accounts for how it is that when a significant-other representation is activated, self-knowledge that is related to the significant-other representation should also come to reside in working memory, influencing the perceiver's perceptions, inferences, affect, and experience of self.

Self-With-Significant-Other Representations

In our model of transference, we assume the existence of multiple aspects of the self, some linked quite specifically to a particular relationship with a significant other. If some aspects of the self are more tightly linked than others to a specific significant other in memory, then these aspects are likely to be evoked when the representation of this significant other is activated. While it is possible that a given significant-other representation is linked to every aspect of the self, it seems more likely that different aspects of the self are especially well linked to particular significant others from one's life (see also Ogilvie & Ashmore, 1991). The representation of the self when *with* a specific individual can be thought of as a "self-with-other" unit in memory. This self-with-other perspective can be brought into the transference context with the prediction that a "self-with-other" unit will be activated upon significant-other activation, and this is in fact supported by the research to be described later (Hinkley & Andersen, 1996).

Although the implications of different self-with-other models vary, in broad strokes, each supports the existence of linkages in memory between self and significant-other representations. The general notion is readily embodied in the concept of *relational schemas* (Baldwin, 1992; Berscheid, 1994; Bugental, 1992). A relational schema is thought to comprise the self and a significant-other representation, along with an interpersonal script involving an expected pattern of interaction between the self and the other, learned through past experience. It is proposed that these three elements of the schema may even be structurally associated in memory such that activation of one element in the structure spreads to others with special efficiency (Baldwin, 1992). A relational schema approach is thus consistent with our thinking about self-with-significant-other linkages in memory, although both our transference and Baldwin's relational models are essentially silent about the exact internal organization of the self and significant-other representations, that is, about their precise cognitive architecture defined in terms of intra-representation associations (see Andersen & Chen, in press).

Interestingly, research outside of the transference context focused on associations between self and significant-other representations offers persuasive evidence for self/significant-other linkages. Specifically, in this work, significant-other activation—based on a priming manipulation—has been shown to lead to changes in an individual's experience of the self, as assessed in terms of self-evaluative responses. For instance, after participants were primed to think of a parental figure, they reported less enjoyment of sexually charged written passages than they did after being primed to think of a friend. That is, the activation of the representation of a familial significant other versus a friend differentially influenced participants' personal self-evaluative standards (Baldwin & Holmes, 1987). In a related study, when psychology graduate students were subliminally exposed to the approving face of their program director, they rated their own research ideas more favorably than when subliminally exposed to his disapproving face (Baldwin, Carrell & Lopez, 1990). Similarly, Roman Catholic female participants, who considered themselves religious, evaluated themselves less positively when subliminally exposed to the face of the Pope versus the face of a nonrelevant other.

Overall, then, considerable theory and evidence supports the existence of linkages in memory between the self and significant others—which we argue are fundamental to the cognitive underpinnings of the interpersonal self. We recognize, of course, that the self may be connected to various others—including, but not only, significant others—and in various ways. Thus, before examining the motivational underpinnings of the intperpersonal self, we consider several other theoretical perspectives from the broader social-cognitive literature on the interpersonal self.

COLLECTIVITY AND IDIOSYNCRACY IN THE SELF

Although it is obvious that knowledge about the self is likely to be mentally represented in some respects in *relation* to others, there are numerous ways of conceptualizing the extent to which the self is bound to others, and numerous levels of analysis that are of importance. Thus, we briefly consider some of these in an effort to better locate our research on transference in the general arena of interpersonal models of the self.

Social identities. One level of analysis can be found in social identity theory, that is, in the distinction between an individual's *personal identity* and his or her *social identities* (Tajfel & Turner, 1979). Social identity refers to the individual's identification with larger groups or collectives (e.g., Brewer, 1991; Huo, Smith & Tyler, 1996; Markus & Kitayama, 1991; Turner & Oakes, 1989; Tyler & Degoey, 1995). Thus, social identity theory and related frameworks focus on the interpersonal self in terms of how one's self-categorizations are related to one's membership in various groups and classes of people. From a social-identity standpoint, an individual's self-esteem is thought to be derived, threatened, maintained, and enhanced differentially depending on whether one's personal versus one's social identity is relevant and thus operative in a given context (Crocker & Major, 1989; Steele, 1988). A common theme in the literature on social identity theory, moreover, is that people seek to distinguish themselves from others, and yet also seek to assimilate into social groups and relationships as well, perhaps to find some optimal balance between personal distinctiveness and group belongingness (Brewer, 1991). A number of recent empirical studies have, in fact, been concerned with the manner in which people identify with particular social groups, and with the role of belonging to particular groups in identity formation and maintenance (e.g., Deaux, 1991, 1993; Turner, 1985).

Overall, considerable theory and research thus suggests that each of us holds a host of social identities, in addition to our own personal or individualized identity. A schematic representation of the distinction between one's personal versus one's social identities appears in FIGURE 1, adapted from a social-psychological model of the self (Brewer, 1991). As reflected in the figure, the self may comprise the personal self as well as numerous social identities, with the personal self depicted at the center of various concentric circles, expanding outward into identities that are increasingly public. In this way, social identities define the self, even though they clearly extend beyond the individualized self, parts of which may remain entirely distinct from the interpersonal self. This illustration is provocative because it depicts one way in which the self is represented in relation to others, with others defined in terms of social groupings.

Conceptualizations of the interpersonal self increasingly recognize cultural and subcultural differences in psychological structures and processes, such as the degree to which social versus personal identities operate. For example, the distinction between the "independent" versus "interdependent" self has been studied in the social-psychological literature on cross-cultural differences in the self (Markus & Kitayama, 1991). Although both forms of self-construction acknowledge that the self is defined, regulated, and experi-

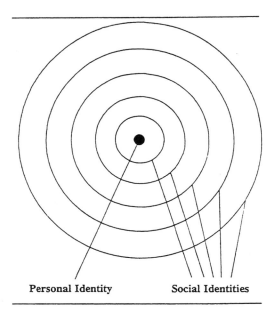

Personal Identity   Social Identities

FIGURE 1. Personal and societal identities. (From Brewer, M. [1991]. Reprinted by permission.)

enced, at least in part, in relation to other persons, the "independent" view, which is relatively Western, holds that the self is autonomous and independent, whereas the relatively non-Western "interdependent" view conceptualizes the self as bound up with specific others. Interestingly, the idea that the self is tightly linked to specific individuals suggests malleability in the self across social contexts as a function of which others are present. We return later to this notion of context-specific selves when we present evidence for just this kind of malleability in the self in the context of transference—that is, when specific significant-other representations are activated and brought to bear on the tasks of perceiving, interpreting, and relating to newly encountered individuals (Hinkley & Andersen, 1996; see also Andersen & Chen, in press). These data suggest that even in a culture that values the "independent" view, such as in the United States, the interdependent processes of transference may nonetheless occur.

Personal identities with significant others. Consistent with the basic proposition that the self is bound to specific individuals in one's life, our research focuses on the self as it is linked to particular "significant others" who one knows or has known—for example, members of one's family of origin (parents, siblings, and extended family), one's spouse or romantic partner, children, or close friends. Returning for a moment to FIGURE 1, we would argue that significant others exist largely in one or two of the *inner*most circles of identity and reflect those specific persons most important to the self. As shown in FIGURE 2, based on our own empirical research, we have argued that the self is linked to multiple significant others in memory (Andersen & Berk, in press). In our view, the self is intimately intertwined with significant others, and with personal relationships, so that the relational dynamics linking the self with these others are also stored in memory (see Sullivan, 1953).

As we described briefly earlier, in our model of significant-other representations and transference, we argue that a mental representation of a significant other can be thought of as a bundle of knowledge stored in memory about the person that can be brought to bear on interpreting new people who somehow resemble a significant other. This notion that past or present relations with significant others may play a role in relations with new people reflects the nearly century-old concept of *transference* (Freud, 1912/1958). The available evidence suggests that transference is a basic process—not a pathological one—and one that we would argue represents a very intimate way in which significant others are related to the self. When transference occurs, one is likely to perceive this new person in terms of the representation, and respond to him or her as one has responded to the significant other (Anderson *et al.*, 1996). Importantly, our model also argues that because the bundle of knowledge about the significant other is linked to that about

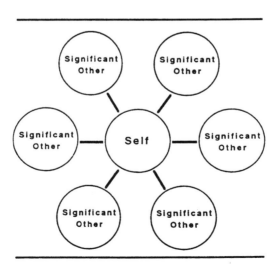

FIGURE 2. Linkages between the self and significant-other representations in memory. (From Andersen, S.M. & Berk, M.S. [in press]. Reprinted by permission.)

the self, those aspects of the self that are associated with a particular significant other are likely to be elicited when the relevant significant-other representation is activated (Hinkley & Andersen, 1996).

Significant others as part of the self. A related line of work that similarly recognizes the relevance of significant-other representations to the self, although it does not focus on transference per se, is also worth considering
here. This framework proposes that *personal* identity may become connected with a particular significant other one loves and to whom one is deeply
attached, for example, in the context of a long term romantic/spousal relationship, so that the significant other comes to be part of the self (Aron,
Aron & Smollen, 1992; Aron, Aron, Tudor & Nelson, 1991). This notion
is depicted in FIGURE 3, which shows how another person can become pro-
gressively included in the self, such that one's self identity may include a
specific other person. This notion extends well beyond our research on
transference because it defines different types of significant-other representations as a function of how much they are incorporated into the self, which
we have yet to study in our research. On theoretical grounds, however, we
would argue that when a significant-other representation is not highly overlapping with the self, that is, when it is solidly a representation of its own,

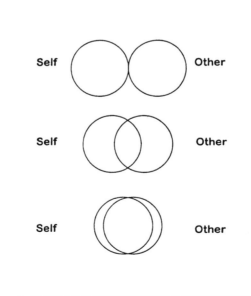

FIGURE 3. Inclusion of a significant other in the self. (Adapted from Aron, Aron &
Smollen, 1992.)

this representation may still be used to interpret new individuals—in transference—in a process akin to the displacement of significant-other-based inferences to a new person (Greenberg & Mitchell, 1983). By contrast, when a self representation is used to interpret a new person, this is more akin to the process of projection (see Catrambone & Markus, 1987), rather than displacement. Indeed, it is interesting that a merging of the self and a significant-other representation may imply that transference involving such a representation would reflect a combination of the two interpretive process—projection and displacement, in a kind of projective displacement—which is a notion that warrants research attention.

Thus far we have described our model of the cognitive underpinnings of the self, highlighting how the self is related to the significant individuals in one's life. We have also considered, however, various other theoretical perspectives on how the self may be bound to others in multiple ways and at multiple levels. We now proceed onto the motivational underpinnings of the interpersonal self before detailing our research in the arena of transference—research that we argue directly speaks to both the cognitive and motivational foundations of the interpersonal self.

THE SELF AND BASIC MOTIVATIONS

Almost any adequate model of the nature of self representations necessarily includes the assumption that motivations of various kinds are pertinent to self-definition. Indeed, most broad-based theories of human personality that have emerged over the course of this century have assumed that particular motivations are central to how the self develops and functions. A small set of basic human motivations has been emphasized in some form or another across these theoretical perspectives. Among these is the fundamental need for human connection, caring, warmth, tenderness, or attachment (see Adler, 1927/1957; Bakan, 1966; Batson, 1990; Baumeister & Leary, 1995; Bowlby, 1969, Deci, 1995; Fairbairn, 1952; Greenberg & Mitchell, 1983; Guisinger & Blatt, 1994; Helgeson, 1994; Horney, 1939, 1945; McAdams, 1985, 1989; Mullahy, 1970; Rogers, 1951; Safran, 1990; Sullivan, 1940, 1953). We focus on this need for connection and consider its special relevance to the interpersonal self. At the same time, we acknowledge that many other human motivations exist, operating simultaneously with this need. For example, the need to be able to *de*tach from others as well as to attach to them has also been proposed (Guidano & Liotti, 1983), as has the need to experience and express psychological autonomy, personal freedom, or self-determination (Deci & Ryan, 1985, 1991). If attachment is to proceed well and if a sense of well-being is to be attained, some capacity to pursue individual aspirations freely is of importance (see Ryan, 1993). Beyond this, considerable research has focused on the need for competence, mastery, or control, showing that it is of great relevance to effective human functioning (e.g., Abramson, Seligman & Teasdale, 1978; Bakan, 1966; Bandura, 1977, 1986; Dweck & Licht, 1980; White, 1959), a notion echoed in numerous theories of personality and behavior (e.g., Horney, 1939; Jung, 1933; Sullivan, 1953). On another level, there also appears to be an overall need to experience a sense of meaning in one's activities—and even to be able to perceive one's life as a whole as meaningful. In theoretical terms, meaning needs have long been considered quite basic (Frankl, 1959; Jung, 1933), and this notion has received some research support (Janoff-Bulman, 1992; Silver & Wortman, 1980). Finally, there is the need for security and safety (Horney, 1939; Sullivan, 1953)—the need to feel comfortable with the self, and to believe that one is and will be all right. Security needs may play out in many ways, for example, in the tendency to see the self in a positive light (e.g., Epstein, 1973; Greenwald, 1980; Taylor & Brown, 1988). Indeed, security may well be an overarching motivation that is relevant to all the others, as reflected in its special role in attachment, as well as in later functioning, notions we elaborate upon below. Together, this set of motivations, noted in FIGURE 4, provides a context for the interpersonal self—constituting the internal moorings that exist alongside connection needs.

Human Connection

The need to feel connected with other human beings, the longing to be close, and the desire to experience tenderness, caring, and warmth from others and to be able to provide it in return may be a fundamental human motivation (see Stern, 1985). This basic need for connection has received considerable empirical support beginning, for example, with the postwar studies on institutionalized children (Appell & Roudinesco, 1951; Robertson, 1953; Spitz, 1945). Human infants separated from their mothers exhibited deep depression and failed to thrive in large anonymous institutions—apparently not because of malnutrition but because of a lack of tender physical care. In fact, even in non-human primates, warmth appears to outweigh physical sustenance in that baby monkeys prefer a cuddly terry-cloth "mother" to one made of wire who dispenses milk (as reflected in

---

Connection
Autonomy
Mastery
Meaning
Security

FIGURE 4. Basic human motivations.

time spent with the "mother," Harlow & Harlow, 1969). Both of these historic lines of work suggest that the need for connection, as reflected in proximity seeking and the pursuit of tender interactions with a caretaker, may be basic to growth in infancy (see also Sullivan, 1953).

Attachment processes. Attachment theory holds that infants are inherently motivated to attach to their caregivers—for survival and for protection from danger—and to elicit complementary responses from caregivers (e.g., Bowlby, 1958). However, it is not only proximity seeking that is relevant, but also "felt security" based on a caregiver's responsiveness or "sensitivity" to the infant (Sroufe & Waters, 1977; Sroufe, 1996). The caregiver is the center of the infant's social and emotional life; in fact, it is the emotional connection with the caregiver that is crucial, and can be seen in the emotional mimicry and turn-taking that occurs in caretaker–infant interactions, processes that are part of effective attachment (e.g., Stern, 1985). Research on attachment in infancy has shown that secure attachment tends to co-occur with parental expressions of sensitivity to the infant (Ainsworth, 1989; Bowlby, 1969, 1973, 1980)—defined in terms of the degree of sensitive, shared activity with the infant, activity geared toward the infant's developing capabilities and within the range of these capabilities. Sensitivity is also thought to involve both provision of an effective set of environmental contingencies that enhance development, as well as relational responsiveness to the infant, shown to be crucial to secure attachment (for a review, see Thompson, in press). Such sensitivity is reflected in the caregiver's attention to the infant's signals, accurate interpretation of their meaning, and an appropriate and prompt response to them (Ainsworth *et al.*, 1974). It is reflected in an empathic and sympathetic orientation to the child (Dix, 1991), and generally, in responsive parenting that shows the adult's ability and willingness to protect and provide for the child (Bowlby, 1969). Overall, it has been shown that mothers who respond positively, consistently, and warmly to the child's signals seem to have securely attached children (Isabella, 1995), suggesting that the basic need for connection and tenderness is clearly important in early development—in the context of attachment. In addition, some research suggests that it is not only the caretaker's actual sensitivity that fosters secure attachment, but also the infant's *subjective appraisal* of this sensitivity. Indeed, constantly intervening with the infant's ongoing actions and efforts, even if in a warm way, may be intrusive or controlling, potentially leading to an avoidant style of attachment. A lack of intervention, however, is also problematic, as unresponsive maternal behavior can lead to a resistant attachment style (Belsky & Cassidy, 1994). Hence, it appears that close and tender interactions that are neither too stimulating and controlling nor too minimal and distant are the most predictive of secure attachment.

Secure attachment. Secure attachment makes it possible for the infant to explore the external world with relatively little conflict or fear by using the caretaker as a "secure base" to explore elsewhere, allowing him or her to *play* with his or her own developing capacities. In this sense, secure attachment facilitates a positive, mutually responsive parent-child relationship that helps children to better regulate their affect (Grossman, Grossman & Schwan, 1986), and may help them later in childhood (Stroufe, 1983; Stroufe, Schork, Motti, Lawroski & LaFreniere, 1984), as well as in adulthood in terms of forming successful relationships (Hazan & Shaver, 1987, 1990). On the other hand, the absence or lack of a comfortable, secure attachment, shown, for example, in infants' inability to soothe themselves, in irreconcilable crying, in manifestations of anxiety and rage, and in unresponsiveness to caregivers, may correspond, in later relationships, to less self-confidence, self-efficacy, social competence, and capacity to regulate negative affect (Carnelley, Pietromonco & Jaffe, 1994; Collins & Read, 1990; Dutton, Saunders, Starzomski & Bartholomew, 1994; Shaver, Collins & Clark, 1996; Woike, Osier & Candela, 1996; for a review, see Thompson, in press).

The harmonious coming together of the child and caretaker, so relevant to attachment, is captured in the concept of "dovetailing", which reflects the interpersonal interplay of child and adult and fosters skill development and, in fact, learning (Kaye, 1984). A child's actions can be considered fully realized or "complete" when linked to reactions from the caretaker and family members, specifically, when the child's actions elicit preferred reactions from caretakers. Hence, the self is intertwined with others at the onset. Such dovetailing provides scaffolding for the child's growth and development, with the child as the apprentice in particular developmental tasks with the caretaker. As the child's representational capacities mature, he or she assumes an increasingly active role in shared activities with significant others and the full nature of the apprentice relation gradually diminishes. The dovetailing concept underscores how the child's behaviors are interlaced with those of caretakers in social-emotional development, grounding the interpersonal self in this interplay. Relatedly, "social referencing" in infancy is linked to dovetailing in that the child actively searches for clarifying information from the caretakers' emotional reactions to his or her behavior (Camps & Sternberg, 1981; Klinnert, Campos, Scorce, Emde & Svejda, 1983), and in this communication process, a shared, socially constructed meaning or reality emerges for the child (see also Hardin & Higgins, 1996; Sullivan, 1953).

Empathy and attachment. Attachment to parenting figures is importantly associated not only with the need for tenderness and connection, but also with the basic need for social competence. One component of such social competence worth considering here is empathy because empathy enables the individual to better relate to others by conveying to others an ability to understand their emotional states and situational predicament, to grasp what they are experiencing (Ickes, 1997). Indeed, children show elementary forms of empathy at an early age (Eisenberg & Mussen, 1989; Hoffman,

1981), a finding that supports the notion that basic empathic abilities may emerge in part because of the basic need to be connected with others. Hence, as a function of how basic connection needs are or are not allowed to play out, the capacity for empathy may be facilitated or inhibited, respectively (Batson, 1991). Indeed, individual differences in empathic abilities have been shown to be associated with secure attachment (Kestenbaum, Faber & Sroufe, 1989), suggesting that both empathy and attachment may reflect the same underlying need for connection.

The importance of empathy as an element of the basic need to connect with others is further revealed by the fact that empathic feelings appear to mediate altruistic behavior, among both adults and children (Coke, Batson & McDavis, 1978; Dovidio, Allen & Schroeder, 1990; Eisenberg & Miller, 1987), and to inhibit aggression (Miller & Eisenberg, 1988; Richardson, Hammack, Smith, Gardner & Signo, 1994). Such evidence is of societal significance in that it suggests that experiencing another's joys and sorrows not only is of social value, but also that it emerges fairly naturally in development. Interestingly, because other human needs are highly relevant to empathy (such as the need for security) it is only when these other needs are simultaneously met that empathic feelings of compassion can occur and facilitate altruism, because people need to be able to regulate the intensity with which they feel another's pain (Eisenberg *et al.*, 1996; Stotland, 1969). Empathetic distress in response to another person can lead more to self-protection than to compassion and altruism (Hoffman, 1988); hence, it is only when empathy develops in a balanced way that it can evoke compassion and sympathy rather than distress, thus facilitating altruism (Batson, 1991; Eisenberg, 1992; Ickes, 1997).

Mental models and attachment. In attachment theory, on the basis of interpersonal interactions with the caretaker, mental models of the self and other are thought to form, containing the child's view of whether or not the attachment figure will respond positively or negatively to his or her bids for emotional support (see also Higgins, 1989b). Contingencies of this kind in relationships with caregivers are reflected in the child's expectancies about how the significant other will respond, with the emphasis on the caretaker's acceptance or rejection of the child (see also Andersen & Glassman, 1996), that is, on whether or not he or she will show interest in the child (Thompson, in press). Expressed nurturance and responsiveness to the child's own agency are especially valuable not only in the development of the child's relational skills, but also in the development of his or her overall competence motivation. Ultimately, people form mental models of the other and of the self (Bartholomew & Horowitz, 1991), portraying the self as someone worthy or unworthy and the other as trustworthy or untrustworthy. The motivations and expectancies experienced toward the significant other are thus thought to be an inherent part of mental models. Such mental models are thus thought to represent both attachment successes and failures in relation to the caretaker such that the caretaker's responsiveness or rejection is represented in the model—especially in the connections between the self and the significant other (Baldwin, 1992; Berscheid, 1994; Bugental, 1992). Once formed, such models influence information processing and are used to interpret new relationships in that they are thought to contain "implicit decision rules for relating to others" (Thompson, in press; see also Markus & Cross, 1990). Indeed, it has been argued that mental models are organized representations based on past experience that exert a selective impact on the entire continuum of information processing—"influencing attention, encoding, storage, retrieval, inference, and planning and anticipation" (Markus & Cross, 1990, p. 583).

Although the attachment literature suggests that both child and adult attachment are mediated by internal models reflecting the self in relation to the primary caretaker, little research has explicitly examined this proposition directly or the nature of such models in a mental representational sense in either children or adults. Hence, it is not known whether or not mental models exist and mediate people's responses to new persons in interpersonal relations. Traditionally, research on the attachment process in child development has focused on the "strange situation" and has examined how children handle separation from the parent in the experimental context, classifying attachment-relevant behaviors into trait-like attachment styles (e.g., Ainsworth, Blehar, Walters & Wall, 1978). Examination of these traits also forms the basis of the adult attachment literature, which has focused on romantic, spousal, and work relationships (e.g., Collins & Read, 1990; Hazan & Shaver, 1987, 1990; Pietromonaco, 1985; Shaver & Rubenstein, 1980; Simpson, 1990). Work on attachment in adulthood has thus tended to focus not on mental models per se, but rather on trait-like attachment styles—although there are some clear exceptions in the recent literature (Baldwin, Fehr, Keedian, Seidel & Thompson, 1993; Baldwin, Keelan, Fehr, Enns & Koh-Rangarajoo, 1996; Collins, 1996; Shaver, Collins & Clark, 1996; Miller & Read, 1991; Zeifman & Hazan, in press).

As described earlier in our work, we conceptualize the self as linked to specific significant others in memory and we examine mental representations of significant others as they play out in transference. Hence, our work is pertinent to attachment theory, and specifically, to theorizing about mental models of significant others stored in relation to the self. In fact, our research is among the first to examine such models directly by focusing on how representations of significant others are represented in memory and activated in relation to new persons, as well as on how these representations are linked to the self. From our point of view, the basic motivation to attach to a caretaker is likely to be stored with the representation of a significant other in memory, so that it is played out with any new person if the significant-other representation is activated and applied to him or her. The basic motivation to bond with this significant other, to feel connected, and to be near, which is so apparent in infants and young children, should thus play out in transference as it occurs in adult encounters and relationships.

Self-regulation and attachment. As implied, attachment not only involves warmth or nurturance, but also safety and security, such as the safety felt or not felt upon separation. Considering attachment processes from a somewhat different perspective, recent research on self-regulatory systems also suggests that these two motivations—namely, nurturance and security—are of crucial importance (Higgins, 1996a, b). In this work, the self-regulatory systems of individuals striving to satisfy their nurturance needs are focused on maximizing the presence of positive outcomes with others, and on preventing the absence of them. The absence of positive outcomes, that is, the withdrawal of nurturance and love, is thought to be associated with depression (Beck & Greenberg, 1974). In comparison, the self-regulatory system that is linked to security concerns focuses on preventing the occurrence of negative outcomes and on making sure of their absence. Anticipating negative outcomes is thought to involve fear and anxiety (see also Lazarus & Averill, 1972). From this view, then, a caregiver may be emotionally important because of the nurturance and security that are or are not experienced with him or her. As an example, individuals whose parents withdraw love when contingencies are not met are more likely to expect emotional abandonment and experience mistrust of and resentment toward others (Moretti & Higgins, in press). The detrimental nature of love withdrawal has been underscored in other research as well, showing that this parenting strategy is associated with low self-esteem, social avoidance, and heightened anxiety in children (Maccoby & Martin, 1983). Overall, a caregiver may foster one or both of the above self-regulatory systems in a child, in similar or differing degrees, by responding to him or her in ways that are receptive to his or her needs for nurturance and security. Recent work on self-regulation thus provides yet another perspective on the role of the motivation for connection with others in the development of the self.

Beyond Human Connection

Autonomy needs. As indicated, there are a number of other basic motivations that research has substantiated. In particular, there is an "opposing" need relative to the motivation for connection, namely, the need for detachment from others in the form of *individual autonomy* and personal freedom (Deci, 1995; Deci & Ryan, 1985, 1991; Ryan, 1993). The need for autonomy, or self-determination, refers to the need to experience one's choices, thoughts, and actions as freely chosen, that is, as emanating from the true or authentic self, a locus of causality that is not only distinguishable from an external locus, but also, importantly, from internal loci that reflect the mere adoption of external forces. Thus, connection and autonomy needs may at times oppose each other insofar as the satisfaction of autonomy needs requires determining one's actions on the basis of one's own personal beliefs, values, standards, and wishes, even if others may disagree; in such cases, the price may be lack of "closeness," if "closeness" is contingent upon particular

acts (Ryan, 1993; see also Higgins, 1989a). The notion that autonomy motives co-exist with the need for connection suggests that the self is not entirely an *inter*personal phenomenon, but has an *intra*personal element as
well (see Andersen, 1984; Andersen & Ross, 1984; Andersen & Williams,
1985). Moreover, the evidence suggests that there are multiple human
needs that play a role in how the need for connection is expressed. In fact, it
has long been argued that optimal satisfaction of either autonomy or connection needs may require that both are pursued and satisfied simultaneously. That is, true connection and true autonomy cannot be experienced in the
absence of each other (Ryan, 1993). Similarly, the attachment literature
suggests that successful adaptation involves a mixture of attachment and detachment, in a secure balance that gives on the ability to tolerate the absence
of others and to trust that they will return (Guidano & Liotti, 1983).

Mastery needs. Beyond the need for autonomy, there is also the basic need
for a sense of *personal mastery*, competence, or control. The need to feel
that one is developing and using one's own skills and talents and bringing
them to fruition has been defined in terms of effectance motivation (White,
1959), self-efficacy (Bandura, 1986), and feelings of competence and control (Dweck, 1975; Dweck & Leggett, 1988; see also Burger, 1985). The
conception of this need is reflected in a long-standing theoretical literature
(e.g., Adler, 1927/1957; Horney, 1939), and when construed in terms of
achievement motivation, it constitutes one of the most widely researched
human motivations (e.g. Atkinson, 1957; Dweck & Licht, 1980; McClel-
land, Atkinson, Clark, & Lowell, 1953).

Interestingly, there has been a recent resurgence in work on human
agency, defined in terms of control and mastery, that has focused on its duality with human belongingness needs (Bakan, 1966; Baumeister & Leary,
1995; Blatt, 1990; Helgeson, 1994; McAdams & Constantin, 1983;
Moskowitz, Suh & Desaulniers, 1994; Wiggins, 1992). Compelling as this
work is, however, it does not always distinguish mastery needs from autonomy or self-determination needs (discussed above), even though these conceptions are distinguishable. That is, one can experience mastery or competence in a particular activity, and nonetheless feel controlled by others,
rather than autonomous and free to choose (Bandura, 1989; Deci, 1995;
Deci & Ryan, 1991).

Meaning needs. On yet another level, various theories of personality have
long made the assumption that there is a basic need for something similar to
mastery, but far broader conceptually, namely, a sense of *meaning*. A basic
need for meaning reflects the motivation to comprehend life, to have some
kind of discernment on the basis of this understanding (Frankl, 1959; Jung,
1993; see also Becker, 1971, 1973). Such a need appears to operate across
cultures. Finding meaning in life involves constructing a broader comprehension and acceptance of life events, and placing life events in perspective
(Janoff-Bulman, 1992; Silver & Wortman, 1980). It also provides a frame-

work for action (Klinger, 1977) and identity (McAdams, 1996). In this sense, the narratives people construct to make sense of their existence may be one way in which they are able to imbue life with meaning (Baumeister, 1991, 1996).

From an existential point of view, constructing meaning and finding a way to lead a meaningful life involves living "authentically" by exercising choice, responsibility, consciousness, self-examination (Heiddeger, 1962; May, Angel & Ellenberger, 1958; Yalom, 1980; see also Charme, 1984). But the need for meaning can be conceptualized at other levels of analysis as well. For instance, on a rather specific level, the meaning systems people construct have been implicated in reducing threat-related responses to the social world, in that people appear to have a need to defend their world views (Greenberg, Pyszczynski & Solomon, 1986; Greenberg, Pyszczynski, Solomon & Chatal, 1992), a tendency that appears to be useful in overall well-being (Silver & Wortman, 1980, Pennebaker, 1988, in press), specifically, in increasing felt security. Hence, meaning needs are widely considered fundamental (Bruner, 1990; Glendin, 1962), and a growing body of work supports this claim.

To further define meaning needs, some have argued that experiencing meaning includes simply gaining a sense of predictability. There are clearly theories of personality, therefore, that highlight meaning needs somewhat indirectly in terms of the predictability that any coherent cognition provides, and hence, in terms of the uncertainty reduction that may be part and parcel of the cognition (Beck, 1976; Kelly, 1955; Guidano Y Liotti, 1983). In cognitive psychology, in fact, information theory suggests that the definition of information is that which further reduces uncertainty (e.g., Atteneave, 1959), and yet is worth noting here that information is not likely to be synonymous with meaning because the sheer amount of information does not specify the content, value, history, or purpose of the information (Krietler & Krietler, 1976). Nonetheless, meaning is largely bestowed by mental processes, and this renders cognition a primary mechanism for making meaning (see also Cummins, 1989; Csikszentmihalyi & Rochberg-Halton, 1981; Nelson, 1985).

Security needs. Beyond the need for meaning, there is also the fundamental need to feel safe and *secure*. As indicated, this motivation for security is reflected in attachment processes, and may emerge in relation to other basic needs as well. Overall, in adulthood, people appear to have a basic need to feel adequate, or even far better than adequate, even inflated (Taylor, 1991). The motivation for security, then, to believe that one is and will be all right, and to experience positive feelings, is clearly reflected in self-serving biases and self-inflation (e.g., Arkin, 1981; Baumgardner & Arkin, 1988; Brown & Gallagher, 1992; Campbell & Fehr, 1990; Greenwald, 1980; Kunda, 1987, 1990; Showers, 1992; Taylor & Brown, 1988). Indeed, such self-bolstering processes are more likely to emerge as a coping mechanism in response to threatening experiences (Greenberg & Pyszczynski, 1985). And it is of great interest that "normal" individuals, relative to depressives, tend to show an "illusory glow" of optimism rather than any special accuracy in their self perceptions (Alloy & Abramson, 1979; Lewinsohn, Mischel, Chaplin & Barton, 1980; Sackeim, 1983; Sackeim & Gur, 1979; Sackeim & Wagner, 1986; Taylor & Brown, 1988), suggesting that nondepressives favor pleasant perceptions over painful ones. Diverse research on related phenomena concurs with this basic assumption, including findings in the area of self-esteem maintenance (Tesser, 1988, 1992), automatic egotism (Paulhus & Levitt, 1987), ego-defensive attributions (Bradley, 1978; Miller & Ross, 1975), and terror-management (Greenberg, Pyszczynski & Solomon, 1986; Greenberg, Pyszczynski, Solomon & Chatel, 1992). Put simply, people are poised to defend their self-esteem where needed and to bolster their sense of adequacy or security by seeing themselves in a highly positive light especially under threat.

Although we do not wish to argue that this list of basic human motivations is *the* list, we believe the literature makes clear that multiple motivations are operative in human behavior, and we believe this is likely to be relevant to the interpersonal nature of the self.

In the remainder of this paper, we describe our research on transference, and consider its implications for how best to conceptualize the interpersonal self. Because this work deals with long-standing clinical theory, we first consider the clinical literature on transference. We then present empirical evidence which speaks not only to the general operation of significant-other representations in transference, but also, more specifically, to the role and consequences of stored linkages between self and significant-other representations in the process. Although we highlight the cognitive underpinnings of the self in relation to significant others in the sections that follow, we aim to make clear the relevance of the motivational foundations of the interpersonal self—in particular, the basic needs for connection and security—to understanding its cognitive representation. That connection and security are fundamental human needs and that stored linkages between self and significant-other representations exist in memory converge in implying that the self is defined and experienced at least in part in relation to the important individuals in one's life, that is, that the self is interpersonal.

SIGNIFICANT-OTHER REPRESENTATIONS AND TRANSFERENCE

Psychodynamic Models

The clinical concept of transference (e.g., Ehrenreich, 1989; Greenson, 1965; Luborsky & Chrits-Christoph, 1990) has received scant empirical examination in psychology, even though the notion that people superimpose old feelings, expectations, and patterns of behavior learned with a past significant other onto new persons in their life, especially a new therapist, is the cornerstone of psychodynamic therapy (e.g., Horney, 1939, 1945; Sullivan, 1940, 1953; Freud, 1912/1958; Greenberg & Mitchell, 1983). The concept of transference has largely been a theoretical one, discussed among clinicians in terms of its manifestations and use in psychotherapy. According to Freud (1912/1958), transference occurs when the "patient" superimposes his or her childhood fantasies and conflicts about a parent onto an "analyst" in the context of psychoanalysis, by weaving "the figure of the physician into one of the series' already constructed in his mind" (Freud, 1912/1963, p. 107; see Andersen & Glassman, 1996).

Although transference is a clinical concept considered essential to psychoanalysis, it is also thought to have profound implications for everyday social life and its vicissitudes, and not to be experienced only in therapy. Although the psychosexual drive-structure model proposed by Freud is not compatible with our information-processing formulation (see Greenberg & Mitchell, 1983), Freud's relatively simple assertion that people hold mental representations of significant others or *imagoes* that influence their relations with *new* individuals, both in therapy and in life (Freud, 1912/1958; Luborsky & Chrits-Christoph, 1990; Schimek, 1983), is largely compatible with our framework, in which we assume that transference can be interpreted in terms of mental representations of significant others, and as such, can be examined in controlled experiments. Although our research is silent about whether the occurrence of transference in therapy is essential in treating psychopathology and suffering, our research does suggest that the phenomenon is ubiquitous.

Our conceptualization of transference is based largely on the model of transference proposed by Harry Stack Sullivan (1953), who argued that children construct "personifications" of self and other. In our view, personifications can be conceptualized as *mental representations* that are linked together in memory (although Sullivan preferred energy-transformation metaphors to mental structures), and the "dynamisms" that reflect the dynamics characterizing the relationship between self and other can also be construed in cognitive terms. Sullivan characterized the transference process as *parataxic distortion*, and emphasized that the formation of personifications and dynamisms is based on simple interpersonal learning in the context of basic motivations and needs. For example, Sullivan argued that needs for security and satisfaction in expressing one's perceptions and emotions, and exercising one's capacities are best addressed in "integrative" encounters. Ideally, one is able to exercise one's own capacities and talents, and to express one's emotions, while remaining close to and "tender" with the other. This enables satisfaction and a sense of security. These needs as experienced in relation to the particular significant other, then, form the basis for the development of idiosyncratic personifications and dynamisms, which then serve as the basis for parataxic distortion or transference. Transference is thus defined as an illusory two-person situation that emerges with a new person, so that what was learned in relation to the significant other is experienced with the new person (although perhaps not as a simple repetition, Wachtel, 1981).

Social-Cognitive Model

In our experimental research on transference, we have adopted, as indicated, a social-cognitive approach (for related conceptual approaches, see Singer, 1985, 1988; Wachtel, 1981; Westen, 1988). We suggest that the basic process of transference involves the activation and application of mental representations of significant others to new people in everyday social relations (Andersen & Glassman, 1996). As part of the process, an activated significant-other representation guides inferences about a new individual, who is perceived in terms of the representation, leading to predictable information-processing consequences, as well as to consequences for affect, evaluation, interpersonal closeness motivation, expectancies concerning acceptance or rejection, and self-experiences. The processes underlying the use of significant-other representations are similar to those governing the activation and use of any social construct (Higgins, 1989a; Higgins & King, 1981; see also Andersen & Klatzky, 1987; Andersen, Klatzky & Murray, 1990), such as those designating other individual-person exemplars or various types of social categories (Smith & Zarate, 1992). We argue, however, that significant-other representations are particularly powerful in that they are chronically ready to be used and are of high importance to the person (Anderson et al., 1995).

Thus far, our research on transference has shown that people use significant-other representations to make inferences about a new person who somehow resembles a significant other—inferring qualities not actually learned but consistent with the significant-other representation (Andersen & Baum, 1994; Andersen & Cole, 1990; Andersen et al., 1995, 1996; Hinkley & Andersen, 1996; for a review, see Andersen & Glassman, 1996). That is, perceivers show a chronic and pronounced tendency to "go beyond the information given" (Bruner, 1957) about new people on the basis of an activated significant-other representation, apparently treating what they *inferred* when learning about the new person as information *learned* (for related work, see Johnson, Hastroudi & Lindsay, 1993; Johnson & Raye, 1981). Beyond inferential and memory effects, transference is also reflected in representation-consistent evaluation, motivation, expectancies, and affect stored with the significant-other representation (Anderson et al., 1996), as indicated, and this research is described here in detail because such effects implicate the self in transference by implying the activation of stored linkages between the self and the significant other when the significant-other representation is activated. The emergence of expectancies for acceptance or rejection and of motivations to be emotionally close or distant in transference points to the powerful relation between the significant other and the self. Still more direct evidence for this relation also exists, showing that changes in self-definition may occur based on significant-other activation by virtue of linkages between the bundle of knowledge representing the significant other and that representing aspects of the self that are particularly related to this other (Hinkley & Andersen, 1996), see also Baldwin, 1992). When the significant-other representation is triggered, its activation spreads to related aspects of the self, so that from the entire pool of self-information stored in memory, the subset reflecting how the self is defined, regulated, and experienced when with the significant other is what comes to mind. It is in these ways that this research on transference speaks to the self/significant-other relation.

We turn now to the empirical evidence that we argue supports the existence and operation of stored self/significant-other linkages—linkages that not only are basic to the cognitive underpinnings of the interpersonal self, but also that reflect some of the fundamental motivational underpinnings of the self in relation to significant others.

TRANSFERENCE INFLUENCES EXPECTANCIES, MOTIVATION, AND AFFECT

The first study we describe speaks to the self in relation to significant others by extending prior work demonstrating schema-triggered evaluation in transference (Andersen & Baum, 1994)—that is, liking or disliking of a new person who resembles a significant other as the significant other is liked or disliked. We extend this research into the motivational domain, focusing in particular on the need for connection (Andersen *et al.*, 1996). We conceptualize this as the desire to emotionally approach or distance from the new person, and our assumption is that this motivation should be experienced with the new other in transference as it is experienced with the significant other. Such a transfer of motivation should occur by means of the basic process of schema-triggered affect (Fiske, 1982; Fiske & Pavelchak, 1986), though this prediction reaches beyond the theory of schema-triggered affect, which was designed to explain how liking and disliking of a new other may emerge from an evaluatively toned representation (typically a stereotype). We assume that it is the emotionally laden nature of significant-other representations that enables their activation to have motivational consequences. In addition, beyond examining closeness and connectedness motivation, we also examined interpersonal expectancies for acceptance or rejection, which are likely to be of relevance to the desire to approach or avoid the other. Finally, we also assessed immediate emotional responses in terms of facially expressed emotion at the moment of encountering (encoding) each piece of information about the new person in transference. Emotions too can be powerful motivators in their own right.

In this research, we used the same between-participants design used in prior work (Andersen & Baum, 1994). Participants in the experimental condition of this design learned about a new person, allegedly seated next door, who resembled their own positively or negatively toned significant other, and participants in the control condition learned about a new person resembling some other participant's positive or negative significant other. In order to control for content differences in features presented about the new person and to draw meaningful conclusions about the effects of significant-other resemblance, each participant in the control condition was systematically paired—that is, yoked—with another participant in the experimental condition (randomly selected without replacement). Such perfect one-to-one yoking across the transference and the non-transference conditions meant that participants in both of these conditions were exposed to exactly the same features, ensuring that any differences observed were not content-driven or derived from evaluative differences (see also Andersen & Baum, 1994). All participants completed sentences to describe their significant others two weeks *before* the actual experiment. More specifically, in the initial session, participants were asked to provide an equal number of positive and negative sentences to describe both their positively and negatively toned significant others, which allowed us to describe the new person using an equal number of positive and negative descriptors in both conditions, diminishing the obviousness of the overall tone of the representation. Importantly, while participants read each descriptive feature about the new person, their ongoing *facial expressions* were covertly videotaped. Hence, nonverbal facial affect at *encoding*, that is, during the precise moment that the participant learned each feature about the new person, was assessed. Our index of facial affect was derived from naive judges' ratings of the pleasantness in participants' facial expressions. After participants learned about the new person, their *motivation* to emotionally approach or avoid this new other was assessed—that is, their motivation for connection with the other. Participants' *expectancies* as to whether the new other would be accepting or rejecting of them were also assessed, as was representation-consistent liking of, and memory about, the new person, as in prior work.

Schema-Triggered Motivation to be Close

We view motivational material *vis-à-vis* significant others as stored in the linkages between the self and the significant other, and hence as material that may be activated and applied to a new other when a significant-other representation is activated. As indicated, in this study, we defined motivation in terms of the longing for interpersonal closeness, operationalizing this basic motivation for connection in terms of participants' self-reported motivation to emotionally approach or avoid the new person. In the initial stimulus-generation phase of the study, when participants named a positively toned significant other, they were asked to name someone whom they felt close to and to whom they *wanted to be still closer*, and when they named a negatively toned significant other, they were asked to name one to whom they did not feel close and from whom they *wanted to be even more distant*. In the experimental session, participants learned about a new person who resembled either this positively or negatively toned significant other, or a yoked participant's positively or negatively toned significant other. Afterward, they reported their desire to be interpersonally close with this person, to be emotionally open, disclosing, and receptive.

As predicted, the results showed that motives pursued in relation to a significant other are activated when the significant-other representation is activated in transference. That is, participants were more motivated to emotionally approach (and not to emotionally distance from) the new person who resembled their own positively toned versus their own negatively toned significant other, a pattern that did not occur in the nontransference-control condition. This demonstrates the occurrence of *schema-triggered motivation* in transference, extending research on schema-triggered affect (e.g., Fiske, 1982) into the motivational domain. These findings are especially important in that the need to be close, to bond, or to attach to others is among the most fundamental, as argued earlier.

Schema-Triggered Expectancies for Acceptance or Rejection

Given the basic need for attachment and connection, it is likely that memory for outcomes received from significant others, in terms of acceptance and responsiveness or rejection and unresponsiveness to one's bids for connection is stored with significant-other representations. Specifically, such outcome expectancies are likely to be stored in the linkages between the self and the significant other in memory, and thus should play out in transference—as *schema-triggered expectancies* (Andersen *et al.*, 1996). For example, if a significant other is harsh and rejecting, this should be stored in the representation of him or her *in relation to* the self and should emerge in transference as an expectancy for rejection from a new person who bears some resemblance to the significant other. In the same study described above, when the new person resembled participants' own positively toned significant other, rather than their own negatively toned significant other, participants expected the person to like and accept them more, a pattern not found when the new person resembled a yoked participant's significant other. Such schema-triggered expectancies are critical, in part, because expectancies about acceptance versus rejection are of considerable relevance in human relations (Downey, Lebolt & Feldman, in press; Feldman & Downey, 1995), and because such outcomes and contingencies are likely to be fundamental to our relations with significant others (e.g., Bandura, 1986; Higgins, 1989b, 1991). Moreover, if such contingencies are activated in transference, it is of importance for theoretical conceptualizations of the interpersonal self because it implies a bi-directional influence in self/significant-other linkages. That is, feelings may run *from* the self *to* the significant other, for example, in the form of representation-consistent evaluations of a new other who resembles a significant other, as well as *from* the significant other *to* the self, in this case, in the form of representation-consistent expectancies regarding whether a new other will be accepting or rejecting of the self. Overall, these data provide another indication that the need for connection helps define what is stored about the significant other in memory and hence what emerges in transference.

Schema-Triggered Facial Affect

In expanding the notion of schema-triggered affect, we also examined emotional responding, testing the hypothesis that the emotional concomitants of transference may be found in momentary facial expressions upon encountering a new person who resembles a significant other. Such momentary facial expressions have important implications in that emotional responses are thought to last only a few seconds (Ekman, 1992), and facial changes are thought to reflect emotion. To the extent that the overall tone of a significant-other representation is expressed affectively when a person is learning a relevant feature about a new person who bears some resemblance to a significant other, facial affect at this moment should reflect the overall tone of the representation rather than the valence of the feature itself. Two trained judges in this research, blind to the participants' condition, rated participants' facial expressions for pleasant versus unpleasant feeling, one feature at a time, and these ratings were examined as our index of transient affect.

As predicted, participants responded with more pleasant facial affect while learning about a new person who resembled their own positively versus negatively toned significant other, a pattern that did not emerge when the new person resembled a yoked participant's significant other. Importantly, the overall tone of the representation was expressed facially regardless of whether the feature itself was positive or negative in valence. Using this virtually instantaneous measure of transient affect, then, the data showed that learning about a new person who resembled a significant other results in representation-consistent facial affect. Indeed, because *self-reported transient mood* effects were *not* observed in this study (although see Andersen & Baum, 1994), facial affect in transference appears to occur fleetingly. Nonetheless, the data clearly demonstrate schema-triggered transient facial affect in transference, extending our prior work into the domain of emotional responses. It may be that it is difficult to observe relatively less transient affect, for example, transient mood, because assessing such affect may be complicated by factors such as participants' desire to protect positive mood states and repair negative ones (e.g., Clark & Isen, 1982), or to increase their self-esteem (e.g., Greenberg & Pyszczynski, 1985; Greenwald, 1980; see also Hinkley & Andersen, 1996). Generally, these findings extend prior work by showing that the overall tone of a significant-other representation predicts facial expressions of affect at encoding in transference, showing the power of the emotional resonance of the experience. Coupled with the closeness motivation and expectancy findings, these data provide strong evidence for the pertinence of the need for connection in understanding transference and its implications for self and personality.

TRANSFERENCE INFLUENCES ONE'S SENSE OF SELF

As indicated, central to our social-cognitive model of transference is the notion that significant-other representations are linked with self-representations in memory. Because significant-other representations are, by definition, of relevance to the self, and have been demonstrated to have important affective and motivational consequences for the self, it is crucial to understand the precise nature of the linkages between self and significant-other representations, and the role of these linkages in transference. We argued above that self/significant-other linkages imply that aspects of the self will be activated when a significant-other representation is activated in transference. A recent study, to be described shortly, directly examined this hypothesis (Hinkley & Andersen, 1996).

When a significant-other representation is activated and applied in the context of significant-other resemblance in a new person, relevant changes in the *working self-concept* should occur—that is, changes in what is currently active in working memory about the self. Specifically, we argue that the activation of a significant-other representation should bring those aspects of the self that reflect the *self when with the particular significant other* (Ogilvie & Ashmore, 1991) into working memory. That is, encountering a new person who bears some resemblance to a significant other should lead a perceiver to experience the self as he or she is when *with* the significant other by virtue of the infusion into the working self-concept of those aspects of self-information that specifically pertain to the self when *with* this significant other. Moreover, because the overall tone of a significant-other representation should be linked to feelings about the self when *with* the significant other, corresponding changes in *self-evaluation* should also occur.

This study made use of the same experimental design as the one used in the study described above in which participants learned about a new person who resembled either their own or a yoked participant's positively or negatively toned significant other. In each condition, participants learned an equal number of positive and negative features about the new person. Again, participants were yoked across the own-significant-other and control conditions on a one-to-one basis so that the exact content of features presented about the new person was identical across these conditions. In the experiment, after learning about the new person, participants were asked to describe themselves "as they are now" (as an index of their working self-concept). They did this by generating sentences to describe themselves, and afterward, classified each of the self-descriptive sentences that they listed as positive or negative (as an index of self-evaluation). Following this, participants completed our standard recognition-memory test about the new person, used to assess representation-consistent memory and inferences.

The above procedures were rendered meaningful by the fact that we collected information about the self from the participants during a pretest session held two weeks prior to the experiment. In this pretest session, before identifying any significant other, participants provided a series of descriptors to characterize the self by completing various sentences to describe themselves "as they are now"—this set of self-descriptors served as a measure of each participant's *pretest* working self-concept. Afterward, participants classified each self-descriptor they had provided as either positive or negative. Next, participants identified a positively and a negatively toned significant other, and completed an equal number of positive and negative sentences to describe each. Finally, they were asked to generate descriptors to characterize the self when *with* each significant other, by listing descriptive sentences about the self when with each of these others. Together, these pretest-session procedures provided the necessary ingredients for testing our hypotheses.

Changes in the Working Self-Concept

By measuring participants' working self-concepts at two points in time— *during* the pretest session and *after* experiencing the experimental manipulation—we could assess changes in the featural content of the working self-concept as a function of significant-other resemblance and transference. In particular, the degree of featural overlap between the "working" self-concept and the self when with the significant other was assessed (a measure adapted from Prentice, 1990, and coded by independent judges) so as to index the extent to which each participant's working self-concept reflected his or her previously assessed self-with-significant-other description. This overlap was calculated at pretest and in the experiment, with the prediction being that the "working" self-concept would change more in the direction of the self when with the significant other, controlling for the same overlap calculated entirely at pretest, *when* the new person resembled the participant's own significant other rather than a yoked participant's significant other. That is, the number of overlapping items between participants' working self-concept and their sense of self when *with* the significant other in the experiment—covarying out pretest overlap—was our primary dependent measure.

As predicted, the working self-concept as freely described by participants in the experiment came to overlap more with their self-when-with-significant-other description—when the new person resembled this particular significant other rather than a yoked participant's significant other. Hence, under the condition of significant-other resemblance and transference, changes in the working self-concept occurred. This effect held, in fact, whether the new person resembled a positively or a negatively toned significant other, and was specific to the relevant significant other, that is, the effect was not simply general across all significant-other representations stored in a given participant's memory.

Changes in Self-Evaluation Based on the Working Self-Concept

To measure changes in the evaluative tone of the working self-concept in transference, participants' positive and negative classifications of their working self-concept descriptors were examined (in both the pretest and experimental sessions). When the new person resembled the participant's own significant other, the newly overlapping aspects of the working self-concept, that is, those that changed in the direction of the self when *with* the significant other, were expected to reflect the overall tone of the relevant significant-other representation. The main analyses of self-evaluative changes in the working self-concept were conducted using these newly *overlapping* items. Indeed, participants perceived these *newly overlapping* working-self-concept features as more positive when the new person resembled their own positively versus negatively toned significant other, an effect that did not occur in the control condition. These data clearly demonstrate that representation-consistent shifts in the working self-concept that occur during transference have self-evaluative implications that are consistent with the overall tone of the significant-other representation.

Interestingly, however, the self-evaluation reflected in the aspects of the working self-concept that did *not* change in the direction of the self when *with* the significant other, changed in exactly the opposite way. That is, for these non-overlapping features, which were, in fact, the majority of the working self-concept features that participants listed, self-evaluation became more *positive* when the new person resembled the participant's own *negatively* versus positively toned significant other, an effect that did not hold when the new person resembled a yoked participant's significant other. Hence, the valence of the items *not* involved in the overlap with the self-with-significant-other representation became most *positive* when the new person resembled the participant's own *negatively* toned significant other. Given that this occurred only in the context of significant-other resemblance in the new person, *positive* aspects of self-knowledge appear to have been marshaled in the context of a negative transference encounter, enabling the self to be experienced and perceived more positively overall in spite of the influx of some negative self-evaluation.

This bolstering of self-evaluation in the overall working self-concept in the negative transference condition enhances the self in the face of threat, in a reversal of our predicted effect—for the non-overlapping features of the self concept versus those that overlapped with participants' self-when-with-the-significant-other descriptions. The fact that this occurred in the negative transference context suggests that some changes in self-evaluation in this kind of transference context may reflect a compensatory response. Such compensatory responses appear to be common in various domains (Greenberg & Pyszczynski, 1985; Steele, 1988; Taylor & Brown, 1988; Taylor & Lobel, 1989; Tesser, 1988), and this may well be operative when negative changes in the working self-concept occur in transference. The "shoring up" of positive self-conceptions in the working self-concept *as a whole* presumably counteracts the negative self-evaluation when *with* the negatively toned significant other that we observed in the negative transference condition in this research.

These data are interesting because the tendency to see oneself in positive light can readily be construed in terms of the basic need for security—the desire to have positive regard for the self. From this standpoint, this evidence is important in part because it suggests yet another way that basic human motivations may be pertinent to what is stored in memory in relation to significant others and what emerges in transference. That is, these data suggest that the basic motivation for security plays a role in transference by implying that the ways in which self-evaluation is experienced and regulated, based in part on the operation of security needs in the context of one's relationship with a significant other, may be experienced in the transference process.

Transference as Representation-Consistent Memory

Consistent with prior research, the basic transference effect was found in this particular study in the form of representation-consistent memory (Andersen & Baum, 1994; Andersen *et al.*, 1995, 1996; Andersen & Cole, 1990). That is, participants showed more representation-consistent memory confidence about the new person who resembled their own significant other. This memory effect held regardless of the overall evaluative tone of the significant-other representation from which the new person's features were derived. Hence, significant-other activation and application clearly occurred when we expected it would—under conditions of significant-other resemblance—showing that the observed changes in the working self-concept occurred in the context of transference.

Taken together, these data support the hypothesis that shifts in the working self-concept occur in the context of transference and indicate that they have complex implications for self-definition and self-evaluation. These data are in fact the first in this line of work to demonstrate unequivocally that self and significant-other representations, along with the linkages between them, are activated in the context of transference. In our view, self/significant-other linkages constitute the cognitive underpinnings of the interpersonal self, as it exists in relation to the significant others in one's life. Upon encountering a new person who in some way resembles a significant other, individuals appear to define and experience themselves as they are when with the relevant significant other. In addition, self-evaluation comes to reflect the tone of the significant-other representation. However, when the self-aspects that are brought to mind upon encountering a new person who resembles a significant other are negative, a compensatory or defensive self-enhancement appears to occur as well. Hence, we argue that the basic need to feel secure, in this case, to feel positively about the self in the face of negative content entering the working self-concept, appears to be relevant in transference. This is important because it suggests yet another linkage between the transference processes and basic needs, a crucial step if transference is to be considered reflective of the interpersonal nature of the self.

CONCLUDING COMMENTS

To summarize, we have argued for a conceptualization of self that is fundamentally interpersonal in nature, focusing in particular on how the self is defined by the specific significant relationships in one's life. Although we do not mean to imply that there is nothing else to the self beyond interpersonal material, we do regard significant relationships as basic to self-definition and experience. Hence, we have discussed basic human needs, arguing that the need for connection with other human beings is primary in personality and behavior, and considered various ways in which the self may be defined in relation both to groups (generalized others) and to specific individuals. We also presented our conceptualization of the cognitive underpinnings of the interpersonal self—that is, how the self may be linked to various significant others in memory—in the context of our social-cognitive conceptualization of transference in everyday social relations. Finally, we offered findings emerging from our experimental social-cognitive research on transference, rooted in our assumptions regarding the cognitive foundations of the self in relation to significant others. In the process, we sought to make clear the relevance of the motivational elements of the interplay between self and significant-other representations in memory, as well as the cognitive underpinnings, to their activation and the consequences they lead to in transference.

Overall, the research we presented demonstrates the phenomenon of transference—the re-experiencing of ideas, motivation, and affect in relation to a new person derived from a relationship with a significant other. Empirical support for the interpersonal nature of the self has been found in this research, most notably in the form of data demonstrating schema-triggered closeness motivations and schema-triggered expectancies for acceptance versus rejection in transference, which imply that such material is stored with the significant other in relation to the self (Andersen *et al.*, 1996). Our research also indicates that the way one views oneself appears to change in the context of transference, such that one becomes more like the self one is when *with* the significant other in this context. Taken as a whole, our findings support an interpersonal model of the self by implying that the need for human connection, so pivotal in development of the self, appears to emerge in transference, as does the need for a sense of security in the form of a bolstering of the self under threatening transferential circumstances. The other basic motivations we have considered—autonomy, competence, and meaning—have not yet been directly examined in the transference context, and warrant future empirical attention since they are also likely to be stored with significant-other representations. Although our model cannot account for all of the variance in self-definition or in contextual changes in an individual's self-concept and self-experience, the model does involve an interpersonal model of the self and postulates a complex web of multiple representations of self linked with multiple representations of significant others that can account both for continuity and malleability in the self, as it exists and operates in relation to others.

ACKNOWLEDGMENTS

Special thanks are extended to Noah Glassman, Kathy Balto, Michele Berk, and Tatiana Friedman for their comments on an earlier draft of this paper.

REFERENCES

ABRAMSON, L. Y., SELIGMAN, M. E. P. & TEASDALE, J. D. (1978). Learned helplessness in humans: Critique and reformation. *Journal of Abnormal Psychology, 87,* 49–74.

ADLER, A. (1957). *Understanding human nature.* New York: Fawcett Premier. (Original work published in 1927).

AINSWORTH, M. D. S. (1989). Attachments beyond infancy. *American Psychologist, 44,* 709–716.

AINSWORTH, M. D. S., BELL, S. M. & STAYTON, D. J. (1974). Infant-mother attachment and social development: Socialization as a product of reciprocal responsiveness to signals. In M. P .M. Richards (Ed.), *The integration of the child into a social world* (pp. 99–135). Cambridge: Cambridge University Press.

AINSWORTH, M. D. S., BLEHAR, M. C., WALTERS, E. & WALL, S. (1978). *Patterns of attachment: A psychological study of the strange situation.* Hillsdale, NJ: Erlbaum.

ALLOY, L. B. & ABRAMSON, L. Y. (1979). Judgment of contingency in depressed and nondepressed students: Sadder but wiser? *Journal of Experimental Psychology: General, 108,* 441–445.

ANDERSEN, S. M. (1984). Self-knowledge and social inference: II. the diagnosticity of cognitive/affective and behavioral data. *Journal of Personality and Social Psychology, 46,* 294–307.

ANDERSEN, S. M. & BAUM, A. B. (1994). Transference in interpersonal relations: Inferences and affect based on significant-other representations. *Journal of Personality, 62,* 4, 460–497.

ANDERSEN, S. M. & BERK, M. S. (in press). Transference in everyday experience: Implications of experimental research for relevant clinical phenomena. *Review of General Psychology.*

ANDERSEN, S. M. & CHEN, S. (in press). Measuring transference in everyday social relations: Theory and evidence using an experimental social-cognitive paradigm. In H. Kurtzman (Ed.), *Cognition and Psychodynamics.* New York: Oxford University Press.

ANDERSEN, S. M. & COLE, S. W. (1990). "Do I know you?": The role of significant others in general social perception. *Journal of Personality and Social Psychology, 59,* 384–399.

ANDERSEN, S. M. & GLASSMAN, N. S. (1996). Responding to significant others when they are not there: Effects on interpersonal inference, motivation, and affect. In R. M. Sorrentino & E. T. Higgins (Eds.), *Handbook of motivation and cognition* (Vol. 3, pp. 262–321). New York: Guilford.

ANDERSEN, S. M., GLASSMAN, N. S., CHEN, S. & COLE, S. W. (1995). Transference in social perception: The role of chronic accessibility in significant-other representations. *Journal of Personality and Social Psychology, 69,* 41–57.

ANDERSEN, S. M. & KLATZKY, R. L. (1987). Traits and social stereotypes: Levels of categorization in person perception. *Journal of Personality and Social Psychology, 53,* 235–246.

ANDERSEN, S. M., KLATZKY, R. L. & MURRAY, J. (1990). Traits and social stereotypes: Efficiency differences in social information processing. *Journal of Personality and Social Psychology, 59,* 192–201.

ANDERSEN, S. M., REZNIK, I. & MANZELLA, L. M. (1996). Eliciting transient affect, motivation, and expectancies in transference: Significant-other representations and the self in social relations. *Journal of Personality and Social Psychology, 71,* 1108–1129.

ANDERSEN, S. M. & ROSS, L. (1984). Self-knowledge and social inference: I. The impact of cognitive/affective and behavioral data. *Journal of Personality and Social Psychology, 46,* 280–293.

ANDERSEN, S. M. & WILLIAMS, M. (1985). Cognitive/affective reactions in the improvement of self-esteem: When thoughts and feelings make a difference. *Journal of Personality and Social Psychology, 48,* 1086–1097.

APPEL, G. & ROUDINESCO, J. (1951). Film: *Maternal deprivation in young children* (16 mm; 30 mins; sound). London: Tavistock Child Development.

ARKIN, R. M. (1981). Self-presentation styles. In T. J. Tedeschi (Ed.), *Impression management theory and social psychological research* (pp. 311–333). New York: Academic Press.

ARON, A., ARON, E. N. & SMOLLEN, D. (1992). Inclusion of others in the self scale and structure of interpersonal closeness. *Journal of Personality and Social Psychology, 63,* 596–612.

ARON, A., ARON, E.N., TUDOR, M. & NELSON, G. (1991). Close relationships as including other in the self. *Journal of Personality and Social Psychology, 60,* 241–253.

ATKINSON, J. W. (1957). Motivational determinants of risk-taking behavior. *Psychological Review, 64,* 359-372.

ATTENEAVE, F. (1959). *Applications of information theory to psychology.* New York: Holt.

BAKAN, D. (1966). *The duality of human existence.* Chicago: Rand-McNally.

BALDWIN, M. W. (1992). Relational schemas and the processing of information. *Psychological Bulletin, 112,* 461–484.

BALDWIN, M. W., CARRELL, S. E. & LOPEZ, D. F. (1990). Priming relationship schemas: My advisor and the Pope are watching me from the back of my mind. *Journal of Experimental Social Psychology, 26,* 435–454.

BALDWIN, M. W. & HOLMES, J. G. (1987). Salient private audiences and awareness of the self. *Journal of Personality and Social Psychology, 52,* 1087–1098.

BALDWIN, M. W., FEHR, B., KEEDIAN, E., SEIDEL, M. & THOMPSON, D. W. (1993). An exploration of the relational schemata underlying attachment styles: Self-report and lexical decision approaches. *Personality and Social Psychology Bulletin, 19,* 746–754.

BALDWIN, M. W., KEELAN, J. P. R., FEHR, B., ENNS, V. & KOH-RANGARAJOO, E. (1996). Social-cognitive conceptualization of attachment working models: Availability and accessibility effects. *Journal of Personality and Social Psychology, 71,* 94–109.

BANAJI, M. R. & PRENTICE, D. A. (1994). The self in social context. *Annual Review of Psychology, 45,* 297–332.

BANDURA, A. (1977). *Social learning theory.* Englewood Cliffs, NJ: Prentice-Hall.

BANDURA, A. (1986). *Social foundations of thought and action: A social cognitive theory.* Englewood Cliffs, NJ: Prentice Hall.

BANDURA, A. (1986). The explanatory and predictive scope of self-efficacy theory. Special issue: Self-efficacy theory in contemporary psychology. *Journal of Social and Clinical Psychology, 4,* 359–373.

BANDURA, A. (1989). Human agency in social-cognitive theory. *American Psychologist, 44,* 1175–1184.

BARGH, J. A. (1989). Condition automaticity: Varieties of automatic influence in social perception and cognition. In J. S. Uleman & J. A. Bargh (Eds.), *Unintended thought* (pp. 3–51). New York: Guilford.

BARSALOU, L.W. (1993). Flexibility, structure, and linguistic vagary in concepts: Manifestations of a compositional system of perceptual symbols. In A. F. Collins, S. E. Gathercol, M. A. Conway, & P. E. Morris (Eds.), *Theories of memory.* Hillsdale, NJ: Erlbaum.

BARTHOLOMEW, K. & HOROWITZ, L. M. (1991). Attachment styles among young adults: A test of a four-category model. *Journal of Personality and Social Psychology, 61,* 226–244.

BATSON, C. D. (1990). How social an animal?: The human capacity for caring. *American Psychologist, 45,* 336–346.

BATSON, C. D. (1991). *The altruism question: Toward a social-psychological answer.* Hillsdale, NJ: Erlbaum.

BAUMGARDNER, A. H. & ARKIN, R. M. (1988). Affective state mediates casual attributions for success and failure. *Motivation and Emotion, 12,* 99–111.

BAUMEISTER, R. F. (1991). *Meaning of life.* New York: Guilford.

BAUMEISTER, R. F. & LEARY, M.R. (1995). The need to belong: Desire for interpersonal attachments as a fundamental human motivation. *Psychological Bulletin, 117,* 497–529.

BECK, A. T. (1976). *Cognitive therapy and the emotional disorders.* New York: Penguin Books/Meridian.

BECK, A.T. & GREENBERG, R.L. (1974). Cognitive therapy with depressed women. In V. Franks & V. Burtle (Eds.), *Women and therapy: New psychotherapies for a changing society* (pp. 113–131). New York: Brunner/Mazel.

BECKER, E. (1971). *The birth and death of meaning.* Second Edition. New York: Free Press.

BECKER, E. (1973). *The denial of death.* New York: Free Press.

BELSKY, J. & CASSIDY, J. (1994). Attachment: Theory and evidence. In M. Rutter & D. Hay (Eds.), *Development through life* (pp. 373–402). Oxford: Blackwell.

BERSCHEID, E. (1994). Interpersonal relationships. *Annual Review of Psychology, 45*, 79–129.

BLATT, S. J. (1990). Interpersonal relatedness and self-definition: Two personality configurations and their implications for psychopathology and psychotherapy. In J. L. Singer (Ed.), *Repression and dissociation: Implications for personality theory, psychopathology, and health*. Chicago, IL: University of Chicago Press.

BOWLBY, J. (1958). The nature of the child's tie to his mother. *International Journal of Psychoanalysis, 39*, 350–373.

BOWLBY, J. (1969). *Attachment and loss: Vol. 1. Attachment*. New York: Basic Books.

BOWLBY, J. (1973). *Attachment and loss: Vol. 2 Separation: Anxiety and anger*. New York: Basic Books.

BOWLBY, J. (1980). *Attachment and loss: Vol. 3 Loss: Sadness and depression*. New York: Basic Books.

BRADLEY, G. W. (1978). Self-serving biases in the attribution process: A reexamination of the fact or fiction question. *Journal of Personality and Social Psychology, 36*, 56–71.

BREAKWELL, G. (1992). *Social psychology of identity and self concept*. San Diego, CA: Academic Press.

BREWER, M. B. (1991). The social self: On being the same and different at the same time. *Personality and Social Psychology Bulletin, 17*, 475–482.

BROWN, J. D. & GALLAGHER, F. M. (1992). Coming to terms with failure: Private self-enhancement and public self-effacement. *Journal of Experimental Social Psychology, 28*, 3–22.

BRUNER, J. (1990). *Acts of meaning*. Cambridge, MA: Harvard University Press.

BRUNER, J. S. (1957). Going beyond the information given. In H. E. Gruber, K. R. Hammond, & R. Jessor, *Contemporary approaches to cognition* (pp. 41–60). Cambridge, MA: Harvard University Press.

BUGENTAL, D. B. (1992). Affective and cognitive processes within threat-oriented family systems. In I. E. Sigel, A. McGillicuddy-de Lissi, & J. Goodnow (Eds.), *Parental belief systems: The psychological consequences for children* (2nd ed., pp. 219–248). Hillsdale, NJ: Erlbaum.

BURGER, J. M. (1985). Desire for control and achievement-related behaviors. *Journal of Personality and Social Psychology, 48*, 1520–1533.

CAMPBELL, J. D. & FEHR, B. (1990). Self-esteem and perceptions of conveyed impressions: Is negative affectivity associated with greater realism? *Journal of Experimental Social Psychology, 58*, 122–133.

CAMPOS, J. J. & STERNBERG, C. R. (1981). Perception, appraisal, and emotion: The onset of social referencing. In M. E. Lamb & L. R. Sherrod (Eds.), *Infant social cognition* (pp. 273–314). Hillsdale, NJ: Erlbaum.

CANTOR, J. & ENGLE, R. W. (1993). Working memory capacity as long term memory activation: An individual differences approach. *Journal of Experimental Psychology, Learning, Memory, and Cognition, 19*, 1101–1114.

CANTOR, N. & KIHLSTROM, J. F. (1987). *Personality and social intelligence*. Englewood Cliffs, NJ: Prentice Hall.

CANTOR, N., MARKUS, H., NIEDENTHAL, P. & NURIUS, P. (1986). On motivation and self-concept. In R. M. Sorrentino and E. T. Higgins (Eds.), *Handbook of motivation and cognition: Foundations of social behavior* (pp. 96–121). New York: Guilford.

CARNELLY, K., PIETROMONACO, P. R. & JAFFE, K. (1994). Depression, working models of other, and relationship functioning. *Journal of Personality and Social Psychology, 66*, 127–140.

CATRAMBONE, R. & MARKUS, H. (1987). The role of self-schemas in going beyond the information given. *Social Cognition, 5,* 349–368.

CHARME, S. T. (1984). *Meaning and myth in the study of lives: A Sartrean perspective.* Philadelphia: University of Pennsylvania Press.

CLARK, M. S. & ISEN, A. M. (1982). Toward understanding the relationship between feeling states and social behavior. In A. Hastorf & A. Isen (Eds.), *Cognitive social psychology* (pp. 73–108). New York: Elsevier North Holland.

COKE, J. S., BATSON, C. D. & McDAVIS, K. (1978). Empathic mediation of helping: A two-stage model. *Journal of Personality and Social Psychology, 36,* 752–766.

COLLINS, N. L. (1996). Working models of attachment: Implications for explanation, emotion, and behavior. *Journal of Personality and Social Psychology, 71,* 810–832.

COLLINS, N. L. & READ, S. J. (1990). Adult attachment, working models, and relationship quality in dating couples. *Journal of Personality and Social Psychology, 58,* 644–663.

CROCKER, J. & MAJOR, B. (1989). Social stigma and self-esteem: The self-protective properties of stigma. *Psychological Review, 96,* 608–630.

CSIKSZENTMIHALYI, M. & ROCHBERG-HALTON, E. (1981). *The meaning of things.* Cambridge: Cambridge University Press.

CUMMINS, R. (1989). *Meaning and mental representation.* Cambridge, MA: MIT Press.

DEAUX, K. (1991). Social identities: Thoughts on structure and change. In R.C. Curtis (Ed.), *The relational self: Theoretical convergencies in psychoanalysis and social psychology* (pp. 77–93). New York: Guilford.

DEAUX, K. (1993). Reconstructing social identity. *Personality and Social Psychology Bulletin, 19,* 4–12.

DECI, E. L. (1995). *Why we do what we do.* New York: Putnam.

DECI, E. L. & RYAN, R. M. (1985). *Intrinsic motivation and self-determination in human behavior.* New York: Plenum.

DECI, E. L. & RYAN, R. M. (1991). A motivational approach to self: Integration in personality. In R. Dienstbier (Ed.), *Nebraska symposium on motivation* (Vol. 38, pp. 237–288). Lincoln, NE: University of Nebraska Press.

DIX, T. (1991). The affective organization of parenting: Adaptive and maladaptive processes. *Psychological Bulletin, 110,* 3–25.

DOVIDIO, J. F., ALLEN, J. L. & SCHROEDER, D. A. (1990). Specificity of empathy-enduced helping: Evidence for altruistic motivation. *Journal of Personality and Social Psychology, 59,* 249–260.

DOWNEY, G., LEBOLT, A. & FELDMAN, S. (in press). The impact of early interpersonal trauma on adult adjustment: The mediating role of rejection sensitivity. In D. Cicchetti & S. Toth (Eds.), *Rochester Symposium on Developmental Psychopathology, Vol. VIII: The effects of trauma on the developmental process.* Rochester, NY: University of Rochester Press.

DUTTON, D. G., SAUNDERS, K., STARZOMSKI, A. & BARTHOLOMEW, K. (1994). Intimacy-anger and insecure attachment as precursors of abuse in intimate relationships. *Journal of Applied Psychology, 24,* 1367–1386.

DWECK, C. S. (1975). The role of expectations and attributions in the alleviation of learned helplessness. *Journal of Personality and Social Psychology, 31,* 674–685.

DWECK, C. S. & LEGGETT, E. L. (1988). A social-cognitive approach to motivation and personality. *Psychological Review, 95,* 256–273.

DWECK, C. S. & LICHT, B. G. (1980). Learned helplessness and intellectual achievement. In J. Garber & M. E. P. Seligman (Eds.), *Human helplessness: Theory and applications* (pp. 197–222). New York: Academic Press.

EHRENREICH, J. H. (1989). Transference: Once concept or many? *The Psychoanalytic Review, 76,* 1989.

EISENBERG, N. (1992). *The caring child.* Cambridge, MA: Harvard University Press.

EISENBERG, N., FABES, R. A., MURPHY, B., KARBON, M., SMITH, M. & MASZK, P. (1996). The relations of children's dispositional empathy-related responding to their emotionality, regulation, and social functioning. *Developmental Psychology, 32,* 195–209.

EISENBERG, N. & MILLER, P. (1987). Empathy and prosocial behavior. *Psychological Bulletin, 101,* 91–119.

EISENBERG, N. & MUSSEN, P. (1989). *The roots of prosocial behavior in children.* Cambridge, England: Cambridge University Press.

EKMAN, P. (1992). Are there basic emotions? *Psychological Review, 99,* 550–553.

ENGLE, R. W., CANTOR, J. & CARULLO, J. J. (1992). Individual differences in working memory and comprehension: A test of four hypotheses. *Journal of Experimental Psychology: Learning, Memory, and Cognition, 18,* 972–992.

EPSTEIN, S. (1973). The self-concept revisited or a theory of a theory. *American Psychologist, 28,* 405–416.

EPSTEIN, S. (1979). The stability of behavior: I. On predicting most of the people much of the time. *Journal of Personality and Social Psychology, 37,* 1097–1126.

FAIRBAIRN, W. R. D. (1952). *Psychoanalytic studies of personality.* London: Tavistock.

FELDMAN, S. & DOWNEY, G. (1995). Rejection sensitivity as a mediator of the impact of childhood exposure to family violence on adult attachment behavior. *Development and Psychopathology, 6,* 231–247.

FISKE, S. T. (1982). Schema-triggered affect: Applications to social perception. In M. S. Clark & S. T. Fiske (Eds.), *Affect and Cognition: The 17th Annual Carnegie Symposium on Cognition* (pp. 55–78). Hillsdale, NJ: Erlbaum.

FISKE, S. T. & PAVELCHAK, M. (1986). Category-based versus piecemeal-based affective responses: Developments in schema-triggered affect. In R. M. Sorrentino & E. T. Higgins (Eds.), *Handbook of motivation and cognition* (pp. 167–203). New York: Guilford.

FRANKL, V. E. (1959). *Man's search for meaning.* Boston, MA: Beacon Press.

FREUD, S. (1958). The dynamics of transference. *Standard edition* (Vol. 12, pp. 99–108). London: Hogarth. (Original work published 1912.)

FREUD, S. (1963). The dynamics of transference. Therapy and technique (pp. 105–115). New York: Macmillan. (Original work published in 1912.)

GLENDIN, E. T. (1962). *Experiencing and the creation of meaning.* Glencoe, IL: Free Press.

GREENBERG, J. & PYSZCZYNSKI, T. (1985). Compensatory self-inflation: A response to the threat to self-regard of public failure. *Journal of Personality and Social Psychology, 49,* 273–280.

GREENBERG, J., PYSZCZYNSKI, T. & SOLOMON, S. (1986). The causes and consequences of a need for self-system: A terror management theory. In R. F. Baumeister (Ed.), *Public self and private self* (pp. 189–212). New York: Springer-Verlag.

GREENBERG, J., PYSZCZYNSKI, T., SOLOMON, S. & CHATEL, D. (1992). Terror management and tolerance: Does mortality salience always intensify negative reactions to others who threaten one's world view? *Journal of Personality and Social Psychology, 58,* 308–318.

GREENBERG, J. R. & MITCHELL, S. A. (1983). *Object relations in psychoanalytic theory.* Cambridge, MA: Harvard University Press.

GREENSON, R. R. (1965). The working alliance and the transference neurosis. *Psychoanalytic Quarterly, 34,* 155–181.

GREENWALD, A. G. (1980). The totalitarian ego. *American Psychologist, 35,* 603–618.

GRIFFIN, D. & BARTHOLOMEW, K. (1994). Models of self and other: Fundamental dimensions underlying measures of adult attachment. *Journal of Personality and Social Psychology, 67,* 430–445.

GROSSMAN, K. E., GROSSMAN, K. & SCHWAN, A. (1986). Capturing the wider view of attachment: A reanalysis of Ainsworth's Strange Situation. In C. E. Izard & P. B. Read (Eds.), *Measuring emotions in infants and children*. (Vol. 2, pp. 124–171). New York: Cambridge University Press.

GUIDANO, V. F. & LIOTTI, G. (1983). *Cognitive processes and emotional disorders*. New York: Guilford.

GUISINGER, S. & BLATT, S. J. (1994). Individuality and relatedness: Evolution of a fundamental dialect. *American Psychologist, 49,* 104–111.

HARDIN, C. D. & HIGGINS, E. T. (1996). Shared reality: How social verification makes the subjective objective. *Handbook of motivation and cognition*. (Vol. 3, pp. 28–84). New York: Guilford.

HARLOW, H. F. & HARLOW, M. K. (1969). Effects of various mother-infant relationships on rhesus monkey behaviors. In B. M. Moss (Ed.), *Determinants of Infant Behavior* (Vol. 4). London: Methuen.

HAZAN, C. & SHAVER, P. (1987). Romantic love conceptualized as an attachment process. *Journal of Personality and Social Psychology, 52,* 511–524.6

HAZAN, C. & SHAVER, P. (1990). Love and work: An attachment-theoretical perspective. *Journal of Personality and Social Psychology, 59,* 270–280.

HEIDEGGER, M. (1962). *Being and time*. New York: Harper & Row.

HELGESON, V. S. (1994). Relation of agency and communion to well-being. Evidence and potential explanations. *Psychological Review, 116*(3), 412–428.

HIGGINS, E. T. (1987). Self-discrepancy theory: A theory relating self and affect. *Psychological Review, 94,* 319–340.

HIGGINS, E. T. (1989a). Knowledge accessibility and activation: Subjectivity and suffering from unconscious sources. In J. S. Uleman & J. A. Bargh (Eds.), *Unintended thought* (pp. 75–123). New York: Guilford.

HIGGINS, E. T. (1989b). Continuities and discontinuities in self-regulatory and self-evaluative processes: A developmental theory relating self and affect. *Journal of Personality, 57,* 407–444.

HIGGINS, E. T. (1990). Personality, social psychology, and person-situation relations: Standards and knowledge activation as a common language. In L. A. Pervin (Ed.), *Handbook of personality* (pp. 301–338). New York: Guilford.

HIGGINS, E. T. (1991). Development of self-regulatory and self-evaluative processes: Costs, benefits, and tradeoffs. In M. R. Gunnar & L. A. Stroufe (Eds.), *Self processes and development: The Minnesota Symposia on Child Development* (Vol. 23). Hillsdale, NJ: Erlbaum.

HIGGINS, E. T. (1996a). Emotional experiences: The pains and pleasures of distinct regulatory systems. In R. D. Kavanaugh, B. Zimmerberg, & S. Fein (Eds.), *Emotion: Interdisciplinary perspectives*. Mahwah, NJ: Erlbaum.

HIGGINS, E. T. (1996b). Ideals, oughts, and regulatory focus: Affect and motivation from distinct pains and pleasures. In P. M. Gollwitzer & J. A. Bargh (Eds.), *The psychology of action: Linking cognition and motivation to behavior*. (pp. 91–114). New York: Guilford.

HIGGINS, E. T. & BARGH, J. A. (1987). Social cognition and social perception. In M. R. Rosenzweig & L. W. Porter (Eds.), *Annual Review of Psychology* (Vol. 38, pp. 369–425). Palo Alto, CA: Annual Reviews.

HIGGINS, E. T. & BRENDL, C. M. (1995). Accessibility and applicability: Some "activation rules" influencing judgment. *Journal of Experimental Social Psychology, 31,* 218–243.

HIGGINS, E. T. & KING, G. A. (1981). Accessibility of social constructs: Information processing consequences of individual and contextual variability. In N. Canto & J. F.

Kihlstrom (Eds.), *Personality, cognition and social interaction* (pp. 69–121). Hillsdale, NJ: Erlbaum.

HIGGINS, E. T., VAN HOOK, E. & DORFMAN, D. (1988). Do self-attributes form a cognitive structure? *Social Cognition, 6,* 177–207.

HINKLEY, K. & ANDERSEN, S. M. (1996). The working self-concept in transference: Significant-other activation and self-change. *Journal of Personality and Social Psychology, 71,* 1279–1295.

HOFFMAN, M. L. (1981). Is altruism part of human nature? *Journal of Personality and Social Psychology, 40,* 121–137.

HOFFMAN, M. L. (1988). Moral development. In M. H. Bornstein & M. E. Lamb (Eds.), *Developmental psychology: An advanced textbook* (pp. 497–548). Hillsdale, NJ: Erlbaum.

HORNEY, K. (1939). *New ways in psychoanalysis.* New York: Norton.

HORNEY, K. (1945). *Our inner conflicts.* New York: Norton.

HOROWITZ, M. J. (ED.) (1991). *Person schemas and maladaptive interpersonal patterns.* Chicago, IL: The University of Chicago Press.

HUO, Y. J., SMITH, H. J., TYLER, T. R. & LIND, E. A. (1996). Subordinate indentification, subgroup identification, and justice concerns: Is separation the problem; Is assimilation the answer? *Psychological Science, 7,* 40–45.

ICKES, W. (in press). *Empathic accuracy.* New York: Guilford Press.

ISABELLA, R. A. (1995). The origins of infant-mother attachment: Maternal behavior and infant development. In R. Vasta (Ed.), *Annals of Child Development,* Vol. 10 (pp. 57–82). London: Jessica Kingsley Publishers, Ltd.

JANOFF-BULMAN, R. (1992). *Shattered assumptions: Towards a new psychology of trauma.* New York: Free Press.

JOHNSON, M. K., HASTROUDI, S. & LINDSAY, D. S. (1993). Source monitoring. *Psychological Bulletin, 114,* 3–28.

JOHNSON, M. K. & RAYE, C. L. (1981). Reality monitoring. *Psychological Review, 88,* 67–85.

JUNG, C. G. (1933). *Modern men in search of soul.* New York: Harcourt, Brace.

JUST, M. A. & CARPENTER, P. A. (1992). A capacity theory of comprehension: Individual differences in working memory. *Psychological Review, 99,* 122–149.

KAYE, K. (1984). Toward a developmental psychology of the family. In L.L'Abate (Ed.), *Handbook of family psychology and psychopathology.* Homewood, IL: Dow Jones-Irwin.

KELLY, G. A. (1955). *The psychology of personal constructs.* New York: Norton.

KESTENBAUM, R., FABER, E. A. & STROUFE, L. A. (1989). Individual differences in empathy among preschoolers: Relation to attachment history. In N. Eisenberg (Ed.), *Empathy and its development: New directions in child development* (Vol. 44, pp. 51–64). New York: Cambridge University Press.

KIHLSTROM, J. G. (1987). The cognitive unconscious. *Science, 237,* 1445–1452.

KLINGER, E. (1977). *Meaning and void.* Minneapolis, MN: University of Minnesota Press.

KLINNERT, M., CAMPOS, J. J., SCORCE, J., EMDE, R. N. & SVEJDA, M. (1983). Emotions as behavior regulators: Social referencing in infancy. In R. Plutchik & H. Kellerman (Eds.), *Emotion: Theory, research, and experience,* Vol. 2. *Emotions in early development* (pp. 57–86). New York: Academic.

KRIETLER, H. & KRIETLER, S. (1976). Cognition, information, and meaning. In H. Krietler & S. Krietler (Eds.), *Cognitive orientation and behavior.* New York: Springer.

KUNDA, Z. (1987). Motivated inferences: Self-serving generation and evaluation of causal theories. *Journal of Personality and Social Psychology, 53,* 636–647.

KUNDA, Z. (1990). The case for motivated reasoning. *Psychological Bulletin, 108,* 480–498.

LAZARUS, R. S. & AVERILL, J. R. (1972). Emotion and cognition with special reference to anxiety. In C. D. Spielberger (Ed.), *Anxiety: Current trends in theory and research* (Vol. 2, pp. 242–283). New York: Academic Press.

LEWINSOHN, P. M., MISCHEL, W., CHAPLIN, W. & BARTON, R. (1980). Social competence and depression: The role of illusory self-perceptions. *Journal of Abnormal Psychology, 89,* 203–212.

LINVILLE, P.W. (1985). Self-complexity and affective extremity: Don't put all your eggs in one cognitive basket. *Social Cognition, 3,* 94–120.

LINVILLE, P. W. (1987). Self-complexity as a cognitive buffer against stress-related illness and depression. *Journal of Personality and Social Psychology, 52,* 663–767.

LINVILLE, P. W. & CARLSTON, D. E. (1994). Social cognition of the self. In P. G. Devine, D. C. Hamilton, & T. M. Ostrom (Eds.), *Social cognition: Impact on social psychology* (pp. 143–193). New York: Academic Press.

LUBORSKY, L. & CRITS-CHRISTOPH, P. (1990). *Understanding transference: The CCRT method.* New York: Basic Books.

MACCOBY, E. E. & MARTIN, J. A. (1983). Socialization in the context of the family: Parent-child interaction. In P. H. Mussen (Ed.), *Handbook of child psychology, volume IV: Socialization, personality, and social development* (pp. 1–101). New York: Wiley.

MARKUS, H. & CROSS, S. (1990). The interpersonal self. In Pervin, L. A. (Ed.), *Handbook of personality.* New York: Guilford.

MARKUS, H. & KITAYAMA, S. (1991). Culture and the self: Implications for cognition, emotion, and motivation. *Psychological Review, 98,* 224–253.

MARKUS, H. & KUNDA, Z. (1986). Stability and malleability of the self concept. *Journal of Personality and Social Psychology, 51,* 858–866.

MARKUS, H. & NURIUS, P. (1986). Possible selves. *American Psychologist, 41,* 954–969.

MAY, R., ANGEL, E. & ELLENBERGER, H. (1958). *Existence.* New York: Basic Books.

McADAMS, D. P. (1985). *Power, intimacy, and the life story: Personological inquiries into identity.* New York: Guilford.

McADAMS, D. P. (1989). *Intimacy: The need to be close.* New York: Doubleday.

McADAMS, D. P. (1996). Personality, modernity, and the storied self: A contemporary framework for studying persons. *Psychological Inquiry, 7,* 295–321.

McADAMS, D. P. & CONSTANTIN, C. A. (1983). Intimacy and affiliation motives in daily living: An experience-sampling analysis. *Journal of Personality and Social Psychology, 45,* 851–861.

MILLER, D. T. & ROSS, M. (1975). Self-serving biases in the attribution of causality: Fact or fiction? *Psychological Bulletin, 82,* 213–225.

MILLER, P. A. & EISENBERG, N. (1988). The relation of empathy to aggressive and externalizing/antisocial behavior. *Psychological Bulletin, 103,* 324–344.

MILLER, L. C. & READ, S. J. (1991). On the coherence of mental models of persons and relationships: A knowledge structure approach. In G. J. O. Fletcher & F. D. Fincham (Eds.), *Cognition in close relationships* (pp. 69–99). Hillsdale, NJ: Erlbaum.

MISCHEL, W. & SHODA, Y. (1995). A cognitive-affective system theory of personality: Reconceptualizing situations, dispositions, dynamics, and invariance in personality structure. *Psychological Review, 102,* 246–268.

MORETTI, M. M. & HIGGINS, E. T. (in press). The self-regulatory role of self-other representations: A self-discrepancy perspective. Chapter to appear in Horowitz, M. J., Segal, Z., Milbrath, C., Andersen, S. & Salovey, P. (Eds.), *Person schemas: Self and interpersonal relationships.* Chicago, IL: University of Chicago Press.

MOSKOWITZ, D. S., SUH, E. J. & DESAULNIERS, J. (1994). Situational influences on gender differences in agency and communion. *Journal of Personality and Social Psychology, 66*(4), 753–761.

MULLAHY, P. (1970). *Psychoanalysis and Interpersonal Psychiatry. The Contributions of Harry Stack Sullivan.* New York: Science House.

NELSON, K. (1985). *Making sense: The acquisition of shared meaning.* New York: Academic Press.

OGILVIE, D. M. & ASHMORE, R. D. (1991). Self-with-other representation as a unit of analysis in self-concept research. In R. C. Curtis (Ed.), *The relational self: Theoretical convergencies in psychoanalysis and social psychology* (pp. 282–314). New York: Guilford Press.

PAULHUS, D. L. & LEWITT, K. (1987). Desirable responding triggered by affect: Automatic egotism? *Journal of Personality and Social Psychology, 52,* 245–259.

PENNEBAKER, J. W. (1988). Confiding traumatic experiences and health. In S. Fisher & J. Reason (Eds.), *Handbook of life stress, cognition, and health* (pp. 669–682). New York: Wiley.

PENNEBAKER, J. W. (in press). Writing about emotional experiences as a therapeutic process. *Psychological Science.*

PIETROMONACO, P. R. (1985). The influence of affect on self-perception in depression. *Social Cognition, 3,* 121–134.

PRENTICE, D. (1990). Familiarity and differences in self-and other-representations. *Journal of Personality and Social Psychology, 59,* 369–383.

READ, S. J. (1984). Analogical reasoning in social judgment: The importance of casual theories. *Journal of Personality and Social Psychology, 46,* 14–25.

READ, S. J. (1987). Similarity and causality in the use of social analogies. *Journal of Experimental Social Psychology, 23,* 189–207.

RICHARDSON, D. R., HAMMACK, G. S., SMITH, S. M., GARDNER, W. & SIGNO, M. (1994). Empathy as a cognitive inhibitor of interpersonal aggression. *Aggressive Behavior, 20,* 275–289.

ROBERTSON, J. (1953). Some responses of young children to loss of maternal care. *Nursing Times, 49,* 382–386.

ROGERS, C. (1951). *Client-centered therapy.* Boston: Houghton-Mifflin.

RYAN, R. M. (1993). Agency and organization: Intrinsic motivation, autonomy, and the self in psychology development. *Nebraska Symposium on Motivation* (Vol. 40, pp. 1–56). Lincoln, NE: University of Nebraska Press.

SACKEIN, H. A. (1983). Self-deception, self-esteem, and depression: The adaptive value of lying to oneself. In J. Masling (Ed.), *Empirical studies of psychoanalytic theory* (pp. 101–157). Hillsdale, NJ: Erlbaum.

SACKEIN, H. A. & GUR, R. C. (1979). Self-deception, other-description, and self-reported psychopathology. *Journal of Consulting and Clinical Psychology, 47,* 213–215.

SACKEIN, H. A. & WEGNER, A. Z. (1986). Attributional patterns in depression and euthymia. *Archives of General Psychiatry, 43,* 553–560.

SAFRAN, J. D. (1990). Toward a refinement of cognitive therapy in light of interpersonal theory: I. Theory. *Clinical Psychology Review, 10,* 87–105.

SAFRAN, J. D. & SEGAL, Z. V. (1990). *Interpersonal processes in cognitive therapy.* New York: Basic Books.

SCHIMEK, J. (1983). The construction of the transference: The relativity of the "here and now" and the "there and then." *Psychoanalysis and Contemporary Thought, 6,* 435–456.

SEDIKIDES, C. & SKOWRONSKI, J. J. (1990). Toward reconciling personality and social psychology: A construct accessibility approach. *Journal of Social Behavior and Personality, 5,* 531–546.

SEDIKIDES, C. & SKOWRONSKI, J. J. (1991). The law of cognitive structure activation. *Psychological Inquiry, 2,* 169–184.

SHAVER, P. R., COLLINS, N. & CLARK, C. L. (1996). Attachment styles and internal working models of self and relationship patterns. In G. J. O. Fletcher & Fitness, J. (Eds.), *Knowledge structures in close relationships: A social psychological approach* (pp. 25–61). Mahwah, NJ: Erlbaum.

SHAVER, P. & RUBENSTEIN, C. (1980). Childhood attachment experience and adult loneliness. In L. Wheeler (Ed.), *Review of personality and social psychology* (Vol. 1, pp. 42–73). Beverly Hills, CA: Sage.

SHOWERS, C. (1992). Compartmentalization of positive and negative self-knowledge: Keeping bad apples out of the bunch. *Journal of Personality and Social Psychology, 62,* 1036–1049.

SILVER, R. C. & WORTMAN, C. B. (1980). Coping with undesirable life events. In J. Garber & M. E. P. Seligman (Eds.), *Human helplessness* (pp. 279–340). New York: Academic Press.

SIMPSON, J. A. (1990). Influence of attachment styles on romantic relationships. *Journal of Personality and Social Psychology, 59,* 971–980.

SINGER, J. L. (1985). Transference and the human condition: A cognitive-affective perspective. *Psychoanalytic Psychology, 2,* 189–219.

SINGER, J. L. (1988). Reinterpreting the transference. In D. C. Turk & P. Salvey (Eds.), *Reasoning, interference, and judgment in clinical psychology* (pp. 182–205). New York: The Free Press.

SMITH, E. R. (1995). What do connectionism and social psychology offer each other? *Journal of Personality and Social Psychology, 70,* 893–912.

SMITH, E. R. & ZARATE, M. A. (1992). Exemplar-based model of social judgment. *Psychological Review, 99,* 3–21.

SMITH, E. R. & ZARATE, M. A. (1990). Exemplar and prototype use in social categorization. *Social Cognition, 8,* 243–262.

SPITZ, R. A. (1945). Hospitalism: An inquiry in the genesis of psychiatric conditions in early childhood. *Psychoanalytic Study of the Child, 1,* 53–73.

STEELE, C. M. (1988). The psychology of self-affirmation: Sustaining the integrity of the self. In L. Berkowitz (Ed.), *Advances in experimental social psychology* (Vol. 21, pp. 261–302). New York: Academic Press.

STERN, D. N. (1985). *The interpersonal world of the infant.* New York: Basic Books.

STOTLAND, L. (1969). Exploratory investigations of empathy. In L. Berkowitz (Ed.), *Advances in experimental social psychology* (Vol. 4, pp. 271–313). New York: Academic Press.

STROUFE, L. A. (1983). Infant-caregiver attachment and patterns of adaptation in preschool: The roots of maladaptation and competence. In M. Perlmutter (Ed.), *Development and policy concerning children with special needs. Minnesota Symposia on Child Psychology,* Vol. 16 (pp. 41–83).

STROUFE, L. A. (1996). *Emotional Development.* Cambridge: Cambridge University Press.

STROUFE, L. A., SCHORK, E., MOTTI, E., LAWROSKI, N. & LaFRENIERE, P. (1984). The role of affect in emerging social competence. In C. Izard, J. Kagan & R. Zajonc (Eds.), *Emotion, cognition and behavior* (pp. 289–319). New York: Cambridge University Press.

STROUFE, L. A. & WATERS, E. (1977). Attachment as an organizational construct. *Child Development, 48,* 1184–1199.

SULLIVAN, H. S. (1940). *Conceptions in modern psychiatry.* New York: Norton.

SULLIVAN, H. S. (1953). *The interpersonal theory of psychiatry.* New York: Norton.

TAJFEL, H. & TURNER, J. C. (1979). An integrative theory of intergroup conflict. In W. G. Austin & S. Worchel (Eds.), *The social psychology of intergroup relations*. Monterey, CA: Brooks/Cole.

TAYLOR, S. E. (1991). Asymmetrical effects of positive and negative events: The mobilization-minimization hypothesis. *Psychological Bulletin, 110*, 67–85.

TAYLOR, S. E. & BROWN, J. D. (1988). Illusion and well-being: A social psychological perspective on mental health. *Psychological Bulletin, 103*, 193–210.

TAYLOR, S. E. & LOBEL, M. (1989). Social comparison activity under threat: Downward evaluation and upward contrasts. *Psychological Review, 96*, 569–575.

TESSER, A. (1988). Toward a self-evaluation maintenance model of social behavior. In L. Berkowitz (Ed.), *Advances in experimental social psychology* (Vol. 21, pp. 181–227). New York: Academic Press.

TESSER, A. (1992). Emotion in social comparison and reflection processes. In L. L. Martin & A. Tesser (Eds.), *The construction of social judgments* (pp. 115–145). Hillsdale, NJ: Erlbaum.

THOMPSON, R. A. (in press). Early sociopersonality development. In W. Damon (Ed.), Handbook of child psychology (5th Ed.), Vol. 3. Social, emotional, and personality development (N. Eisenberg, Vol. Ed.). New York: Wiley.

TURNER, J. C. (1985). Social categorization and self-concept: A social cognitive theory of group behavior. In E. J. Lawler (Ed.), *Advances in group processes* (Vol. 2, pp. 77–121). Greenwich, CT: JAI Press.

TURNER, J. C. & OAKES, P. J. (1989). Self-categorization theory and social influence. In P. B. Paulus (Ed.), *The psychology of group influence* (pp. 233–275). Hillsdale, NJ: Erlbaum.

TYLER, T. R. & DEGOEY, P. (1995). Facilitating collective good in the community and in the family: The psychological dynamics of procedural and social identification. In G. Melton (Ed.), *Nebraska symposium on motivation*. Lincoln, Nebraska: University of Nebraska Press.

WACHTEL, P. L. (1981). Transference, schema, and assimilation: The relevance of Piaget to the psychoanalytic theory of transference. *The Annual of Psychoanalysis, 8*, 59–76.

WESTEN, D. (1988). Transference an information processing. *Clinical Psychology Review, 8*, 161–179.

WHITE, R. W. (1959). Motivation reconsidered: The concept of competence. *Psychological Review, 66*, 297–333.

WIGGINS, J. S. (1992). Agency and communion as conceptual coordinates for the understanding and measurement of interpersonal behavior. In W. M. Grove and D. Cicchetti (Eds.), *Thinking clearly about psychology* (pp. 89–113). Minneapolis: University of Minnesota Press. (Original work published 1912.)

WOIKE, B. A., OSIER, T. J. & CANDELA, K. (1996). Attachment styles and violent imagery in thematic stories about relationships. *Personality and Social Psychology Bulletin, 22*(10), 1030–1034.

YALOM, I. D. (1980). *Existential psychotherapy*. New York: Basic Books.

ZEIFMAN, D. & HAZAN, C. (in press). A process model of adult attachment formation. In S. Duck (Ed.), *Handbook of personal relationships* (2nd Ed.). New York: Wiley.

Part VI: Do We Really Know What We Have Been Talking About?

Introduction

ROBERT L. THOMPSON

Department of Psychology
Hunter College, and the Graduate School
City University of New York
New York, New York 10021

Some of the original presentations before the Psychology Section of the New York Academy of Sciences included invited commentators, but in most cases a diverse audience provided a lively discussion period that touched upon an even wider range of "the self across psychology" than appears in this volume. Papers by the formal discussants follow in this final part.

Michael Lewis wisely cautions against the too-early attribution of mental states to infants and illustrates their logical inconsistency with other established stages and processes of social cognition. He suggests that Neisser's five kinds of self-knowledge (see *Philosophical Psychology*, 1988, *1*, 35–59) may be incorrectly interpreted as a developmental sequence. Lewis recognizes a language trap. Our language practices mislead us when we try to understand the implications for the infant of its perceptions of the world and its perceptions of the successes and failures of its behavior in the world.

That our language habits create difficulties in dealing objectively with the extraordinarily fuzzy notion of self is emphasized by Robert L. Thompson. For Thompson, the problem calls for an experimental analysis that must include identification of those properties of behavior (of others as well as one's own) that evoke "self" words in our own verbal behavior. The difficulties become acute in studying nonhuman animal (nonverbal) cognition and behavior. It is widely acknowledged that cognitive processes in animals, particularly primates, have come to be an unexpectedly fertile area of research that has revealed unanticipated complexities. However, problems centering about the attribution of self-recognition, self-awareness, and a self concept have not enjoyed, until recently, the best of operational understanding. Problems remain with the methodology and interpretation of the widely used mirror mark test, and in assessment of its reliability and generality.

Carol Fleisher Feldman takes off from the papers by Bruner and Miller to pursue issues in the universality (or universalizability) of individual cognitive attributes within a cross-cultural perspective. Culture, for Feldman, is in no way an independent variable in the simple sense of the term. In a relevant earlier paper she wrote of the linguistic construction of cognitive representations, that is, thought from language, a phrasing which provides a timely contrast with a central theme in the discussions above of human infant and nonhuman animal cognition, namely, thought without language.

The Development of a Self

Comments on the Paper of Neisser

MICHAEL LEWIS

Institute for the Study of Child Development
Robert Wood Johnson Medical School
University of Medicine and Dentistry of New Jersey
97 Paterson Street
New Brunswick, New Jersey 08903

Ulric Neisser has been thinking about what a self might be for some time (Neisser, 1988) and his thoughtful paper reflects his continued concern for exploring its composition and the development of it. Most recently he has warned us to be careful in regard to what we mean when we say *self*. He has suggested that "the term self becomes psychologically interesting only when the activity in question is cognitive as well as reflexive, when there is self-awareness, self-consciousness, self-knowledge" (Neisser, 1995, p. 17).

Neisser, along with many before him, has articulated some of the features of a self and has suggested five kinds of self-knowledge (see also James, 1890; Lewis, 1991; Mead, 1934; Merleau-Ponty, 1964; Stern, 1985). While there is agreement that the term *self* represents an array of skills and abilities, when it comes to the study of the development of the self, agreement appears to disappear. I suspect this is because we have little appreciation of what a self developing might mean. For example, does a self come into being at once or does it emerge in pieces? If it emerges over time, does the development of a self follow some order, an order reflecting the increased complexity of the set of skills or abilities that have been articulated?

In this present paper Neisser seems to suggest that the process of development is likely to follow the ordering inherent in his discussion of the five kinds of self-knowledge. To be sure, such an analysis appears reasonable. However, as I have argued before (Lewis, 1990, 1992; Lewis & Brooks-Gunn, 1979), we must be careful in discussing earlier forms of self that we do not fall into a language trap, the result of which is to give to the infant's early capacities of self, skills reserved for later ones. Toward this end I have suggested that we distinguish the earlier features of a self as basic processes related to all complex systems (the machine of self), reserving the term *self* for a particular mental state (Lewis, 1995). The latter is what I assume Neisser means by the conceptual self. Thus, using Neisser's stages, I would caution that the capacities inherent in the conceptual self cannot be given to the ecological or interpersonal self, aspects of the self that in his scheme emerge earlier than the conceptual self.

This cautionary plea is necessary since the error I describe appears often. For example, consider a recent paper by Acquarone (1992), discussing a 3-month-old infant with cerebral palsy:

> The baby came in hanging on mother's left arm, looking at the therapist very briefly but intently and intelligently, even though her body was lifeless, thus giving hints of a potential to develop and a *wish to link with the therapist* [italics added]. We sat on the floor. Baby, with a twisted, half-fallen head, looked briefly at the therapist, half-smiled, and then looked startled. The therapist took it as some faint wish for contact in a very uncoordinated way. Thereafter, the therapist held both stiff little hands and helped her clench her fist, which produced another twisted look, and half-smile. Holding the baby's hands, the therapist talked gently about how nice it feels to be touched and firmly held and the baby jerked uncoordinatedly and stiffened. The therapist noticed the baby's overall joy and that *the infant wanted her legs touched and massaged, even though the baby's growth prevented direct contact* [italics added]. Mother asked the therapist what she was seeing in the child. The therapist observed that the baby had *some determination in linking with people, with her, but she needed to go through stages such as finding her own body boundaries, her identity, her mother's* [italics added]. Mother asked whether she could help. Mother's request for advice on how to help the baby was answered by observations about the baby being looked at, talked to, being held, and closing her hands, having her legs and body touched and massaged (p. 47).

Here we see in the therapeutic situation the writer imputing complex mental states in this handicapped three-month-old infant. The child's motor behavior is interpreted as reflecting mental states unlikely to occur in a child of this age. Similar difficulties can be found elsewhere. For example, Crittenden (1994), in talking about the organization of infant behavior, writes

> For example, an infant might conclude *"When I signal how I feel, my mother behaves in ways that are comforting,"* rather than, *"When I cry, my mother picks me up."* [italics added] Under less auspicious conditions, an infant might encode the more complex and discouraging information that, "When I signal, my mother rejects me," or "When I am quiet, she does not bother me." These examples show how behaviors can be perceived and encoded in procedural models as a function of classes rather than reflexes or links between specific self and other behaviors. These inferred mental states would seem to exist as basic properties of a self, even as the self develops and moves toward mental state capacities, such as are found in the experience of emotion, or as found in the idea of me (p. 82).

Also consider these mental states taken from the same paper: "For example, a securely attached child might have the paired generalizations that, 'My mother loves and understands me,' and 'I am lovable and capable of being understood'" (p. 83). Crittenden, like many others, clearly is willing to attribute these complex mental states to young infants, "even as the self develops." Thus, before the idea of *me* or conceptual self occurs, the infant can have mental states that need the concept of *me*. This type of logical error is found throughout the literature.

Stern's idea about the development of self (1985) contains this same difficulty. He states that, "There is no confusion between self and other in the beginning, or at any point during infancy" (p. 10). This is not a problem since, as I have tried to indicate, this is likely to be a property of all systems, and therefore could exist at the beginning of life (Lewis, 1995). However, this systems idea is not what Stern is addressing. In fact, he is willing to ascribe to the newborn complex mental states because the ability to experience itself is a mental state: "I am suggesting that the infant can experience the process of emerging organization as well as the result, and it is this experience of emerging organization that I call the emergent sense of self. It is the experience of a process as well as a product" (p. 45). For Stern, the self, even from the beginning, has extraordinary mental capacities. It can view itself coming into existence. I think there are some difficulties with such a view of self-development. First, it must rest on the belief that infants are highly capable not only of actions, including perceptions, thoughts, and learning, but also of complex mental states concerning themselves and their existence. While the infant has been shown to be highly capable in terms of some early capacities, these appear to be more reflexive in nature than cognitively based. There is no direct evidence of such mental states, nor are we ever informed as to how we might show there is.

Moreover, this view of the self does not allow for much self-development—certainly the development of the mental states of self. If, by birth, the child is capable of experiencing the self, then this self is a self capable of objective self-awareness (Duval & Wicklund, 1972) at the same time that the self is coming into existence. It experiences itself being created. This difficulty, especially as it relates to self, has historically been a problem.

Kernberg (1976) and Lacan (1968) also claim that the young infant is capable of experiencing its emergent self and, therefore, of experiencing anxiety over its nonexistence. This is similar to Otto Rank's notion of birth anxiety (1929/1952). Freud, in his critique of this view, rightly points out that anxiety is a signal, and as such, has to be experienced. Only the ego can experience: "The id cannot be afraid as the ego can; it is not an organization and cannot estimate situations of danger" (Freud, 1936/1963, p. 80). Since the ego emerges only slowly, certainly not at birth, there can be no objective experience. The problem resides in the fact that any anxiety over nonexistence or experiencing the emerging self, as an adult might experience it, cannot occur to an organism who has no objective self-awareness or mental state of its own existence. It is not possible for an organism to experience itself or to be anxious about its existence prior to the capacity to think about itself as existing, that is, prior to being able to experience itself and prior to its being able to imagine its nonexistence.

The core self and the issue of intersubjectivity, also as discussed by others (see Stern, 1985), presents a similar problem. Intersubjectivity, as Stern and others have defined it, is related to mental states of two selves and the connection between them. It might be possible to have intersubjectivity without a mental state if we think of intersubjectivity as contagion; for example, smiling when another smile appears. This social contagion—as when one bird flies off, all others on the telephone wire do so, or when laughter produces laughter—does not rest on mental states and none needs be evoked. Under such a definition, intersubjectivity becomes a set of complex behavior patterns that are triggered by other behaviors. Intersubjectivity is less controlled by mental states, and more by simple rules, such as circular reactions, as proposed by Piaget. It is not based on intentions in terms of complex means and representations, but is more like automatic social responses. Intersubjectivity between a mother and her six-month-old can take place as a function of a complex pattern system, one that may be present in any species. However, intersubjectivity, which involves a mental state based on the ideas of me, you, and our relationship, should not be possible at this age. Certainly, there is no support for it, and the confusion between mental states and contagion is not often even tested.

Part of the problem is what we might mean when we use such terms as awareness, intention, or intersubjectivity. It is the confusion between the machinery of the self leading to complex patterns of social behavior and the development of mental states. Self-awareness can be used simply to reflect the machine's capacity to monitor aspects of itself; our bodies monitor our temperature or our blood sugar levels. Such capacities do not need a mental state. Unfortunately, often self-awareness is meant to imply a mental state. It is this confusion in our terms and in our conceptions that leads us to assume that the behaviors in early infancy reflect analogous, if not identical, processes and functions that we usually assign to adults. This problem of confusing machine self with the idea of me, a mental state, leads to many difficulties. While the interactive behavior between a three- to six-month-old infant and its mother might be viewed as an early example of intersubjectivity, that is, the ability of the family members to share experiences to match, align, or attune their behavior to each other, it might, on the other hand, reflect much simpler processes. These processes may not involve mental states, but instead, indicate simple rules of contagion or attention-getting and -holding; it may be only the interactions between a dyad, one of whom possesses complex mental states and the other biological capacities.

I have tried to argue that our language, when we think of the self, often fails us. Terms like awareness, intention, regulation, and ideas about self–other impart important information since each of these aspects (or if one prefers, functions or skills) can occur in very different ways. Thus, if we differentiate them, a true developmental model is possible.

REFERENCES

ACQUARONE, S. (1992). What shall I do to stop him crying? Psychoanalytic thinking about the treatment of excessively crying infants and their mothers/parents. *Journal of Child Psychotherapy, 18*(1), 33–56.

CRITTENDEN, P. M. (1994). Peering into the black box: An exploratory treatise on the development of self in young children. In D. Cicchetti & S. Toth (Eds.), *Rochester Symposium on Developmental Psychopathology, Vol. 5: The self and its disorders* (pp. 79–148). Rochester, NY: University of Rochester Press.

DUVAL, S. & WICKLUND, R. A. (1972). *A theory of objective self-awareness.* New York: Academic Press.

FREUD, S. (1963). *The problem of anxiety* [originally published in 1936]. New York: Norton.

JAMES, W. (1890). *The principles of psychology.* New York: Holt.

LEWIS, M. (1990). Thinking and feeling—The elephant's tail. In C. A. Maher, M. Schwebel & N. S. Fagley (Eds.), *Thinking and problem solving in the developmental process: International perspectives (the WORK)* (pp. 89–110). Hillsdale, NJ: Lawrence Erlbaum.

LEWIS, M. (1990). Social knowledge and social development. *Merrill-Palmer Quarterly* [special issue], *36*(1), 93–116.

LEWIS, M. (1991). Ways of knowing: Objective self-awareness or consciousness. *Developmental Review, 11,* 231–243.

LEWIS, M. (1992). *Shame, The exposed self.* New York: The Free Press.

LEWIS, M. (1995). Aspects of self: From systems to ideas. In P. Rochat (Ed.), *The self in early infancy: Theory and research* (pp. 95–115). Advances in Psychology series. North Holland: Elsevier Science Publishers.

LEWIS, M. & BROOKS-GUNN, J. (1979). *Social cognition and the acquisition of self.* New York: Plenum.

MEAD, G. H. (1934). *Mind, self and society: From the standpoint of a social behaviorist.* Chicago: University of Chicago Press.

MERLEAU-PONTY, M. (1964). *Primacy of Perception,* edited by J. Eddie and translated by W. Cobb. Evanston, IL: Northwestern University Press.

NEISSER, U. (1988). Five kinds of self-knowledge. *Philosophical Psychology, 1,* 35–59.

NEISSER, U. (1995). Criteria for an ecological self. In P. Rochat (Ed.), *The self in infancy: Theory and research* (pp. 17–32). Amsterdam: Elsevier Science Publishers.

RANK, O. (1952). *The trauma of birth.* London: Kegan Paul [original work published 1929].

STERN, D. N. (1985). *The interpersonal world of the infant.* New York: Basic Books.

The Human Self and the Animal Self: Behavioral Problems with Few Answers

Comments on the Papers of Mitchell, Swartz, and Gallup

A s part of the proceedings of the thirty-ninth annual meeting of the American Psychopathological Association, there was published in 1950 what became a classic paper by W. N. Schoenfeld titled "An Experimental Approach to Anxiety, Escape and Avoidance Behavior." Skinner's reinforcement theory was capturing national attention and Schoenfeld sought the essential behavioral bottom line in a field cloudy with experimental and clinical concepts of anxiety and its management. For all the definition-defying multiple meanings of the term *anxiety,* its manifestations and management, there must be some fundamental behavioral operations that capture the essence of its causes, onset at any given time, maintenance, termination, or better, prevention. Schoenfeld delineated these basic paradigms in terms of unconditioned and conditioned aversive stimuli in relation to one another and in relation to classes of instrumental behavior that were noncontingently affected, or that stood in contingent relationships to the termination or forestalling of one or both of the stimulus classes or their connectivity. In anticipation of critics inhospitable to a behavioral analysis Schoenfeld (1950) commented, " . . . a word is no better in science than its clarity and unity of meaning, and by this token anxiety in its multifarious non-operational meanings is a perfectly bad word . . ." (p. 74). But it appears that humankind still cannot do without sin, and so for the present paper it is held that the word *self,* standing alone or as a reflexive prefix in a large number of psychological terms, is also a perfectly bad word.

Reber (1995) opened his 5.6-page dictionary entry for *self* this way:

One of the more dominant aspects of human experience is the compelling sense of one's unique existence, what philosophers have traditionally called the issue of personal identity or of the *self.* Accordingly, this term finds itself rather well represented in psychological theory,

[a]Address for correspondence: Robert L. Thompson, Department of Psychology, Hunter College, 695 Park Avenue, New York, New York 10021; telephone: 212/772-5533/-5621; fax: 212/772-5620.

particularly in the areas of social and developmental psychology, the study of personality and the field of psychopathology. The diversity of uses, not surprisingly, is extremely broad and rather unsystematic and the meaning intended is often confounded by the fact that the term may be used in many ways which interact subtly with grammatical forms. (p. 699)

Therein lies a major problem. Is the self in self-recognition, self-awareness, self concept, the self-image, the self-perceived, the self-esteemed, the self-deceived, and so on all the same self? Undoubtedly not! It is widely recognized that the notion of "self" is many-faceted and that no single measurement scheme captures enough of what is intended or suspected by use of the term. Sometimes "it" appears as an independent variable, sometimes as a dependent variable, more often as an intervening variable, still more often as a hypothetical construct. In one text, self is an object, in another a process. It is spoken of as a phenomenological imperative and as an illusion, an artifact of language, an upgraded name for the soul or psyche. For William James (1890) self was both the agent of consciousness and part of the contents of consciousness. It has been observed that there are as many understandings of self as there are understanders. If its meaning is self-evident to the folk psychologist, it is a thorn in the side of one occupied with questions of construct validity. If this confusion seems an impediment to attempts to understand the nonlinguistic animal self, it may yet hold promise for unifying the many branches of human cognitive studies (see Kihlstrom in this volume).

The kind of effort Schoenfeld made to identify fundamental behavioral operations pertaining to the concepts of anxiety and its management has had a less successful history in the matter of self-recognition, self-awareness, and self-conception. Perhaps this reflects the elusive, long-standing, underlying problem of an experimental analysis of consciousness, and perhaps it reflects a misconception of the problem altogether. Swartz in this volume points at such a misconception when she questions whether we are misguided to use the chimpanzee mirror self-recognition model in comparative research with other species. A paper by Hauser, Kralik, Botto-Mahan, Garrett, and Oser (1995), discussed later, raises similar questions.

It is a telling weakness of all accounts of the emergence or development of mirror self-recognition that the necessary and sufficient behavioral contingencies continue to elude us. Kinesthetic-visual matching sounds materialistic enough, but just what one must do to establish such generalized matching as part of the behavioral repertoire is not known. Earlier work on visual-tactile cross-modal discrimination training in monkeys and chimpanzees should be consulted. The "spontaneous" appearance of mirror self-recognition in some of the apes tested thus far is cited often, almost as if it confers some awesome cognitive achievement on the creatures. However, impressive, to label the acquisition of a skill as "spontaneous" is essentially a way of admitting ignorance of the relevant variables. (Spontaneous in the present sense is to be distinguished from spontaneous/emergent behavior as occurs in the context of training an equivalence class.) All three of the authors addressed in this commentary acknowledge that some (or many?) great apes do not show mirror self-recognition under the conventional testing procedures. Do these negative cases reflect problems with the procedure or with the apes? To my knowledge, only Boatright-Horowitz (1993) (see also Thompson & Boatright-Horowitz, 1994) has looked for quantitative differences in how positive and negatively mark-testing chimpanzees orient to a mirror.

If a skill is properly analyzed behaviorally, it takes nothing away from the skill to attempt to train it explicitly rather than to leave its occurrence up to unknown circumstances. Certainly a child's acquisition of identity is in large part under the tutelage of its parents. Thompson and Boatright-Horowitz (1994) described an attempt to induce the criterion responding of the mark test in two pigtailed macaques. As Mitchell, Swartz, and Gallup believe, the results remain controversial. If interpreted as positive, the performance on the mark test was certainly not as robust as occurs in some chimpanzees. Swartz questioned whether one monkey that we judged as passing the mark test (without inferring a self-concept) used the mirror to direct behavior to the mark. Monkeys often respond with glances and movements so rapid that they may go undetected by a human observer. And once the mirror contingencies are learned, mirror-indicated responding may suffice for what started as mirror-guided responding (Platt, Thompson & Boatright, 1991). Further, as appears to have been overlooked by Mitchell and Swartz, our monkey did inspect (sniff?) its hand after touching the mark, a component of the positive response sequence that is regarded as very important since it is said to imply that the animal perceived the mark on its own body. But in spite of our compelling intuition and identification with the animals, other than facial expressions, marks on the head may lack salience (cf. Hauser *et al.*, 1995). (And some facial expressions may lack social significance.)

Arboreal clambering (Povinelli & Cant, 1995) is an intuitively compelling hypothesis to account for the evolution of self-awareness as body awareness, but it calls for a finer analysis in behavioral terms of the events favoring emergence of self-awareness, particularly in regard to outcomes of success or failure early in development as the infant orangutan (or, for a "thought experiment," the now extinct common ancestor of all apes) ventured away from its mother. Whether a similar formulation might apply to arboreal monkeys should not be dismissed too soon. Given that clambering is not an apt description of their getting about, however fixed or stereotyped their patterns of locomotion, surely there is some "trial and error," some modifiability through experience, in the arboreal gamboling of monkeys, young and old. We have still to come to terms with the continuity or discontinuity of monkey-ape cognitive/behavioral capacities, particularly in the present context of discriminations based on one's own behavior. In any case, arboreal clambering comes to our attention as an unanticipated and ingenious turn in the road to ways of understanding how self-awareness emerges from self-agency.

In human experience, language is prominent in modulating and altering the functional relations among inputs and outputs (stimuli and responses) in learning of all kinds (e.g., Forsyth & Eifert, 1996). But language will play no role in the untutored chimpanzee's acquisition of mirror self-recognition, so greater emphasis must be given to the integration of visual attentive processes and somatosensory processes. (For convenience in the present case, by somatosensory I wish to include proprioception, skin senses, vestibular senses, and, unconventionally, those visceral sensations that may be relevant and that can be discriminated.) A recent collection of papers from a variety of perspectives including the philosophical, neuropsychological, physiological, and developmental, focusses on the self as constructed from somatosensory experience and points up important lessons to be had from somatosensory pathologies (Bermudez, Marcel & Eilan, 1995). Heyes (1994) suggests that many vertebrate species evidence a self-concept in the form of a body/spatial concept. Creatures ordinarily don't bump into objects as they make their way about.

The concept of a self-concept appears throughout these papers but there is no attempt to pin down the stimulus classes that must compose a concept if it is to be described in behavioral terms. What are the classes within which generalization occurs, and the classes between which discrimination occurs? What is the size and membership of these sets?

Surely a self-concept has many facets. Stern (1985) made a case for a four-component core sense of self in the developing infant that seems equally applicable to nonhuman animals. Stern spoke of *self-agency,* learning the authorship of one's actions, that is, acquiring effective operant behavior; *self-coherence,* the sense of being a physical whole with boundaries, that is, effectively getting about in one's environment (cf. Heyes, 1994); *self-affectivity,* experiencing affect correlated with other experiences of self, that is, having fun, managing hurt, adapting to and integrating the emotional (respondent) effects attendant upon certain stimulus conditions, contingencies, and response consequences such that other behavior is less disrupted and effectively goal-directed; and *self-history,* the sense of enduring from noting the regularities in the flow of events, that is, acquiring temporal discriminations and various perceptual constancies. Stern's core is not language-dependent and appears to translate easily to behavioral/operational/functional terms without doing violence to his categories. It could be taken to argue for a minimal sense of self in many species, some kind of a maturational step, getting some minimal "it" all together.

In the domain of learning and cognition in nonhuman animals the claims for inferring some kind of selfhood are of recent vintage. Such claims are sometimes held with vigor and passion, particularly in the case of the great apes (and some aquatic mammals), and the negative claim denying self-conception for the lesser primates may be held with equal force. Because of the almost irresistible urge to identify with the great apes, whether on grounds of evolution, appearance, or sociality, a (usually unintentional) anthropomorphism infuses some of the prominent literature (Kennedy, 1992; but see also Rumbaugh, 1994). A number of movies and works of fiction depicting extraordinary sensitivity, intelligence, and language skills in individual chimpanzees, gorillas, and orangutans play upon our cognitive unconscious, however much we may want to resist. Until quite recently, virtually the sole empirical foundation for the attribution of self-recognition, self-awareness, and a self-concept to at least some members of the three genera of great apes was in the mirror self-recognition task introduced by Gallup (1970) and indexed by mirror-mediated, mark-directed responding. Details of the mirror self-recognition task (commonly referred to as the mark test) are found in Gallup (1970, 1994, and this volume) and in the papers by Mitchell and by Swartz also in this volume. The reader is also referred to the volume edited by Parker, Mitchell, and Boccia (1994), *Self-Awareness in Animals and Humans: Developmental Perspectives,* for a broad comparative sampling.

Gallup's mark test enjoys considerable currency in spite of (not always well-founded) criticism of its methodology and other methodologies related to mental state attribution by Heyes (1993, 1994). (Contrary to Gallup's assertion, Heyes' criticisms do not stem from radical behaviorism. Rather, they represent a very conservative adherence to rigorous principles of experimental design and the principle of parsimony long associated with conventional or methodological behaviorism.) However, Heyes (1993) does effectively criticize the inferences drawn from the mark test about the presence or absence of self-conception in apes and monkeys, respectively, and finds those inferences unsupported. For her, passing the mark test reveals nothing more than successful mirror-guided body inspection. A similar view was propounded by Jaynes (1978) and emerges also from Mitchell's interpretation of kinesthetic-visual matching. For additional consideration of criteria for competence in mirror use and related matters see Platt *et al.* (1991).

Claims for phyletic constraints on discriminations of self-derived stimuli remain controversial. Much depends on what kind of self-knowledge one would attribute to what species. A paper by Hauser *et al.* (1995) reported positive results from a modified mark test with cotton-top tamarin monkeys whose white, top-of-the-head hair was color-dyed, altering a distinctive species-typical feature. The authors suggest that species differences in self-recognition among the primates may be attributable to the relative saliency of the marked body part. Further, they join other critics in suggesting that the mark test "may not be sufficient for assessing the concept of self or mental state attribution in nonlinguistic organisms" (p. 10811).

In another context, the roles of contingencies of movement and appearance in discriminating oneself or others in mirror (or video) presentations is in need of more research. Kitchen, Denton, and Brent (1996) used regular mirrors, distorting mirrors, and mark tests with six chimpanzees. Successful mirror-mediated mark-directed responding in the presence of distorting mirrors was taken to indicate that mirror self-recognition by chimpanzees may depend more on the detection of contingent movement cues than on feature recognition.

Major questions remain concerning what the mark test can reveal, how we may conceive an animal's self-conception, and how we can place all this is an experimental and behaviorally effective context. How ironic that (at least for some of us) the name for the "compelling sense of one's unique existence" is so troublesome. Until answers are forthcoming, we stay anxious about the "S-word" because in all its multifarious non-operational meanings, "self" remains a perfectly bad but unavoidable and unescapable word.

REFERENCES

BERMUDEZ, J. L., MARCEL, A. & EILAN, N. (Eds.) (1995). *The body and the self.* Cambridge, MA: MIT Press.

BOATRIGHT-HOROWITZ, S. L. (1992). Mirror behavior and "selfhood" among primates. *Dissertation Abstracts International, 53,* 2047B. (University Microfilms No. DA9224796).

FORSYTH, J. P. & EIFERT, G. H. (1996). The language of feeling and the feeling of anxiety. Contributions of the behaviorisms toward understanding the function-altering effects of language. *Psychological Record, 45,* 607–649.

GALLUP, G. G., JR. (1970). Chimpanzees: Self-recognition. *Science, 167,* 86–87.

GALLUP, G. G., JR. (1991). Toward a comparative psychology of self-awareness: Species limitations and cognitive consequences. In G. R. Goethals & J. Strauss (Eds.), *The self: An interdisciplinary approach* (pp. 121–135). New York: Springer-Verlag.

HAUSER, M. D., KRALIK, J., BOTTO-MAHAN, C., GARRETT, M. & OSER, J. (1995). Self-recognition in primates: Phylogeny and the salience of species-typical features. *Proceedings of the National Academy of Sciences, 92,* 10811–10814.

HEYES, C. M. (1993). Anecdotes, training, trapping and triangulating: Do animals attribute mental states? *Animal Behaviour, 46,* 177–188.

HEYES, C. M. (1994). Reflections on self-recognition in primates. *Animal Behaviour, 47,* 909–919.

JAMES, W. (1890). *Principles of psychology.* New York: Henry Holt.

JAYNES, J. (1978). In a manner of speaking. *Behavioral and Brain Sciences, 4,* 578–579.

KENNEDY, J. S. (1992). *The new anthropomorphism.* New York: Cambridge University Press.

KITCHEN, A., DENTON, D. & BRENT, L. (1996). Self-recognition and abstraction abilities in the common chimpanzee studied with distorting mirrors. *Proceedings of the National Academy of Sciences, 93,* 7405–7408.

PARKER, S. T., MITCHELL, R. W. & BOCCIA, M. L. (Eds.) (1994). *Self-awareness in animals and humans: Developmental perspectives.* New York: Cambridge University Press.

PLATT, M. M., THOMPSON, R. L. & BOATRIGHT, S. L. (1991). Monkeys and mirrors: Questions of methodology. In L. M. Fedigan & P. J. Asquith (Eds.), *The monkeys of Arashiyama: Thirty-five years of research in Japan and the West* (pp. 274–290). Albany: State University of New York Press.

POVINELLI, D. J. & CANT, J. G. H. (1995). Arboreal clambering and the evolution of self-conception. *Quarterly Review of Biology, 70,* 393–421.

REBER, A. S. (1995). *The Penguin dictionary of psychology* (2nd ed.). New York: Penguin Books.

RUMBAUGH, D. M. (1994). Anthropomorphism revisited. *Quarterly Review of Biology, 69,* 248–251.

SCHOENFELD, W. N. (1950). An experimental approach to anxiety, escape and avoidance behavior. In P. H. Hoch & J. Zubin (Eds.), *Anxiety.* New York: Grune & Stratton.

STERN, D. (1985). *The interpersonal world of the infant.* New York: Basic Books.

THOMPSON, R. L. & BOATRIGHT-HOROWITZ, S. L. (1994). The question of mirror-mediated self-recognition in apes and monkeys: Some new results and reservations. In S. T. Parker, R. W. Mitchell & M. L. Boccia (Eds.), *Self-awareness in animals and humans: Developmental perspectives* (pp. 330–349). New York: Cambridge University Press.

Carol Fleisher Feldman is a research scientist in the Department of Psychology at New York University, where she collaborates with Jerome Bruner on studies of interpretive thinking. Professor Feldman's work has concentrated principally on the relation between language and thought, viewed as a problem in pragmatics, whose methods she introduced into psychology from philosophy. Her work with Eskimo and Hawaiian children revealed how the culture in both societies hinders the expression of abstract logical thought in the classroom. She has served on the faculties of Harvard, Yale, and the University of Chicago.

Self-Making as Cultural Cognition[a]

Comments on the Papers of Miller and Bruner

CAROL FLEISHER FELDMAN

Department of Psychology
New York University
New York, New York 10003

I was originally asked to write a reply to Joan Miller's paper, but, as the volume evolved, I was asked to comment on Bruner's paper, too, notwithstanding our close connection. The two papers have a good deal in common, in taking the processes of self-making to be both cultural and cognitive, a view that I share, and one I think too little has been said about, for it seems that these two categories are often regarded as mutually exclusive. My comment, then, is a response to both Miller and Bruner, and a plea for redirection to an expanded notion of cognition that includes cultural patterns and, conversely, for a focus on culture that considers it as part of mental life.

Let me begin with a confession, and a gratuitous one at that, for the fact that this paper uses the two papers it "discusses" as the slimmest of pretexts to talk about matters particularly preoccupying to me at the moment (see, for example, Feldman, 1994) would be clear in a matter of a few sentences in any case. What I want to do here is to defend the view that cultural psychology is classically cognitive in every respect—that it is capable of undergoing growth on the basis of non-social, endogenous processes; that it is held in the privacy of a single mind; that it does not differ in its underlying structure in each and every culture, nor *a fortiori* across individuals within a culture; and that it therefore can and does express itself in cognitive universals. Nevertheless, the occasion for my plea is not inapposite, for my belief that there is a cognitive core of cultural psychology is one that both Miller and Bruner share. As Miller says, "The perspective of cultural psychology rejects the stance of viewing culture as an independent variable . . . [but] (e)qually it rejects . . . treating psychological processes as purely discursive phenomena."

Where cultural psychology modifies the picture from classical cognition is chiefly by adding additional areas to our picture of cognitive life: namely, the interpretive patterns of thinking used when the problem at hand is to discover the meaning of such things as the self and the utterances of friends in everyday life, rather than, say, to discover the singular truth of a mathe-

[a]This work was supported by a grant from the Spencer Foundation to Jerome Bruner in support of a research project on "Meaning Making in Context," 1995–1999.

matical computation or a demonstration in Newtonian physics. As such, it asks us to note the existence of other kinds of thinking than the algorithmic and predictive patterns of classical cognition, and to begin to study them empirically so as to discover their patterns and forms. It says that there is more cognition, that there are additional cognitive capacities that enter our understanding of real-world phenomena—more not less. And more but not different. For, as I have tried to show elsewhere, it says that the cognition used to understand intentional events is patterned in much the same way as our experience of objects in space and time–only that the particular patterns used to organize it are different ones, new to cognitive psychology. They include the self genres of literature, stories of fate and plight that circulate in everyday life, familiar plots, and even ways of talking. These interpretive patterns are found in the culture around us, and in an individual life they probably come by learning through exposure to it. That is the sense in which they are cultural. But, we go on to use them as tools of interpretive *thinking,* and then they are cognitive, as cognitive as thinking in fractions, or predicting the arc of a pendulum.

As everyone knows, C. S. Peirce coined the word *pragmaticism,* a word "ugly enough to be safe from kidnappers," when he found that William James' version of pragmatism, which he found inimical, was displacing his own. It is an interesting fact for the present case that the form of that inimical reading of pragmatism was as a praxis of action in the public forum of observable behavior. Peirce had something more private and mental in mind. And so in the current context do the three of us, Bruner, Miller and I.

We could follow Peirce's lead and add a syllable here or there, say calling cultural psychology "enculturated" psychology. But we know what happened to Peirce's idea, which perhaps offers a lesson about yielding clear labels to take up unclear ones. We should, I think, hold our ground and attack the kidnappers instead. A cultural psychology that is not cognitive is not psychology, and perhaps neither was James's inimical pragmatism. If all the important processes under discussion go on in public, in the space defined by two or more publicly interacting people, this is cultural *sociology,* a nice neat phrase with no extra syllables.

Let me now turn to the substance of a cognitive cultural psychology and try to say here what I think we all three think cultural psychology is, and why studies in cultural psychology are also studies in cognitive psychology, simply a new extension of cognition to take further capacities of mind into account. I begin with Bruner's paper.

Bruner has taken on the hardest possible case for my claim, for versions of the self are at the outer reach of what we can imagine as classically cognitive. They seem arbitrary and quirky, or idiosyncratic. And they sometimes seem to be poorly formed, rather than following well-formed patterns in a workmanlike way. In fact, they are rather rough constructions, as Bruner notes.

Nevertheless, even in our ideas about our "self," signs of cognitive process leap out. First, as it is evident that selves are not found just lying around, it is plain that they must be made. And, if made, then made by each of us according to some construction rules. "Construction rules" gives it away—the self must be patterned along some lines or other. The constraints on these patterns have a cognitive origin, first, in the possible forms that the person narrating can conceive. But, second, because we create the self-conscious version of ourselves in order to tell about it to others (and to ourselves), the possible forms these construction rules can take are also given by the cognitive possibilities for comprehension by our intended audience, whether others or our own selves at some later time.

The first batch of rules controls what can be produced, the second places constraints on the universe of possible self-constructions, limiting the set of useful ones to the ones among those possibilities that can be understood intersubjectively. It is this requirement that the selves we construct enter into discourse with other or successor selves that places the greatest pressures for regularity on their shape.

Indeed, it could be said that "the self" is made chiefly so that we will have the entry ticket into a certain kind of discourse and connection with others. We may, for example, be capable of a self-construction that is a Zen koan, but give it up in favor of a more explicit statement of paradox for the sake of sharing the self with an interlocutor, particularly one not inside our own head. A construction with key references that are private, or whose pattern is too confusingly aligned with the culturally canonical patterns of self-stories, will not be recognizable. Or a self that is too badly formed, too internally inconsistent, will not be recalled correctly, but rather regularized by its audience with time. So self-construction cannot be entirely idiosyncratic—it must be well-enough formed to remember, and canonical enough to be recognized, and perhaps meet other criteria as well.

Self-constructions appear not just in told autobiographies, but they sneak out in bits and pieces into communication with others that is apparently about other topics. For the very deep structure of utterances, whether oral or written, whether for the self or others, whether dialogic or monologic, whether in discourse or not, is that they contain, first, some proposition about the world, and, second, some (usually pragmatically marked) indication of the speaker's point of view toward it. I have written about this elsewhere (Feldman, 1974), and this is not the place to elaborate the point, but let me say just another word about it here: When utterances are examined for their functional structure, for what chores the speaker is doing by means of them, they can be seen as having two major functional constituents. The first is saying something about something, in its simplest form referring to a thing outside of discourse, in more elaborated form describing or mentioning some fact outside of discourse.[b] The second function normally accompa-

---

[b]In the simple case of utterances that contain only a subject and a predicate, the predicate often serves as a stance-taking comment on the topical subject. In the more typical complex case of utterances containing subject and predicate, and a pragmatic marker, subject

nies the first. It says, but usually not explicitly, something about how the speaker who refers to the thing, or mentions the fact, views it from his or her own point of view. These stance indications are pervasive in many discourse forms, particularly in ordinary conversation, where the naked reporting of facts and events is relatively rare and is often socially unacceptable. And they constitute in their totality the steady emanation of bits and pieces of self as it is invoked by the topical context.

The self version we construct and put forward, whether in the pragmatic markers of ordinary conversation or in autobiographical stories, is not inconsequential, as any Asperger's patient will tell you. For one thing the very high-functioning autistic people with this disorder agree on the loneliness of their solitary lives, a loneliness that in no small measure seems the consequence of their too-different way of talking about experience, a discourse defect that drives potential normal interlocutors away. That is, we are under social pressures to make ourselves known to others as the price of their company. The normal other fears strange-sounding self-constructions as he fears the uncanny, the impenetrable. And he avoids it. This leaves those who cannot tell a canonical enough narrative of the self alone, often much more alone then they want to be.

Bruner believes that self-narrations are cognitively based, but not in the sense that they reflect a schema in place when we start to talk, for we are making the story as we go, and remaking it each time. The variability among self-constructions across ontogenetic and historic time, and their evidence of work-in-progress ("their ziggings and zaggings, their isolated episodes and events, their undigested details," as Bruner has put it) indicates that it is not "a stored internal schema" that "guides our self accounts." Instead, the basis in cognition takes the form of construction rules for self-making along acceptably patterned lines—that is, the nature of the cognition involved follows from their nature as constructions. Miller agrees with this. She says, "From a semiotic perspective, cultural meanings are viewed as including representational information, such as shared knowledge about the co-variational structure of human experience, as well as directive information, such as normative expectations. What is most significant about the semiotic perspective, however, is its recognition that culture includes as well constitutive meanings that serve to define and thereby create realities."

For Bruner, as the self is constructed each time, the cognitive task is one of taking "bits and pieces," turning around on them, and putting them together into a narrative structure that has some cognitive form, "like reconceiving some familiar territory in order to put it into a more general topography." In this sense, Bruner sees the cognitive processes involved in self-

---

and predicate together may be used to mention a fact or event, while the pragmatic marker conveys the speaker's stance toward it as a comment on the fact taken as topic. I discuss this at length in Feldman (1987).

making as "meta-cognitive: We impose bold and imaginative meta-structure on local details to achieve coherence." These narrative meta-structures include the clinician's theories, the priest's doctrines of repentance and redemption—the canonical story types of our culture.

Nevertheless, Self is an area where each of us is invited to differentiate ourself, one from the other. There is almost a requirement of distinctiveness. We use the tools of narrative in self-making, then, not only to say what familiar story we can be understood as fitting, but also how we differ from it. Does this make it any less cognitive?

The narrative patterning can be expected to differ creatively, but it must also differ comprehensibly from canonical patterns, for, after all, one main function of these deviations is, as I have noted, to make our distinctiveness understood by someone else. At the other extreme from self narratives are highly canonical interpretive contexts, such as courts, where the judge interpreter is invited to think nothing that has not been thought before, as expressed in the doctrine of *stare decisis*. Different contexts, then, invite different degrees of creativity in the application of the canon of narrative patterns, but they must all be attentive to the canon and the expectations it sets up, and hence must all be based on cognition in two senses: that they make use of the rules of narrative construction and interpretation both to honor them and also to violate them in principled ways.

The creativity necessary for applying the rules of narrative construction to self-making, its emphasis on rule-breaking, may seem on the surface to make self-making cognition too different from classical cognition to be called cognition at all. But is it really? Since Chomsky (1965), syntactic understanding has been seen both as prototypically cognitive, and as being highly creative knowledge within a rule-bound domain. A little thought makes it clear that for nearly every area of patterned thought, mastery includes a capacity to deviate systematically from canon in contexts that invite it—the gambler who tries to create a new system for beating the odds, the upper-level court that takes as its duty the reinterpretation of old principles so as to apply them to new situations unforeseen at the time of their writing, the poet who uses syntactical knowledge creatively in order to "make the familiar strange." So, though classical cognition orients to canonical patterns, it always contains within it the creative possibilities inherent in breaching them. It is no different from interpretive cognition in this regard, or even the idiosyncratic interpretive cognition of self-making. Any differences are just a matter of degree, not of kind.

Miller's case is a bit easier to grind in my mill for it deals with an area, moral development, that has been seen as essentially cognitive, at least since the time of Piaget's and Kohlberg's important foundational work. However, moral development was always seen as deviant, in seeming to pull in substantive matters from way out in the social domain, substantive matters that might not themselves have any cognitive basis. Analyses of moral development, then, were often seen as showing the cognitive operational core of one area of social life, given in classically mathematical terms. To reason morally, it was thought, one added to this mathematical core some social knowledge that might not be cognitive, something like social sensitivity. It was the social component that was the cultural one. So like self-making, moral development too, at least as it was classically conceived, does not constitute an easy case for claiming that cultural psychology is essentially cognitive.

And yet, as Miller makes clear, the social aspects of moral development can themselves be seen as cognitively based, showing that the cognitive basis of morality goes well beyond the simple discovery of operational thinking typical of the various stages of classical moral reasoning. Miller identifies further cognitive patterns within the stages in social structure—collectivism in India and individualism in the West—that give moral reasoning at each stage its distinctive cast in each cultural context. Thus, Miller sees moral reasoning not only as having a cognitive core attributable to the operational level, but also as having a cognitive core attributable to the particular cultural construal of the stage within individualism or collectivism. Miller says, "From the perspective of cultural psychology, psychological processes are understood to be patterned, in part, by cultural meanings and practices." Her way of looking at moral development, by including a cultural dimension, is meant as a step on the road to discovering more about its cognitive patterning, not less.

For Miller, the individualism of the West expresses a system of reasoning, as does the collectivism of the East. The systems are pervasive, general, highly patterned, known to individuals. Moreover, I note that even these cross-cultural differences can be seen as being, in principle, universalizable, which matters. For universalizability is something of an acid test for whether any putative mental event is really a candidate for being considered a cognitive structure. And cultural thought, or at least cross-culturally divergent thought, might seem to be the prototype of the local, which no doubt it sometimes is. But not so moral reasoning of Miller's two kinds.

For we can all imagine thought experiments that could elicit each pattern from members of the other group, given conditions where they are faced with the right hypothetical situation. Moreover, note that it is not just the Western version of the morality of caring that we elicit in this thought experiment, but rather the distinctively Indian way of thinking as Miller defines it. Miller sees the defining difference between the two approaches this way: the Eastern approach sees individuals as naturally social, and duty as congruent with individual inclinations, while Western views tend to see social duty and individual inclinations as naturally opposed.

The Eastern view, as Miller defines it, is, I will argue, universalizable. The Indian collectivist form could be elicited in Westerners in special settings— say Marines under fire or people acting in theater groups, where duty and individual inclination seem to converge. That is, Indian collectivism could be evoked by certain Western settings where each individual's welfare depends on that of everyone else in the group. This is the distinctively Indian way of thinking as Miller defines it.

The universalizability of the "Indian" view need not imply that these forms of thought are not culturally derived. Rather it suggests that we should look for the informing culture, in this case in mini-culture and subculture, rather than at the level of national social structure. In the cases of both the Marines and the theater group, we can understand their collectivism not by eschewing culture, but by focusing on the local group culture where their lives have meaning. Certainly both the Marines and the theater group can be thought of as mini-cultures with their own norms within the Western range of variation. Conversely, we don't even need such an experiment to find the Western antinomy between the individual and his duty in the East. It arises all the time when people see themselves as being outside the community where this culture is defining—namely, with strangers. No community, no culture of community. And individualistic patterns of thinking, otherwise seemingly absent, express themselves and prove to have been potential forms of thinking all along. Both individualism and collectivism, then, have the universalizability that Chomsky has taught us to demand of cognitive systems.

Finally, I want to say a word in defense of a cognitive cultural psychology from another angle. If culture is not just praxis, mind is also not just brain. The middle level is where the heart of psychology lies. From every angle, it is this middle level—let's call it "thinking"—that is attached, and I have to suppose that thinking itself is very threatening in some way, perhaps because of the freedom it implies. But all the attacks essentially take the same form: They note that thinking is an intangible substance, while brain or discourse is not, and then they suggest that thinking is "irreal." And so it is with the self. The battle is always, at bottom, and rather unsuitably, metaphysical.

Metaphysical battles have no proper place in science—they are the stuff of religion and dogma. If someone is thinking, and someone else is studying how, the only legitimate questions to ask are epistemological: What is the thinker doing? How did the study go about looking at it? What did it claim to discover? How does it know? On what basis do it claims rest? How secure are the grounds? and so on.

Attacking thinking as suspicious because it has no material being is, simply, a cheap shot. It's too easy to make suspicions of the unseen attractive. But this appeal to irreality cannot be made to the scientist within us, for no science can or does get by without such entities, physics and psychology being perhaps the most extreme cases.

So this is finally an appeal on behalf of poor cognition, everywhere and always under threat. And for the celebration of mental life and its scientific study—mental life that understands the self, morality, and human intentions more generally, but also science and math, not to mention theater and art, music and baking, architecture and computers—the whole range of cultural products. And it is not simply that we are cognitively enabled consumers, capable of *understanding* such matters, but that we can make them and re-make them, too. For these cultural products did not come from nature. They had to be made. And thought of first by their makers, and remakers. It is culturally informed cognition that equips us to understand them, and it is cognition that *made* them, too.

ACKNOWLEDGMENT

I want to thank Rochel Gelman for first making, and then explaining, an inadvertent remark that suggested the agenda for this paper.

REFERENCES

CHOMSKY, N. (1965). *Aspects of the theory of syntax.* Cambridge, MA: MIT Press.

FELDMAN, C. (1974). Pragmatic features of natural language. In M. W. LaGaly, R. A. Fox & A. Bruck (Eds.), *Papers from the Tenth Regional Meeting of the Chicago Linguistic Society* (pp. 151–160). Chicago: Chicago Linguistic Society.

FELDMAN, C. F. (1987). Thought from language: The linguistic construction of cognitive representations. In J. Bruner & H. Haste (Eds.), *Making sense: The child's construction of the world* (pp. 131–146). London: Methuen.

FELDMAN, C. F. (1994). Genres as mental models. In M. Ammaniti & D. N. Stern (Eds.), *Psychoanalysis and development: Representations and narratives* (pp. 111–121). New York: New York University Press.

Index of Contributors